AMC/Renault Alliance & Encore Automotive Repair Manual

by Curt Choate
and John H Haynes Member of the Guild of Motoring Writers

Models covered:
AMC/Renault Alliance & Encore
with 1.4 liter, 1.7 liter and 2.0 liter gasoline engines
Covers manual and automatic transmissions

(9P1 - 934)   ABCDE FGHI

Haynes Publishing Group
Sparkford Nr Yeovil
Somerset BA22 7JJ England

Haynes Publications, Inc
861 Lawrence Drive
Newbury Park
California 91320 USA

Acknowledgements

We are grateful for the help and cooperation of the American Motors Corporation and Chrysler Corporation for their assistance with technical information, certain illustrations and vehicle photos, and the Champion Spark Plug Company who supplied the illustrations of various spark plug conditions.

A book in the **Haynes Automotive Repair Manual Series**

Printed by J.H. Haynes & Co., Ltd. Sparkford Nr. Yeovil, Somerset BA22 7JJ, England

ISBN 1 85010 532 4

Library of Congress Catalog Card Number 88-82108

Contents

Page

The AMC/Renault Alliance L Convertible

The AMC/Renault Encore GS

About this manual

Its purpose

The purpose of this manual is to help you get the best value from your vehicle. It can do so in several ways. It can help you decide what work must be done, even if you choose to have it done by a dealer service department or a repair shop; it provides information and procedures for routine maintenance and servicing; and it offers diagnostic and repair procedures to follow when trouble occurs.

It is hoped that you will use the manual to tackle the work yourself. For many simpler jobs, doing it yourself may be quicker than arranging an appointment to get the vehicle into a shop and making the trips to leave it and pick it up. More importantly, a lot of money can be saved by avoiding the expense the shop must pass on to you to cover its labor and overhead costs. An added benefit is the sense of satisfaction and accomplishment that you feel after having done the job yourself.

Using the manual

The manual is divided into Chapters. Each Chapter is divided into numbered Sections, which are headed in bold type between horizontal lines. Each Section consists of consecutively numbered paragraphs.

The two types of illustrations used (figures and photographs), are referenced by a number preceding their caption. Figure reference numbers denote Chapter and numerical sequence within the Chapter; (i.e. Fig. 3.4 means Chapter 3, figure number 4). Figure captions are followed by a Section number which ties the figure to a specific portion of the text. All photographs apply to the Chapter in which they appear and the reference number pinpoints the pertinent Section and paragraph; i.e., 3.2 means Section 3, paragraph 2.

Procedures, once described in the text, are not normally repeated. When it is necessary to refer to another Chapter, the reference will be given as Chapter and Section number i.e. Chapter 1/16). Cross references given without use of the word 'Chapter' apply to Sections and/or paragraphs in the same Chapter. For example, 'see Section 8' means in the same Chapter.

Reference to the left or right side of the vehicle is based on the assumption that one is sitting in the driver's seat, facing forward.

Even though extreme care has been taken during the preparation of this manual, neither the publisher nor the author can accept responsibility for any errors in, or omissions from, the information given.

Introduction to the Alliance/Encore

The Alliance/Encore is an AMC-built version of a Renault-designed vehicle with numerous changes incorporated to make it ready for the North American market. The Alliance, which is a sedan version, was introduced first. After its initial success (it was named 'Car of the Year' by *Motor Trend* magazine), the hatchback version Encore was introduced a year later.

The Alliance/Encore is front wheel drive and utilizes MacPherson strut suspension at the front and a rather unique torsion bar suspension at the rear. Transmissions used include a four or five-speed manual and a three-speed automatic.

General dimensions

Overall length .... 163.8 in
Overall width .... 65 in
Overall height .... 54.5 in
Wheelbase .... 97.8 in

Vehicle identification numbers

Modifications are a continuing and unpublicized process in vehicle manufacturing. Since spare parts manuals and lists are compiled on a numerical basis, the individual vehicle numbers are essential to correctly identify the component required.

Vehicle identification number (VIN)

This very important identification number is located on a plate attached to the top left corner of the dashboard and can easily be seen while looking through the windshield from the outside of the vehicle (photo). The VIN also appears on the Vehicle Certificate of Title and Registration. It contains valuable information such as where and when the vehicle was manufactured, the model year and the body style.

Code plate

This plate is located on the left-hand strut tower in the engine compartment. Like the VIN, it contains valuable information concerning the production of the vehicle, as well as information about the way in which the vehicle is equipped. This plate is especially useful for matching the color and type of paint during repair work.

The Vehicle Identification Number (VIN) is located on the driver's side of the dashboard and is visible through the windshield

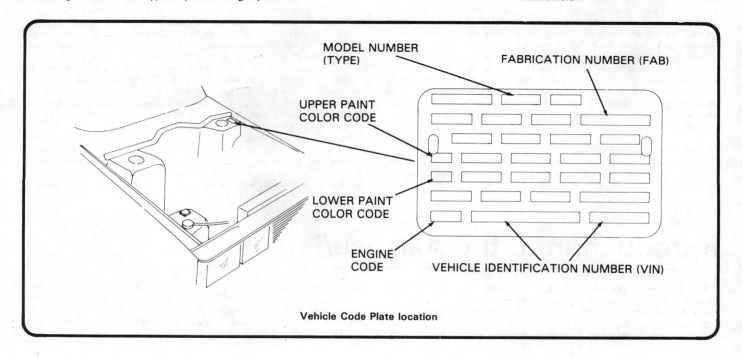

MODEL NUMBER (TYPE)

FABRICATION NUMBER (FAB)

UPPER PAINT COLOR CODE

LOWER PAINT COLOR CODE

ENGINE CODE

VEHICLE IDENTIFICATION NUMBER (VIN)

Vehicle Code Plate location

Vehicle fabrication plate

All 1984 and later vehicles (built after late March, 1984) are equipped with a vehicle fabrication plate, which is riveted to the passenger side strut tower. It contains the VIN, sequential fabrication number and month/day/year of production.

Engine identification numbers

On the 1.4 liter engine, the ID number is attached to the cylinder block above the oil filter. On the 1.7 liter engine it is attached to the flywheel end of the block, near the oil dipstick.

Automatic transmission number

The transmission ID number plate is attached to the transmission case just to the left of the fluid dipstick tube.

Manual transmission number

The manual transmission number is stamped on a plate held in place by one of the bellhousing bolts

Emissions Control Information label

The Emissions Control Information label is attached to the radiator fan shroud.

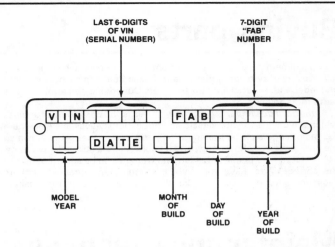

Later models have a Vehicle Fabrication Plate fastened to the passenger side strut tower in the engine compartment

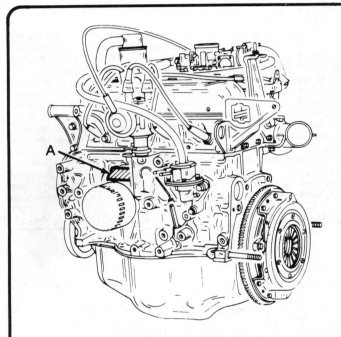

Engine ID number location

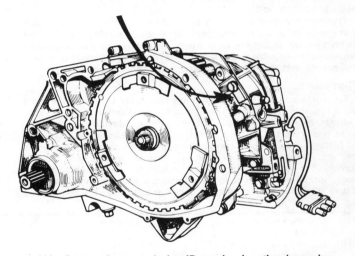

(A) Automatic transmission ID number location (arrow)

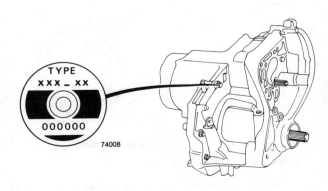

Manual transmission ID number location

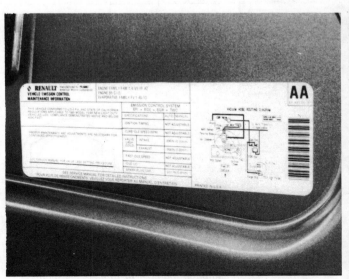

The Vehicle Emission Control Information label contains valuable engine tune-up specifications

Buying parts

Replacement parts are available from many sources, which generally fall into one of two categories — authorized dealer parts departments and independent retail auto parts stores. Our advice concerning these parts is as follows:

Authorized dealer parts department: This is the best source for parts which are unique to your vehicle and not generally available elsewhere (i.e. major engine parts, transmission parts, trim pieces, etc.). It is also the only place you should buy parts if your vehicle is still under warranty, as non-factory parts may invalidate the warranty. To be sure of obtaining the correct parts, have your vehicle's engine and chassis numbers available and, if possible, take the old parts along for positive identification.

Retail auto parts stores: Good auto parts stores will stock frequently needed components which wear out relatively fast (i.e. clutch components, exhaust systems, brake parts, tune-up parts, etc.). These stores often supply new or reconditioned parts on an exchange basis, which can save a considerable amount of money. Discount auto parts stores are often very good places to buy materials and parts needed for general vehicle maintenance (i.e. oil, grease, filters, spark plugs, belts, touch-up paint, bulbs, etc.). They also usually sell tools and general accessories, have convenient hours, charge lower prices, and can often be found not far from your home.

Maintenance techniques, tools and working facilities

Maintenance techniques

There are a number of techniques involved in maintenance and repair that will be referred to throughout this manual. Application of these techniques will enable the home mechanic to be more efficient, better organized and capable of performing the various tasks properly, which will ensure that the repair job is thorough and complete.

Fasteners

Fasteners are nuts, bolts, studs and screws used to hold two or more parts together. There are a few things to keep in mind when working with fasteners. Almost all of them use a locking device of some type, either a lock washer, locknut, locking tab or thread adhesive. All threaded fasteners should be clean and straight, with undamaged threads and undamaged corners on the hex head where the wrench fits. Develop the habit of replacing all damaged nuts and bolts with new ones. Special locknuts with nylon or fiber inserts can only be used once. If they are removed, they lose their locking ability and must be replaced with new ones.

Rusted nuts and bolts should be treated with a penetrating fluid to ease removal and prevent breakage. Some mechanics use turpentine in a spout-type oil can, which works quite well. After applying the rust penetrant, let it "work" for a few minutes before trying to loosen the nut or bolt. Badly rusted fasteners may have to be chiseled or sawed off or removed with a special nut breaker, available at tool stores.

If a bolt or stud breaks off in an assembly, it can be drilled and removed with a special tool commonly available for this purpose. Most automotive machine shops can perform this task, as well as other repair procedures (such as repair of threaded holes that have been stripped out).

Flat washers and lock washers, when removed from an assembly, should always be replaced exactly as removed. Replace any damaged washers with new ones. Always use a flat washer between a lock washer and any soft metal surface (such as aluminum), thin sheet metal or plastic.

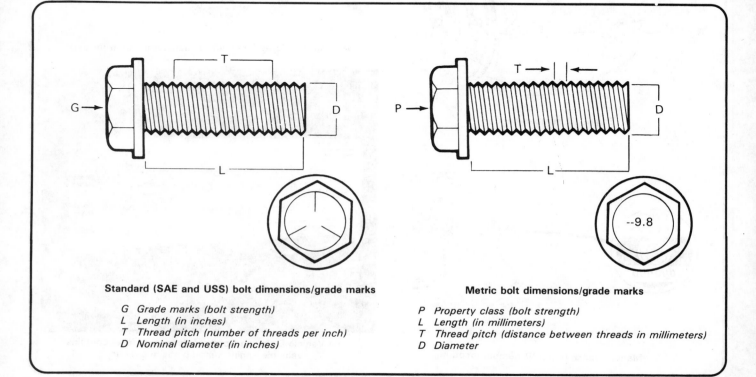

Standard (SAE and USS) bolt dimensions/grade marks

G Grade marks (bolt strength)
L Length (in inches)
T Thread pitch (number of threads per inch)
D Nominal diameter (in inches)

Metric bolt dimensions/grade marks

P Property class (bolt strength)
L Length (in millimeters)
T Thread pitch (distance between threads in millimeters)
D Diameter

Fastener sizes

For a number of reasons, automobile manufacturers are making wider and wider use of metric fasteners. Therefore, it is important to be able to tell the difference between standard (sometimes called U.S., English or SAE) and metric hardware, since they cannot be interchanged.

All bolts, whether standard or metric, are sized according to diameter, thread pitch and length. For example, a standard 1/2 — 13 x 1 bolt is 1/2 inch in diameter, has 13 threads per inch and is 1 inch long. An M12 — 1.75 x 25 metric bolt is 12 mm in diameter, has a thread pitch of 1.75 mm (the distance between threads) and is 25 mm long. The two bolts are nearly identical, and easily confused, but they are not interchangeable.

In addition to the differences in diameter, thread pitch and length, metric and standard bolts can also be distinguished by examining the bolt heads. To begin with, the distance across the flats on a standard bolt head is measured in inches, while the same dimension on a metric bolt is measured in millimeters (the same is true for nuts). As a result, a standard wrench should not be used on a metric bolt and a metric wrench should not be used on a standard bolt. Also, most standard bolts have slashes radiating out from the center of the head to denote the grade or strength of the bolt (which is an indication of the amount of torque that can be applied to it). The greater the number of slashes, the greater the strength of the bolt (grades 0 through 5 are commonly used on automobiles). Metric bolts have a property class (grade) number, rather than a slash, molded into their heads to indicate bolt strength. In this case, the higher the number, the stronger the bolt (property class numbers 8.8, 9.8 and 10.9 are commonly used on automobiles).

Strength markings can also be used to distinguish standard hex nuts from metric hex nuts. Many standard nuts have dots stamped into one side, while metric nuts are marked with a number. The greater the number of dots, or the higher the number, the greater the strength of the nut.

Metric studs are also marked on their ends according to property class (grade). Larger studs are numbered (the same as metric bolts),

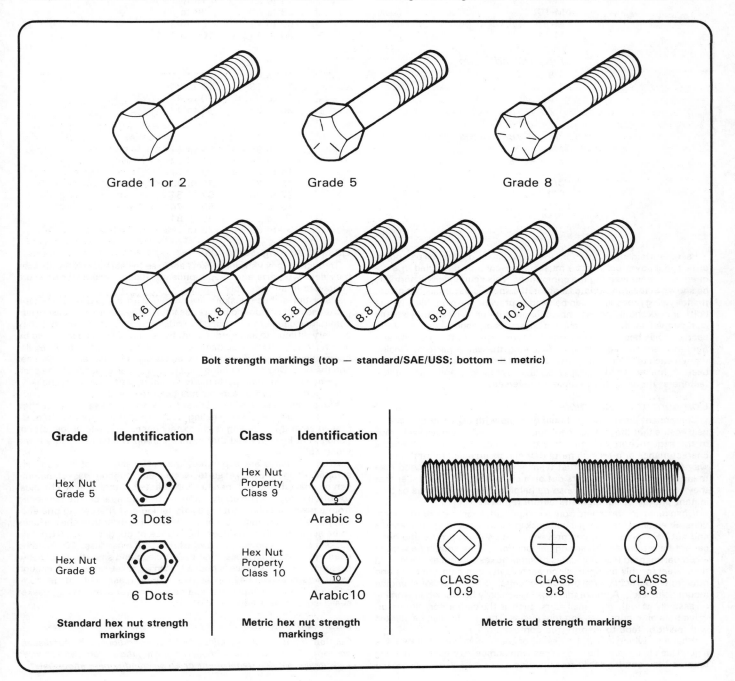

Grade 1 or 2   Grade 5   Grade 8

4.6   4.8   5.8   8.8   9.8   10.9

Bolt strength markings (top — standard/SAE/USS; bottom — metric)

Grade	Identification
Hex Nut Grade 5	3 Dots
Hex Nut Grade 8	6 Dots

Standard hex nut strength markings

Class	Identification
Hex Nut Property Class 9	Arabic 9
Hex Nut Property Class 10	Arabic 10

Metric hex nut strength markings

CLASS 10.9   CLASS 9.8   CLASS 8.8

Metric stud strength markings

while smaller studs carry a geometric code to denote grade.

It should be noted that many fasteners, especially Grades 0 through 2, have no distinguishing marks on them. When such is the case, the only way to determine whether it is standard or metric is to measure the thread pitch or compare it to a known fastener of the same size.

Standard fasteners are often referred to as SAE, as opposed to metric. However, it should be noted that SAE technically refers to a non-metric *fine thread* fastener only. Coarse thread non-metric fasteners are referred to as USS sizes.

Since fasteners of the same size (both standard and metric) may have different strength ratings, be sure to reinstall any bolts, studs or nuts removed from your vehicle in their original locations. Also, when replacing a fastener with a new one, make sure that the new one has a strength rating equal to or greater than the original.

Tightening sequences and procedures

Most threaded fasteners should be tightened to a specific torque value (torque is a twisting force). Over-tightening the fastener can weaken it and cause it to break, while under-tightening can cause it to eventually come loose. Bolts, screws and studs, depending on the material they are made of and their thread diameters, have specific torque values (many of which are noted in the Specifications at the beginning of each Chapter). Be sure to follow the torque recommendations closely. For fasteners not assigned a specific torque, a general torque value chart is presented here as a guide. As was previously mentioned, the size and grade of a fastener determine the amount of torque that can safely be applied to it. The figures listed here are approximate for Grade 2 and Grade 3 fasteners (higher grades can tolerate higher torque values).

	Ft-lb	Nm
Metric thread sizes		
M-6	6 to 9	9 to 12
M-8	14 to 21	19 to 28
M-10	28 to 40	38 to 54
M-12	50 to 71	68 to 96
M-14	80 to 140	109 to 154
Pipe thread sizes		
1/8	5 to 8	7 to 10
1/4	12 to 18	17 to 24
3/8	22 to 33	30 to 44
1/2	25 to 35	34 to 47
U.S. thread sizes		
1/4 — 20	6 to 9	9 to 12
5/16 — 18	12 to 18	17 to 24
5/16 — 24	14 to 20	19 to 27
3/8 — 16	22 to 32	30 to 43
3/8 — 24	27 to 38	37 to 51
7/16 — 14	40 to 55	55 to 74
7/16 — 20	40 to 60	55 to 81
1/2 — 13	55 to 80	75 to 108

Fasteners laid out in a pattern (i.e. cylinder head bolts, oil pan bolts, differential cover bolts, etc.) must be loosened or tightened in a sequence to avoid warping the component. This sequence will normally be shown in the appropriate Chapter. If a specific pattern is not given, the following procedures can be used to prevent warping. Initially, the bolts or nuts should be assembled finger-tight only. Next, they should be tightened one full turn each, in a crisscross or diagonal pattern. After each one has been tightened one full turn, return to the first one and tighten them all one-half turn, following the same pattern. Finally, tighten each of them one-quarter turn at a time until each fastener has been tightened to the proper torque. To loosen and remove the fasteners, the procedure would be reversed.

Component disassembly

Component disassembly should be done with care and purpose to help ensure that the parts go back together properly. Always keep track of the sequence in which parts are removed. Make note of special characteristics or marks on parts that can be installed more than one way (such as a grooved thrust washer on a shaft). It is a good idea to lay the disassembled parts out on a clean surface in the order that they were removed. It may also be helpful to make sketches or take instant photos of components before removal.

When removing fasteners from a component, keep track of their locations. Sometimes threading a bolt back in a part, or putting the washers and nut back on a stud, can prevent mix-ups later. If nuts and bolts cannot be returned to their original locations, they should be kept in a compartmented box or a series of small boxes. A cupcake or muffin tin is ideal for this purpose, since each cavity can hold the bolts and nuts from a particular area (i.e. oil pan bolts, valve cover bolts, engine mount bolts, etc.). A pan of this type is especially helpful when working on assemblies with very small parts, such as the carburetor, alternator, valve train or interior dash and trim pieces. The cavities can be marked with paint or tape to identify the contents.

Whenever wiring looms, harnesses or connectors are separated, it's a good idea to identify the two halves with numbered pieces of masking tape so they can be easily reconnected.

Gasket sealing surfaces

Throughout any vehicle, gaskets are used to seal the mating surfaces between two parts and keep lubricants, fluids, vacuum or pressure contained in an assembly.

Many times these gaskets are coated with a liquid or paste-type gasket sealing compound before assembly. Age, heat and pressure can sometimes cause the two parts to stick together so tightly that they are very difficult to separate. Often, the assembly can be loosened by striking it with a soft-faced hammer near the mating surfaces. A regular hammer can be used if a block of wood is placed between the hammer and the part. Do not hammer on cast parts or parts that could be easily damaged. With any particularly stubborn part, always recheck to make sure that every fastener has been removed.

Avoid using a screwdriver or bar to pry apart an assembly, as they can easily mar the gasket sealing surfaces of the parts (which must remain smooth). If prying is absolutely necessary, use an old broom handle, but keep in mind that extra clean-up will be necessary if the wood splinters.

After the parts are separated, the old gasket must be carefully scraped off and the gasket surfaces cleaned. Stubborn gasket material can be soaked with rust penetrant or treated with a special chemical to soften it so it can be easily scraped off. A scraper can be fashioned from a piece of copper tubing by flattening and sharpening one end. Copper is recommended because it is usually softer than the surfaces to be scraped, which reduces the chance of gouging the part. Some gaskets can be removed with a wire brush, but regardless of the method used, the mating surfaces must be left clean and smooth. If for some reason the gasket surface is gouged, then a gasket sealer thick enough to fill scratches will have to be used during reassembly of the components. For most applications, a non-drying (or semi-drying) gasket sealer should be used.

Hose removal tips

Caution: *If the vehicle is equipped with air conditioning, do not disconnect any of the A/C hoses without first having the system depressurized by a dealer service department or an air conditioning specialist.*

Hose removal precautions closely parallel gasket removal precautions. Avoid scratching or gouging the surface that the hose mates against or the connection may leak. This is especially true for radiator hoses. Because of various chemical reactions, the rubber in hoses can bond itself to the metal spigot that the hose fits over. To remove a hose, first loosen the hose clamps that secure it to the spigot. Then, with slip-joint pliers, grab the hose at the clamp and rotate it around the spigot. Work it back and forth until it is completely free, then pull it off. Silicone or other lubricants will ease removal if they can be applied between the hose and the outside of the spigot. Apply the same lubricant to the inside of the hose and the outside of the spigot to simplify installation.

As a last resort (and if the hose is to be replaced with a new one anyway), the rubber can be slit with a knife and the hose peeled from the spigot. If this must be done, be careful that the metal connection is not damaged.

If a hose clamp is broken or damaged, do not reuse it. Wire-type clamps usually weaken with age, so it is a good idea to replace them with screw-type clamps whenever a hose is removed.

Tools

A selection of good tools is a basic requirement for anyone who plans to maintain and repair his or her own vehicle. For the owner who has few tools, if any, the initial investment might seem high, but when compared to the spiraling costs of professional auto maintenance and repair, it is a wise one.

To help the owner decide which tools are needed to perform the tasks detailed in this manual, the following tool lists are offered: *Maintenance and minor repair, Repair and overhaul* and *Special*. The newcomer to practical mechanics should start off with the *Maintenance and minor repair tool kit*, which is adequate for the simpler jobs performed on a vehicle. Then, as confidence and experience grow, the owner can tackle more difficult tasks, buying additional tools as they are needed. Eventually the basic kit will be expanded into the *Repair and overhaul tool set*. Over a period of time, the experienced do-it-yourselfer will assemble a tool set complete enough for most repair and overhaul procedures and will add tools from the *Special* category when it is felt that the expense is justified by the frequency of use.

Maintenance and minor repair tool kit

The tools in this list should be considered the minimum required for performance of routine maintenance, servicing and minor repair work. We recommend the purchase of combination wrenches (box-end and open-end combined in one wrench); while more expensive than open-ended ones, they offer the advantages of both types of wrench.

Combination wrench set (1/4 in to 1 in or 6 mm to 19 mm)
Adjustable wrench — 8 in
Spark plug wrench (with rubber insert)
Spark plug gap adjusting tool
Feeler gauge set

Brake bleeder wrench
Standard screwdriver (5/16 in x 6 in)
Phillips screwdriver (No. 2 x 6 in)
Combination pliers — 6 in
Hacksaw and assortment of blades
Tire pressure gauge
Grease gun
Oil can
Fine emery cloth
Wire brush
Battery post and cable cleaning tool
Oil filter wrench
Funnel (medium size)
Safety goggles
Jackstands (2)
Drain pan

Note: *If basic tune-ups are going to be part of routine maintenance, it will be necessary to purchase a good quality stroboscopic timing light and combination tachometer/dwell meter. Although they are included in the list of Special tools, it is mentioned here because they are absolutely necessary for tuning most vehicles properly.*

Repair and overhaul tool set

These tools are essential for anyone who plans to perform major repairs and are in addition to those in the *Maintenance and minor repair tool kit*. Included is a comprehensive set of sockets which, though expensive, are invaluable because of their versatility (especially when various extensions and drives are available). We recommend the 1/2-inch drive over the 3/8-inch drive. Although the larger drive is bulky and more expensive, it has the capacity of accepting a very wide range of large sockets (ideally, the mechanic would have a 3/8-inch drive set and a 1/2-inch drive set).

Socket set(s)
Reversible ratchet
Extension — 10 in
Universal joint
Torque wrench (same size drive as sockets)
Ball peen hammer — 8 oz
Soft-faced hammer (plastic/rubber)
Standard screwdriver (1/4 in x 6 in)
Standard screwdriver (stubby — 5/16 in)
Phillips screwdriver (No. 3 x 8 in)
Phillips screwdriver (stubby — No. 2)
Pliers — vise grip
Pliers — lineman's
Pliers — needle nose
Pliers — snap-ring (internal and external)
Cold chisel — 1/2 in
Scriber
Scraper (made from flattened copper tubing)

Micrometer set

Dial indicator set

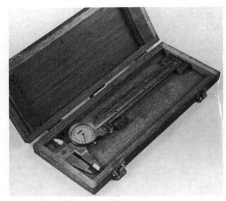

Dial caliper

Hand-operated vacuum pump

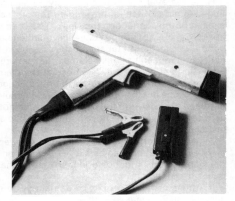

Timing light

Compression gauge with spark plug
hole adapter

Damper/steering wheel puller

General purpose puller

Hydraulic lifter removal tool

Valve spring compressor

Valve spring compressor

Ridge reamer

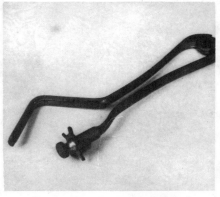

Piston ring groove cleaning tool

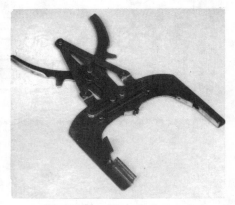

Ring removal/installation tool

Ring compressor

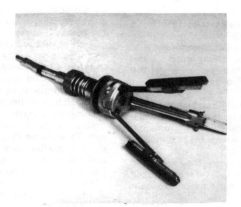

Cylinder hone

Brake hold-down spring tool

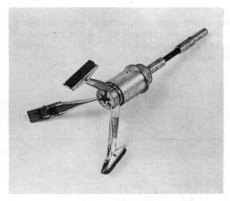

Brake cylinder hone

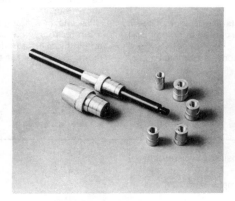

Clutch plate alignment tool

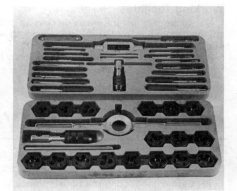

Tap and die set

Center punch
Pin punches (1/16, 1/8, 3/16 in)
Steel rule/straightedge — 12 in
Allen wrench set (1/8 to 3/8 in or 4 mm to 10 mm)
A selection of files
Wire brush (large)
Jackstands (second set)
Jack (scissor or hydraulic type)

Note: *Another tool which is often useful is an electric drill motor (with a chuck capacity of 3/8-inch) and a set of good-quality drill bits.*

Special tools

The tools in this list include those which are not used regularly, are expensive to buy, or which need to be used in accordance with their manufacturer's instructions. Unless these tools will be used frequently, it is not very economical to purchase many of them. A consideration would be to split the cost and use between yourself and a friend or friends. In addition, most of these tools can be obtained from a tool rental shop on a temporary basis.

This list contains only those tools and instruments widely available to the public, and not those special tools produced by the vehicle manufacturer for distribution to dealer service departments. Occasionally, references to the manufacturer's special tools are included in the text of this manual. Generally, an alternative method of doing the job without the special tool is offered. However, sometimes there is no alternative to their use. Where this is the case, and the tool cannot be purchased or borrowed, the work should be turned over to the dealer service department or an automotive repair shop.

Valve spring compressor
Piston ring groove cleaning tool
Piston ring compressor
Piston ring installation tool
Cylinder compression gauge
Cylinder ridge reamer

Cylinder surfacing hone
Cylinder bore gauge
Micrometer(s) and/or dial calipers
Hydraulic lifter removal tool
Balljoint separator
Universal-type puller
Impact screwdriver
Dial indicator set
Stroboscopic timing light (inductive pick-up)
Hand-operated vacuum/pressure pump
Tachometer/dwell meter
Universal electrical multimeter
Cable hoist
Brake spring removal and installation tools
Floor jack

Buying tools

For the do-it-yourselfer who is just starting to get involved in vehicle maintenance and repair, there are a number of options available when purchasing tools. If maintenance and minor repair is the extent of the work to be done, the purchase of individual tools is satisfactory. If, on the other hand, extensive work is planned, it would be a good idea to purchase a modest tool set from one of the large retail chain stores. A set can usually be bought at a substantial savings over the individual tool prices (and they often come with a tool box). As additional tools are needed, add-on sets, individual tools and a larger tool box can be purchased to expand the tool selection. Building a tool set gradually allows the cost of the tools to be spread over a longer period of time and gives the mechanic the freedom to choose only those tools that will actually be used.

Tool stores will often be the only source of some of the special tools that are needed, but regardless of where tools are bought, try to avoid cheap ones (especially when buying screwdrivers and sockets) because they won't last very long. The expense involved in replacing cheap tools will eventually be greater than the initial cost of quality tools.

Care and maintenance of tools

Good tools are expensive, so it makes sense to treat them with respect. Keep them clean and in usable condition and store them properly when not in use. Always wipe off any dirt, grease or metal chips before putting them away. Never leave tools lying around in the work area. Upon completion of a job, always check closely under the hood for tools that may have been left there (so they don't get lost during a test drive).

Some tools, such as screwdrivers, pliers, wrenches and sockets, can be hung on a panel mounted on the garage or workshop wall, while others should be kept in a tool box or tray. Measuring instruments, gauges, meters, etc. must be carefully stored where they cannot be damaged by weather or impact from other tools.

When tools are used with care and stored properly, they will last a very long time. Even with the best of care, tools will wear out if used frequently. When a tool is damaged or worn out, replace it; subsequent jobs will be safer and more enjoyable if you do.

Working facilities

Not to be overlooked when discussing tools is the workshop. If anything more than routine maintenance is to be carried out, some sort of suitable work area is essential.

It is understood, and appreciated, that many home mechanics do not have a good workshop or garage available and end up removing an engine or doing major repairs outside. It is recommended, however, that the overhaul or repair be completed under the cover of a roof.

A clean, flat workbench or table of comfortable working height is an absolute necessity. The workbench should be equipped with a vise that has a jaw opening of at least four inches.

As mentioned previously, some clean, dry storage space is also required for tools, as well as the lubricants, fluids, cleaning solvents, etc. which soon become necessary.

Sometimes waste oil and fluids, drained from the engine or cooling system during normal maintenance or repairs, present a disposal problem. To avoid pouring them on the ground or into a sewage system, simply pour the used fluids into large containers, seal them with caps and take them to an authorized disposal site or recycling center. Plastic jugs (such as old antifreeze containers) are ideal for this purpose.

Always keep a supply of old newspapers and clean rags available. Old towels are excellent for mopping up spills. Many mechanics use rolls of paper towels for most work because they are readily available and disposable. To help keep the area under the vehicle clean, a large cardboard box can be cut open and flattened to protect the garage or shop floor.

Whenever working over a painted surface (such as when leaning over a fender to service something under the hood), always cover it with an old blanket or bedspread to protect the finish. Vinyl covered pads, made especially for this purpose, are available at auto parts stores.

Booster battery (jump) starting

Certain precautions must be observed when using a booster battery to 'jump start' a vehicle.

a) Before connecting the booster battery, make sure that the ignition switch is in the Off position.
b) Turn off the lights, heater and other electrical loads.
c) The eyes should be shielded; safety goggles are a good idea.
d) Make sure the booster battery is the same voltage as the dead one in the vehicle.
e) The two vehicles must not touch each other.
f) Make sure the transmission is in Neutral (manual transmission) or Park (automatic transmission).

Connect the red jumper cable to the *positive* (+) terminals of each battery.

Connect one end of the black jumper cable to the *negative* (−) terminal of the booster battery. The other end of this cable should be connected to a good ground on the vehicle to be started, such as a bolt or bracket on the engine block. Use caution to ensure that the cables will not come into contact with the fan, drivebelts or other moving parts of the engine.

Start the engine using the booster battery, then, with the engine running at idle speed, disconnect the jumper cables in the reverse order of connection.

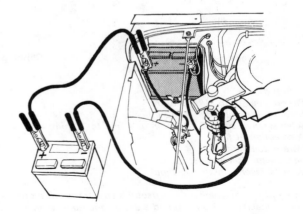

Booster battery cable connections (note that the negative cable is *not* attached to the negative terminal of the dead battery)

Jacking and towing

Jacking

The jack supplied with the vehicle should only be used for raising the vehicle when changing a tire or placing jackstands under the frame. **Caution:** *Never work under the vehicle or start the engine while this jack is being used as the only means of support.*

The vehicle should be on level ground with the wheels blocked and the transmission in Park (automatic) or Reverse (manual). Pry off the hub cap (if equipped) using the tapered end of the lug wrench. Loosen the wheel nuts one-half turn and leave them in place until the wheel is raised off the ground.

Place the jack under the side of the vehicle at the jack point nearest the wheel to be removed. Raise the jack until the jack head contacts the body. Turn the jack handle in a clockwise direction until the wheel is raised off the ground. Remove the wheel nuts, pull off the wheel and replace it with the spare.

With the beveled side in, replace the wheel nuts and tighten them until snug. Turn the jack handle counterclockwise to lower the vehicle. Remove the jack and tighten the nuts in a crisscross sequence by turning the wrench clockwise. Replace the hub cap (if equipped) by placing it into position and using the heel of your hand or a rubber mallet to seat it.

Towing

The vehicle should be towed only with the front wheels off the ground, or with all four wheels off the ground. **Note:** *Rear towing with the front wheels on the ground is not recommended. If damage prevents front towing, use wheel dollies or a flat bed truck.*

Towing equipment specifically designed for this purpose should be used and should be attached to the main structural members of the vehicle and not the bumper or driveaxles.

Safety is a major consideration when towing and all applicable state and local laws must be obeyed. A safety chain system must be used for all towing.

While towing, the parking brake should be released and the steering must be unlocked (ignition switch in the Off position). Remember that power steering and power brakes will not work with the engine off.

If equipped, be sure to remove the air dam (spoiler) before towing the vehicle.

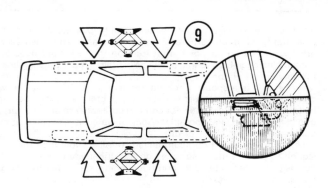

Jack lifting points

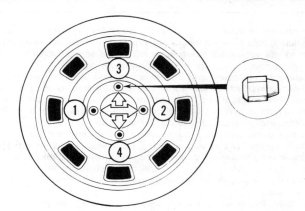

When installing the wheel, make sure the lug nuts are tightened in a criss-cross pattern (follow the numbered sequence)

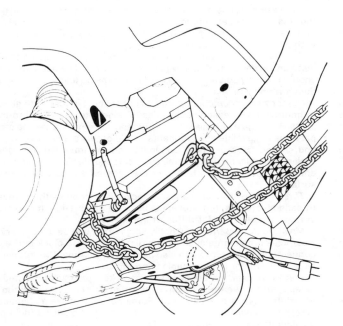

Commercial tow truck hook-up for 1983 vehicles only

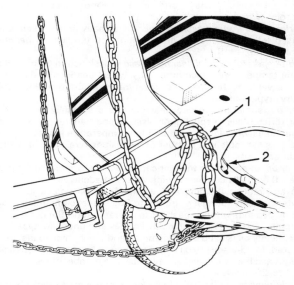

Commercial tow truck hook-up for 1984 and later vehicles (attach the primary chains [1] to the eyes [2])

Automotive chemicals and lubricants

A number of automotive chemicals and lubricants are available for use during vehicle maintenance and repair. They include a wide variety of products ranging from cleaning solvents and degreasers to lubricants and protective sprays for rubber, plastic and vinyl.

Contact point/spark plug cleaner is a solvent used to clean oily film and dirt from points, grime from electrical connectors and oil deposits from spark plugs. It is oil free and leaves no residue. It can also be used to remove gum and varnish from carburetor jets and other orifices.

Carburetor cleaner is similar to contact point/spark plug cleaner but it is a stronger solvent and may leave a slight oily residue. It is not recommended for cleaning electrical components or connections.

Brake system cleaner is used to remove grease or brake fluid from brake system components where clean surfaces are absolutely necessary and petroleum-based solvents cannot be used. It also leaves no residue.

Silicone-based lubricants are used to protect rubber parts such as hoses, weatherstripping and grommets, and are used as lubricants for hinges and locks.

Multi-purpose grease is an all-purpose lubricant used wherever grease is more practical than a liquid lubricant such as oil. Some multi-purpose grease is white and specially formulated to be more resistant to water than ordinary grease.

Bearing grease/wheel bearing grease is a heavy grease used where increased loads and friction are encountered (i.e. wheel bearings, universal joints, etc.).

High-temperature wheel bearing grease is designed to withstand the extreme temperatures encountered by wheel bearings in disc-brake equipped vehicles. It usually contains molybdenum disulfide, which is a 'dry' type lubricant.

Gear oil (sometimes called gear lube) is a specially designed oil used in differentials, manual transmissions and transfer cases, as well as other areas where high-friction, high-temperature lubrication is required. It is available in a number of viscosities (weights) for various applications.

Motor oil, of course, is the lubricant specially formulated for use in engines. It normally contains a wide variety of additives to prevent corrosion and reduce foaming and wear. Motor oil comes in various weights (viscosity ratings) of from 5 to 80. The recommended weight of the oil depends on the seasonal temperature and the demands on the engine. Light oil is used in cold climates and under light load conditions; heavy oil is used in hot climates and where high loads are encountered. Multi-viscosity oils are designed to have characteristics of both light and heavy oils and are available in a number of weights from 5W-20 to 20W-50.

Oil additives range from viscosity index improvers to slick chemical treatments that purportedly reduce friction. It should be noted that most oil manufacturers caution against using additives with their oils.

Gas additives perform several functions, depending on their chemical makeup. They usually contain solvents that help dissolve gum and varnish that build up on carburetor and intake parts. They also serve to break down carbon deposits that form on the inside surfaces of the combustion chambers. Some additives contain upper cylinder lubricants for valves and piston rings.

Brake fluid is a specially formulated hydraulic fluid that can withstand the heat and pressure encountered in brake systems. Care must be taken that this fluid does not come in contact with painted surfaces or plastics. An opened container should always be resealed to prevent contamination by water or dirt.

Undercoating is a petroleum-based, tar-like substance that is designed to protect metal surfaces on the underside of a vehicle from corrosion. It also acts as a sound-deadening agent by insulating the bottom of the vehicle.

Weatherstrip cement is used to bond weatherstripping around doors, windows and trunk lids. It is sometimes used to attach trim pieces as well.

Degreasers are heavy-duty solvents used to remove grease and grime that may accumulate on engine and chassis components. They can be sprayed or brushed on and, depending on the type, are rinsed off with either water or solvent.

Solvents are used alone or in combination with degreasers to clean parts and assemblies during repair and overhaul. The home mechanic should use only solvents that are non-flammable and that do not produce irritating fumes.

Gasket sealing compounds may be used in conjunction with gaskets, to improve their sealing capabilities, or alone, to seal metal-to-metal joints. Many gasket sealers can withstand extreme heat, some are impervious to gasoline and lubricants, while others are capable of filling and sealing large cavities. Depending on the intended use, gasket sealers either dry hard or stay relatively soft and pliable. They are usually applied by hand, with a brush, or are sprayed on the gasket sealing surfaces.

Thread cement is an adhesive locking compound that prevents threaded fasteners from loosening because of vibration. It is available in a variety of types for different applications.

Moisture dispersants are usually sprays that can be used to dry out electrical components such as the distributor, fuse block and wiring connectors. Some types can also be used as treatment for rubber and as a lubricant for hinges, cables and locks.

Waxes and polishes are used to help protect painted and plated surfaces from the weather. Different types of paint may require the use of different types of wax polish. Some polishes utilize a chemical or abrasive cleaner to help remove the top layer of oxidized (dull) paint on older vehicles. In recent years many non-wax polishes that contain a wide variety of chemicals such as polymers and silicones have been introduced. These non-wax polishes are usually easier to apply and last longer than conventional waxes and polishes.

Safety first!

Regardless of how enthusiastic you may be about getting on with the job at hand, take the time to ensure that your safety is not jeopardized. A moment's lack of attention can result in an accident, as can failure to observe certain simple safety precautions. The possibility of an accident will always exist, and the following points should not be considered a comprehensive list of all dangers. Rather, they are intended to make you aware of the risks and to encourage a safety conscious approach to all work you carry out on your vehicle.

Essential DOs and DON'Ts

DON'T rely on a jack when working under the vehicle. Always use approved jackstands to support the weight of the vehicle and place them under the recommended lift or support points.

DON'T attempt to loosen extremely tight fasteners (i.e. wheel lug nuts) while the vehicle is on a jack — it may fall.

DON'T start the engine without first making sure that the transmission is in Neutral (or Park where applicable) and the parking brake is set.

DON'T remove the radiator cap from a hot cooling system — let it cool or cover it with a cloth and release the pressure gradually.

DON'T attempt to drain the engine oil until you are sure it has cooled to the point that it will not burn you.

DON'T touch any part of the engine or exhaust system until it has cooled sufficiently to avoid burns.

DON'T siphon toxic liquids such as gasoline, antifreeze and brake fluid by mouth, or allow them to remain on your skin.

DON'T inhale brake lining dust — it is potentially hazardous (see *Asbestos* below)

DON'T allow spilled oil or grease to remain on the floor — wipe it up before someone slips on it.

DON'T use loose fitting wrenches or other tools which may slip and cause injury.

DON'T push on wrenches when loosening or tightening nuts or bolts. Always try to pull the wrench toward you. If the situation calls for pushing the wrench away, push with an open hand to avoid scraped knuckles if the wrench should slip.

DON'T attempt to lift a heavy component alone — get someone to help you.

DON'T rush or take unsafe shortcuts to finish a job.

DON'T allow children or animals in or around the vehicle while you are working on it.

DO wear eye protection when using power tools such as a drill, sander, bench grinder, etc. and when working under a vehicle.

DO keep loose clothing and long hair well out of the way of moving parts.

DO make sure that any hoist used has a safe working load rating adequate for the job.

DO get someone to check on you periodically when working alone on a vehicle.

DO carry out work in a logical sequence and make sure that everything is correctly assembled and tightened.

DO keep chemicals and fluids tightly capped and out of the reach of children and pets.

DO remember that your vehicle's safety affects that of yourself and others. If in doubt on any point, get professional advice.

Asbestos

Certain friction, insulating, sealing, and other products — such as brake linings, brake bands, clutch linings, torque converters, gaskets, etc. — contain asbestos. *Extreme care must be taken to avoid inhalation of dust from such products since it is hazardous to health.* If in doubt, assume that they *do* contain asbestos.

Fire

Remember at all times that gasoline is highly flammable. Never smoke or have any kind of open flame around when working on a vehicle. But the risk does not end there. A spark caused by an electrical short circuit, by two metal surfaces contacting each other, or even by static electricity built up in your body under certain conditions, can ignite gasoline vapors, which in a confined space are highly explosive. Do not, under any circumstances, use gasoline for cleaning parts. Use an approved safety solvent.

Always disconnect the battery ground (–) cable *at the battery* before working on any part of the fuel system or electrical system. Never risk spilling fuel on a hot engine or exhaust component.

It is strongly recommended that a fire extinguisher suitable for use on fuel and electrical fires be kept handy in the garage or workshop at all times. Never try to extinguish a fuel or electrical fire with water.

Fumes

Certain fumes are highly toxic and can quickly cause unconsciousness and even death if inhaled to any extent. Gasoline vapor falls into this category, as do the vapors from some cleaning solvents. Any draining or pouring of such volatile fluids should be done in a well ventilated area.

When using cleaning fluids and solvents, read the instructions on the container carefully. Never use materials from unmarked containers.

Never run the engine in an enclosed space, such as a garage. Exhaust fumes contain carbon monoxide, which is extremely poisonous. If you need to run the engine, always do so in the open air, or at least have the rear of the vehicle outside the work area.

If you are fortunate enough to have the use of an inspection pit, never drain or pour gasoline and never run the engine while the vehicle is over the pit. The fumes, being heavier than air, will concentrate in the pit with possibly lethal results.

The battery

Never create a spark or allow a bare light bulb near the battery. The battery normally gives off a certain amount of hydrogen gas, which is highly explosive.

Always disconnect the battery ground (–) cable *at the battery* before working on the fuel or electrical systems.

If possible, loosen the filler caps or cover when charging the battery from an external source. Do not charge at an excessive rate or the battery may burst.

Take care when adding water and when carrying a battery. The electrolyte, even when diluted, is very corrosive and should not be allowed to contact clothing or skin.

Always wear eye protection when cleaning the battery to prevent the caustic deposits from entering your eyes.

Household current

When using an electric power tool, inspection light, etc., which operates on household current, always make sure that the tool is correctly connected to its plug and that, where necessary, it is properly grounded. Do not use such items in damp conditions and, again, do not create a spark or apply excessive heat in the vicinity of fuel or fuel vapor.

Secondary ignition system voltage

A severe electric shock can result from touching certain parts of the ignition system (such as the spark plug wires) when the engine is running or being cranked, particularly if components are damp or the insulation is defective. In the case of an electronic ignition system, the secondary system voltage is much higher and could prove fatal.

Troubleshooting

Contents

This section provides an easy-reference guide to the more common problems which may occur during the operation of your vehicle. These problems and possible causes are grouped under various components or systems i.e. Engine, Cooling system, etc., and also refer to the Chapter and/or Section which deals with the problem.

Remember that successful troubleshooting is not a mysterious 'black art' practiced only by professional mechanics; it's simply the result of a bit of knowledge combined with an intelligent, systematic approach to the problem. Always work by a process of elimination, starting with the simplest solution and working through to the most complex — and never overlook the obvious. Anyone can forget to fill the gas tank or leave the lights on overnight, so don't assume that you are above such oversights.

Finally, always get clear in your mind why a problem has occurred and take steps to ensure that it doesn't happen again. If the electrical system fails because of a poor connection, check all other connections in the system to make sure that they don't fail as well; if a particular fuse continues to blow, find out why — don't just go on replacing fuses. Remember, failure of a small component can often be indicative of potential failure or incorrect functioning of a more important component or system.

Engine

1 Engine will not rotate when attempting to start

1 Battery terminal connections loose or corroded. Check the cable terminals at the battery; tighten the cable or remove corrosion as necessary.
2 Battery discharged or faulty. If the cable connections are clean and tight on the battery posts, turn the key to the On position and switch on the headlights and/or windshield wipers. If they fail to function, the battery is discharged.
3 Automatic transmission not completely engaged in Park or clutch not completely depressed.
4 Broken, loose or disconnected wiring in the starting circuit. Inspect all wiring and connectors at the battery, starter solenoid and ignition switch. **Note:** *A service bulletin has been issued for these vehicles pertaining to loose, dirty or paint-coated connections at the battery or starter solenoid terminals. If a no-crank condition persists, contact your dealer for more information and possible replacement of the nut and washer used on the solenoid terminal.*
5 Starter motor pinion jammed in flywheel ring gear. If manual transmission, place transmission in gear and rock the vehicle to manually turn the engine. Remove starter and inspect pinion and flywheel at earliest convenience.
6 Starter solenoid faulty (Chapter 5).
7 Starter motor faulty (Chapter 5).
8 Ignition switch faulty (Chapter 10).

2 Engine rotates but will not start

1 Fuel tank empty.
2 Battery discharged (engine rotates slowly). Check the operation of electrical components as described in previous Section.
3 Battery terminal connections loose or corroded. See previous Section.
4 Fuel injector or fuel pump faulty (Chapter 4).
5 Excessive moisture on, or damage to, ignition components (Chapter 5).
6 Worn, faulty or incorrectly gapped spark plugs (Chapter 1).
7 Broken, loose or disconnected wiring in the starting circuit (see previous Section).
8 Broken, loose or disconnected wiring at the coil or faulty coil (Chapter 5).
9 Intake air leaks (check all hoses and connections).
10 Faulty cold start injector, thermo-time switch, supplementary air regulator, air or coolant temperature sensor, airflow meter, TPS, or ECU (Chapter 4).
11 Loosen injection system wire harness or ground connection.

3 Starter motor operates without rotating engine

1 Starter pinion sticking. Remove the starter (Chapter 5) and inspect.
2 Starter pinion or flywheel teeth worn or broken. Remove the cover at the rear of the engine and inspect.

4 Engine hard to start when cold

1 Battery discharged or low. Check as described in Section 1.
2 Fuel injection system in need of attention (Chapter 4).
3 Distributor rotor carbon tracked and/or advance mechanism malfunctioning (Chapter 5).

5 Engine hard to start when hot

1 Air filter clogged (Chapter 1).
2 Fuel not reaching the injector (Chapter 4).

6 Starter motor noisy or excessively rough in engagement

1 Pinion or flywheel gear teeth worn or broken. Remove the cover at the rear of the engine (if so equipped) and inspect.
2 Starter motor mounting bolts loose or missing.

7 Engine starts but stops immediately

1 Loose or faulty electrical connections at distributor, coil or alternator.
2 Insufficient fuel reaching the fuel injector(s). Check the pump output as described in Chapter 4.
3 Vacuum leak at the gasket surfaces of the intake manifold and/or fuel injector unit. Make sure that all mounting bolts (nuts) are tightened securely and that all vacuum hoses connected to the fuel injection unit and manifold are positioned properly and in good condition.

8 Engine lopes while idling or idles erratically

1 Vacuum leakage. Check mounting bolts (nuts) at the fuel injection unit and intake manifold for tightness. Make sure that all vacuum hoses are connected and in good condition. Use a stethoscope or a length of fuel hose held against your ear to listen for vacuum leaks while the engine is running. A hissing sound will be heard. A soapy water solution will also detect leaks. Check the fuel injection unit and intake manifold gasket surfaces.
2 Supplementary air regulator not operating correctly (Chapter 4).
3 Leaking EGR valve or plugged PCV valve (see Chapters 1 and 6).
4 Air filter clogged (Chapter 1).
5 Fuel pump not delivering sufficient fuel to the fuel injector (see Section 7).
6 Leaking head gasket. If this is suspected, take the vehicle to a repair shop or dealer where the engine can be pressure checked.
7 Timing chain/belt and/or sprockets worn (Chapter 2).
8 Camshaft lobes worn (Chapter 2).
9 Defective airflow meter, air or coolant temperature sensor, TPS, injector(s) or ECU (Chapter 4).
10 Air bypass screw incorrectly adjusted.
11 Loose injection system wire harness or ground connection.

9 Engine misses at idle speed

1 Spark plugs worn or not gapped properly (Chapter 1).
2 Faulty spark plug wires (Chapter 1).
3 Compression low (Chapter 1).
4 Intake air leaks. Check all hoses and connections.
5 Leaking cold start injector.

6   Incorrect fuel system pressure (check pressure regulator).
7   Supplementary air regulator valve not operating correctly.
8   Defective air or coolant temperature sensor.
9   Defective TPS.
10   Defective injectors, airflow meter or ECU.
11   Air bypass screw incorrectly adjusted.
12   Loose wire harness connectors or system ground.

10   Engine misses throughout driving speed range

1   Fuel filter clogged and/or impurities in the fuel system (Chapter 1). Also check fuel output (see Section 7).
2   Faulty or incorrectly gapped spark plugs (Chapter 1).
3   Incorrect ignition timing (Chapter 1).
4   Check for cracked distributor cap, disconnected distributor wires and damaged distributor components (Chapter 1).
5   Leaking spark plug wires (Chapter 1).
6   Faulty emissions system components (Chapter 6).
7   Low or uneven cylinder compression pressures. Remove spark plugs and test compression with gauge (Chapter 1).
8   Weak or faulty ignition system (Chapter 5).
9   Vacuum leaks at fuel injection unit, intake manifold or vacuum hoses (see Section 8).
10   Defective ECU or loose wire harness or system ground connection.
11   Defective fuel injector(s).

11   Engine stalls

1   Idle speed incorrect (Chapter 1).
2   Fuel filter clogged and/or water and impurities in the fuel system (Chapter 1). Also check the fuel system pressure and make sure the cold start injector is not leaking.
3   Distributor components damp or damaged (Chapter 5).
4   Faulty emissions system components (Chapter 6).
5   Faulty or incorrectly gapped spark plugs (Chapter 1). Also check spark plug wires (Chapter 1).
6   Vacuum leak at the fuel injection unit, intake manifold or vacuum hoses. Check as described in Section 8.
7   Valve clearances incorrectly set (Chapter 1).
8   Supplementary air regulator, ECU, air or coolant temperature sensor or airflow meter defective (Chapter 4).
9   Air bypass screw incorrectly adjusted.
10   Loose injection wire harness or system ground connection.

12   Engine lacks power

1   Incorrect ignition timing (Chapter 1).
2   Excessive play in distributor shaft. At the same time, check for worn rotor, faulty distributor cap, wires, etc. (Chapters 1 and 5).
3   Faulty or incorrectly gapped spark plugs (Chapter 1).
4   Fuel injection unit not adjusted properly or excessively worn (Chapter 4).
5   Faulty coil (Chapter 5).
6   Brakes binding (Chapter 1).
7   Automatic transmission fluid level incorrect (Chapter 1).
8   Clutch slipping (Chapter 8).
9   Fuel filter clogged and/or impurities in the fuel system (Chapter 1). Also check the fuel system pressure.
10   Emissions control system not functioning properly (Chapter 6).
11   Use of sub-standard fuel. Fill tank with proper octane fuel.
12   Low or uneven cylinder compression pressures. Test with compression tester, which will detect leaking valves and/or blown head gasket (Chapter 1).
13   Defective airflow meter, TPS, injectors or ECU (Chapter 4).

13   Engine backfires

1   Emissions system not functioning properly (Chapter 6).
2   Ignition timing incorrect (Chapter 1).

3   Faulty secondary ignition system (cracked spark plug insulator, faulty plug wires, distributor cap and/or rotor) (Chapters 1 and 5).
4   Fuel injection in need of adjustment or worn excessively (Chapter 4).
5   Vacuum leak at fuel injection unit, intake manifold or vacuum hoses. Check as described in Section 8.
6   Valve clearances incorrectly set, and/or valves sticking (Chapter 2).

14   Pinging or knocking engine sounds during acceleration or uphill

1   Incorrect grade of fuel. Fill tank with fuel of the proper octane rating.
2   Ignition timing incorrect (Chapter 1).
3   Fuel injection unit in need of adjustment (Chapter 4).
4   Improper spark plugs. Check plug type against Emissions Control Information label located in engine compartment. Also check plugs and wires for damage (Chapter 1).
5   Worn or damaged distributor components (Chapter 5).
6   Faulty emissions system (Chapter 6).
7   Vacuum leak. Check as described in Section 8.

15   Engine 'diesels' (continues to run) after switching off

1   Idle speed too high (Chapter 1).
2   Ignition timing incorrectly adjusted (Chapter 1).
3   Thermo-controlled air cleaner heat valve not operating properly (Chapter 1).
4   Excessive engine operating temperature. Probable causes of this are malfunctioning thermostat, clogged radiator, faulty water pump (Chapter 3).

16   Engine starts hard in sub-zero temperatures

An American Motors dealer technical service bulletin concerning this problem has been issued. Take the vehicle to your dealer and inform him of the problem.

Engine electrical system

17   Battery will not hold a charge

1   Alternator drivebelt defective or not adjusted properly (Chapter 1).
2   Electrolyte level low or battery discharged (Chapter 1).
3   Battery terminals loose or corroded (Chapter 1).
4   Alternator not charging properly (Chapter 5).
5   Loose, broken or faulty wiring in the charging circuit (Chapter 5).
6   Short in vehicle wiring causing a continual drain on battery.
7   Battery defective internally.

18   Ignition light fails to go out

1   Fault in alternator or charging circuit (Chapter 5).
2   Alternator drivebelt defective or not properly adjusted (Chapter 1).

19   Ignition light fails to come on when key is turned on

1   Warning light bulb defective (Chapter 10).
2   Alternator faulty (Chapter 5).
3   Fault in the printed circuit, dash wiring or bulb holder (Chapter 10).

Fuel system

20   Excessive fuel consumption

1   Incorrect fuel system pressure (Chapter 4).

2   Air bypass screw incorrectly adjusted (Chapter 4).
3   Defective cold start injector, air or coolant temperature sensor or airflow meter (Chapter 4).
4   Incorrectly set ignition timing or low cylinder compression (Chapter 1).
5   Fuel injection internal parts excessively worn or damaged (Chapter 4).
6   Low tire pressure or incorrect tire size (Chapter 1).

21   Fuel leakage and/or fuel odor

1   Leak in a fuel feed or vent line (Chapter 4).
2   Tank overfilled. Fill only to automatic shut-off.
3   Emissions system filter clogged (Chapter 1).
4   Vapor leaks from system lines (Chapter 4).
5   Fuel injection internal parts excessively worn or out of adjustment (Chapter 4).

Engine cooling system

22   Overheating

Note: *If overheating has occurred, certain components of the cooling system must be carefully checked and replaced. An American Motors dealer service bulletin concerning this matter has been issued. Take the vehicle to your dealer and inform him of the problem.*

1   Insufficient coolant in system (Chapter 1).
2   Water pump drivebelt defective or not adjusted properly (Chapter 1).
3   Radiator core blocked or radiator grille dirty and restricted (Chapter 3).
4   Thermostat faulty (Chapter 3).
5   Fan blades broken or cracked (Chapter 3).
6   Remote filler cap not maintaining proper pressure. Have cap pressure tested by gas station or repair shop.
7   Ignition timing incorrect (Chapter 1).

23   Overcooling

1   Thermostat faulty (Chapter 3).
2   Inaccurate temperature gauge (Chapter 10)

24   External coolant leakage

1   Deteriorated or damaged hoses. Loosen clamps at hose connections (Chapter 1).
2   Water pump seals defective. If this is the case, water will drip from the 'weep' hole in the water pump body (Chapter 1).
3   Leakage from radiator core or header tank. This will require the radiator to be professionally repaired (see Chapter 3 for removal procedures).
4   Engine drain plugs or water jacket core plugs leaking (see Chapter 2).

25   Internal coolant leakage

Note: *Internal coolant leaks can usually be detected by examining the oil. Check the dipstick and inside of the rocker arm cover(s) for water deposits and an oil consistency like that of a milkshake.*

1   Leaking cylinder head gasket. Have the cooling system pressure-tested.
2   Cracked cylinder bore or cylinder head. Dismantle engine and inspect (Chapter 2).

26   Coolant loss

1   Too much coolant in system (Chapter 1).
2   Coolant boiling away due to overheating (see Section 15).
3   Internal or external leakage (see Sections 24 and 25).
4   Faulty remote filler cap. Have the cap pressure-tested.

27   Poor coolant circulation

1   Inoperative water pump. A quick test is to pinch the top radiator hose closed with your hand while the engine is idling, then let it loose. You should feel the surge of coolant if the pump is working properly (Chapter 1).
2   Restriction in cooling system. Drain, flush and refill the system (Chapter 1). If necessary, remove the radiator (Chapter 3) and have it reverse-flushed.
3   Water pump drivebelt defective or not adjusted properly (Chapter 1).
4   Thermostat sticking (Chapter 3).

Clutch

28   Fails to release (pedal pressed to the floor — shift lever does not move freely in and out of Reverse)

Note: *If the clutch fails to release (indicated by gear clash or difficult gear shifting), the clutch cable travel may be insufficient. An American Motors dealer service bulletin concerning this matter has been issued. Take the vehicle to your dealer and inform him of the problem.*
1   Improper linkage free play adjustment (Chapter 8).
2   Clutch fork off ball stud. Look under the vehicle, on the left side of transmission.
3   Clutch plate warped or damaged (Chapter 8).

29   Clutch slips (engine speed increases with no increase in vehicle speed)

1   Linkage out of adjustment (Chapter 8).
2   Clutch plate oil soaked or lining worn. Remove clutch (Chapter 8) and inspect.
3   Clutch plate not seated. It may take 30 or 40 normal starts for a new one to seat.

30   Grabbing (chattering) as clutch is engaged

1   Oil on clutch plate lining. Remove (Chapter 8) and inspect. Correct any leakage source.
2   Worn or loose engine or transmission mounts. These units move slightly when clutch is released. Inspect mounts and bolts.
3   Worn splines on clutch plate hub. Remove clutch components (Chapter 8) and inspect.
4   Warped pressure plate or flywheel. Remove clutch components and inspect.

31   Squeal or rumble with clutch fully engaged (pedal released)

1   Improper adjustment; no free play (Chapter 1).
2   Release bearing binding on transmission bearing retainer. Remove clutch components (Chapter 8) and check bearing. Remove any burrs or nicks, clean and relubricate before reinstallation.
3   Weak linkage return spring. Replace the spring.

32   Squeal or rumble with clutch fully disengaged (pedal depressed)

1   Worn, defective or broken release bearing (Chapter 8).

2   Worn or broken pressure plate springs (or diaphragm fingers) (Chapter 8).

33   Clutch pedal stays on floor when disengaged

1   Bind in cable or release bearing. Inspect cable and remove clutch components as necessary.

Manual transmission

34   Noisy in Neutral with engine running

1   Input shaft bearing worn.
2   Damaged main drive gear bearing.
3   Worn countershaft bearings.
4   Worn or damaged countershaft end play shims.

35   Noisy in all gears

1   Any of the above causes, and/or:
2   Insufficient lubricant (see checking procedures in Chapter 1).

36   Noisy in one particular gear

1   Worn, damaged or chipped gear teeth for that particular gear.
2   Worn or damaged synchronizer for that particular gear.

37   Slips out of high gear

1   Transmission loose on clutch housing (Chapter 7).
2   Shift rod not working freely (Chapter 7).
3   Worn selector fork.
4   Worn or improperly adjusted linkage (Chapter 7).
5   Worn selector shaft detent grooves or broken plunger or ball spring.
6   Dirt between transmission case and engine or misalignment of transmission (Chapter 7).

38   Difficulty in engaging gears

1   Clutch not releasing completely (see clutch adjustment in Chapter 1).
2   Loose, damaged or out-of-adjustment shift linkage. Make a thorough inspection, replacing parts as necessary (Chapter 7).

39   Oil leakage

1   Excessive amount of lubricant in transmission (see Chapter 1 for correct checking procedures). Drain lubricant as required.
2   Speedometer oil seal in need of replacement (Chapter 7).

Automatic transmission

Note: *Due to the complexity of the automatic transmission, it is difficult for the home mechanic to properly diagnose and service this component. For problems other than the following, the vehicle should be taken to a dealer or reputable mechanic.*

40   General shift mechanism problems

1   Chapter 7 deals with checking and adjusting the shift linkage on automatic transmissions. Common problems which may be attributed to poorly adjusted linkage are:

   Engine starting in gears other than Park or Neutral.

   Indicator on shifter pointing to a gear other than the one actually being used.
   Vehicle moves when in Park.
2   Refer to Chapter 7 to adjust the linkage.

41   Fluid leakage

1   Automatic transmission fluid is a deep red color. Fluid leaks should not be confused with engine oil, which can easily be blown by air flow to the transmission.
2   To pinpoint a leak, first remove all built-up dirt and grime from around the transmission. Degreasing agents and/or steam cleaning will achieve this. With the underside clean, drive the vehicle at low speeds so air flow will not blow the leak far from its source. Raise the vehicle and determine where the leak is coming from. Common areas of leakage are:
   a) Pan: Tighten mounting bolts and/or replace pan gasket as necessary (see Chapters 1 and 7).
   b) Filler pipe: Replace the rubber seal where pipe enters transmission case.
   c) Transmission fluid lines: Tighten connectors where lines enter transmission case and/or replace lines.
   d) Vent pipe: Transmission overfilled and/or water in fluid (see checking procedures, Chapter 1).
   e) Speedometer connector: Replace the O-ring where speedometer cable enters transmission case (Chapter 7).

42   Transmission will not downshift with accelerator pedal pressed to the floor

   Vacuum modulator faulty or out of adjustment.

43   Engine will start in gears other than Park or Neutral

   Shift linkage out of adjustment (Chapter 7). Have the neutral start switch checked as well.

44   Transmission slips, shifts rough, is noisy or has no drive in forward or reverse gears

1   There are many probable causes for the above problems, but the home mechanic should be concerned with only one possibility — fluid level.
2   Before taking the vehicle to a repair shop, check the level and condition of the fluid as described in Chapter 1. Correct fluid level as necessary or change the fluid and filter if needed. If the problem persists, have a professional diagnose the probable cause.

Drive axles

45   Clicking noise in turns

1   Worn or damaged outboard CV joint. Check for cut or damaged boot. Repair as necessary (Chapter 8).

46   Knock or clunk when accelerating from a coast

1   Worn or damaged inboard CV joint. Check for cut or damaged boot. Repair as necessary (Chapter 8).

47   Shudder or vibration during acceleration

1   Worn or damaged inboard or outboard joints. Repair or replace as

necessary (Chapter 8).
2   Sticking inboard joint assembly. Correct or replace as necessary (Chapter 8).

Brakes

Note: *Before assuming that a brake problem exists, make sure that the tires are in good condition and inflated properly (see Chapter 1), that the front end alignment is correct and that the vehicle is not loaded with weight in an unequal manner.*

48   Vehicle pulls to one side during braking

1   Defective, damaged or oil contaminated disc brake pads on one side. Inspect as described in Chapter 9.
2   Excessive wear of brake pad material or disc on one side. Inspect and correct as necessary.
3   Loose or disconnected front suspension components. Inspect and tighten all bolts to the specified torque (Chapter 11).
4   Defective caliper assembly. Remove caliper and inspect for stuck piston or other damage (Chapter 9).

49   Noise (high-pitched squeal without the brakes applied)

Disc brake pads worn out. The noise comes from the wear sensor rubbing against the disc (does not apply to all vehicles). Replace pads with new ones immediately (Chapter 9).

50   Excessive brake pedal travel

1   Partial brake system failure. Inspect entire system (Chapter 9) and correct as required.
2   Insufficient fluid in master cylinder. Check (Chapter 1), add fluid and bleed system if necessary (Chapter 9).
3   Rear brakes not adjusting properly. Make a series of starts and stops while the vehicle is in Reverse. If this does not correct the situation, remove drums and inspect self-adjusters (Chapter 9).

51   Brake pedal feels spongy when depressed

1   Air in hydraulic lines. Bleed the brake system (Chapter 9).
2   Faulty flexible hoses. Inspect all system hoses and lines. Replace parts as necessary.
3   Master cylinder mounting bolts/nuts loose.
4   Master cylinder defective (Chapter 9).

52   Excessive effort required to stop vehicle

1   Power brake booster not operating properly (Chapter 9).
2   Excessively worn linings or pads. Inspect and replace if necessary (Chapter 9).
3   One or more caliper pistons or wheel cylinders seized or sticking. Inspect and rebuild as required (Chapter 9).
4   Brake linings or pads contaminated with oil or grease. Inspect and replace as required (Chapter 9).
5   New pads or shoes installed and not yet seated. It will take a while for the new material to seat against the drum (or rotor).

53   Pedal travels to the floor with little resistance

Little or no fluid in the master cylinder reservoir caused by leaking wheel cylinder(s), leaking caliper piston(s), loose, damaged or disconnected brake lines. Inspect entire system and correct as necessary.

54   Brake pedal pulsates during brake application

1   Wheel bearings not adjusted properly or in need of replacement (Chapter 1).
2   Caliper not sliding properly due to improper installation or obstructions. Remove and inspect (Chapter 9).
3   Rotor defective. Remove the rotor (Chapter 9) and check for excessive lateral runout and parallelism. Have the rotor resurfaced or replace it with a new one.

55   Clunking noise during light brake pedal application or when driving over rough roads at low speed

An American Motors dealer technical service bulletin concerning this problem has been issued. Take the vehicle to your dealer and inform him of the problem.

56   Low frequency noise during light to moderate brake application (may range from a wire brush sound to a low pich squeal)

An American Motors dealer technical service bulletin concerning this problem has been issued. Take the vehicle to your dealer and inform him of the problem.

Suspension and steering systems

57   Vehicle pulls to one side

1   Tire pressures uneven (Chapter 1).
2   Defective tire (Chapter 1).
3   Excessive wear in suspension or steering components (Chapter 11).
4   Front end in need of alignment.
5   Front brakes dragging. Inspect brakes as described in Chapter 9.

58   Shimmy, shake or vibration

1   Tire or wheel out-of-balance or out-of-round. Have professionally balanced.
2   Loose, worn or out-of-adjustment wheel bearings (Chapters 1 and 8).
3   Shock absorbers and/or suspension components worn or damaged (Chapter 11).

59   Excessive pitching and/or rolling around corners or during braking

1   Defective shock absorbers. Replace as a set (Chapter 11).
2   Broken or weak springs and/or suspension components. Inspect as described in Chapter 11.

60   Excessively stiff steering

1   Lack of fluid in power steering fluid reservoir (Chapter 1).
2   Incorrect tire pressures (Chapter 1).
3   Front end out of alignment.
4   See also section titled *Lack of power assistance.*

61   Excessive play in steering

1   Excessive wear in suspension or steering balljoints (Chapter 11).
2   Steering gearbox worn (Chapter 11).

62 Lack of power assistance

1   Steering pump drivebelt faulty or not adjusted properly (Chapter 1).
2   Fluid level low (Chapter 1).
3   Hoses or lines restricted. Inspect and replace parts as necessary.
4   Air in power steering system. Bleed system (Chapter 11).

63 Excessive tire wear (not specific to one area)

1   Incorrect tire pressures (Chapter 1).
2   Tires out of balance. Have professionally balanced.
3   Wheels damaged. Inspect and replace as necessary.
4   Suspension or steering components excessively worn (Chapter 11).

64 Excessive tire wear on outside edge

1   Inflation pressures incorrect (Chapter 1).

2   Excessive speed in turns.
3   Front end alignment incorrect (excessive toe-in). Have professionally aligned.
4   Suspension arm bent or twisted (Chapter 11).

65 Excessive tire wear on inside edge

1   Inflation pressures incorrect (Chapter 1).
2   Front end alignment incorrect (toe-out). Have professionally aligned.
3   Loose or damaged steering components (Chapter 11).

66 Tire tread worn in one place

1   Tires out of balance.
2   Damaged or buckled wheel. Inspect and replace if necessary.
3   Defective tire (Chapter 1).

Chapter 1   Tune-up and routine maintenance

Contents

Specifications

Recommended lubricants and fluids

Engine oil
    Type . . . . API type SF only
    Viscosity
        Above 14°F 10W40
        Below 14°F 10W30
        Below −4°F . . . . 5W20 or 5W30
    Capacity
        1.4 liter engine . . . . 4 US quarts
        1.7 liter engine . . . . 5.5 US quarts
Coolant type . . . . 50/50 mix of distilled water and antifreeze (ALUGARD 340-2 on the label)

Coolant capacity
    1.4 liter engine
        With air conditioner . . . . 4.8 US quarts
        Without air conditioner . . . . 4.4 US quarts
    1.7 liter engine . . . . 7.0 US quarts
Brake fluid type . . . . DOT 3 or SAE J-1703F
Manual transmission oil type
    Normal use . . . . SAE 80W90 API GL-5 gear oil
    Sustained use below 14°F . . . . SAE 75W90 API GL-5 gear oil
Manual transmission oil capacity
    4-speed . . . . 3.4 US quarts
    5-speed . . . . 3.6 US quarts
Automatic transmission fluid
    Type . . . . Dexron II or Mobil 220
    Capacity . . . . 3.75 US quarts
Power steering fluid type . . . . Dexron II
Windshield washer fluid . . . . Water and/or special windshield cleaner

Drivebelt deflection

1.4 liter engine	
Alternator	4 to 5 mm
Water pump/air conditioner	3.5 to 4.5 mm
1.7 liter engine	Must be checked with gauge (see dealer service department)

Brakes

Front pad thickness	9/32 in (7 mm) minimum (including metal shoe)
Rear brake lining thickness	1/32 in (0.5 mm) minimum (above rivet head or shoe)

Engine

Idle speed	Check Vehicle Emission Control Information label in the engine compartment
Spark plugs	
Type	
1.4 liter engine	Champion RN12YC
1.7 liter engine	Champion RN9YC
Gap	0.032 in
Ignition timing*	
1.4 liter engine	$8 \pm 1°$ BTDC
1.7 liter engine	Check Vehicle Emission Control Information label in engine compartment
Cylinder compression	130 psi
Valve clearances	
1.4 liter engine	
Intake	0.006 in
Exhaust	0.008 in
1.7 liter engine	
Intake	0.008 in
Exhaust	0.016 in

* Not adjustable, see text

Torque specifications	**Ft-lbs**
Oil pan drain plug	16
Spark plugs	21

1 Introduction to routine maintenance

This Chapter was designed to help the home mechanic maintain his (or her) vehicle for peak performance, economy, safety and long life.

On the following pages you will find a maintenance schedule along with Sections which deal specifically with each item on the schedule. Included are visual checks, adjustments and item replacements.

Servicing your vehicle using the time/mileage maintenance schedule and the sequenced Sections will give you a planned program of maintenance. Keep in mind that it is a full plan, and maintaining only a few items at the specified intervals will not give you the same results.

You will find as you service your vehicle that many of the procedures can, and should, be grouped together, due to the nature of the job at hand. Examples of this are as follows:

If the vehicle is fully raised for a chassis lubrication, for example, this is the ideal time for the following checks: manual transmission oil; exhaust system; suspension; steering and the fuel system.

If the tires and wheels are removed, as during a routine tire rotation, go ahead and check the brakes at the same time.

If you must borrow or rent a torque wrench, it is a good idea to replace the spark plugs at the same time to save both time and money.

The first step of this or any maintenance plan is to prepare yourself before the actual work begins. Read through the appropriate Sections for all work that is to be performed before you begin. Gather together all necessary parts and tools. If it appears that you could have a problem during a particular job, don't hesitate to seek advice from your local parts man or dealer service department.

2 Routine maintenance schedule

The following recommendations are given with the assumption that the vehicle owner will be doing the maintenance or service work (as opposed to having a dealer service department do the work). The following are factory maintenance recommendations; however, subject to the preference of the individual owner, in the interest of keeping his or her vehicle in peak condition at all times and with the vehicle's ultimate resale in mind, many of these operations may be performed more often. We encourage such owner initiative.

When the vehicle is new, it should be serviced initially by a factory authorized dealer service department to protect the factory warranty. In most cases the initial maintenance check is done at no cost to the owner.

Every 250 miles or weekly, whichever comes first

Check the engine oil level (Sec 5)
Check the engine coolant level (Sec 5)
Check the windshield washer fluid level (Sec 5)
Check the tires and tire pressures (Sec 4)

Every 6000 miles or 6 months, whichever comes first

Check the automatic transmission fluid level (Sec 5)
Check the power steering fluid level (Sec 5)
Change the engine oil and oil filter (Sec 16)
Check the cooling system (Sec 8)
Check and replace (if necessary) the underhood hoses (Sec 9)
Check the exhaust system (Sec 12)
Check the steering and suspension components (Sec 13)
Check and adjust (if necessary) the engine drivebelts (Sec 7)
Check the brake master cylinder fluid level (Sec 5)
Check the manual transmission oil level (Sec 5)
Check the disc brake pads (Sec 14)
Check the brake system (Sec 14)
Check and service the battery (Sec 6)
Check and replace (if necessary) the windshield wiper blades (Sec 10)
Check the driveaxle rubber boots for cracks and damage (Sec 28)

Every 12000 miles or 12 months, whichever comes first

Check the drum brake linings (Sec 14)
Check the parking brake (Sec 14)
Check the clutch pedal free play (Sec 20)
Rotate the tires (Sec 19)
Check the fuel system components (Sec 17)
Replace the fuel filter (Sec 18)
Check/adjust the valve clearances (1.4 liter engine) (Sec 30)
Drain, flush and refill the cooling system (Sec 21)

Every 18000 miles or 18 months, whichever comes first

Change the automatic transmission fluid and filter (if driven mainly in heavy city traffic in hot climates, in hilly or mountainous areas, or for frequent trailer pulling) (Sec 22)

Every 24000 miles or 24 months, whichever comes first

Replace the air filter (Sec 24)
Replace the spark plugs (Sec 26)
Check the spark plug wires, distributor cap and rotor (Sec 27)
Check the ignition timing (Sec 25)
Change the automatic transmission fluid (if driven under severe conditions, change at 18000 miles) (Sec 22)
Change the automatic transmission oil (Sec 23)
Check the engine compression (Sec 29)
Check/adjust the valve clearances (1.7 liter engine) (Sec 30)

Every 80000 miles

Replace the timing belt with a new one (1.7 liter engine) (Chapter 2)

3   Tune-up sequence

The term 'tune-up' is loosely used for any general operation that puts the engine back in its proper running condition. A tune-up is not a specific operation, but rather a combination of individual operations, such as replacing the spark plugs and air filter and checking the ignition timing, etc.

If, from the time the vehicle is new, the routine maintenance schedule (Section 2) is followed closely and frequent checks are made of fluid levels and high wear items, as suggested throughout this manual, the engine will be kept in relatively good running condition and the need for additional tune-ups will be minimized.

More likely than not, however, there will be times when the engine is running poorly due to lack of regular maintenance. This is even more likely if a used vehicle (which has not received regular and frequent maintenance checks) is purchased. In such cases, an engine tune-up will be needed outside of the regular routine maintenance intervals.

The following series of operations are those most often needed to bring a generally poor running engine back into a proper state of tune.

Minor tune-up
Clean, inspect and test battery (Sec 6)
Check all engine-related fluids (Sec 5)
Check engine compression (Sec 29)
Check and adjust drivebelts (Sec 7)
Replace spark plugs (Sec 26)
Inspect distributor cap and rotor (Sec 27)
Inspect spark plug and coil wires (Sec 27)
Check ignition timing (Sec 25)
Replace fuel filter (Sec 18)
Check cooling system (Sec 8)

Major tune-up
(the above operations and those listed below)
Check EGR system (Chapter 6)
Check ignition system (Chapter 5)
Check charging system (Chapter 5)
Check fuel system (Sec 17)

4   Tire and tire pressure checks

1   Periodically inspecting the tires may not only prevent you from being stranded with a flat tire, but can also give you clues as to possible problems with the steering and suspension systems before major damage occurs.
2   Proper tire inflation adds miles to the lifespan of the tires, allows the vehicle to achieve maximum miles per gallon figures and contributes to the overall quality of the ride.
3   When inspecting the tires, first check the wear of the tread. Irregularities in the tread pattern (cupping, flat spots, more wear on one side than the other) are indications of front end alignment and/or balance problems. If any of these conditions are noted, take the vehicle to a reputable repair shop to correct the problem.
4   Also check the tread area for cuts and punctures. Many times a nail or tack will embed itself into the tire tread and yet the tire will hold its air pressure for a short time. In most cases, a repair shop or gas station can repair the punctured tire.
5   It is also important to check the sidewalls of the tires, both inside and outside. Check for deteriorated rubber, cuts, and punctures. Also inspect the inboard side of the tire for signs of brake fluid leakage, indicating that a thorough brake inspection is needed immediately.
6   Incorrect tire pressure cannot be determined merely by looking at the tire. This is especially true for radial tires. A tire pressure gauge must be used. If you do not already have a reliable gauge, it is a good idea to purchase one and keep it in the glovebox. Built-in pressure gauges at gas stations are often unreliable.
7   Always check tire inflation when the tires are cold. Cold, in this case, means the vehicle has not been driven more than one mile after sitting for three hours or more. It is normal for the pressure to increase four to eight pounds or more when the tires are hot.
8   Unscrew the valve cap protruding from the wheel or hubcap and press the gauge firmly onto the valve stem. Observe the reading on the gauge and compare the figure to the recommended tire pressure listed on the tire placard. The tire placard is usually attached to the driver's door or the glovebox door.
9   Check all tires and add air as necessary to bring them up to the recommended pressure levels. Do not forget the spare tire. Be sure to reinstall the valve caps (which will keep dirt and moisture out of the valve stem mechanism).

5   Fluid level checks

1   There are a number of components on a vehicle which rely on the use of fluids to perform their job. During normal operation of the vehicle,

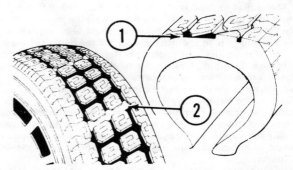

Fig. 1.1 The tread wear indicators are molded into the tread grooves (1) — if the wear indicator is exposed (2), the tire should be replaced (Sec 4)

5.4   After wiping off the engine oil dipstick, make sure it is reinserted all the way before withdrawing it for the oil level check

5.6   The oil filler cap is located on the rocker arm cover

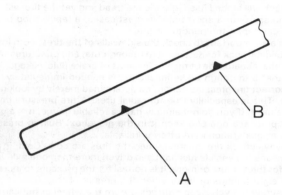

Fig. 1.2 The oil dipstick has an *Add* (A) and a *Full* (B) mark on it (Sec 5)

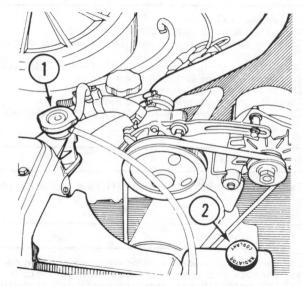

Fig. 1.3 Earlier models have a remote filler cap (1) and a reservoir cap (2) (Sec 5)

these fluids are used up and must be replenished before damage occurs. See *Recommended lubricants and fluids* at the front of this Chapter for the specific fluid to be used when addition is required. When checking fluid levels, it is important to have the vehicle on a level surface. **Note:** *Some models are equipped with a systems Sentry monitoring and warning system which will indicate low fluid levels by illuminating a red light on the instrument panel. The fluid levels can be checked manually as described below, but be sure to disconnect the sensor wires from the dipstick or cap before removing them. Refer to your owner's handbook for more information on this sytem.*

Engine oil
2   The engine oil level is checked with a dipstick which is located at the side of the engine block (which is actually the 'front' of the engine since the engine is mounted sideways in these vehicles). The dipstick travels through a tube and into the oil pan to the bottom of the engine.
3   The oil level should be checked preferably before the vehicle has been driven, or about 15 minutes after the engine has been shut off. If the oil is checked immediately after driving the vehicle, some of the oil will remain in the upper engine components, producing an inaccurate reading on the dipstick.
4   Pull the dipstick from the tube (photo) and wipe all the oil from the end with a clean rag. Insert the clean dipstick all the way back into the oil pan and pull it out again. Observe the oil at the end of the dipstick. At its highest point, the level should be between the *Add* and *Full* marks.
5   It takes approximately one quart of oil to raise the level from the *Add* mark to the *Full* mark on the dipstick. Do not allow the level to drop below the *Add* mark as engine damage due to oil starvation may occur. On the other hand, do not overfill the engine by adding oil above

the *Full* mark since it may result in oil-fouled spark plugs, oil leaks or oil seal failures.
6   Oil is added to the engine after removing a twist-off cap located on the rocker arm cover (photo). The cap should be marked *Engine oil* or *Oil*. An oil can spout or funnel will reduce spills as the oil is poured in.
7   Checking the oil level can also be an important preventative maintenance step. If you find the oil level dropping abnormally, it is an indication of oil leakage or internal engine wear which should be corrected. If there are water droplets in the oil, or if it is milky looking, component failure is indicated and the engine should be checked immediately. The condition of the oil can also be checked along with the level. With the dipstick removed from the engine, take your thumb and index finger and wipe the oil up the dipstick, looking for small dirt or metal particles which will cling to the dipstick. This is an indication that the oil should be drained and fresh oil added (Section 16).

Engine coolant
8   All vehicles covered by this manual are equipped with a pressurized coolant recovery system which makes coolant level checks very easy. A clear or white coolant reservoir attached to the inner fender panel is connected by a hose to the remote filler cap (on later models, the filler cap is part of the reservoir). As the engine heats up during operation, coolant is forced from the system, through the connecting tube

5.9A   The coolant reservoir on later models is located on the right side of the firewall

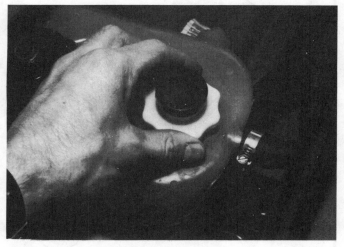

5.9B   On later models, the remote filler cap is integral with the reservoir (it must be removed to add coolant to the system)

5.15   The windshield washer reservoir is tucked into the right front corner of the engine compartment (do not fill it completely if freezing weather is expected)

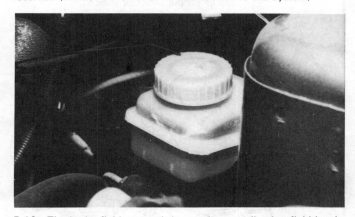

5.19   The brake fluid reservoir is translucent, allowing fluid level checks at a glance

and into the reservoir. As the engine cools, the coolant is automatically drawn back into the system to keep the level correct.

9   The coolant level should be checked when the engine is hot. Merely observe the level of fluid in the reservoir, which should be at or near the *Full* mark on the side of the reservoir (photo). If the system is completely cool, also check the level in the remote filler assembly by removing the cap (photo).

10 **Caution:** *Under no circumstances should either the radiator cap or the remote filler cap be removed when the system is hot, because escaping steam and scalding coolant could cause serious personal injury. In the case of the remote filler cap, wait until the system has cooled completely, then wrap a thick cloth around the cap and turn it to the first stop. If any steam escapes, wait until the system has cooled further, then remove the cap. The radiator cap may also be removed after the engine has cooled completely.*

11 If only a small amount of coolant is required to bring the system up to the proper level, regular water can be used. However, to maintain the proper antifreeze/water mixture in the system, both should be mixed together to replenish a low level. High-quality antifreeze offering protection to −20 °F should be mixed with water in the proportion specified on the container. Do not allow antifreeze to come in contact with your skin or painted surfaces of the vehicle. Flush contacted areas immediately with plenty of water.

12 Coolant should be added to the reservoir until it reaches the *Full* mark.

13 As the coolant level is checked, note the condition of the coolant. It should be relatively clear. If it is brown or a rust color, the system should be drained, flushed and refilled (Section 21).

14 If the cooling system requires repeated additions to maintain the proper level, have the remote filler cap checked for proper sealing ability.

Also check for leaks in the system (cracked hoses, loose hose connections, leaking gaskets, etc.).

Windshield washer fluid

15 Fluid for the windshield washer system is located in a plastic reservoir (photo). The level in the reservoir should be maintained at the *Full* mark, except during periods when freezing temperatures are expected, at which times the fluid level should be maintained no higher than 3/4 full to allow for expansion should the fluid freeze. The use of an additive designed for windshield washer systems will help lower the freezing point of the fluid and will result in better cleaning of the windshield surface. Do not use antifreeze because it will cause damage to the vehicle's paint.

16 Also, to help prevent icing in cold weather, warm the windshield with the defroster before using the washer.

Battery electrolyte

17 All vehicles with which this manual is concerned are equipped with a 'maintenance-free' battery which is permanently sealed (except for vent holes) and has no filler caps. Water does not have to be added to these batteries at any time.

Brake fluid

18 The master cylinder is mounted directly on the firewall (manual brake models) or on the front of the power booster unit (power brake models) in the engine compartment.

19 The master cylinder reservoir is made of translucent plastic, which allows checking of the brake fluid level without removal of the reservoir cap. The level should be maintained between the *Max* and *Min* marks (photo).

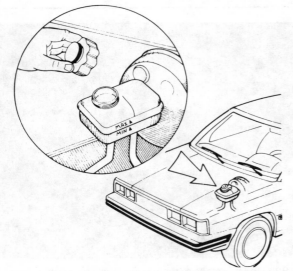

Fig. 1.4 Make sure the brake fluid level is between the
marks on the reservoir (Sec 5)

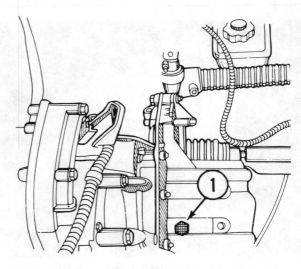

Fig. 1.5 Manual transmission check/fill plug location (1)
(Sec 5)

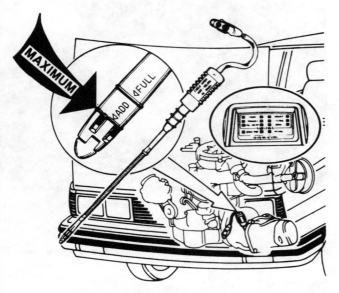

Fig. 1.6 Automatic transmission dipstick used on vehicles
with *Systems Sentry* (Sec 5)

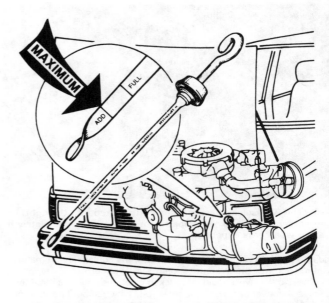

Fig. 1.7 Type I automatic transmission dipstick (no longer
used) (Sec 5)

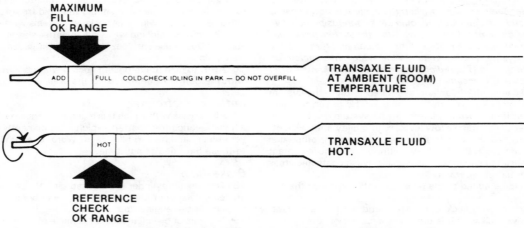

Fig. 1.8 Type II automatic transmission dipstick (Sec 5)

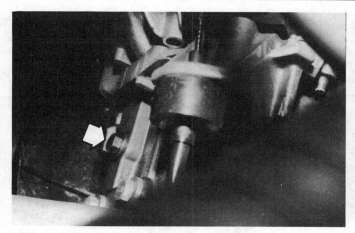

5.26 The check/fill plug is located on the front of the manual transmission

5.45 The power steering fluid reservoir has a sight glass built into the side so the fluid level can be easily checked

20 If a low level is indicated, be sure to wipe the top of the reservoir with a clean rag, to prevent contamination of the brake system, before removing the cap. Also, be sure to disconnect the wire (if equipped) from the cap before removing it.
21 When adding fluid, pour it carefully into the reservoir, taking care not to spill any onto surrounding painted surfaces. Be sure the specified fluid is used, since mixing different types of brake fluid can cause damage to the system. See *Recommended lubricants and fluids* or your owner's manual.
22 At this time the fluid and master cylinder can be inspected for contamination. Normally, the brake system will not need periodic draining and refilling, but if rust deposits, dirt particles or water droplets are seen in the fluid, the system should be dismantled, drained and refilled with fresh fluid.
23 After filling the reservoir to the proper level, make sure the cap is properly seated to prevent fluid leakage and/or system contamination.
24 The brake fluid in the master cylinder will drop slightly as the brake shoes or pads at each wheel wear down during normal operation. If the master cylinder requires repeated replenishing to keep it at the proper level, this is an indication of leakage in the brake system, which should be corrected immediately. Check all brake lines and connections, along with the wheel cylinders and booster (see Section 14 for more information).
25 If upon checking the master cylinder fluid level you discover one or both reservoirs empty or nearly empty, the brake system should be bled (Chapter 9).

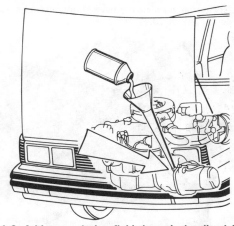

Fig. 1.9 Add transmission fluid through the dipstick hole (use a funnel to prevent spills) (Sec 5)

Manual transmission oil
26 Manual shift transmissions do not have a dipstick. The oil level is checked with the engine cold by removing a plug from the side (front) of the transmission case (photo). Locate the plug and use a rag to clean the plug and the area around it, then remove it with a wrench.
27 If oil immediately starts leaking out, thread the plug back into the transmission because the level is all right. If there is no leakage, completely remove the plug and place your little finger inside the hole. The oil level should be just at the bottom of the plug hole.
28 If the transmission needs more oil, use a syringe to squeeze the appropriate lubricant into the plug hole until the level is correct.
29 Thread the plug back into the transmission and tighten it securely.
30 Drive the vehicle a short distance, then check to make sure the plug is not leaking.

Automatic transmission fluid
31 The level of the automatic transmission fluid should be carefully maintained. Low fluid level can lead to slipping or loss of drive, while overfilling can cause foaming and loss of fluid. The fluid level should be checked only when the engine is completely cool.
32 With the parking brake set, start the engine, then move the shift lever through all the gear ranges, ending in Park. The fluid level must be checked with the vehicle level and the engine running at idle (don't let the engine run very long before making the check or the transmission fluid will heat up).
33 Locate the dipstick at the front of the transmission and pull it out of the filler tube.

34 Wipe the fluid from the dipstick and push it back into the filler tube until the cap seats.
35 Pull the dipstick out again and note the fluid level.
36 On models with a *Systems Sentry* or a *type I* dipstick (see accompanying illustration), the correct fluid level is at but not above the *Add* mark.
37 On models with a *type II* dipstick, the correct level is between the *Add* and *Full* marks. **Note:** *The type II dipstick can be used in all automatic transmissions.*
38 Add just enough of the recommended fluid to fill the transmission to the proper level. It takes about one-half (1/2) pint to raise the level from the *Add* mark to the *Full* mark, so add the fluid a little at a time and keep checking the level until it is correct.
39 The condition of the fluid should also be checked along with the level. If the fluid at the end of the dipstick is a dark reddish-brown color, or if the fluid has a burnt smell, the transmission fluid should be changed. If you are in doubt about the condition of the fluid, purchase some new fluid and compare the two for color and smell.

Power steering fluid
40 Unlike manual steering, the power steering system relies on fluid which may, over a period of time, require replenishing.
41 The reservoir for the power steering pump is attached to the left-hand (passenger) side fender well in the engine compartment.
42 For the check, the front wheels should be pointed straight ahead and the engine should be off.
43 Use a clean rag to wipe off the reservoir and the area around the cap. This will help prevent any foreign matter from entering the reservoir if the cap must be removed to add fluid.
44 Make sure the engine is at normal operating temperature.
45 Check the fluid level on the side of the reservoir. It should be at the *Full* mark (photo).

6.4A Battery terminal corrosion usually appears as a white fluffy powder

6.4B Removing the cable from the battery post (always remove the ground cable first and hook it up last)

6.4C Cleaning the battery post with a special tool

6.4D Cleaning the battery cable clamp

46 If it isn't, remove the cap (disconnect the wire first — if equipped) and add the recommended fluid until the level is correct. A funnel will help prevent spills.

47 If the reservoir requires frequent fluid additions, all power steering hoses, hose connections, the power steering pump and the steering gear should be carefully checked for leaks.

6   Battery check and maintenance

1 A sealed *maintenance-free* battery is standard equipment on all vehicles with which this manual is concerned. Although this type of battery has many advantages over the older, capped cell type and never requires the addition of water, it should be routinely maintained according to the procedures which follow. **Warning:** *Hydrogen gas in small quantities is present in the area of the two small side vents on sealed batteries, so keep lighted tobacco and open flames or sparks away from them.*

2 The external condition of the battery should be monitored periodically for damage such as a cracked case or cover.

3 Check the tightness of the battery cable clamps to ensure good electrical connections and check the entire length of each cable for cracks and frayed conductors.

4 If corrosion (visible as white, fluffy deposits) is evident, remove the cables from the terminals, clean them with a battery brush and reinstall the cables (photos). Corrosion can be kept to a minimum by

6.5 Make sure the positive battery terminal cover (if originally equipped) is in place and in good condition.

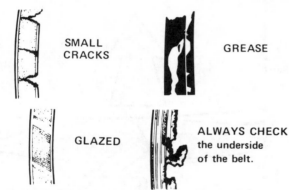

Fig. 1.10 Some of the common types of drivebelt deterioration (check them carefully to prevent an untimely breakdown) (Sec 7)

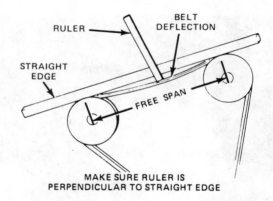

Fig. 1.11 Drivebelt tension can be checked with a straightedge and ruler (1.4 liter engine) (Sec 7)

applying a layer of petroleum jelly or grease to the terminals and cable clamps after they are assembled.

5   Make sure that the rubber/plastic protector (if so equipped) over the positive terminal is not torn or missing. It should completely cover the terminal (photo).

6   Make sure that the battery carrier is in good condition and that the hold-down clamp bolt is tight. If the battery is removed from the carrier, make sure that no parts remain in the bottom of the carrier when the battery is reinstalled. When reinstalling the hold-down clamp bolt, do not overtighten it.

7   Corrosion on the hold-down components, battery case and surrounding areas may be removed with a solution of water and baking soda, but take care to prevent any solution from coming in contact with your eyes, skin or clothes, as it contains acid. Protective gloves should be worn. Thoroughly wash all cleaned areas with plain water.

8   Any metal parts of the vehicle damaged by corrosion should be covered with a zinc-based primer, then painted after the affected areas have been cleaned and dried.

9   Further information on the battery, charging and jump-starting can be found in Chapter 5.

7 Drivebelt check and adjustment

1   The drivebelts, or V-belts as they are sometimes called, are located at the front of the engine (in this case, the *front* is actually the right-hand side, since the engine is mounted sideways) and play an important role in the overall operation of the vehicle and its components. Due to their function and material make-up, the belts are prone to failure after a period of time and should be inspected and adjusted periodically to prevent major engine damage.

2   The number of belts used on a particular vehicle depends on the accessories installed. Drivebelts are used to turn the alternator, power steering pump, water pump and air-conditioning compressor. Depending on the pulley arrangement, a single belt may be used to drive more than one of these components. **Note:** *A single belt is used to drive all of the components on the 1.7 liter engine. Due to the need for a special tension measuring tool, the belt on these engines should be checked and adjusted by a dealer service department.*

3   With the engine off, open the hood and locate the various belts at the front of the engine. Using your fingers (and a flashlight, if necessary), move along the belts checking for cracks and separation of the belt plies. Also check for fraying and glazing, which gives the belt a shiny appearance. Both sides of the belt should be inspected, which means you will have to twist the belt to check the underside.

4   The tension of each belt is checked by pushing on the belt at a distance halfway between the pulleys. Push firmly with your thumb and see how much the belt moves down (deflects). A rule of thumb is that if the distance from pulley center-to-pulley center is between 7 and 11 inches, the belt should deflect 1/4-inch. If the belt is longer and travels between pulleys spaced 12 to 16 inches apart, the belt should deflect 1/2-inch.

5   If it is necessary to adjust the belt tension, either to make the belt tighter or looser, it is done by moving the belt-driven accessory on the bracket.

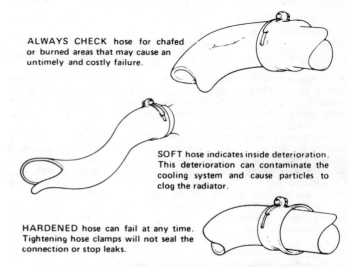

ALWAYS CHECK hose for chafed or burned areas that may cause an untimely and costly failure.

SOFT hose indicates inside deterioration. This deterioration can contaminate the cooling system and cause particles to clog the radiator.

HARDENED hose can fail at any time. Tightening hose clamps will not seal the connection or stop leaks.

Fig. 1.12 Simple checks can detect cooling system hose defects (Sec 8)

6   For each component there will be an adjustment or strap bolt and a pivot bolt. Both bolts must be loosened slightly to enable you to move the component.

7   After the two bolts have been loosened, move the component away from the engine (to tighten the belt) or toward the engine (to loosen the belt). Hold the accessory in position and check the belt tension. If it is correct, tighten the two bolts until just snug, then recheck the tension. If it is all right, tighten the bolts.

8   It will often be necessary to use some sort of pry bar to move the accessory while the belt is adjusted. If this must be done to gain the proper leverage, be very careful not to damage the component being moved or the part being pried against.

8 Cooling system check

Caution: *The electric cooling fan can activate at any time, even when the ignition switch is in the Off position. Disconnect the fan motor wire or negative battery cable when working in the vicinity of the fan.*

1   Many major engine failures can be attributed to a faulty cooling system. If the vehicle is equipped with an automatic transmission, the cooling system also plays an important role in prolonging its life.

2   The cooling system should be checked with the engine cold. Do this before the vehicle is driven for the day or after it has been shut off for at least three hours.

3   Remove the remote filler cap and thoroughly clean the cap (inside and out) with clean water. Also clean the neck in the remote filler assembly. All traces of corrosion should be removed.

8.4   Although this radiator hose appears to be in good condition, it should still be periodically checked for cracks (more easily noticed when the hose is squeezed)

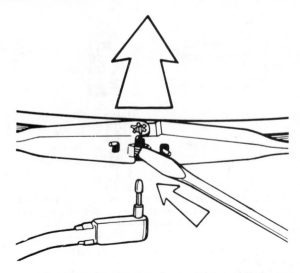

Fig. 1.13 Windshield wiper blade removal (early models) (Sec 10)

4   Carefully check the upper and lower radiator hoses along with the smaller diameter heater hoses. Inspect each hose along its entire length, replacing any hose which is cracked, swollen or shows signs of deterioration. Cracks may become more apparent if the hose is squeezed (photo).
5   Also make sure that all hose connections are tight. A leak in the cooling system will usually show up as white or rust colored deposits on the areas adjoining the leak.
6   Use compressed air or a soft brush to remove bugs, leaves, etc. from the front of the radiator or air-conditioning condenser. Be careful not to damage the delicate cooling fins or cut yourself on them.
7   Finally, have the cap and system pressure tested. If you do not have a pressure tester, most gas stations and repair shops will do this for a minimal charge.

9   Underhood hose check and replacement

Caution: *Replacement of air-conditioner hoses must be left to a dealer service department or an air-conditioning technician who can depressurize the system and perform the work safely.*
1   The high temperatures present under the hood can cause deterioration of the numerous rubber and plastic hoses.
2   Periodic inspection should be made for cracks, loose clamps and leaks because some of the hoses are part of the emissions control systems and can affect the engine's performance.
3   Remove the air cleaner if necessary and trace the entire length of each hose. Squeeze each hose to check for cracks and look for swelling, discoloration and leaks.
4   If the vehicle has considerable mileage or if one or more of the hoses is deteriorated, it is a good idea to replace all of the hoses at one time.
5   Measure the length and inside diameter of each hose and obtain and cut the replacement to size. Since original equipment hose clamps are often good for only one or two uses, it is a good idea to replace them with worm-drive clamps.
6   Replace each hose one at a time to eliminate the possibility of confusion. Hoses attached to the heater and radiator contain coolant, so newspapers or rags should be kept handy to catch the spills when they are disconnected.
7   After installation, run the engine until it reaches operating temperature, shut it off and check for leaks. After the engine has cooled, retighten all of the worm-drive clamps.

10   Windshield wiper blade inspection and replacement

1   The windshield wiper and blade assembly should be inspected

periodically for damage, loose components and cracked or worn blade elements.
2   Road film can build up on the wiper blades and affect their efficiency so they should be washed regularly with a mild detergent solution.
3   The action of the wiping mechanism can loosen the fasteners so they should be checked and tightened, as necessary, at the same time the wiper blades are checked.
4   If the wiper blade elements are cracked, worn or warped, they should be replaced with new ones. Use a small screwdriver to depress the retaining spring, then pull the blade assembly off the pin on the arm. Install the new blade by positioning it over the wiper arm pin and pressing on it until it snaps into place. **Note:** *Later model wiper blade assemblies can be separated from the arm by grasping the arm and pivoting the blade away from it.*
5   The wiper blade element is locked in place at either end of the wiper blade assembly by a spring-loaded retainer and metal tabs. To remove the element, squeeze the retainer and slide the element up, out of the tabs.
6   To install, slide the element into the retaining tabs, lining up the slot in the element with the tabs, and snap the element into place.
7   Snap the blade assembly into place on the wiper arm pin.

11   Body lubrication

1   Raise the vehicle and support it securely on jackstands.
2   Clean and lubricate the brake cable, along with the cable guides and levers. This can be done by smearing some chassis grease onto the cable and its related parts with your fingers. Place a few drops of light engine oil on the transmission shift linkage rods and swivels.
3   Lower the vehicle to the ground for the remaining body lubrication process.
4   Open the hood and smear a little chassis grease on the hood latch mechanism. Have an assistant pull the release lever from inside the vehicle as you lubricate the cable at the latch.
5   Lubricate all the hinges (door, hood, hatch) with a few drops of light engine oil to keep them in proper working order.
6   Finally, the key lock cylinders can be lubricated with spray-on graphite which is available at auto parts stores.

12   Exhaust system check

1   With the engine cold (at least three hours after the vehicle has been driven), check the complete exhaust system from its starting point at the engine to the end of the tailpipe. This should be done on a hoist where unrestricted access is available.

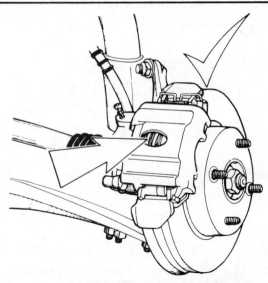

Fig. 1.14 The disc brake pads are checked by looking through the hole in the center of the caliper (Sec 14)

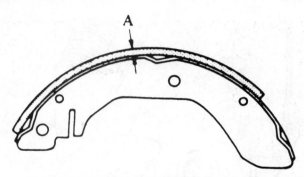

Fig. 1.15 The lining thickness of the rear brake shoes (A) is measured from the surface of the lining to the metal shoe or rivets (Sec 14)

2   Check the pipes and connections for signs of leakage and/or corrosion indicating a potential failure. Make sure that all brackets and hangers are in good condition and tight.
3   At the same time, inspect the underside of the body for holes, corrosion, open seams, etc. which may allow exhaust gases to enter the passenger compartment. Seal all body openings with silicone or body putty.
4   Rattles and other noises can often be traced to the exhaust system, especially the mounts and hangers. Try to move the pipes, muffler and catalytic converter. If the components can come in contact with the body or suspension parts, secure the exhaust system with new mounts.
5   This is also an ideal time to check the running condition of the engine by inspecting inside the very end of the tailpipe. The exhaust deposits here are an indication of engine state-of-tune. If the pipe is black and sooty or coated with white deposits, the engine may be in need of a tune-up (including a thorough fuel injection inspection and adjustment).

13   Suspension and steering check

1   Whenever the front of the vehicle is raised for service, it is a good idea to visually check the suspension and steering components for wear.
2   Indications of a fault in these systems are excessive play in the steering wheel before the front wheels react, excessive sway around corners, body movement over rough roads or binding at some point as the steering wheel is turned.
3   Before the vehicle is raised for inspection, test the shock absorbers by pushing down to rock the vehicle at each corner. If you push down and the vehicle does not come back to a level position within one or two bounces, the shocks/struts are worn and must be replaced. As this is done, check for squeaks and strange noises coming from the suspension components. Additional information on suspension components can be found in Chapter 11.
4   Now raise the front end of the vehicle and support it firmly on jackstands placed under the frame rails. Because of the work to be done, make sure the vehicle cannot fall from the stands.
5   Crawl under the vehicle and check for loose bolts, broken or disconnected parts and deteriorated rubber bushings on all suspension and steering components. Look for grease or fluid leaking from around the steering gear. Check the power steering hoses and connections for leaks. Check the balljoints for wear by checking for movement at the joint (pry gently between the balljoint and the mount).
7   Have an assistant turn the steering wheel from side-to-side and check the steering components for free movement, chafing and binding. If the steering does not react with the movement of the steering wheel, try to determine where the slack is located.

14   Brake check

1   The brakes should be inspected every time the wheels are removed or whenever a defect is suspected. Indications of a potential brake system defect are: the vehicle pulls to one side when the brake pedal is depressed; noises coming from the brakes when they are applied; excessive brake pedal travel; pulsating pedal; and leakage of fluid, usually seen on the inside of the tire or wheel.

Disc brakes
2   The front disc brakes can be visually checked without removing any parts except the wheels.
3   Raise the vehicle and place it securely on jackstands. Remove the wheels (see *Jacking and towing* at the front of the manual, if necessary).
4   The disc brake calipers, which contain the pads, are now visible. There is an outer pad and an inner pad in each caliper. All pads should be inspected.
5   Check the pad thickness by looking at each end of the caliper and through the inspection hole in the caliper body. If any pad is 9/32-inch or less in thickness, all pads should be replaced. Keep in mind that the lining material is riveted or bonded to a metal backing shoe; in this particular case, the metal portion is very definitely included in this measurement.
6   Since it will be difficult, if not impossible, to measure the exact thickness of the remaining lining material, remove the pads for further inspection or replacement (Chapter 9) if you are in doubt as to the quality of the pad.
7   Before installing the wheels, check for leakage around the brake hose connections leading to the caliper and damage (cracking, splitting, etc.) to the brake hose. Replace the hose or fittings as necessary, referring to Chapter 9.
8   Also check the condition of the rotor. Look for scoring, gouging and burnt spots. If these conditions exist, the rotor should be removed for servicing.

Drum brakes
9   Since the brake drums must be removed to check the shoe lining thickness, first refer to Chapter 9, Section 6, and remove the drums.
10 With the drum removed, carefully brush away any accumulations of dirt and dust.
Warning: *Do not blow the dust out with compressed air. Make an effort not to inhale the dust because it contains asbestos and is harmful to your health.*
11 Note the thickness of the lining material on both the front and rear brake shoes. If the material has worn away to within 1/16-inch of the recessed rivets or metal plate, the shoes should be replaced. If the linings look worn, but you are unable to determine their exact thickness, compare them with a new set at an auto parts store. The shoes should also be replaced if they are cracked, glazed (shiny surface) or contaminated with brake fluid.
12 Check to see that all the brake assembly springs are connected and in good condition.
13 Check the brake components for signs of fluid leakage. With your finger, carefully pry back the rubber boots on the wheel cylinder located

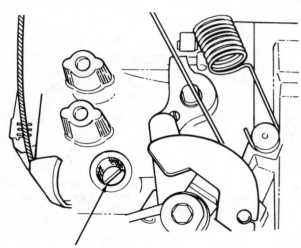

Fig. 1.16 Idle speed adjusting screw location (multi-point injection system) (Sec 15)

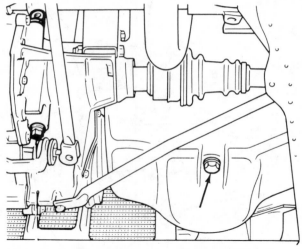

Fig. 1.17 Engine oil drain plug location (1.4 liter engine) (Sec 16)

at the top of the brake shoes. Any leakage is an indication that the wheel cylinders should be overhauled immediately (Chapter 9). Also check the hoses and connections for signs of leakage.

14 Wipe the inside of the drum with a clean rag and denatured alcohol. Again, be careful not to breathe the dangerous asbestos dust.

15 Check the inside of the drum for cracks, scores, deep scratches and hard spots which will appear as small discolored areas. If imperfections cannot be removed with fine emery cloth, the drum must be taken to a machine shop for resurfacing.

16 After the inspection process, if all parts are found to be in good condition, reinstall the brake drum (Chapter 9). Install the wheel and lower the vehicle to the ground.

Parking brake

17 The easiest way to check the operation of the parking brake is to park the vehicle on a steep hill with the parking brake set and the transmission in Neutral. If the parking brake cannot prevent the vehicle from rolling, it is in need of adjustment (see Chapter 9).

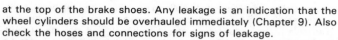

15 Engine idle speed check and adjustment

Multi-point fuel injection system

1 The idle speed adjustment screw is located on top of the throttle plate housing.

2 Start the engine and allow it to reach normal operating temperature, then shut it off (all accessories must be off as well).

3 Connect a tachometer to the diagnostic connector (terminals D1-1 and D1-3; see Chapter 4 for detailed information). Start the engine and wait for the electric cooling fan to cycle on and then off. Turn the idle speed screw as required to obtain the specified idle speed.

TBI system

4 Since the idle speed on these models is controlled electronically by the ISC, the idle speed should never require adjustment. In the event that the idle speed is incorrect, have it checked by a dealer service department.

16 Engine oil and filter change

1 Frequent oil changes may be the best form of preventative maintenance available to the home mechanic. When engine oil ages, it gets diluted and contaminated, which ultimately leads to premature engine wear.

2 Although some sources recommend oil filter changes every other oil change, we feel that the minimal cost of an oil filter and the relative ease with which it is installed dictate that a new filter be used whenever the oil is changed.

3 The tools necessary for a normal oil and filter change are a wrench

to fit the drain plug at the bottom of the oil pan, an oil filter wrench to remove the old filter, a container with at least a six-quart capacity to drain the old oil into and a funnel or oil can spout to help pour fresh oil into the engine.

4 In addition, you should have plenty of clean rags and newspapers handy to mop up any spills. Access to the underside of the vehicle is greatly improved if the vehicle can be lifted on a hoist, driven onto ramps or supported by jackstands. **Warning:** *Do not work under a vehicle which is supported only by a bumper, hydraulic or scissors-type jack.*

5 If this is your first oil change on the vehicle, it is a good idea to crawl underneath and familiarize yourself with the locations of the oil drain plug and the oil filter. The engine and exhaust components will be warm during the actual work, so it is a good idea to figure out any potential problems before the engine and its accessories are hot.

6 Allow the engine to warm up to normal operating temperature. If the new oil or any tools are needed, use this warm-up time to gather everything necessary for the job. The correct type of oil to buy for your application can be found in *Recommended lubricants and fluids* near the front of this Chapter.

7 With the engine oil warm (warm engine oil will drain better and more built-up sludge will be removed with the oil), raise and support the vehicle. Make sure it is firmly supported. If jackstands are used, they should be placed toward the front of the frame rails which run the length of the vehicle.

8 Move all necessary tools, rags and newspapers under the vehicle. Position the drain pan under the drain plug. Keep in mind that the oil will initially flow from the engine with some force, so place the pan accordingly.

9 Being careful not to touch any of the hot exhaust pipe components, use the wrench to remove the drain plug near the bottom of the oil pan. Depending on how hot the oil has become, you may want to wear gloves while unscrewing the plug the final few turns.

10 Allow the old oil to drain into the pan. It may be necessary to move the pan farther under the engine as the oil flow slows to a trickle.

11 After all the oil has drained, wipe off the drain plug with a clean rag. Small metal particles may cling to the plug and would immediately contaminate the new oil.

12 Clean the area around the drain plug opening and reinstall the plug. **Note:** *Replace the copper gasket on the drain plug with a new one each time the plug is removed. Tighten the plug securely with the wrench. If a torque wrench is available, use it to tighten the plug.*

13 Move the drain pan into position under the oil filter.

14 Now use the filter wrench to loosen the oil filter. Chain or metal band-type filter wrenches may distort the filter canister, but this is of no concern as the filter will be discarded anyway.

15 Sometimes the oil filter is on so tight it cannot be loosened, or it is positioned in an area which is inaccessible with a filter wrench. As a last resort, you can punch a metal bar or long screwdriver directly through the bottom of the canister and use it as a T-bar to turn the filter. If so, be prepared for oil to spurt out of the canister as it is punctured.

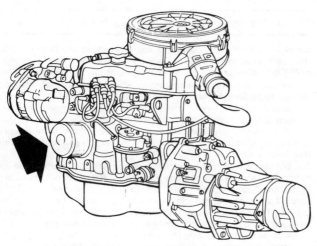

Fig. 1.18 Oil filter location (1.4 liter engine) (Sec 16)

Fig. 1.19 Before installing the new oil filter, spread a thin coat of clean engine oil on the rubber gasket (Sec 16)

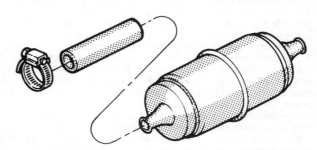

Fig. 1.20 Fuel filter components — exploded view (Sec 18)

16 Completely unscrew the old filter. Be careful, it is full of oil. Empty the oil inside the filter into the drain pan.
17 Compare the old filter with the new one to make sure they are the same type. **Note:** *Beginning in May, 1984, all engines were equipped with metric thread oil filters (earlier models had standard threads). All engines equipped with a metric filter have an identification label on the engine. The filter is also marked with the metric thread size (M20 x 1.50). The metric and older non-metric filters are not interchangeable.*
18 Use a clean rag to remove all oil, dirt and sludge from the area where the oil filter mounts to the engine. Check the old filter to make sure the rubber gasket is not stuck to the engine mounting surface. If the gasket is stuck to the engine (use a flashlight if necessary), remove it.
19 Open one of the cans of new oil and apply a light coat of oil to the rubber gasket of the new oil filter.
20 Attach the new filter to the engine following the tightening directions printed on the filter canister or packing box. Most filter manufacturers recommend against using a filter wrench due to the possibility of overtightening and damaging the seal.
21 Remove all tools, rags, etc. from under the vehicle, being careful not to spill the oil in the drain pan, then lower the vehicle.
22 Move to the engine compartment and locate the oil filler cap on the rocker arm cover (the cap will most likely be labeled *Engine Oil* or *Oil*).
23 If an oil can spout is used, push the spout into the top of the oil can and pour the fresh oil through the filler opening. A funnel may also be used.
24 Pour about four (4) quarts of fresh oil into the engine. Wait a few minutes to allow the oil to drain into the pan, then check the level on the oil dipstick (see Section 5 if necessary). If the oil level is at or near the lower *Add* mark, start the engine and allow the new oil to circulate.
25 Run the engine for only about a minute and then shut it off. Immediately look under the vehicle and check for leaks at the oil pan drain plug and around the oil filter. If either is leaking, tighten with a bit more force.
26 With the new oil circulated and the filter now completely full, recheck the level on the dipstick and add enough oil to bring the level to the *Full* mark on the dipstick.
27 During the first few trips after an oil change, make it a point to check frequently for leaks and proper oil level.
28 The old oil drained from the engine cannot be reused in its present state and should be disposed of. Oil reclamation centers, auto repair shops and gas stations will normally accept the oil, which can be refined and used again. After the oil has cooled, it can be drained into a suitable container (capped plastic jugs, topped bottles, milk cartons, etc.) for transport to one of these disposal sites.

17 Fuel system check

Caution: *There are certain precautions to take when inspecting or servicing the fuel system components. Work in a well-ventilated area and do not allow open flames (cigarettes, appliance pilot lights, etc.) to get near the work area. Mop up spills immediately and do not store fuel-soaked rags where they could ignite.*
1 The fuel system is under pressure, so if any fuel lines are disconnected for servicing, be prepared to catch the fuel as it spurts out. Plug all disconnected fuel lines immediately after disconnection to prevent the tank from emptying itself.
2 The fuel system is most easily checked with the vehicle raised on a hoist so the components underneath the vehicle are readily visible and accessible.
3 If the smell of gasoline is noticed while driving or after the vehicle has been in the sun, the system should be thoroughly inspected immediately.
4 Remove the gas filler cap and check for damage, corrosion and an unbroken sealing imprint on the gasket. Replace the cap with a new one, if necessary.
5 With the vehicle raised, inspect the gas tank and filler neck for punctures, cracks and other damage. The connection between the filler neck and the tank is especially critical. Sometimes a rubber filler neck will leak due to loose clamps or deteriorated rubber, problems a home mechanic can usually rectify. **Caution:** *Do not, under any circumstances, try to repair a fuel tank yourself (except rubber components) unless you have had considerable experience. A welding torch or any open flame can easily cause the fuel vapors to explode if the proper precautions are not taken.*
6 Carefully check all rubber hoses and metal lines leading away from the fuel tank. Check for loose connections, deteriorated hoses, crimped lines and other damage. Follow the lines up to the front of the vehicle, carefully inspecting them all the way. Repair or replace damaged sections as necessary.

18 Fuel filter replacement

Warning: *Gasoline is extremely flammable so extra precautions must be taken when working on any part of the fuel system. Do not smoke or allow open flames or bare light bulbs near the work area. Also, do not work in a garage if a natural gas-type appliance with a pilot light is present.*
1 The fuel filter is attached to the right-rear frame member. Raise the vehicle and support it securely on jackstands.

2   Carefully pinch off the rubber fuel hoses attached to the filter with Vise-grip pliers (pad the jaws with tape or sections of rubber hose to avoid damage to the fuel hoses).
3   Loosen the hose clamps and detach the hoses from the filter.
4   Remove the bolts attaching the fuel filter bracket to the frame.
5   Position the new filter and install the bracket bolts (make sure the arrow indicating the direction of fuel flow is facing the front of the vehicle).
6   Slip the hoses onto the filter fittings and tighten the clamps, then remove the Vise-grip pliers.
7   Start the engine and check for leaks at the filter hoses.

19   Tire rotation

1   The tires should be rotated at the specified intervals and whenever uneven wear is noticed. Since the vehicle will be raised and the tires removed anyway, this is a good time to check the brakes (Section 14).
2   Refer to the accompanying illustration for the *preferred* and *optional* tire rotation patterns. Do not include *Temporary Use Only* spare tires in the rotation sequence. The *optional* X-rotation procedure is acceptable when required for more uniform tire wear.
3   Refer to the information in *Jacking and towing* at the front of this manual for the proper procedures to follow when raising the vehicle and changing a tire; however, if the brakes are to be checked, do not apply the parking brake as stated. Make sure the tires are blocked to prevent the vehicle from rolling.
4   Preferably, the entire vehicle should be raised at the same time. This can be done on a hoist or by jacking up each corner and then lowering the vehicle onto jackstands placed under the frame rails. Always use four jackstands and make sure the vehicle is firmly supported.
5   After rotation, check and adjust the tire pressures as necessary and be sure to check the lug nut tightness.

20   Clutch pedal free play check

Note: *The clutch pedal free play is automatically adjusted by a mechanism attached to the top of the pedal and the cable end. The free play can be checked as described here, but if it is incorrect, the only thing that can be done is to check for broken adjustment mechanism components and a frayed cable.*
1   Basically, free play is the distance the clutch pedal moves before all play in the linkage is removed and the clutch begins to disengage. It is measured at the pedal pad.
2   Slowly depress the pedal and determine how far it moves before resistance is felt.
3   The pedal should move at least 3/4-inch before the play is removed from the linkage.

21   Cooling system servicing (draining, flushing and refilling

Caution: *The electric cooling fan can activate at any time, even when the ignition switch is in the Off position. Disconnect the fan motor wire or the negative battery cable when working in the vicinity of the fan.*
1   Periodically, the cooling system should be drained, flushed and refilled to replenish the antifreeze mixture and prevent formation of rust and corrosion, which can impair the performance of the cooling system and ultimately cause engine damage.
2   At the same time the cooling system is serviced, all hoses and the radiator/remote filler cap(s) should be inspected and replaced if defective (see Section 9).
3   Since antifreeze is a corrosive and poisonous solution, be careful not to spill any of the coolant mixture on the vehicle's paint or your skin. If this happens, rinse immediately with plenty of clean water. Also, consult your local authorities about the dumping of antifreeze before draining the cooling system. In many areas, reclamation centers have been set up to collect automobile oil and drained antifreeze/water mixtures rather than allowing them to be added to the sewage system.
4   With the engine cold, remove the remote filler cap.
5   Move a large container under the radiator to catch the coolant as it is drained.
6   Drain the radiator. Most models are equipped with a drain petcock at the bottom. If this drain has excessive corrosion and cannot be turned

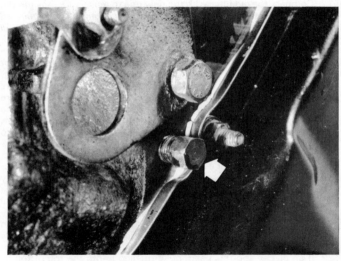

21.7   The engine block drain plug on 1.4 liter engines is located below the water pump

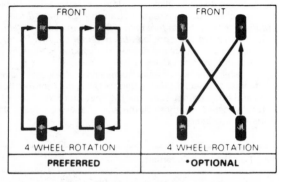

Do not include "temporary use only" spare tire in rotation.
* The optional "X" rotation pattern for radials is acceptable when required for more uniform tire wear.

Fig. 1.21 Tire rotation diagram (Sec 19)

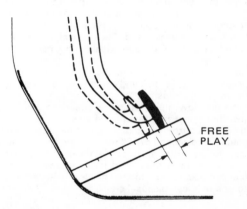

Fig. 1.22 Checking clutch pedal free play with a ruler (Sec 20)

easily, or if the radiator is not equipped with a drain, disconnect the lower radiator hose to allow the coolant to drain. Be careful that none of the solution is splashed on your skin or into your eyes.

7 Remove the engine drain plug or open the petcock. On the 1.4 liter engine it is located behind the accessory drive idler pulley (loosen the pulley for access to the drain, if necessary) (photo). On the 1.7 liter engine it is located on the back side of the engine, near the crankshaft pulley end. This will allow the coolant to drain from the engine itself.

8 Disconnect the hose from the coolant reservoir and remove the reservoir. Flush it out with clean water.

9 Place a garden hose in the remote filler neck and flush the system until the water runs clear at all drain points.

10 In severe cases of contamination or clogging of the radiator, remove it (see Chapter 3) and reverse flush it. This involves simply inserting the hose in the bottom radiator outlet to allow the clear water to run against the normal flow, draining through the top. A radiator repair shop should be consulted if further cleaning or repair is necessary.

11 When the coolant is regularly drained and the system refilled with the correct antifreeze/distilled water mixture, there should be no need to use chemical cleaners or descalers.

12 To refill the system, close the drain petcock(s) (or reconnect the radiator hose) and install the drain plug securely in the engine. Special thread-sealing tape (available at auto parts stores) should be used on the drain plug. Install the reservoir and the overflow hose where applicable. Tap the plastic T-fitting to ensure proper operation of the ball check valve vent. On vehicles equipped with a 1.7 liter engine, open the bleed screw on the radiator by turning the knob counterclockwise.

13 Add coolant to the remote filler very slowly to allow displaced air to escape (do not add coolant to the radiator when refilling the system). Continue to slowly add coolant until the remote filler assembly is full (just below the overflow hose port) or until coolant flows out of the

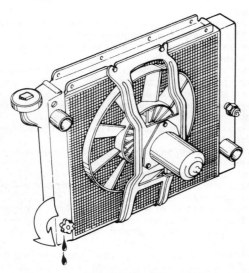

Fig. 1.23 Radiator drain location (Sec 21)

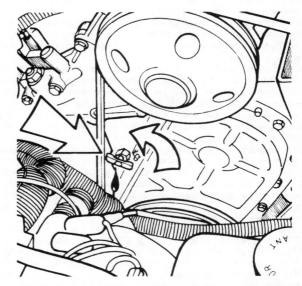

Fig. 1.24 Some engines may have a drain petcock threaded into the block instead of a plug (Sec 21)

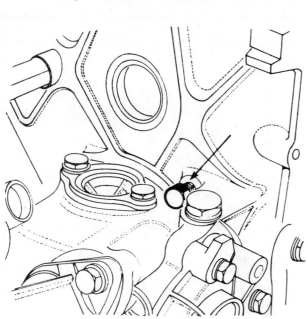

Fig. 1.25 Engine block drain plug location (1.7 liter engine) (Sec 21)

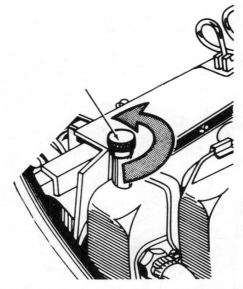

Fig. 1.26 On the 1.7 liter engine, open the radiator bleed screw by turning it counterclockwise before filling the cooling system (Sec 21)

radiator bleed screw (1.7 liter engine). Add more coolant to the reservoir until it reaches the mark. Install the remote filler and reservoir caps.

14 Run the engine until normal operating temperature is reached and, with the engine idling, check carefully for leaks at the drain and hose connections.

15 Always refill the system with a mixture of high quality antifreeze and distilled water in the proportion called for on the antifreeze container or in your owner's manual. Chapter 3 also contains information on antifreeze mixtures.

16 Keep a close watch on the coolant level and the various cooling system hoses during the first few miles of driving. Tighten the hose clamps and/or add more coolant as necessary.

22 Automatic transmission fluid change

1 At the specified time intervals, the transmission fluid should be drained and new fluid added.

2 Before draining, purchase the specified transmission fluid (see *Recommended lubricants and fluids*).

3 Tools necessary for this job include jackstands to support the vehicle in a raised position, a wrench to remove the fluid drain plugs, a drain pan capable of holding at least five quarts, newspapers and clean rags.

4 The fluid should be drained immediately after the vehicle has been driven. This will remove any built-up sediment better than if the fluid were cold. Because of this, it may be wise to wear protective gloves (fluid temperature can exceed 350°F in a hot transmission).

5 After it has been driven to warm up the fluid, raise the vehicle and place it on jackstands for access underneath. Make sure it is firmly supported by four stands placed under the frame rails.

6 Move the necessary equipment under the vehicle, being careful not to touch any of the hot exhaust components.

7 Position the newspapers and drain pan under the transmission and remove the drain plugs from the transmission and differential. Let the fluid drain into the pan as long as possible, then reinstall and tighten the plugs.

8 Lower the vehicle to the ground.

9 Open the hood and remove the dipstick from the transmission.

10 Add fluid to the transmission a little at a time, continually checking the level with the dipstick, until the level is correct (see Section 5).

11 With the selector lever in Park, apply the parking brake and start the engine without depressing the accelerator pedal (if possible). Do

not race the engine at a high speed; run it at slow idle only.

12 Depress the brake pedal and shift the transmission through each gear. Place the selector back into Park and look under the vehicle for leaks around the drain plugs, then recheck the fluid level.

13 Drive the vehicle to reach normal operating temperature (15 miles of highway driving or its equivalent in the city), then park it and allow it to cool completely before checking the fluid level one last time as described in Section 5.

23 Manual transmission oil change

1 At the specified time intervals, the transmission oil should be changed to ensure trouble-free transmission operation. Before proceeding, purchase the specified transmission oil.

2 Tools necessary for this job generally include jackstands to support the vehicle in a raised position, a wrench to remove the drain plug, a drain pan capable of holding at least five quarts, newspapers and clean rags.

3 The oil should be drained immediately after the vehicle has been driven. This will remove any contaminants better than if the oil were cold. Because of this, it may be wise to wear protective gloves while removing the drain plug.

4 After the vehicle has been driven to warm up the oil, raise it and place it on jackstands for access underneath. make sure it is firmly supported and as level as possible.

5 Move the necessary equipment under the vehicle, being careful not to touch any of the hot exhaust components.

6 Spread out the newspapers and position the drain pan under the transmission.

7 Remove the drain plug and allow the oil to drain into the pan as long as possible. Remove the oil level check plug from the side of the transmission to speed the draining.

8 After the oil has drained completely, reinstall the drain plug and tighten it securely.

9 Using a hand pump or squeeze bottle, fill the transmission to the bottom of the oil level check hole with the recommended grade of oil.

10 Reinstall the plug and tighten it securely, then lower the vehicle and start the engine.

11 After test driving the vehicle, check for leaks around the plugs.

12 Pour the old oil into a capped container and dispose of it at a service station or reclamation center.

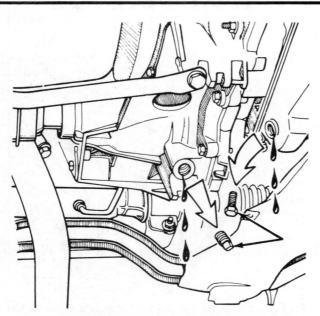

Fig. 1.27 Automatic transmission drain plug locations (Sec 22)

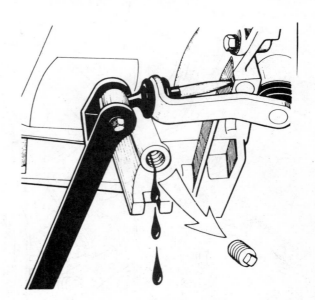

Fig. 1.28 Manual transmission drain plug location (Sec 23)

24 Air filter replacement

1 At the specified intervals, the air filter should be replaced with a new one. A thorough program of preventative maintenance would call for the filter to be inspected between changes.

TBI injection system

2 The air filter on TBI equipped models (49-state) is located inside the air cleaner housing on the top of the engine. The filter is generally replaced by removing the wing nut at the top of the air cleaner assembly, releasing the spring clips and lifting off the top plate (photo).

3 While the top plate is off, be careful not to drop anything down into the throttle body.

4 Lift the air filter element out of the housing.

5 To check the filter, hold it up to strong sunlight or place a flashlight or droplight on the inside of the filter. If you can see light coming through the paper element, the filter is all right. Check all the way around the filter.

6 Wipe out the inside of the air cleaner housing with a clean rag.

7 Place the old filter (if in good condition) or the new filter (if the specified interval has elapsed) back into the air cleaner housing. Make sure it seats properly in the bottom of the housing.

8 Install the top plate and the wing nut.

Multi-point injection system

9 On multi-point injection equipped models (California), the air filter is located in the housing on the left-hand side of the engine compartment.

10 Remove the wing nuts or clips, lift off the cover, remove the old filter and install the new one.

11 Position the cover and install the wing nuts or clips.

25 Ignition timing check

Note: *It is imperative that the procedures included on the Vehicle Emissions Control Information label be followed when checking the ignition timing. The label will include all information concerning preliminary steps to be performed before checking the timing, as well as the timing specifications. The timing is not adjustable on these engines, so if it is not as specified, have the ignition system checked by a dealer service department.*

1 Locate the VECI label under the hood and read through and perform all preliminary instructions concerning ignition timing. Be sure to disconnect the vacuum hose from the distributor vacuum advance unit and plug the end of the hose.

2 Locate the timing marks and window at the rear (transmission end) of the engine (photo). The mark on the far left represents top dead center (TDC) and each graduation is equal to two (2) degrees. The flywheel/driveplate has a timing mark stamped into it as well.

3 Locate the mark on the flywheel and highlight it with chalk or a dab of paint so it will be visible under the timing light.

4 With the ignition off, connect the pick-up lead of the timing light to the number 1 spark plug (the number 1 spark plug is the one at the rear [transmission end] of the engine). Use either a jumper lead between the wire and plug or an inductive-type pick-up. Do not pierce the wire or attempt to insert a wire between the boot and the wire. Connect the timing light power leads according to the manufacturer's instructions.

5 Start the engine, aim the timing light at the window and marks and note which timing mark the notch on the flywheel is lining up with.

6 If the notch is not lining up with the correct mark, the initial timing is off and the ignition system should be checked by a dealer service department.

7 Turn off the engine and disconnect the timing light. Reconnect the number 1 spark plug wire, if removed, and the vacuum hose.

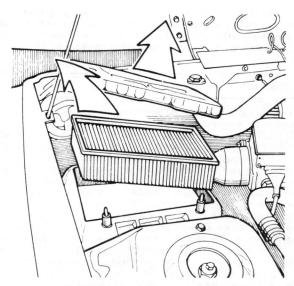

Fig. 1.29 Multi-point injection system air filter location (Sec 24)

24.2 The air cleaner cover is held in place with a wing nut and several spring clips

25.2 The timing marks are clearly visible at the transmission end of the engine

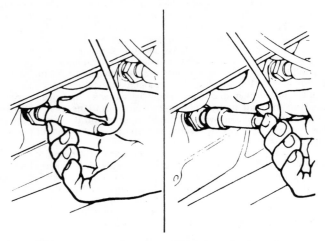

Fig. 1.30 When disconnecting the spark plug wires, always pull on the boot at the end of the wire (left), not on the wire itself (right) — if you twist the wire slightly while pulling, it will come free much easier (Sec 26)

26.11 A handy helper for installing spark plugs is a length of 5/16-inch rubber hose

26 Spark plug replacement

1   The spark plugs are located on the front of the engine and are easily accessible for removal.
2   In most cases, the tools necessary for a spark plug replacement job include a plug wrench or spark plug socket which fits onto a ratchet wrench (this special socket will be padded inside to protect the plug) and a feeler gauge to check and adjust the spark plug gaps. Also, a special spark plug wire removal tool is available for separating the wires from the spark plugs. To ease installation, obtain a piece of 5/16-inch inside diameter rubber hose, 8 to 12 inches in length.
3   The best procedure to follow when replacing the spark plugs is to purchase the new spark plugs beforehand, adjust them to the proper gap and then replace each plug one at a time. When buying the new spark plugs, it is important to obtain the correct plugs for your specific engine. This information can be found in the Specifications at the front of this Chapter, but should be checked against the information found on the Emissions Control Information label located under the hood or in the owner's manual. If differences exist between these sources, purchase the spark plug type specified on the Emissions Control label because the information was printed for your specific engine.
4   With the new spark plugs at hand, allow the engine to cool completely before attempting plug removal. During this time, each of the new spark plugs can be inspected for defects and the gaps can be checked.
5   The gap is checked by inserting the proper thickness gauge between the electrodes at the tip of the plug. The gap between the electrodes should be the same as that given in the Specifications or on the Emissions Control label. The wire should just touch each of the electrodes. If the gap is incorrect, use the notched adjuster on the feeler gauge to bend the curved side electrode slightly until the proper gap is achieved. If the side electrode is not exactly over the center electrode, use the notched adjuster to align the two. Also at this time check for cracks in the porcelain insulator, indicating the spark plug should not be used.
6   Cover the fenders of the vehicle to prevent damage to the paint.
7   With the engine cool, remove the spark plug wire from one spark plug. Do this by grabbing the boot at the end of the wire, not the wire itself. Sometimes it is necessary to use a twisting motion while the boot and plug wire are pulled free. Using a plug wire removal tool is the easiest and safest method.
8   If compressed air is available, use it to blow any dirt or foreign material away from the spark plug area. A common bicycle pump will also work. The idea here is to eliminate the possibility of material falling into the cylinder as the spark plug is removed.
9   Now place the spark plug wrench or socket over the plug and remove it from the engine by turning in a counterclockwise direction.
10   Compare the spark plug with those shown in the accompanying

color photos to get an indication of the overall running condition of the engine.
11   Due to the angle at which the spark plugs must be installed on most engines, installation will be simplified by inserting the plug wire end of the new spark plug into the 5/16-inch rubber hose, mentioned previously (photo), before it is installed in the cylinder head. This procedure serves two purposes: the rubber hose gives you flexibility for establishing the proper angle of plug insertion in the head and, should the threads be improperly lined up, the rubber hose will merely slip on the spark plug when it meets resistance, preventing damage to the cylinder head threads.
12   After installing the plug to the limit of the hose grip, tighten it with the socket. It is a good idea to use a torque wrench for this to ensure that the plug is seated correctly. The correct torque figure is included in the Specifications.
13   Before pushing the spark plug wire onto the end of the plug, inspect it following the procedures outlined in Section 27.
14   Attach the plug wire to the new spark plug, again using a twisting motion on the boot until it is firmly seated on the spark plug. Make sure the wire is routed away from the exhaust manifold.
15   Follow the above procedure for the remaining spark plugs, replacing them one at a time to prevent mixing up the spark plug wires.

27 Spark plug wires, distributor cap and rotor — check and replacement

1   Begin this procedure by making a visual check of the spark plug wires while the engine is running. In a darkened garage (make sure there is ventilation) start the engine and observe each plug wire. Be careful not to come into contact with any moving engine parts. If there is a break in the wire, you will see arcing or a small spark at the damaged area. If arcing is noticed, make a note to obtain new wires, then allow the engine to cool and check the distributor cap and rotor.
2   Detach the distributor cap by removing the mounting screws (photo). With the screws removed, separate the cap from the distributor (or in the case of the 1.7 liter engine, from the head) with the spark plug wires still attached.
3   Inspect the cap for cracks and other damage. Closely examine the contacts on the inside of the cap for excessive corrosion. Slight scoring is normal. Deposits on the contacts may be removed with a small file.
4   If the inspection reveals damage to the cap, make a note to obtain a replacement for your particular engine, then examine the rotor.
5   The rotor is visible, with the cap removed, at the end of the distributor shaft. On the 1.4 liter engine it is pressed onto the shaft and can be removed by pulling on it. The rotor on the 1.7 liter engine is bonded to the end of the camshaft and will have to be destroyed to remove it (use a pliers). When a new rotor is installed, it must be glued to the shaft.

Measuring plug gap. A feeler gauge of the correct size (see ignition system specifications) should have a slight 'drag' when slid between the electrodes. Adjust gap if necessary

Adjusting plug gap. The plug gap is adjusted by bending the earth electrode inwards, or outwards, as necessary until the correct clearance is obtained. Note the use of the correct tool

Normal. Grey-brown deposits, lightly coated core nose. Gap increasing by around 0.001 in (0.025 mm) per 1000 miles (1600 km). Plugs ideally suited to engine, and engine in good condition

Carbon fouling. Dry, black, sooty deposits. Will cause weak spark and eventually misfire. Fault: over-rich fuel mixture. Check: carburettor mixture settings, float level and jet sizes; choke operation and cleanliness of air filter. Plugs can be re-used after cleaning

Oil fouling. Wet, oily deposits. Will cause weak spark and eventually misfire. Fault: worn bores/piston rings or valve guides; sometimes occurs (temporarily) during running-in period. Plugs can be re-used after thorough cleaning

Overheating. Electrodes have glazed appearance, core nose very white – few deposits. Fault: plug overheating. Check: plug value, ignition timing, fuel octane rating (too low) and fuel mixture (too weak). Discard plugs and cure fault immediately

Electrode damage. Electrodes burned away; core nose has burned, glazed appearance. Fault: pre-ignition. Check: as for 'Overheating' but may be more severe. Discard plugs and remedy fault before piston or valve damage occurs

Split core nose (may appear initially as a crack). Damage is self-evident, but cracks will only show after cleaning. Fault: pre-ignition or wrong gap-setting technique. Check: ignition timing, cooling system, fuel octane rating (too low) and fuel mixture (too weak). Discard plugs, rectify fault immediately

27.2 The distributor cap is held in place with two screws (1.4 liter engine shown)

6 Inspect the rotor for cracks and other damage. Carefully check the condition of the metal contact at the top of the rotor for excessive burning and pitting.

7 If it is determined that a new rotor is required, make a note to that effect. If the rotor and cap are in good condition, reinstall them at this time.

8 If the cap must be replaced, do not reinstall it. Leave it off the distributor with the wires still connected.

9 If the spark plug wires are being replaced, now is the time to obtain a new set, along with a new cap and rotor as determined in the checks above. Purchase a wire set for your particular engine, pre-cut to the proper size, with the rubber boots already installed.

10 If the spark plug wires passed the check in Step 1, they should be checked further as follows.

11 Examine the wires one at a time to avoid mixing them up.

12 Disconnect the plug wire from the spark plug. A removal tool can be used for this, or you can grab the rubber boot, twist slightly and then pull the wire free. Do not pull on the wire itself, only on the rubber boot.

13 Inspect inside the boot for corrosion, which will look like a white crusty powder. Some models use a conductive white silicone lubricant which should not be mistaken for corrosion.

14 Now push the wire and boot back onto the end of the spark plug. It should be a tight fit on the plug end. If not, remove the wire and

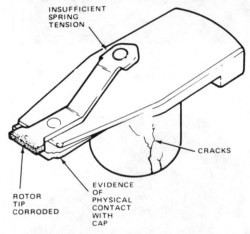

Fig. 1.32 The rotor has a different set of defects to look for, most notably wear and corrosion at the tip (if in doubt, replace it with a new one) (Sec 27)

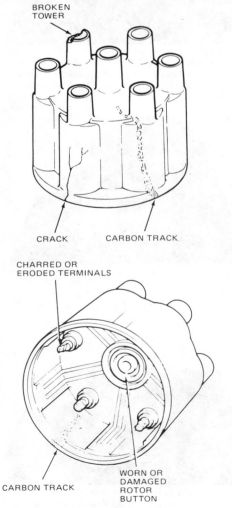

Fig. 1.31 Here's what to look for when inspecting the distributor cap (if in doubt, buy a new one — the cost is not very high) (Sec 27)

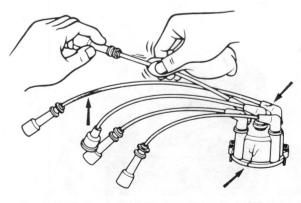

Fig. 1.33 Before the spark plug wires can be inspected, they must be wiped clean (check for cracks, burned areas and damage at the locations indicated by the arrows) (Sec 27)

use pliers to carefully crimp the metal connector inside the wire boot until the fit is snug.

15 Now, using a clean rag, clean the entire length of the wire. Remove all built-up dirt and grease. As this is done, check for burns, cracks and any other form of damage. Bend the wires in several places to ensure that the conductive wire inside has not hardened.

16 Next, the wires should be checked at the distributor cap in the same manner.

17 If the wires appear to be in good condition, make sure that all wires are secure at both ends. If the cap and rotor are also in good condition, the check is finished.

18 If it was determined that new wires are required, obtain them at this time, along with a new cap and rotor (if so determined in the checks above).

19 Attach the rotor to the distributor. Make sure that the carbon brush is properly installed in the cap, as a wide gap between the carbon brush and the rotor will cause rotor burn-through and/or damage to the distributor cap.

20 If new wires are being installed, replace them one at a time. **Note:** *It is important to replace the wires one at a time, noting the routing as each wire is removed and installed, to maintain the correct firing order and to prevent short-circuiting.*

21 Attach the cap to the distributor.

28 Driveaxle rubber boot inspection

1 If the driveaxle rubber boots are damaged or deteriorated, serious and costly damage can occur to the CV joints the rubber boots are designed to protect. Therefore the boots should be inspected very carefully at the recommended intervals.

2 Raise the front of the vehicle and support it securely on jackstands.

3 Crawl under the vehicle and check the four driveaxle boots (two on each axle) very carefully for cracks, tears, holes, deteriorated rubber and loose or missing clamps. If the boots are dirty, wipe them clean before beginning the inspection.

4 If damage or deterioration is evident, the boots must be replaced with new ones as soon as possible.

29 Compression check

1 A compression check will tell you what mechanical condition the engine is in. Specifically, it can tell you if the compression is down due to leakage caused by worn piston rings, defective valves and seats or a blown head gasket.

2 Begin by cleaning the area around the spark plugs before you remove them. This will keep dirt from falling into the cylinders while you are performing the compression test.

3 Remove the coil high-tension lead from the distributor and ground it on the engine block. Make sure the throttle is wide open.

4 With the compression gauge in the number 1 cylinder's spark plug hole, crank the engine over at least four compression strokes and observe the gauge (the compression should build up quickly in a healthy engine). Low compression on the first stroke, followed by gradually increasing pressure on successive strokes, indicates worn piston rings. A low compression reading on the first stroke, which does not build

up during successive strokes, indicates leaking valves or blown head gasket (a cracked head could also be the cause). Record the highest gauge reading obtained.

5 Repeat the procedure for the remaining cylinders and compare the results to the Specifications. Compression readings approximately 10% above or below the specified amount can be considered normal.

6 Pour a couple of teaspoons of engine oil (a squirt can works great for this) into each cylinder, through the spark plug hole, and repeat the test.

7 If the compression increases after the oil is added, the piston rings are definitely worn. If the compression does not increase significantly, the leakage is occurring at the valves or head gasket. Leakage past the valves may be caused by burned valve seats or faces, warped, cracked or bent valves or valves that require adjustment.

8 If two adjacent cylinders have equally low compression, there is a strong possibility that the head gasket between them is blown. The appearance of coolant in the combustion chambers or the crankcase would verify this condition.

9 If the compression is higher than normal, the combustion chambers are probably coated with carbon deposits. If that is the case, the cylinder head should be removed and decarbonized.

10 If compression is way down or varies greatly between cylinders, it would be a good idea to have a leak-down test performed by a reputable automotive repair shop. This test will pinpoint exactly where the leakage is occurring and how severe it is.

30 Valve clearance check and adjustment

Note: *The following procedure can become difficult for the novice home mechanic. If you are unfamiliar with the task of adjusting valves, read through the entire procedure to acquaint yourself with the steps and components involved. It may be a good idea to have a knowledgeable person (such as a mechanic) perform the job while you watch, then you will be better prepared to tackle the job at subsequent maintenance intervals. The clearances must be checked/adjusted with the engine completely cool, so let the vehicle stand overnight before beginning the procedure.*

1.4 liter engine

1 The only special tool required (in addition to common hand tools) is a small wrench to fit the adjusting screw on each pushrod (a very small adjustable wrench may work). A new rocker arm cover gasket should be purchased in advance so it is on hand when the cover is reinstalled.

2 If the vehicle is equipped with a manual transmission, place the shift lever in Neutral and set the parking brake. Remove the air cleaner assembly or intake duct, disconnect all necessary wires and hoses and remove the rocker arm cover from the top of the engine. Label the wires and hoses to simplify installation.

3 Position the number 1 piston at Top Dead Center (TDC) on the compression stroke. To do this, first number each spark plug wire (1 through 4, from the rear [transmission] end of the engine to the front), then remove all of the spark plugs from the engine. Locate the number 1 cylinder plug wire and trace it back to the distributor cap (the number 1 cylinder is the one at the transmission end of the engine). Write a number 1 on the distributor body directly below the terminal where the number 1 plug wire is attached to the cap. Do this for the other cylinders (using numbers 2, 3 and 4) as well, then remove the cap and wires from the distributor as an assembly.

4 Slip a wrench or socket/ratchet over the large bolt at the front of the crankshaft and slowly turn it in a clockwise direction until the beveled tooth on the flywheel/driveplate is aligned with the TDC mark below the timing window at the rear of the engine. The distributor rotor should be pointing directly at the number 1 you made on the distributor body. If it isn't, turn the crankshaft one more complete revolution (360°) in a clockwise direction. If the rotor is now pointing at the 1 on the distributor body, then the number 1 piston is at TDC on the compression stroke and the valve clearances can be adjusted.

5 Starting at the rear (driver's side) of the engine, the valves are arranged E-I-I-E-E-I-I-E (E = exhaust and I = intake). Keep in mind as the clearances are checked and adjusted that the intake and exhaust valves require different clearances (refer to the Specifications at the front of this Chapter).

6 Insert the specified size feeler gauge between the first valve stem

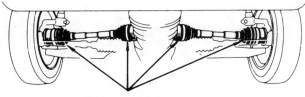

Fig. 1.34 The driveaxle rubber boots are vulnerable because of their location on the underside of the vehicle (if they are damaged, replace them immediately to prevent damage to the CV joints) (Sec 28)

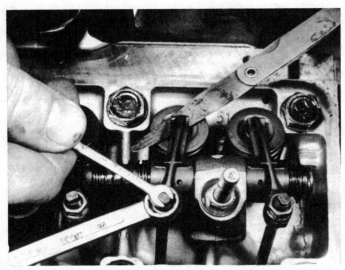

30.7   Adjusting the valve clearance on a 1.4 liter engine

and rocker arm (number 1 cylinder exhaust valve). If the gauge fits between the valve and rocker arm with a slight drag, then the clearance is correct and no adjustment is required.

7   If the feeler gauge will not fit between the valve and rocker arm, or if it is loose, loosen the adjusting screw locknut with a wrench and carefully tighten or loosen the screw until you can feel a slight drag on the feeler gauge as it is withdrawn from between the valve and rocker arm (photo).

8   Hold the screw with the wrench to keep it from turning and tighten the locknut securely. Recheck the clearance to make sure it didn't change when the nut was tightened.

9   Repeat the procedure for the second valve (which is the intake valve for the number 1 cylinder). Note that the specified clearance is different so a different size feeler gauge will be required.

10   Turn the crankshaft 180° clockwise and watch the distributor rotor. It should move 90° and stop pointing at the number 3 you made on the distributor body.

11   Repeat the valve clearance check/adjustment at the valves in the number 3 cylinder. Remember to keep track of the intake and exhaust valves and use the correct size feeler gauge.

12   Turn the crankshaft an additional 180° clockwise and make sure the rotor moves 90° and stops pointing at the number 4 you made on the distributor. Check/adjust the valve clearances at the valves in the number 4 cylinder (number 4 is at the front of the engine).

13   Turn the crankshaft 180° clockwise and make sure the rotor is pointing at the number 2 on the distributor. Check/adjust the valve clearances at the valves in the number 2 cylinder.

14   Install the rocker arm cover (use a new gasket) and tighten the

mounting nuts evenly and securely.

15   Reconnect all wires and hoses and install the air cleaner assembly or duct, then start the engine and check for oil leaks around the edge of the rocker arm cover.

1.7 liter engine

Note: *The valve adjustment procedure for this engine is quite involved and requires special tools and an assortment of shims to be done correctly. As a result, it should be done by a dealer service department or properly equipped repair shop. You can, however, check the clearances with feeler gauges and take the vehicle to a shop if adjustment is required.*

16   Refer to the procedure under the 1.4 liter engine heading and follow steps 1 through 4.

17   Starting at the rear (driver's side) of the engine, the valves are arranged E-I-I-E-E-I-I-E (E = exhaust and I = intake). Keep in mind as the clearances are checked and adjusted that the intake and exhaust valves require different clearances (refer to the Specifications at the front of this Chapter).

18   The cam lobes for the number 1 cylinder should be pointing up, away from the valve tappets. Insert the specified size feeler gauge between the heel of the first cam lobe and the shim on top of the valve tappet (number 1 cylinder exhaust valve). If the gauge fits between the shim and cam lobe with a slight drag, then the clearance is correct and no adjustment is required.

19   If the feeler gauge will not fit between the shim and cam lobe, or if it is loose, a different size shim is required (have the shims replaced by a dealer service department or a properly equipped repair shop after all of the clearances have been checked).

20   Repeat the procedure for the second valve (which·is the intake valve for the number 1 cylinder). Note that the specified clearance is different so a different size feeler gauge will be required.

21   Turn the crankshaft 180° clockwise and watch the distributor rotor. It should move 90° and stop pointing at the number 3 you made on the distributor body.

22   Repeat the valve clearance check at the cam lobes for the number 3 cylinder. Remember to keep track of the intake and exhaust valves and use the correct size feeler gauge.

23   Turn the crankshaft an additional 180° clockwise and make sure the rotor moves 90° and stops pointing at the number 4 you made on the distributor. Check the valve clearances at the lobes for the number 4 cylinder (number 4 is at the front of the engine).

24   Turn the crankshaft 180° clockwise and make sure the rotor is pointing at the number 2 on the distributor. Check the valve clearances at the lobes for the number 2 cylinder.

25   If the clearances are not correct, install the rocker arm cover and take the vehicle to a dealer service department or repair shop to have shims installed which will correct the clearances.

26   Install the rocker arm cover (use a new gasket) and tighten the mounting nuts evenly and securely.

27   Reconnect all wires and hoses and install the air cleaner assembly or duct, then start the engine and check for oil leaks around the edge of the rocker arm cover.

Chapter 2 Part A   1.4 liter engine

Contents

Specifications

General

Bore	2.992 in
Stroke	3.031 in
Displacement	85.24 cu in (1397 cc)
Compression ratio	9:1
Oil pressure	
Idle speed	10 psi
4000 rpm	50 psi
Cylinder numbers	1-2-3-4 (from flywheel end)
Number 1 cylinder	Flywheel end of engine
Firing order	1-3-4-2

Cylinder head

Maximum warpage	0.002 in
Maximum resurfacing cut	0.020 in

Valves and related components

Valve face and seat angle
    Intake . . . . 60°
    Exhaust . . . . 45°
Valve stem diameter . . . . 0.275 in
Valve guide inside diameter . . . . 0.276 in
Stem-to-guide clearance . . . . 0.001 in
Valve seat width
    Intake . . . . 0.043 to 0.055 in
    Exhaust . . . . 0.055 to 0.067 in
Valve margin width (minimum) . . . . 1/32 in
Valve spring free length . . . . 1.638 in
Valve spring length under load
    45 Ft-lbs . . . . 1.248 in
    81 Ft-lbs . . . . 0.975 in
Pushrod length . . . . 6.876 in
Follower diameter (std.) . . . . 0.741 in
Valve clearances (engine cold)
    Intake . . . . 0.006 in
    Exhaust . . . . 0.008 in

Crankshaft and connecting rods

Crankshaft end play
    1983 . . . . 0.004 to 0.009 in
    1984 on . . . . 0.002 to 0.009 in
Connecting rod end play (side clearance) . . . . 0.012 to 0.023 in
Main bearing journal diameter . . . . 2.157 in
Main bearing journal minimum regrind diameter . . . . 2.147 in
Main bearing oil clearance . . . . 0.0004 to 0.0014 in
Connecting rod journal diameter . . . . 1.732 in
Connecting rod journal minimum regrind diameter . . . . 1.720 in
Connecting rod bearing oil clearance . . . . 0.0010 to 0.0026 in
Crankshaft journal taper/out-of-round limit . . . . Check with dealer service department or automotive machine shop

Engine block

Cylinder liner bore diameter . . . . 2.992 in
Out-of-round/taper limit . . . . Check with dealer service department or automotive machine shop
Cylinder liner protrusion . . . . 0.001 to 0.004 in

Pistons and rings

Piston ring side clearance . . . . Check with dealer service department or automotive machine shop
Piston-to-bore clearance . . . . Check with dealer service department or automotive machine shop
Piston ring end gap . . . . Pre-set (do not change)

Camshaft

Bearing journal diameter . . . . 1.482 in
Bearing oil clearance . . . . Check with dealer service department or automotive machine shop
Camshaft end play (retaining plate-to-journal face clearance) . 0.002 to 0.005 in

Oil pump

Gear-to-body clearance . . . . 0.007 in maximum
Gear-to-gear clearance (trochoidal-type pump only)*
    Dimension A . . . . 0.002 to 0.011 in
    Dimension B . . . . 0.001 to 0.006 in
* See accompanying illustration (Fig. 2A.16)

Torque specifications	Ft-lbs
Cylinder head bolts	42
Connecting rod cap nuts	31
Main bearing cap bolts	44
Rocker arm shaft nuts/bolts	13
Flywheel bolts	37
Driveplate bolts	50
Transmission-to-engine bolts	31
Engine mount nuts/bolts	30
Camshaft sprocket bolt	21
Camshaft retaining plate bolts	6
Crankshaft pulley hub bolt	81
Intake/exhaust manifold nuts	12
Rocker arm cover nuts	27 in-lbs
Oil pan bolt	9
Oil pump mounting bolts	6

1   General information

The 1.4 liter engine is an in-line, overhead valve four cylinder mounted transversely in the engine compartment. The cast iron block has replaceable wet liners (cylinders) and the crankshaft is supported by five insert-type main bearings. Thrust bearings are installed at the center main to control crankshaft end play.

The connecting rods ride in insert-type bearings at the crankshaft and are attached to the pistons by interference fit pins. The pistons are made of aluminum and are equipped with two compression rings and one oil control ring.

The camshaft is chain driven from the crankshaft and operates the rocker arms through pushrods. The valves are equipped with one spring each and ride in guides which are pressed into the head. The valves are actuated directly by the rocker arms.

Lubrication is provided by a gear or trochoidal-type oil pump driven off the camshaft and located in the crankcase.

2   Repair operations possible with the engine in the vehicle

Many major repair operations can be accomplished without removing the engine from the vehicle.

It is a very good idea to clean the engine compartment and the exterior of the engine with some type of pressure washer before any work is begun. A clean engine will make the job easier and will prevent the possibility of getting dirt into internal areas of the engine.

Remove the hood (Chapter 11) and cover the fenders to provide as much working room as possible and to prevent damage to the painted surfaces.

If oil or coolant leaks develop, indicating a need for gasket or seal replacement, the repairs can generally be made with the engine in the vehicle. The oil pan gasket, the cylinder head gasket, intake and exhaust manifold gaskets, timing chain cover gaskets and the front crankshaft oil seals are accessible with the engine in place.

Exterior engine components, such as the water pump, the starter motor, the alternator and the distributor, as well as the intake and exhaust manifolds, are quite easily removed for repair with the engine in place.

Since the cylinder head can be removed without pulling the engine, valve component servicing can also be accomplished with the engine in the vehicle.

Replacement of, repairs to or inspection of the timing gears and chain and the oil pump are all possible with the engine in place.

In extreme cases caused by a lack of necessary equipment, repair or replacement of piston rings, pistons, connecting rods and rod bearings and reconditioning of the cylinder bores is possible with the engine in the vehicle. However, this practice is not recommended because of the cleaning and preparation work that must be done to the components involved.

Detailed removal, inspection, repair and installation procedures for the above mentioned components can be found in the appropriate Part of Chapter 2 or the other Chapters in this manual.

3   Engine overhaul — general information

It is not always easy to determine when, or if, an engine should be completely overhauled, as a number of factors must be considered.

High mileage is not necessarily an indication that an overhaul is needed, while low mileage, on the other hand, does not preclude the need for an overhaul. Frequency of servicing is probably the single most important consideration. An engine that has had regular (and frequent) oil and filter changes, as well as other required maintenance, will most likely give many thousands of miles of reliable service. Conversely, a neglected engine may require an overhaul very early in its life.

Excessive oil consumption is an indication that piston rings and/or valve guides are in need of attention (make sure that oil leaks are not responsible before deciding that the rings and guides are bad). Have a cylinder compression or leak-down test performed by an experienced tune-up mechanic to determine for certain the extent of the work required.

If the engine is making obvious knocking or rumbling noises, the con-necting rod and/or main bearings are probably at fault. Check the oil pressure with a gauge (installed in place of the oil pressure sending unit) and compare it to the Specifications. If it is extremely low, the bearings and/or oil pump are probably worn out.

Loss of power, rough running, excessive valve train noise and high fuel consumption rates may also point to the need for an overhaul (especially if they are all present at the same time). If a complete tune-up does not remedy the situation, major mechanical work is the only solution.

An engine overhaul generally involves restoring the internal parts to the specifications of a new engine. During an overhaul, the piston rings are replaced and the cylinder walls are reconditioned (rebored and/or honed). If a rebore is done, then new pistons are also required. The main and connecting rod bearings are replaced with new ones and, if necessary, the crankshaft may be reground to restore the journals. Generally, the valves are serviced as well, since they are usually in less-than-perfect condition at this point. While the engine is being overhauled other components, such as the distributor, starter and alternator can be rebuilt as well. The end result should be a like-new engine that will give as many trouble-free miles as the original.

Before beginning the engine overhaul, read through the entire procedure to familiarize yourself with the scope and requirements of the job. Overhauling an engine is not that difficult, but it is time consuming. Plan on the vehicle being tied up for a minimum of two weeks, especially if parts must be taken to an automotive machine shop for repair or reconditioning. Check on availability of parts and make sure that any necessary special tools and equipment are obtained in advance. Most work can be done with typical shop hand tools, although a number of precision measuring tools are required for inspecting parts to determine if they must be replaced. Often a reputable automotive machine shop will handle the inspection of parts and offer advice concerning reconditioning and replacement. **Note:** *Always wait until the engine has been completely disassembled and all components, especially the engine block, have been inspected before deciding what service and repair operations must be performed by an automotive machine shop. Since the block's condition will be the major factor to consider when determining whether to overhaul the original engine or buy a rebuilt one, never purchase parts or have machine work done on other components until the block has been thoroughly inspected. As a general rule, time is the primary cost of an overhaul, so it does not pay to install worn or sub-standard parts.*

As a final note, to ensure maximum life and minimum trouble from a rebuilt engine, everything must be assembled with care in a spotlessly clean environment.

4   Engine rebuilding alternatives

The do-it-yourselfer is faced with a number of options when performing an engine overhaul. The decision to replace the engine block, piston/connecting rod assemblies and crankshaft depends on a number of factors, with the number one consideration being the condition of the block. Other considerations are cost, access to machine shop facilities, parts availability, time required to complete the project and experience.

Some of the rebuilding alternatives include:

Individual parts — If the inspection procedures reveal that the engine block and most engine components are in reusable condition, purchasing individual parts may be the most economical alternative. The block, crankshaft and piston/connecting rod assemblies should all be inspected carefully. Even if the block shows little wear, the cylinder bores should receive a finish hone; a job for an automotive machine shop.

Master kit (crankshaft kit) — This rebuild package usually consists of a reground crankshaft and a matched set of pistons and connecting rods. The pistons will already be installed on the connecting rods. Piston rings and the necessary bearings may or may not be included in the kit. These kits are commonly available for standard cylinder bores, as well as for engine blocks which have been bored to a regular oversize.

Short block — A short block consists of an engine block with a crankshaft and piston/connecting rod assemblies already installed. All new bearings are incorporated and all clearances will be correct. Depending on where the short block is purchased, a guarantee may be included. The existing camshaft, valve train components, cylinder

head and external parts can be bolted to the short block with little or
no machine shop work necessary.

Long block — A long block consists of a short block plus an oil pump,
oil pan, cylinder head, rocker arm cover, camshaft and valve train components, timing sprockets and chain or belt and timing chain or belt
cover. All components are installed with new bearings, seals and
gaskets incorporated throughout. The installation of manifolds and external parts is all that is necessary. Some form of guarantee is usually
included with the purchase.

Give careful thought to which alternative is best for you and discuss
the situation with local automotive machine shops, auto parts dealers
or dealership partsmen before ordering or purchasing replacement parts.

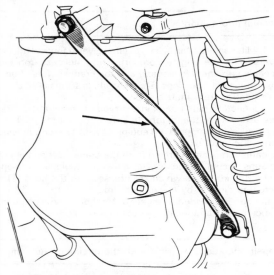

**Fig. 2A.1 Remove the engine-to-transmission support rod
(Sec 6)**

5   Engine removal — methods and precautions

If it has been decided that an engine must be removed for overhaul
or major repair work, certain preliminary steps should be taken.

Locating a suitable work area is extremely important. A shop is, of
course, the most desirable place to work. Adequate work space, along
with storage space for the vehicle, is very important. If a shop or garage
is not available, at the very least a flat, level, clean work surface made
of concrete or asphalt is required.

Cleaning the engine compartment and engine prior to removal will
help keep tools clean and organized.

An engine hoist or A-frame will also be necessary. Make sure that
the equipment is rated in excess of the combined weight of the engine
and its accessories. Safety is of primary importance, considering the
potential hazards involved in lifting the engine out of the vehicle.

If the engine is being removed by a novice, a helper should be
available. Advice and aid from someone more experienced would also
be helpful. There are many instances when one person cannot
simultaneously perform all of the operations required when lifting the
engine out of the vehicle.

Plan the operation ahead of time. Arrange for or obtain all of the tools
and equipment you will need prior to beginning the job. Some of the
equipment necessary to perform engine removal and installation safely
and with relative ease are (in addition to an engine hoist) a heavy duty
floor jack, complete sets of wrenches and sockets as described in the
front of this manual, wooden blocks and plenty of rags and cleaning
solvent for mopping up the inevitable spills. If the hoist is to be rented,
make sure that you arrange for it in advance and perform beforehand
all of the operations possible without it. This will save you money and
time.

Plan for the vehicle to be out of use for a considerable amount of
time. A machine shop will be required to perform some of the work
which the do-it-yourselfer cannot accomplish due to a lack of special
equipment. These shops often have a busy schedule, so it would be
wise to consult them before removing the engine in order to accurately
estimate the amount of time required to rebuild or repair components
that may need work.

Always use extreme caution when removing and installing the engine.
Serious injury can result from careless actions. Plan ahead. Take your
time and a job of this nature, although major, can be accomplished
successfully.

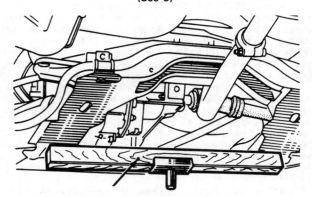

**Fig. 2A.2 Support the engine cradle with a length of
4x4 lumber and a jack (Sec 6)**

6   Engine — removal

Note: *The engine and transmission can be removed as an assembly,
but it is easier to detach them and remove the engine as a separate unit.*

1   Remove the hood if not already done (Chapter 11) and disconnect
the battery cables from the battery.
2   Remove the air cleaner assembly.
3   Drain the cooling system (Chapter 1) and remove the radiator
(Chapter 3).
4   Label and disconnect all wires, hoses and cables attached to the
engine (except for air conditioning hoses — see Chapter 3).
5   Raise the vehicle and support it on jackstands, then drain the oil
(Chapter 1).
6   Remove the exhaust pipe clamp and the engine-to-transmission
support rod.
7   Remove the flywheel cover.
8   Remove the engine drivebelts (Chapter 1).
9   Refer to Chapter 3 and remove the water pump.

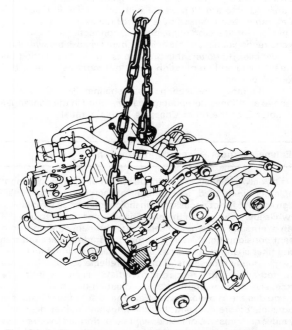

**Fig. 2A.3 The chain or cable should be attached to the
engine brackets at each end and looped over the hoist hook
(Sec 6)**

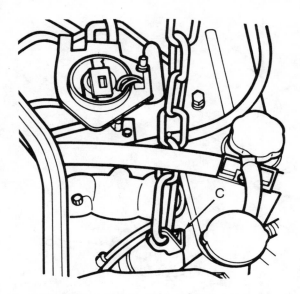

Fig. 2A.4 On later model vehicles without cruise control, the hoist bracket (C) is attached to the exhaust manifold (Sec 6)

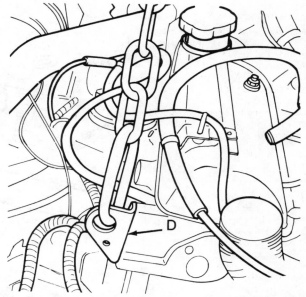

Fig. 2A.5 On all later model vehicles, the hoist bracket (D) is installed in place of the ignition coil wire bracket (Sec 6)

10 Remove the crankshaft pulley and hub from the front of the crankshaft.
11 Remove the torque converter-to-driveplate bolts (vehicles with automatic transmission).
12 On vehicles with air conditioning, remove the compressor from the mounts without disconnecting the hoses and position it out of the way (do not strain the hoses).
13 Support the engine cradle with a jack and length of 4x4 lumber (see accompanying illustration).
14 Disconnect the clutch cable from the fork on the bellhousing.
15 Refer to Chapter 5 and remove the TDC sensor from the bellhousing.
16 Remove the remaining engine-to-transmission bolts. The two studs must be removed also to provide enough room for the engine to be separated from the transmission.
17 Position a jack under the right-hand mounting pad to support the transmission and prevent it from tilting.
18 Attach a hoist to the engine and take up the weight. **Note:** *On later models, lifting brackets should be attached to the engine first and the chain or cable connected to them. For vehicles without cruise control, move the fuel line and bracket and attach the hoist bracket to the exhaust manifold. For vehicles with cruise control, remove the cruise control cable bracket and install the hoist bracket in its place. Remove the ignition coil wire bracket and install the hoist bracket in its place.*
19 Remove the front engine mount bolts.
20 Lift up on the engine, separate it from the transmission and remove it from the engine compartment.

7 Engine overhaul disassembly sequence

1 It is much easier to disassemble and work on the engine if it is mounted on a portable engine stand. These stands can often be rented for a reasonable fee from an equipment rental yard. Before the engine is mounted on a stand, the flywheel/driveplate should be removed from the engine (refer to Section 18.)
2 If a stand is not available, it is possible to disassemble the engine with it blocked up on a sturdy workbench or on the floor. Be extra careful not to tip or drop the engine when working without a stand.
3 If you are going to obtain a rebuilt engine, all external components must come off first in order to be transferred to the replacement engine (just as they will if you are doing a complete engine overhaul yourself). These include:
  Alternator and brackets
  Emissions control components

  Distributor, spark plug wires and spark plugs
  Water pump
  Fuel injection components
  Intake/exhaust manifolds
  Oil filter
  Engine mounts
  Flywheel/driveplate
Note: *When removing the external components from the engine, pay close attention to details that may be helpful or important during installation. Note the installed position of gaskets, seals, spacers, pins, washers, bolts and other small items.*
4 If you are obtaining a short block (which consists of the engine block, crankshaft, pistons and connecting rods all assembled), then the cylinder head, oil pan and oil pump will have to be removed also. See *Engine rebuilding alternatives* for additional information regarding the different possibilities to be considered.
5 If you are planning a complete overhaul, the engine must be disassembled and the internal components removed in the following order:
  Rocker arm cover
  Cylinder head and pushrods
  Valve followers
  Timing chain/gear cover
  Timing chain gears
  Camshaft
  Oil pan
  Oil pump
  Piston/connecting rod assemblies (and cylinder liners)
  Crankshaft
6 Before beginning the disassembly and overhaul procedures, make sure the following items are available:
  Common hand tools
  Small cardboard boxes or plastic bags for storing parts
  Gasket scraper
  Vibration damper puller
  Micrometers
  Small hole gauges
  Telescoping gauges
  Dial indicator set
  Valve spring compressor
  Cylinder surfacing hone
  Piston ring groove cleaning tool
  Electric drill motor
  Tap and die set
  Wire brushes
  Cleaning solvent

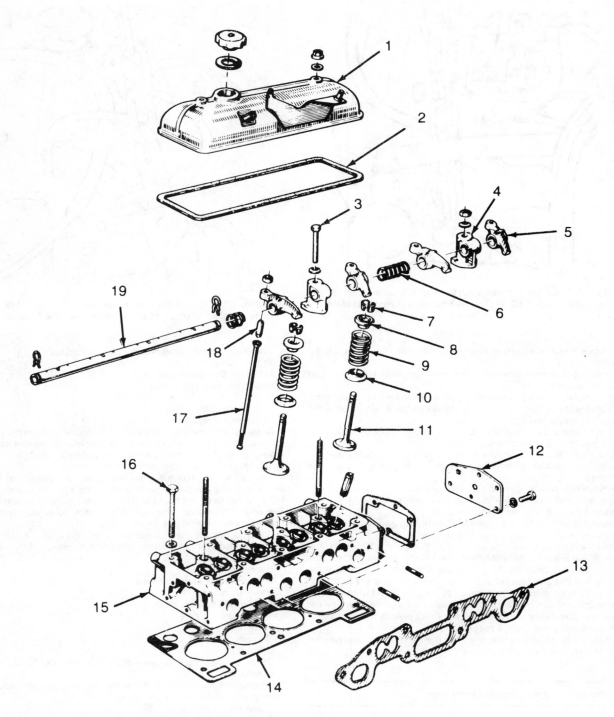

Fig. 2A.6 Cylinder head components — exploded view (Sec 8)

1	Rocker arm cover	6	Rocker arm shaft spring	11	Valve
2	Gasket	7	Valve keepers	12	Water jacket plate
3	Bolt	8	Retainer	13	Manifold gasket
4	Rocker arm shaft pedestal	9	Valve spring	14	Cylinder head gasket
5	Rocker arm	10	Spring seat	15	Cylinder head

16	Head bolt
17	Pushrod
18	Valve adjustment screw
19	Rocker arm shaft

8 Cylinder head — removal (engine in vehicle)

1 Disconnect the negative battery cable from the battery.
2 Refer to Chapter 1 and drain the cooling system.
3 Remove the air cleaner assembly.
4 Separate the spark plug wires from the spark plugs, then remove the distributor cap and wires as an assembly (Chapter 1).
5 Disconnect the wire from the coolant temperature sending unit on the water pump (photo).
6 Loosen the alternator mounting and adjustment bolts, push the alternator towards the engine and slip off the drivebelt (photo).
7 Remove the adjustment arm mounting bolt and swing the alternator carefully away from the engine.
8 Remove the clamps and separate the heater hoses from the water pump fittings (photo).
9 Remove the clamp and separate the radiator hose from the water pump (photo).
10 Refer to Chapter 4 and remove the fuel injection components from the intake manifold (on multi-point injection systems, the injectors should be removed as well).
11 Disconnect the power brake vacuum hose from the manifold.
12 Separate the exhaust pipe from the manifold.
13 Remove the nuts and separate the rocker arm cover from the cylinder head. Remove the gasket.
14 Remove the bolts/nuts and separate the rocker arm assembly from the head (photo).

8.5   Disconnect the wire from the coolant temperature sending unit

8.6   Loosen the alternator bolts and slip off the belt

8.8   Disconnect the heater hoses . . .

8.9   . . . and the upper radiator hose at the water pump

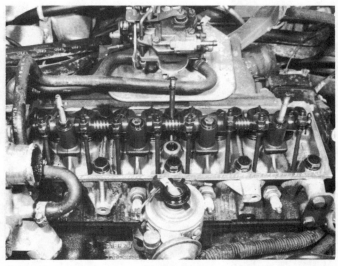

8.14   Remove the nuts and bolts, then separate the rocker arm shaft assembly from the cylinder head

8.15   Lift out the pushrods and store them in order

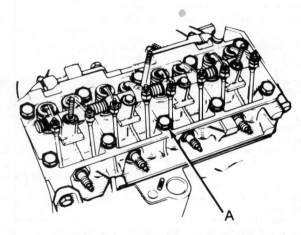

Fig. 2A.7 DO NOT remove the center head bolt (A) on the
distributor side of the engine (Sec 8)

15   Lift out each of the pushrods, using a twisting motion to separate
them from the cam followers (photo). Number them from 1 to 8 (starting at the flywheel end of the engine) to ensure that they are reinstalled
in their original locations.
16   Refer to the cylinder head bolt tightening diagram and loosen each
of the bolts 1/2-turn in the reverse order of the tightening sequence.
Remove all of the bolts except for the one next to the distributor (center
bolt on the distributor side).
17   Using a soft-faced hammer, tap the side of each end of the head
to pivot it around the remaining bolt and break the gasket seal. **Caution:**
*Do not attempt to lift the head off the engine until the gasket seal is
broken as described above. If it is lifted up, the seal at the base of each
cylinder liner will be broken and debris will enter the oil pan.*
18   After breaking the gasket seal, remove the remaining bolt and lift
the head off the engine. **Note:** *The crankshaft must not be turned with
the head off or the cylinder liner seals will be broken. If the crankshaft
must be turned, screw bolts with large washers under the heads into
the head bolt holes.*

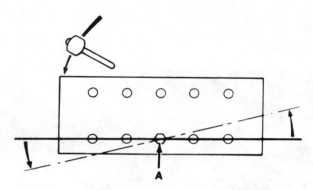

Fig. 2A.8 Tap the head on each end until it can pivot
around the remaining head bolt (A), which will break the
gasket seal (Sec 8)

9   Cylinder head — removal (engine on stand)

The procedure is nearly identical to the one described in Section 8
with the exception of not having to disconnect as many components.
Refer to Section 8 and modify it as needed.

10.3   Use a valve spring compressor to compress the valve
springs, then remove the keepers from the valve stem

10   Cylinder head — disassembly

Note: *New and rebuilt cylinder heads are commonly available for most
engines at dealerships and auto parts stores. Due to the fact that some
specialized tools are necessary for the disassembly and inspection procedures, and replacement parts may not be readily available, it may
be more practical and economical for the home mechanic to purchase
a replacement head rather than taking the time to disassemble, inspect
and recondition the original head.*
1   Cylinder head disassembly involves removal and disassembly of
the intake and exhaust valves and their related components. Remove
the clip from the end of the rocker arm shaft, then slide off the springs,
rocker arms and pedestals. Keep the parts in order to ensure installation
in their original locations.
2   Before the valves are removed, arrange to label and store them,
along with their related components, so they can be kept separate and
reinstalled in the same valve guides they are removed from.
3   Compress the valve spring on the first valve with a spring compressor and remove the keepers (photo). Carefully release the valve
spring compressor and remove the retainer, the spring, the valve guide
seal, the spring seat and the valve from the head. If the valve binds
in the guide (won't pull through), push it back into the head and deburr
the area around the keeper groove with a fine file or whetstone.
4   Repeat the procedure for the remaining valves. Remember to keep
together all the parts for each valve so they can be reinstalled in the
same locations.
5   Once the valves have been removed and safely stored, the head
should be thoroughly cleaned and inspected. If a complete engine
overhaul is being done, finish the engine disassembly procedures before
beginning the cylinder head cleaning and inspection process.

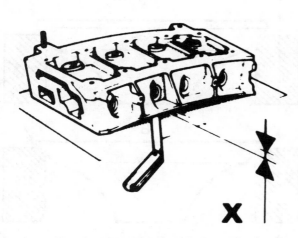

Fig. 2A.9 Try to slip various thickness feeler gauges
between the head and a surface plate or straightedge to
determine the amount of warpage (X) (Sec 11)

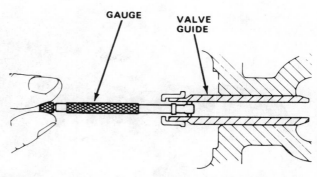

Fig. 2A.10 Use a small hole gauge to determine the inside
diameter of the valve guides (the gauge is then measured
with a micrometer) (Sec 11)

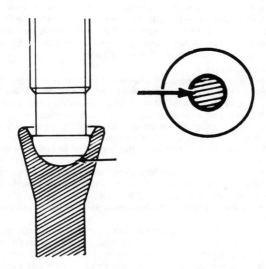

Fig. 2A.11 If the center of the pushrod recess (arrow) is
worn, the pushrod(s) should be replaced with new ones
(Sec 11)

11   Cylinder head — cleaning and inspection

1   Thorough cleaning of the cylinder head and related valve train components, followed by a detailed inspection, will enable you to decide how much valve service work must be done during the engine overhaul.

Cleaning

2   Scrape away all traces of old gasket material and sealing compound from the head gasket sealing surfaces.
3   Remove any built-up scale around the coolant passages.
4   Run a stiff wire brush through the oil holes to remove any deposits that may have formed in them.
5   It is a good idea to run an appropriate size tap into each of the threaded holes to remove any corrosion and thread sealant that may be present. If compressed air is available, use it to clear the holes of debris produced by this operation.
6   Clean the rocker arm shaft bolt or stud threads with a wire brush.
7   Next, clean the cylinder head with solvent and dry it thoroughly.

Compressed air will speed the drying process and ensure that all holes and recessed areas are clean. **Note:** *Decarbonizing chemicals are available and may prove very useful when cleaning cylinder heads and valve train components. They are very caustic and should be used with caution. Be sure to follow the instructions on the container.*
8   Clean the rocker arms and pushrods with solvent and dry them thoroughly. Compressed air will speed the drying process and can be used to clean out the oil passages.
9   Clean all the valve springs, keepers, retainers and spring seats with solvent and dry them thoroughly. Do the components from one valve at a time to avoid mixing up the parts.
10   Scrape off any heavy deposits that may have formed on the valves, then use a motorized wire brush to remove deposits from the valve heads and stems. Again, make sure the valves do not get mixed up.

Inpection

Cylinder head

11   Inspect the head very carefully for cracks, evidence of coolant leakage or other damage. If cracks are found, a new cylinder head should be obtained.
12   Using a straightedge or surface plate and feeler gauge, check the head gasket mating surface for warpage. If the warpage exceeds 0.006-inch over the length of the head, it can be resurfaced at an automotive machine shop.
13   Examine the valve seats in each of the combustion chambers. If they are pitted, cracked or burned, the head will require valve service that is beyond the scope of the home mechanic.
14   Measure the inside diameters of the valve guides (at both ends and the center of each guide) with a small hole gauge and a 0-to-1-inch micrometer. Record the measurements for future reference. These measurements, along with the valve stem diameter measurements, will enable you to compute the valve stem-to-guide clearances. These clearances, when compared to the Specifications, will be one factor that will determine the extent of valve service work required. The guides are measured at the ends and at the center to determine if they are worn in a bell-mouth pattern (more wear at the ends). If they are, guide reconditioning or replacement is necessary.

Rocker arm components

15   Check the rocker arm and adjusting screw faces (that contact the pushrod ends and valve stems) for pits, wear and rough spots. Check the pivot contact areas as well. Check the shaft for wear at the rocker arm pivot points.
16   Inspect the pushrod ends for scuffing and excessive wear. Make sure the center portion of the end that contacts the valve adjustment screw is unworn. Roll the pushrod on a flat surface, such as a piece of glass, to determine if it is bent.
17   Any damaged or excessively worn parts must be replaced with new ones.

Valves

18   Carefully inspect each valve face for cracks, pits and burned spots. Check the valve stem and neck for cracks. Rotate the valve and check for any obvious indication that it is bent. Check the end of the stem for pits and excessive wear. The presence of any of these conditions indicates the need for valve service by a properly equipped professional.

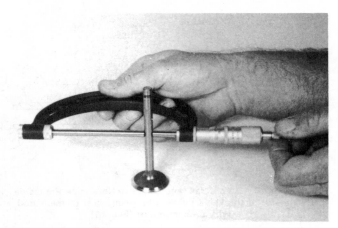

11.20   Measure the diameter of each valve stem at three points

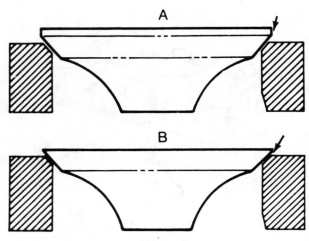

Fig. 2A.12 The valve margin width (A — arrow) must be as specified; if no margin exists (B — arrow), the valve must be replaced (Sec 11)

11.21a   Measure the free length of each valve stem with a dial or Vernier caliper

19 Measure the valve stem diameter (photo). By subtracting the stem diameter from the corresponding valve guide diameter, the valve stem-to-guide clearance is obtained. Compare the results to the Specifications. If the stem-to-guide clearance is greater than specified, the guides will have to be reconditioned and new valves may have to be installed, depending on the condition of the old valves.

Valve components

20 Check each valve spring for wear (on the ends) and pits. Measure the free length (photo) and compare it to the Specifications. Any springs that are shorter than specified have sagged and should not be reused. Stand the spring on a flat surface and check it for squareness (photo).
21 Check the spring retainers and keepers for obvious wear and cracks. Any questionable parts should be replaced with new ones, as extensive damage will occur in the event of failure during engine operation.
22 If the inspection process indicates that the valve components are in generally poor condition and worn beyond the limits specified, which is usually the case in an engine that is being overhauled, reassemble the valves in the cylinder head and refer to Section 12 for valve servicing recommendations.
23 If the inspection turns up no excessively worn parts, and if the valve faces and seats are in good condition, the valve train components can be reinstalled in the cylinder head without major servicing. Refer to the appropriate Section for cylinder head reassembly procedures.

12   Valves — servicing

1   Because of the complex nature of the job and the special tools and equipment needed, servicing of the valves, the valve seats and the valve guides (commonly known as a 'valve job') is best left to a professional.
2   The home mechanic can remove and disassemble the head, do the initial cleaning and inspection, then reassemble and deliver the head to a dealer service department or a reputable automotive machine shop for the actual valve servicing.
3   The dealer service department, or automotive machine shop, will remove the valves and springs, recondition or replace the valves and valve seats, recondition the valve guides, check and replace the valve springs, spring retainers and keepers (as necessary), replace the valve seals with new ones, reassemble the valve components and make sure the installed spring height is correct. The cylinder head gasket surface will also be resurfaced if it is warped.
4   After the valve job has been performed by a professional, the head will be in like-new condition. When the head is returned, be sure to clean it again, very thoroughly (before installation on the engine), to remove any metal particles and abrasive grit that may still be present from the valve service or head resurfacing operations. Use compressed air, if available, to blow out all the oil holes and passages.

11.21b   Check each valve spring for squareness

13.2   Remove the bolts to separate the oil pan from the block

13   Oil pan — removal

1   If the oil pan is being removed with the engine in the vehicle, first carry out the following operations:
   a)   Remove the two bolts and detach the engine-to-transmission support rod (note the location of the spacer).
   b)   Remove the bolts and separate the flywheel/driveplate cover from the bellhousing.
   c)   Drain the engine oil.
   d)   Disconnect the wires from the oil level sensor at the front of the oil pan (if so equipped).
2   Remove the oil pan-to-engine bolts (photo).
3   Tap the oil pan with a soft-faced hammer to break the seal, then separate it from the engine. Note that on some engines a gasket is not used, only a gasket sealing compound. On other engines, cork side gaskets and rubber end seals are used.

14   Oil pump — removal

1   If the oil pump must be removed with the engine in the vehicle, refer to Section 13 and remove the oil pan.
2   Remove the mounting bolts (photo) and carefully withdraw the oil pump and drive gear.

15   Timing cover, sprockets and chain — removal

1   If the engine is in the vehicle, remove the alternator drivebelt and the oil pan. Refer to the valve adjustment procedure in Chapter 1 and position the number 1 piston at TDC on the compression stroke as described there.
2   Using a large wrench or socket/breaker bar combination, remove the large bolt from the front of the crankshaft and slip off the pulley. Keep the crankshaft from turning by jamming a large screwdriver or pry bar in the ring gear teeth. **Caution:** *If the cylinder head has been removed, the crankshaft must not be allowed to turn. If it does, the cylinder liner seals will be broken and debris will fall into the oil pan.*
3   Remove the pulley hub from the crankshaft with a puller (photo).
4   Remove the bolts and carefully separate the timing cover from the engine block. Note that no gasket is used on some engines and a cork gasket is used on other engines.
5   Remove the timing chain tensioner Allen head bolt, hold the slipper and spring arm together and carefully separate the tensioner assembly from the block.
6   Bend back the locking tab and remove the camshaft sprocket retaining bolt.
7   Remove the sprockets and chain as an assembly (photo). If they are tight on the shafts, lever them off very carefully with two large screwdrivers.
8   Make sure the Woodruff key in the end of the crankshaft is snug in the keyway. If it is loose, remove it and store it where it will not get lost.

14.2   The oil pump is attached to the block with three bolts

15.3   A puller may be required to remove the crankshaft pulley hub

15.7   Separate the timing chain and sprockets from the camshaft/crankshaft as as assembly

16.2   Lift out the cam followers and store them in order

16.3   Remove the retaining plate bolts and carefully withdraw the camshaft from the block

16   Camshaft and followers — removal

1   Wedge a section of wood dowel into the distributor drive gear and extract it from the engine block.
2   Remove the camshaft followers by withdrawing them through the top of the block (photo). Label or store them in order to ensure that they are reinstalled in their original locations.
3   Remove the camshaft retaining plate bolts (photo) and carefully withdraw the camshaft from the block (try to avoid nicking or gouging the bearings).

17   Cylinder liners, pistons and connecting rods — removal

1   If the engine is in the vehicle, carry out the following operations first:
   a)   Remove the oil pan.
   b)   Remove the oil pump (to improve access).
   c)   Remove the cylinder head (not necessary if only the main bearings are being removed).
2   Turn the crankshaft until the end throws are at their lowest point.
Caution: *If the liners are not being removed, make sure they are clamped in place as described in the cylinder head removal procedure before turning the crankshaft.* If the connecting rods and caps are not marked, number them and mark the block so the rods, caps and liners can be returned to their original locations. If they are marked, number 1 should be the cylinder nearest the flywheel end of the engine.
3   Remove the nuts and withdraw the rod cap from the first connecting rod. If only the rod bearings are being replaced, push the rod away from the crankshaft and remove the upper bearing insert. Keep the rod cap and bearings together (don't mix them up).
4   Remove the cylinder liner clamp bolts you installed earlier and withdraw the liner, piston and connecting rod as an assembly through the top of the block. Mark the liner so it will be reinstalled in its original location.
5   Pull the rod down and remove the piston assembly from the liner.
6   Repeat the procedure to remove the three remaining liner, piston and rod assemblies.

18   Flywheel/driveplate — removal

1   Lock the crankshaft with a strip of angle iron between the ring gear teeth and the transmission mounting stud or by wedging a large block of wood between the crankcase and one of the crankshaft throws.
2   Mark the flywheel/driveplate in relationship to the crankshaft, then remove the bolts and pull it off the crankshaft.

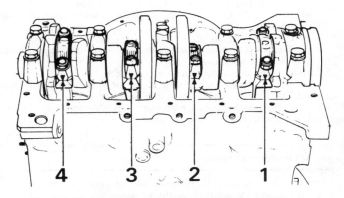

4   3   2   1

Fig. 2A.13   Mark the connecting rods and caps before removing them (Sec 17)

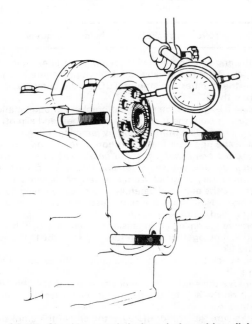

Fig. 2A.14   Checking crankshaft end play with a dial indicator (Sec 19)

19.3   The crankshaft end play can also be checked with feeler gauges

19.4   The main bearing caps should be numbered in order with number 1 at the flywheel end of the engine

19   Crankshaft — removal

1   Before the crankshaft is removed, check the end play as follows. Mount a dial indicator with the stem in line with the crankshaft and just touching the end (see accompanying illustration).
2   Push the crankshaft all the way to the rear and zero the dial indicator. Next, pry the crankshaft to the front as far as possible and check the reading on the dial indicator. The distance that it moves is the end play. If it is greater than specified, check the crankshaft thrust surfaces for wear. If no wear is apparent, new thrust bearings should correct the end play.
3   If a dial indicator is not available, feeler gauges can be used. Gently pry or push the crankshaft all the way to the front of the engine. Slip feeler gauges between the crankshaft and the front face of the thrust bearing (photo) to determine the clearance (which is equivalent to crankshaft end play).
4   Loosen each of the main bearing cap bolts 1/4-turn at a time, until they can be removed by hand. Check the main bearing caps to see if they are marked as to their locations. They are usually numbered consecutively (beginning with 1) from the rear of the engine to the front (photo). If they are not, mark them with number stamping dies or a center punch.
5   Gently tap the caps with a soft-faced hammer, then separate them from the engine block. If necessary, use the main bearing cap bolts as levers to remove the caps. Try not to drop the bearing insert if it comes out with the cap. Note that the oil dipstick tube is held in place by one of the bolts (photo).
6   Carefully lift the crankshaft out of the engine. It is a good idea to have an assistant available, since the crankshaft is quite heavy. With the bearing inserts in place in the engine block and in the main bearing caps, return the caps to their respective locations on the engine block and tighten the bolts finger tight.

20   Crankshaft rear oil seal — replacement

1   The oil seal can be replaced without removing the crankshaft, although the engine must be out of the vehicle (or the transmission must be removed). Detach the flywheel/driveplate from the crankshaft.
2   Clean the area around the seal, then carefully pry it out of the recess with a screwdriver. Do not scratch the seal mating surface on the crankshaft.
3   Wipe out the recess to remove all traces of oil and sludge.

19.5   The oil dipstick tube is held in place by the main bearing cap bolt

4   Apply moly-based grease to the seal lip and lubricate the outer edge with engine oil.
5   Position the seal over the end of the crankshaft with the open side facing in. Carefully drive the seal into the recess with a hammer and section of pipe the same diameter as the seal (a block of wood can be used against the seal as well, but you must be very careful to drive the seal in squarely).
6   Normally, the seal would be driven in until it is flush with the engine block. However, if only the seal is being replaced and the original crankshaft is being used, the seal must be driven in until it is 0.118-inch below the block surface. This will ensure that the seal lip contacts the crankshaft in a different location than the original seal.
7   Reinstall the flywheel/driveplate.

21   Engine mounts — replacement

Front mounts

1   Position a jack (with a block of wood on the jack head) under the oil pan if the right-hand mount is being removed or under the transmis-

21.2   Engine mount-to-frame nut location

21.4   The engine mount bracket is attached to the engine with three bolts

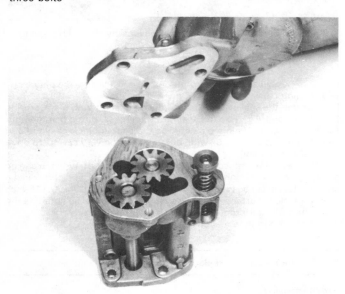

22.1   Remove the screws and separate the cover from the oil pump (gear-type pump shown)

sion if the left-hand mount is being removed. Raise the jack just enough to take up the weight of the engine and transmission.
2   Remove the rubber mount-to-frame nut and washer (photo).
3   Remove the mounting nuts/bolts and separate the mount from the engine or transmission brackets.
4   Remove the bolts securing the bracket to the engine or transmission (photo), lift off the bracket and withdraw the rubber mount.
5   Installation is the reverse of removal.

Rear mount
6   Disconnect the negative battery cable from the battery and remove the air cleaner assembly.
7   Position a jack (with a block of wood on the jack head) under the transmission and raise the jack just enough to take up the weight of the unit.
8   Remove the nut and washer securing the rubber mount to the transmission bracket.
9   Remove the two bolts securing the mounting bracket to the frame, slide out the bracket and remove the rubber mount.
10   Installation is the reverse of removal.

---

22   Oil pump — inspection and repair

---

1   Remove the bolts and separate the cover from the pump (photo). Be careful not to lose the pressure relief valve components, which may be ejected by the spring.
2   Remove the pressure relief valve ball seat, ball, spring and spring seat from the pump body (photos).
3   Lift out the idler gear and the drive gear and shaft. **Note:** *If your engine is equipped with a trochoidal-type pump, the 'gears' will not look like the ones in the photos but the disassembly/reassembly procedure is the same.*
4   Clean the components with solvent and carefully examine the gears, pump body and relief valve ball and seat for wear and damage. Replace the pump with a new one if evidence of wear or damage exists.
5   If the components are in good condition, check the clearances as follows.
6   On gear-type pumps, measure the clearance between the body and gears with a feeler gauge (photo). If the clearance is excessive, replace the pump with a new one.

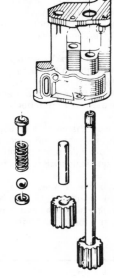

Fig. 2A.15   Gear-type oil pump components — exploded view (Sec 22)

7   On trochoidal-type pumps, measure the clearance between the outer gear and pump body and between the inner and outer gears as shown in the accompanying illustration. If the clearances are excessive, replace the pump with a new one.

8   If the clearances are as specified and no wear or damage is evident, reassemble the pump. Fill it with clean engine oil before installing the cover.

23   Crankshaft — inspection

1   Clean the crankshaft with solvent and dry it thoroughly. Be sure to clean the oil holes with a stiff brush and flush them with solvent. Check the main and connecting rod bearing journals for uneven wear, scoring, pitting or cracks. Check the remainder of the crankshaft for cracks and damage.

2   Using an appropriate size micromoeter, measure the diameter of

22.2a   Remove the pressure relief valve ball seat and ball, . . .

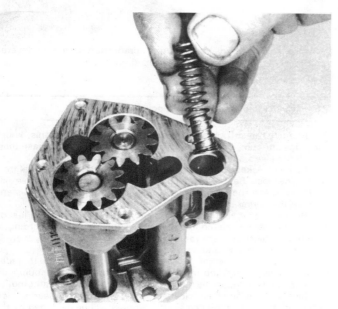

22.2b   . . . followed by the spring and spring seat

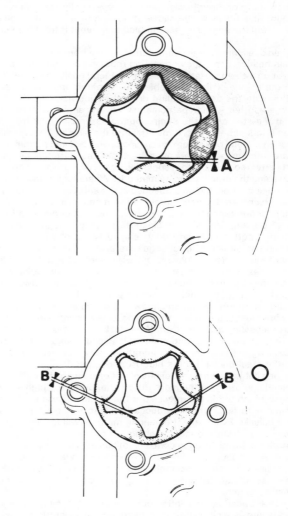

Fig. 2A.16 On trochoidal-type oil pumps, check the gear clearance (A and B) with the gears positioned in two different ways (Sec 22)

22.6   Checking the gear-to-body clearance with a feeler gauge(gear-type pump shown)

the main and connecting rod journals (photo) and compare the results to the Specifications. By measuring trhe diameter at a number of points around the journal's circumference, you will be able to determine whether or not the journal is out of round. Take the measurement at each end of the journal, near the crank counterweights, to determine whether the journal is tapered.

3   If the crankshaft journals are damaged, tapered, out of round or worn beyond the limits given in the Specifications, have the crankshaft reground by a reputable automotive machine shop. Be sure to use the correct undersize bearing inserts if the crankshaft is reconditioned.

4   Refer to Section 24 and examine the main and rod bearing inserts. If the bearing inserts and journals are all in good condition, do not decide to reuse the bearings until the oil clearances have been checked.

5   Check the pilot bearing in the rear end of the crankshaft for wear and damage. If replacement is necessary, thread a large tap into the bearing to remove it (the tap will cut threads in the bearing and push it out when it bottoms in the crankshaft hole). Use a hammer and socket or section of pipe to tap the new bearing into place.

23.2   Measure the diameter of each crankshaft journal at several points to detect taper and out-of-round conditions

24   Main and connecting rod bearings — inspection

1   Even though the main and connecting rod bearings should be replaced with new ones during the engine overhaul, the old bearings should be retained for close examination, as they may reveal valuable information about the condition of the engine.

2   Bearing failure occurs mainly because of lack of lubrication, the presence of dirt or other foreign particles, overloading the engine and corrosion. Regardless of the cause of bearing failure, it must be corrected before the engine is reassembled to prevent it from happening again.

3   When examining the bearings, remove them from the engine block, the main bearing caps, the connecting rods and the rod caps and lay them out on a clean surface in the same general position as their location in the engine. This will enable you to match any noted bearing problems with the corresponding crankshaft journal.

4   Dirt and other foreign particles get into the engine in a variety of ways. If may be left in the engine during assembly, or it may pass through filters or breathers. It may get into the oil, and from there into the bearings. Metal chips from machining operations and normal engine wear are often present. Abrasives are sometimes left in engine components after reconditioning, especially when parts are not thoroughly cleaned using the proper cleaning methods. Whatever the source, these foreign objects often end up embedded in the soft bearing material and are easily recognized. Large particles will not embed in the bearing and will score or gouge the bearing and shaft. The best prevention for this cause of bearing failure is to clean all parts thoroughly and keep everything spotlessly clean during engine assembly. Frequent and regular engine oil and filter changes are also recommended.

5   Lack of lubrication (or lubrication breakdown) has a number of interrelated causes. Excessive heat (which thins the oil), overloading (which squeezes the oil from the bearing face) and oil leakage or throwoff (from excessive bearing clearances, worn oil pump or high engine speeds) all contribute to lubrication breakdown. Blocked oil passages, which usually are the result of misaligned oil holes in a bearing shell, will also oil-starve a bearing and destroy it. When lack of lubrication is the cause of bearing failure, the bearing material is wiped or extruded from the steel backing of the bearing. Temperatures may increase to the point where the steel backing turns blue from overheating.

6   Driving habits can have a definite effect on bearing life. Full-throttle, low-speed operation (or 'lugging' the engine) puts very high loads on bearings, which tends to squeeze out the oil film. These loads cause the bearings to flex, which produces fine cracks in the bearing face (fatigue failure). Eventually the bearing material will loosen in pieces and tear away from the steel backing.

7   Short-trip driving leads to corrosion of bearings because insufficient engine heat is produced to drive off the condensed water and corrosive gases. These products collect in the engine oil, forming acid and sludge. As the oil is carried to the engine bearings, the acid attacks and corrodes the bearing material.

8   Incorrect bearing installation during engine assembly will lead to bearing failure as well. Tight-fitting bearings leave insufficient bearing oil clearance and will result in oil starvation. Dirt or foreign particles trapped behind a bearing insert result in high spots on the bearing which lead to failure.

25   Cylinder liners and engine block — cleaning

1   Remove the soft plugs from the engine block. To do this, knock the plugs into the block (using a hammer and punch), then grasp them with large pliers and pull them back through the holes.

2   Using a gasket scraper, remove all traces of gasket material from the engine block. Be very careful not to nick or gouge the gasket sealing surfaces. Clean the cylinder liner-to-block bore mating surfaces and remove the O-ring seals from the liners.

3   Remove the main bearing caps and separate the bearing inserts from the caps and the engine block. Tag the bearings according to which cylinder they were removed from (and whether they were in the cap or the block) and set them aside.

4   Using a hex wrench of the appropriate size, remove the threaded oil gallery plugs from the front and back of the block (if equipped).

5   If the engine is extremely dirty it should be taken to an automotive machine shop to be steam cleaned or hot tanked. Any bearings left in the block (such as the camshaft bearings) will be damaged by the cleaning process, so plan on having new ones installed while the block is at the machine shop.

6   After the block is returned, clean all oil holes and oil galleries one more time (brushes for cleaning oil holes and galleries are available at most auto parts stores). Flush the passages with warm water until the water runs clear, dry the block thoroughly and wipe all machined surfaces with a light, rust-preventative oil. If you have access to compressed air, use it to speed the drying process and to blow out all the oil holes and galleries.

7   If the block is not extremely dirty or sludged up, you can do an adequate cleaning job with warm soapy water and a stiff brush. Take plenty of time and do a thorough job. Regardless of the cleaning method used, be very sure to thoroughly clean all oil holes and galleries, dry the block completely and coat all machined surfaces with light oil.

8   The threaded holes in the block must be clean to ensure accurate torque readings during reassembly. Run the proper size tap into each of the holes to remove any rust, corrosion, thread sealant or sludge and to restore any damaged threads. If possible, use compressed air to clear the holes of debris produced by this operation. Now is a good time to thoroughly clean the threads on the head bolts and the main bearing cap bolts as well.

9   Reinstall the main bearing caps and tighten the bolts finger tight.

10 After coating the sealing surfaces of the new soft plugs with a good quality gasket sealer, install them in the engine block. Make sure they are driven in straight and seated properly or leakage could result. Special tools are available for this purpose, but equally good results can be obtained using a large socket (with an outside diameter that will just slip into the soft plug) and a hammer.

11 If the engine is not going to be reassembled right away, cover it with a large plastic trash bag to keep it clean.

|

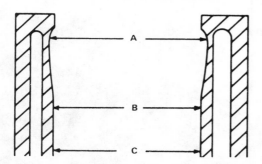

Fig. 2A.17 Measure the diameter of each cylinder liner just under the wear ridge (A), at the center (B) and at the bottom (C) (Sec 26)

26   Cylinder liners and engine block — inspection

1   Thoroughly clean the engine block as described in Section 25.
2   Visually check the block for cracks, rust and corrosion. Look for stripped threads in the threaded holes. It is also a good idea to have the block checked for hidden cracks by an automotive machine shop that has the special equipment to do this type of work. If defects are found, have the block repaired, if possible, or replaced.
3   Check the cylinder liners for scuffing and scoring. Look for cracks as well.
4   Using the appropriate precision measuring tools, measure each liner's diameter at the top (just under the ridge), center and bottom of the liner's bore, parallel to the crankshaft axis. Next, measure each liner's diameter at the same three locations across the crankshaft axis. Compare the results to the Specifications. If the cylinder liners are badly scuffed or scored, or if they are out-of-round or tapered beyond the limits given in the Specifications, have them rebored and honed at an automotive machine shop. If a rebore is done, oversize pistons and rings will be required.
5   If the cylinders are in reasonably good condition and not worn to the outside of the limits, and if the piston-to-cylinder clearances can be maintained properly, then they do not have to be rebored; honing is all that is necessary.
6   Before honing the cylinders, clamp them into the block with large bolts and washers (see Section 36).
7   To perform the honing operation you will need the proper size flexible hone (with fine stones), plenty of light oil or honing oil, some rags and an electric drill motor. Mount the hone in the drill motor, compress the stones and slip the hone into the first cylinder at a pace which will produce a fine cross-hatch pattern on the cylinder walls (with the cross-hatch lines intersecting at approximately a 60° angle). Be sure to use plenty of lubricant and do not take off any more material than is absolutely necessary to produce the desired finish. Do not withdraw the hone from the cylinder while it is running. Instead, shut off the drill and continue moving the hone up and down in the cylinder until it comes to a complete stop, then compress the stones and withdraw the hone. Wipe the oil out of the cylinder and repeat the procedure on the remaining cylinders. Remember, do not remove too much material from the cylinder wall. If you do not have the tools or do not desire to perform the honing operation, most automotive machine shops will do it for a reasonable fee.
8   After the honing job is complete, chamfer the top edges of the cylinder bores with a small file.
9   The entire engine block must be thoroughly washed again with warm, soapy water to remove all traces of the abrasive grit produced during the honing operation. Be sure to run a brush through all oil holes and galleries and flush them with running water. After rinsing, dry the block and apply a coat of light rust preventative oil to all machined surfaces. Wrap the block in a plastic trash bag to keep it clean and set it aside until reassembly.

27   Cylinder liner protrusion — measurement

1   Regardless of whether new or original cylinder liners will be installed when the engine is reassembled, the liner protrusion above the

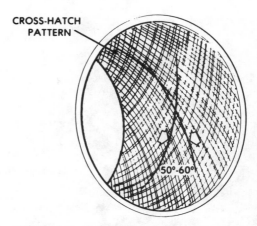

Fig. 2A.18 The cylinder hone should leave a cross-hatch pattern with the lines intersecting at approximately a 60° angle (Sec 26)

27.4   Measuring the cylinder liner protrusion with a straightedge and feeler gauge

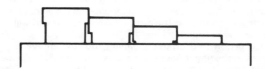

Fig. 2A.19 The cylinder liners must be arranged in ascending order of protrusion with the liner having the greatest protrusion at the flywheel end of the engine (Sec 27)

block must be measured.
2   Before checking the liner protrusion, make sure the mating/sealing surfaces of the liners and block bores are perfectly clean. Remove the original O-ring seals if not already done.
3   If the original liners are being checked, install them in their original locations. If new liners are being installed, install them initially at random. With the liners in place, keep the matched pistons together with them. With the liners in place, the flats on liners 1 and 2 must face each other and the flats on liners 3 and 4 must face each other.
4   Lay a straightedge across the first liner and measure the gap between the straightedge and the top of the block with a feeler gauge (photo). This is the liner protrusion (make sure it is within the specified limit listed in the Specifications at the front of this Chapter).
5   Repeat the procedure for the remaining cylinders.
6   If new liners are being installed, the height variation between cylinders must also be checked. The liners must be arranged so that

28.4   Cleaning the piston ring grooves with a ring groove cleaning tool (available at auto parts stores)

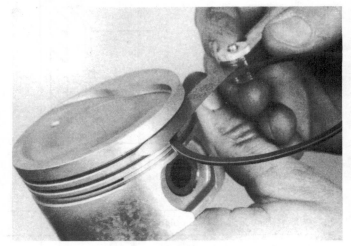

28.10   Checking the piston ring side clearance with a feeler gauge

the one with the greatest protrusion (within the specified limits) is installed in the number 1 cylinder (the cylinder nearest to the flywheel end of the engine). The remaining liners must be stepped down, in order, so that the one with the least protrusion becomes number 4. Make sure when moving a liner from one cylinder to another that the matched piston stays with it.

7   Once the liner positions have been finalized, mark them (along with the pistons) from 1 to 4 to ensure installation in the correct cylinder.

28   Piston/connecting rod assembly — inspection

1   Before the inspection process can be carried out, the piston/connecting rod assemblies must be cleaned and the original piston rings removed from the pistons. **Note:** *Always use new piston rings when the engine is reassembled.*
2   Using a piston ring installation tool, carefully remove the rings from the pistons. Do not nick or gouge the pistons in the process.
3   Scrape all traces of carbon from the top (or crown) of the piston. A hand-held wire brush or a piece of fine emery cloth can be used once the majority of the deposits have been scraped away. Do not, under any circumstances, use a wire brush mounted in a drill motor to remove deposits from the pistons. The piston material is soft and will be eroded away by the wire brush.
4   Use a piston ring groove cleaning tool to remove any carbon deposits from the ring grooves. If a tool is not available, a piece broken off the old ring will do the job. Be very careful to remove only the carbon deposits. Do not remove any metal and do not nick or scratch the sides of the ring grooves (photo).
5   Once the deposits have been removed, clean the piston/rod assemblies with solvent and dry them thoroughly. Make sure that the oil hole in the big end of the connecting rod and the oil return holes in the back sides of the ring grooves are clear.
6   If the pistons are not damaged or worn excessively, and if the liners are not rebored, new pistons will not be necessary. Normal piston wear appears as even vertical wear on the piston thrust surfaces and slight looseness of the top ring in its groove. New piston rings, on the other hand, should always be used when an engine is rebuilt.
7   Carefully inspect each piston for cracks around the skirt, at the pin bosses and at the ring lands.
8   Look for scoring and scuffing on the thrust faces of the skirt, holes in the piston crown and burned areas at the edge of the crown. If the skirt is scored or scuffed, the engine may have been suffering from overheating and/or abnormal combustion, which caused excessively high operating temperatures. The cooling and lubrication systems should be checked thoroughly. A hole in the piston crown is an indication that abnormal combustion (preignition) was occurring. Burned areas at the edge of the piston crown are usually evidence of spark knock (detonation). If any of the above problems exist, the causes must

28.11   Measuring the piston diameter (note that the measurement is taken 90° from the pin)

be corrected or the damage will occur again.
9   Corrosion of the piston (evidenced by pitting) indicates that coolant is leaking into the combustion chamber and/or the crankcase. Again, the cause must be corrected or the problem may persist in the rebuilt engine.
10   Measure the piston ring side clearance by laying a new piston ring in each ring groove and slipping a feeler gauge in between the ring and the edge of the ring groove (photo). Check the clearance at three or four locations around each groove. Be sure to use the correct ring for each groove; they are different. If the side clearance is greater than specified, new pistons and/or rings will have to be used.
11   Check the piston-to-bore clearance by measuring the bore (see Section 26) and the piston diameter. Make sure that the pistons and bores are correctly matched. Measure the piston across the skirt, on the thrust faces (at a 90° angle to the piston pin). Subtract the piston diameter from the bore diameter to obtain the clearance. If it is greater than specified, the liners will have to be rebored and new pistons and rings installed. Check the piston-to-rod clearance by twisting the piston and rod in opposite directions. Any noticeable play indicates that there is excessive wear, which must be corrected. The piston/connecting rod assemblies should be taken to an automotive machine shop to have new piston pins installed and the pistons and connecting rods rebored.
12   If the pistons must be removed from the connecting rods, such as when new pistons must be installed, or if the piston pins have too

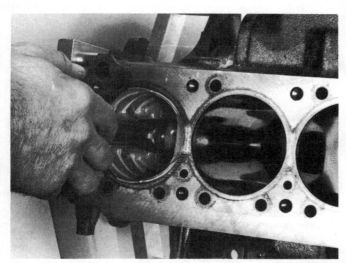

29.3a   Use the piston to square the ring in the cylinder prior to checking the ring end gap

29.3b   Measure the ring end gap with a feeler gauge

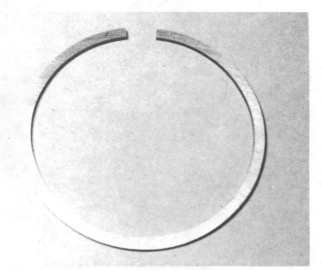

29.11   The word TOP stamped into the number 2 ring must face up when the ring is installed

much play in them, they should be taken to an automotive machine shop. While they are there have the connecting rods checked for bend and twist, as automotive machine shops have special equipment for this purpose. Unless new pistons or connecting rods must be installed, do not disassemble the pistons from the connecting rods.
13   Check the connecting rods for cracks and other damage. Temporarily remove the rod caps, lift out the old bearing inserts, wipe the rod and cap bearing surfaces clean and inspect them for nicks, gouges or scratches. After checking the rods, replace the old bearings, slip the caps into place and tighten the nuts finger tight.

29   Piston rings — installation

1   Before installing the new piston rings, the ring end gaps must be checked. It is assumed that the piston ring side clearance has been checked and verified correct (Section 28).
2   Lay out the piston/connecting rod assemblies and the new ring sets so the ring sets will be matched with the same piston and cylinder during the end gap measurement and engine assembly.
3   Insert the top (number one) ring into the first cylinder and square it up with the cylinder walls by pushing it in with the top of the piston (photo). The ring should be near the bottom of the cylinder at the lower

limit of ring travel. To measure the end gap, slip a feeler gauge between the ends of the ring (photo). Compare the measurement to the Specifications.
4   If the gap is larger or smaller than specified, double-check to make sure that you have the correct rings before proceeding.
5   If the gap is too small, consult with your dealer service department as the rings are pre-gapped and should not be filed.
6   Excess end gap is not critical unless it is greater than 0.040-inch (1 mm). Again, double-check to make sure you have the correct rings for your engine.
7   Repeat the procedure for each ring that will be installed in the first cylinder and for each ring in the remaining cylinders. Remember to keep rings, pistons and cylinders matched up.
8   Once the ring end gaps have been checked/corrected, the rings can be installed on the pistons.
9   The oil control ring (lowest one on the piston) is installed first.
10   After the oil ring has been installed, check to make sure that it can be turned smoothly in the ring groove.
11   The number two (middle) ring is installed next. It should be stamped with a mark so it can be readily distinguished from the top ring. **Note:** *Always follow the instructions printed on the ring package or box — different manufacturers may require different approaches. Do not mix up the top and middle rings, as they have different cross sections.*
12   Use a piston ring installation tool and make sure that the identification mark is facing the top of the piston, then slip the ring into the middle groove on the piston. Do not expand the ring any more than is necessary to slide it over the piston.
13   Finally, install the number one (top) ring in the same manner.
14   Repeat the procedure for the remaining pistons and rings. Be careful not to confuse the number one and number two rings.

30   Camshaft, bearings and followers — inspection and bearing replacement

Camshaft

1   After the camshaft has been removed from the engine, cleaned with solvent and dried, inspect the bearing journals for uneven wear, pitting and evidence of seizure. If the journals are damaged, the bearing inserts in the block are probably damaged as well. Both the camshaft and bearings will have to be replaced with new ones. Measure the inside diameter of each camshaft bearing and record the results (take two measurements, 90° apart, at each bearing).
2   Measure the bearing journals with a micrometer (photo) to determine if they are excessively worn or out-of-round. If they are more than 0.001-inch out-of-round, the camshaft should be replaced with a new one. Subtract the bearing journal diameter(s) from the

30.2   The camshaft bearing journal diameter (shown being measured) is subtracted from the bearing inside diameter to obtain the oil clearance

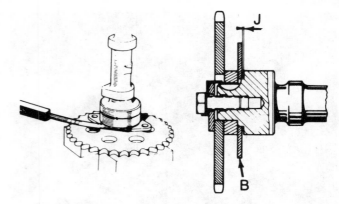

Fig. 2A.20 Checking camshaft end play (J) by inserting a feeler gauge between the retainer plate (B) and the face of the bearing journal (Sec 30)

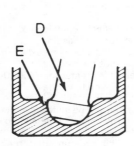   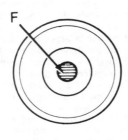

Fig. 2A.21 If the center of the follower recess is worn, it should be replaced with a new one (Sec 30)

D Pushrod   F Center (bottom) of recess
E Follower

31.3   Use a large socket or section of pipe to install the new timing chain cover oil seal

corresponding bearing inside diameter measurement to obtain the oil clearance. If it is excessive, new bearings must be installed.
3   Check the camshaft lobes for heat discoloration, score marks, chipped areas, pitting and uneven wear. If the lobes are in good condition the camshaft can be reused.
4   If the camshaft is usable, temporarily install the sprocket and tighten the bolt. Using a feeler gauge, measure the clearance between the retaining plate and the outer face of the bearing journal. If the clearance is excessive, install a new retaining plate. To do this, remove the sprocket and draw the old plate off with a puller. Install the new plate and collar with a hammer and section of pipe.

Followers
5   Clean the followers with solvent and dry them with compressed air *without mixing them up*.
6   Check the follower camshaft mating surface for score marks, scuffing and uneven wear.
7   Check the recess inside the follower and the end of the pushrod (if not already done). The center of the recess should not be worn at all.
8   Replace the follower(s) and pushrod(s) if the center recess is worn at the bottom.

Bearing replacement
9   Camshaft bearing replacement requires special tools and expertise that place it outside the scope of the do-it-yourselfer. Take the block to an automotive machine shop to ensure that the job is done correctly.

31   Timing cover, sprockets and chain — inspection

1   Check the sprocket teeth for wear and damage. If they are 'hooked', replace the sprockets and chain with new parts. If the engine has a lot of miles on it, replace the sprockets and chain as a matter of course.
2   Check the tensioner slipper chain contact surface for wear and damage and make sure the spring is in good condition.
3   Drive the old seal out of the timing cover and install a new one with a hammer and block of wood or large socket (photo). Make sure the open side of the seal faces in.

32   Flywheel/driveplate — inspection and repair

1   Check the flywheel for score marks and overheating of the clutch plate surface and check the ring gear for chipped or worn teeth. If the clutch plate surface is worn or damaged, it can be resurfaced at an automotive machine shop. If the ring gear is worn or damaged, have it replaced by your dealer service department or an automotive machine shop.
2   Check the driveplate carefully for distortion and cracks around the bolt holes or radiating out from the center.

34.6   The thrust bearings must be installed with the oil grooves facing OUT

34.12   A torque wrench MUST be used when tightening the main bearing cap bolts

33 Engine overhaul — reassembly sequence

1   Before beginning engine reassembly, make sure you have all the necessary new parts, gaskets and seals as well as the following items on hand:
    Common hand tools
    A 1/2-inch drive torque wrench
    Piston ring installation tool
    Piston ring compressor
    Short lengths of rubber or plastic hose to fit over connecting rod bolts
    Plastigage
    Feeler gauges
    A fine-tooth file
    New engine oil
    Engine assembly lube or moly-based grease
    RTV-type gasket sealant
    Anaerobic-type gasket sealant
    Thread locking compound
2   In order to save time and avoid problems, engine reassembly must be done in the following order.
    Crankshaft and main bearings
    Rear main oil seal
    Piston rings
    Piston/connecting rod assemblies
    Oil pump
    Oil pan
    Camshaft
    Timing chain/sprockets
    Timing chain/sprocket
    Valve followers
    Cylinder head and pushrods
    Oil filter
    Rocker arm cover
    Flywheel/driveplate

34 Crankshaft — installation and main bearing oil clearance check

1   Crankshaft installation is generally one of the first steps in engine reassembly; it is assumed at this point that the engine block and crankshaft have been cleaned, inspected and repaired or reconditioned.
2   Position the engine with the bottom facing up.
3   Remove the main bearing cap bolts and lift out the caps. Lay them out in the proper order to help ensure that they are installed correctly.
4   If they are still in place, remove the old bearing inserts from the block and the main bearing caps. Wipe the main bearing surfaces of the block and caps with a clean, lint-free cloth (they must be kept spotlessly clean).

5   Clean the back sides of the new main bearing inserts and lay one bearing half in each main bearing saddle in the block. Lay the other bearing half from each bearing set in the corresponding main bearing cap. Make sure the tab on the bearing insert fits into the recess in the block or cap. Also, the oil holes in the block and cap must line up with the oil holes in the bearing insert. Do not hammer the bearing into place and do not nick or gouge the bearing faces. No lubrication should be used at this time. **Note:** *If all five bearing inserts have two oil holes, they can be installed in any location. If two of the bearings have one oil hole, install them in the number 1 and 3 saddles. Install the remaining bearings in any locations.*
6   The thrust bearings must be installed in the number three (3) saddle (photo).
7   Clean the faces of the bearings in the block and the crankshaft main bearing journals with a clean, lint-free cloth. Check or clean the oil holes in the crankshaft, as any dirt here can go only one way — straight through the new bearings.
8   Once you are certain that the crankshaft is clean, carefully lay it in position in the main bearings with the counterweights lying sideways.
9   Before the crankshaft can be permanently installed, the main bearing oil clearance must be checked.
10   Trim several pieces of the appropriate size of Plastigage (so they are slightly shorter than the width of the main bearings) and place one piece on each crankshaft main bearing journal, parallel with the journal axis. Do not lay them across the oil holes.
11   Clean the faces of the bearings in the caps and install the caps in their respective positions (do not mix them up). Make sure the tabs on the bearing inserts in the caps and block are on the same side. Do not disturb the Plastigage.
12   Starting with the center main and working out toward the ends, tighten the main bearing cap bolts, in three steps, to the specified torque (photo). *Do not rotate the crankshaft at any time during this operation.*
13   Remove the bolts and carefully lift off the main bearing caps. Keep them in order. Do not disturb the Plastigage or rotate the crankshaft. If any of the main bsearing caps are difficult to remove, tap them gently from side-to-side with a soft-faced hammer to loosen them.
14   Compare the width of the crushed Plastigage on each journal to the scale printed on the Plastigage container to obtain the main bearing oil clearance. Check the Specifications to make sure it is correct.
15   If the clearance is not correct, double-check to make sure you have the right size bearing inserts. Also, make sure that no dirt or oil was between the bearing inserts and the main bearing caps or the block when the clearance was measured.
16   Carefully scrape all traces of the Plastigage material off the main bearing journals and/or the bearing faces. Do not nick or scratch the bearing faces.
17   Carefully lift the crankshaft out of the engine. Clean the bearing faces in the block, then apply a thin, uniform layer of clean, high-quality moly-based grease or engine assembly lube to each of the bearing surfaces. Be sure to coat the thrust faces of the thrust bearing.

35.5a   The arrow on the piston crown must face the flywheel when the piston/liner/connecting rod assemblies are installed

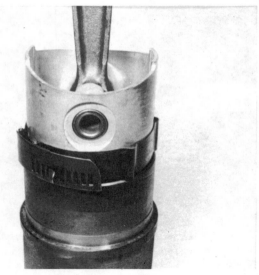

35.5b   Installing the piston/connecting rod assembly in the liner

36.3   The tab on the bearing insert must fit into the recess in the cap or rod

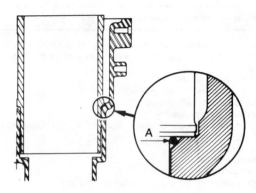

Fig. 2A.22 The O-ring seal (A) on the cylinder liner must not be twisted or it may leak (Sec 36)

18   Make sure the crankshaft journals are clean, then lay the crankshaft back in place in the block. Clean the faces of the bearings in the caps, then apply a thin, uniform layer of clean, moly-based grease to each of the bearing faces. Install the caps in their respective positions. Make sure the dipstick tube bracket is in place at the number 2 bearing cap. Install the bolts and tighten them to the specified torque, starting with the center main and working out toward the ends. Work up to the final torque in three steps.
19   Rotate the crankshaft a number of times by hand and check for any obvious binding.
20   Check the crankshaft end play with a feeler gauge or a dial indicator as described in Section 19.
21   Refer to Section 20 and install the new rear oil seal.

35   Pistons — installation in cylinder liners

1   If not already done, check the cylinder liner protrusion and install the piston rings on the pistons (refer to the appropriate Section).
2   Lay the four liners face down in a row on the bench in their correct order (1 through 4). Turn them as necessary so that the flats on liners 1 and 2 face each other and the flats on liners 3 and 4 face each other.
3   Lubricate the pistons and rings, then match them up with the correct liner.
4   Beginning with assembly number 1, make sure the piston ring end gaps are 120° apart (do not align the oil ring gap with a return hole in the piston). Compress the rings with a ring compressor.
5   Insert the piston into the liner with the arrow on the piston facing the flywheel end of the engine (photos). If the liners are laid out cor-

rectly, the arrow on piston number 1 should face away from the other liners. Carefully tap the piston into the liner with a soft-faced hammer until the top of the piston is approximately 1-inch from the top of the liner.
6   Repeat the procedure for the remaining piston/connecting rod/liner assemblies.
7   Install new base O-rings on each of the cylinder liners (make sure they are not twisted).
8   Install the liner/piston/connecting rod assemblies in the engine and check the bearing clearances as described in Section 36.

36   Cylinder liner, piston and connecting rod assemblies — installation and bearing oil clearance check

1   Remove the connecting rod cap from the end of the number one connecting rod. Remove the old bearing inserts and wipe the bearing surfaces of the connecting rod and cap with a clean, lint-free cloth (they must be kept spotlessly clean).
2   Clean the back side of the new upper bearing half, then lay it in place in the connecting rod. Make sure that the tab on the bearing fits into the recess in the rod. Do not hammer the bearing insert into place and be very careful not to nick or gouge the bearing face. Do not lubricate the bearing at this time.
3   Clean the back side of the other bearing insert and install it in the rod cap (photo). Again, make sure the tab on the bearing fits into the recess in the cap, and do not apply any lubricant. It is critically important that the mating surfaces of the bearing and connecting rod are perfectly clean and oil-free when they are assembled. Slip a section of plastic

36.6 Installing the liner/piston/connecting rod assembly in the block

36.7 The liners must be clamped in place with large bolts and washers

36.9a Install the connecting rod bearing/cap . . .

36.9b . . . and tighten the nuts with a torque wrench

or rubber hose over the connecting rod cap bolts.

4   Rotate the crankshaft until the number one connecting rod journal is as far from the number one cylinder as possible (bottom dead center).

5   Clean the number one connecting rod journal on the crankshaft and the bearing faces in the rod.

6   Make sure the O-ring is in place on the liner, then slide the number 1 liner/piston/connecting rod assembly into the block while guiding the end of the rod into place on the crankshaft (photo). Be sure that the arrow on the piston is pointing to the flywheel end of the engine and that the flat on the liner is positioned as described earlier.

7   Once the piston/connecting rod/liner assembly is installed, the connecting rod bearing oil clearance must be checked before the rod cap is permanently bolted in place. Before this is done, secure the liner in the bore with large bolts and washers (thread the bolts into the head bolt holes) (photo).

8   Cut a piece of the appropriate size Plastigage slightly shorter than the width of the connecting rod bearing and lay it in place on the number one connecting rod journal, parallel with the journal axis (it must not cross the oil hole in the journal) (photo).

9   Clean the connecting rod cap bearing face, remove the protective hoses from the connecting rod bolts and gently install the rod cap in place (photo). Make sure the mating mark on the cap is on the same side as the mark on the connecting rod. Also, the mark (number) on the cap/rod must be located on the side of the engine opposite the camshaft. Install the nuts and tighten them to the specified torque, working up to it in three steps (photo). Do not rotate the crankshaft at any time during this operation.

10 Remove the rod cap, being very careful not to disturb the Plastigage. Compare the width of the crushed Plastigage to the scale printed on the Plastigage container to obtain the oil clearance (photo).

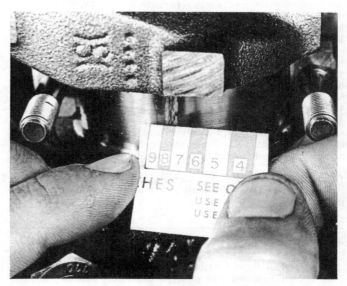

36.10 The crushed Plastigage is compared to the scale printed on the container to obtain the bearing oil clearance

37.1   When installing the camshaft, be very careful not to damage the bearings

38.2   Use thread locking compound on the flywheel bolts and tighten them in a criss-cross pattern

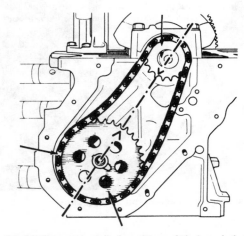

Fig. 2A.23 Correct installed position of timing chain and sprockets (note the positions of the marks on the sprockets) (Sec 39)

Compare it to the Specifications to make sure the clearance is correct. If the clearance is not correct, double-check to make sure that you have the correct size bearing inserts. Also, recheck the crankshaft connecting rod journal diameter and make sure that no dirt or oil was between the bearing inserts and the connecting rod or cap when the clearance was measured.

11   Carefully scrape all traces of the Plastigage material off the rod journal and/or bearing face (be very careful not to scratch the bearing — use your fingernail or a piece of hardwood). Make sure the bearing faces are perfectly clean, then apply a uniform layer of clean, high quality moly-based grease or engine assembly lube to both of them. You will have to push the piston into the cylinder to expose the face of the bearing insert in the connecting rod; be sure to slip the protective hoses over the rod bolts first.

12   Slide the connecting rod back into place on the journal, remove the protective hoses from the rod cap bolts, install the rod cap and tighten the nuts to the specified torque. Again, work up to the torque in three steps.

13   Repeat the entire procedure for the remaining piston/connecting rod/liner assemblies. Keep the back sides of the bearing inserts and the inside of the connecting rod and cap perfectly clean when assembling them. Make sure you have the correct assembly for the cylinder and that the arrow on the piston faces to the rear (flywheel end) of the engine when installed. Also, when installing the rod caps for the final time, be sure to lubricate the bearing faces adequately.

14   After all the piston/connecting rod assemblies have been properly installed, rotate the crankshaft a number of times by hand and check for any obvious binding.

15   As a final step, check the end play as follows. Mount a dial indicator with its stem in line with the crankshaft and touching the side of the number one cylinder connecting rod cap.

16   Push the connecting rod forward, as far as possible, and zero the dial indicator. Next, push the connecting rod all the way to the rear and check the reading on the dial indicator. The distance that it moves is the end play. If the play exceeds the service limit, a new connecting rod will be required. Repeat the procedure for the remaining connecting rods.

17   An alternative method is to slip feeler gauges between the connecting rod and the crankshaft throw until the play is removed. The end play is equal to the thickness of the feeler gauge(s).

37   Camshaft and followers — installation

Coat each of the cam lobes and bearing journals with engine assembly lube or moly-based grease, then carefully slide the camshaft into the block (photo). Be very careful not to damage the bearings.

2   Install the retaining plate bolts and tighten them to the specified

torque. Make sure the camshaft turns smoothly.

3   Apply engine assembly lube or moly-based grease to the followers and install them in their original locations in the block.

38   Flywheel/driveplate — installation

1   Clean the back of the flywheel and the end of the crankshaft, then position the flywheel and align the marks that were made during removal.

2   Apply thread locking compound to the bolt threads, then install and tighten them to the specified torque (photo). Follow a criss-cross pattern to avoid warping the flywheel.

39   Timing cover, sprockets and chain — installation

1   Install the Woodruff key in the groove in the end of the crankshaft, then tap the crankshaft sprocket into position. Make sure the timing mark on the sprocket faces out.

2   If the engine is in the vehicle, position the number 1 piston at TDC (refer to the valve adjustment procedure in Chapter 1 for more information). If the engine is out of the vehicle, turn the crankshaft until pistons number 1 and 4 are at the tops of the cylinders.

39.4 When correctly installed, the marks on the sprockets will face each other and the chain will have an equal amount of slack in each run

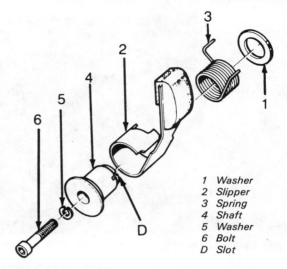

1 Washer
2 Slipper
3 Spring
4 Shaft
5 Washer
6 Bolt
D Slot

Fig. 2A.24 Timing chain tensioner components — exploded view (Sec 39)

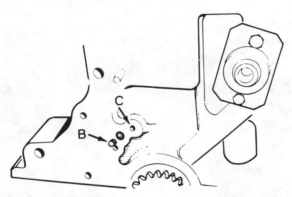

Fig. 2A.25 The dowel pin in the block (B) must fit into the slot in the shaft and the spring end must fit into the hole (C) when installing the tensioner assembly (Sec 39)

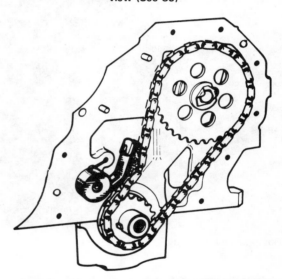

Fig. 2A.26 When correctly installed, the tensioner will take the slack out of the top run of the chain (Sec 39)

3   Temporarily install the camshaft sprocket and turn the camshaft until the timing marks on both sprockets face each other and coincide with an imaginary line drawn through the camshaft and crankshaft centers (see the accompanying ilustration). Remove the camshaft sprocket.
4   Position the chain over the camshaft sprocket, then loop it around the crankshaft sprocket while attaching the sprocket to the camshaft. Make sure the marks are properly aligned when there is an equal amount of slack in each side of the chain (photo).
5   Install the camshaft sprocket bolt and a new locking tab. Tighten the bolt to the specified torque and bend up the locking tab.
6   Install the chain tensioner assembly and tighten the bolt. The spring ends must fit in the hole in the block and against the slipper to apply tension to the chain. The dowel pin in the block fits into the slot in the tensioner shaft.
7   Make şure the gasket mating surfaces of the cover are clean (remove any old gasket material with a scraper and wipe off the residue with lacquer thinner).
8   Apply a bead of RTV-type gasket sealant to the cover flange (photo), then position it on the block over the dowels and studs. Install the bolts/nuts and tighten them in a criss-cross pattern
to the specified torque (work up to it in three steps). **Note:** *Some engines are equipped with cork gaskets at the timing chain cover. If you are installing new cork gaskets, apply a thin coat of sealant to each side of the gasket and do not overtighten the bolts.*

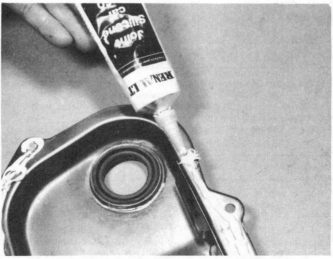

39.8 Apply RTV-type sealant to the timing cover flange

39.9   Install the pulley hub, . . .

39.10a   . . . followed by the pulley . . .

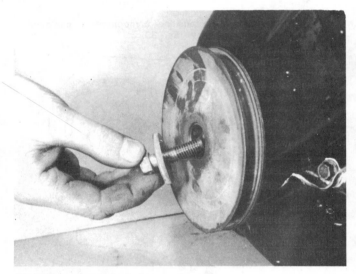

39.10b   . . . and the bolt

40.1   Installing the oil pump

9   Lubricate the crankshaft pulley hub with moly-based grease and carefully slide it onto the end of the crankshaft (photo).
10   Place the pulley in position, install the bolt and tighten it to the specified torque (photos).
11   If the engine is in the vehicle, install the oil pan and the alternator drivebelt.

40   Oil pump — installation

1   Install the oil pump drive shaft in the block bore. If the engine is in the vehicle, engage it with the distributor drive gear (photo).
2   Push the pump into contact with the block, then install and tighten the bolts. Note that no gasket is used.
3   If the engine is in the vehicle, install the oil pan.

41   Oil pan — installation

1   Make sure that the gasket mating surfaces are clean (remove any old gasket material with a scraper and wipe off the residue with lacquer thinner).
2   Apply a uniform bead of RTV-type gasket sealant to the oil pan flange. Build it up thicker at the corners and areas that contact the timing cover and number 1 bearing cap. Also apply the sealant to the boss and corners of the number 1 main bearing cap (flywheel end).

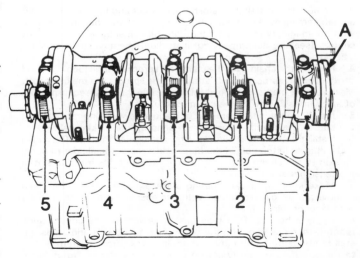

Fig. 2A.27   Make sure the sealant is applied to the boss (A) on the flywheel end main bearing cap (Sec 41)

41.3 Carefully lower the oil pan into place on the block (do not disturb the gaskets — if used)

42.1 Lubricate the stem and install the valve in the guide

42.2a Install the spring seat over the guide

42.2b The closely-wound coils on the spring must be next to the head

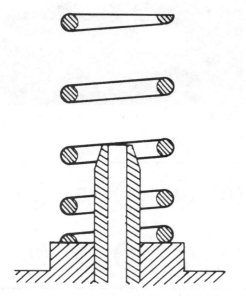

Fig. 2A.28 The valve springs must be installed with the closely-wound coils next to the cylinder head (Sec 42)

Note: *Some engines were equipped with cork gaskets and rubber seals at the oil pan. If you are installing new cork/rubber gaskets, apply a thin layer of sealant to each side of the cork gaskets and retain them with the dowels at the ends. Also, the cork gaskets must cover the ends of the main bearing rubber seals. Apply RTV-type sealant to the joints between the cork and rubber gaskets. Do not overtighten the bolts or the cork gaskets will be crushed and oil leaks will result.*

3   Carefully lower the oil pan onto the block (photo). Do not disturb the sealant or gaskets.

4   Install the bolts and tighten them in a criss-cross pattern to the specified torque (work up to it in three steps).

5   If the engine is in the vehicle, install the support rod, the flywheel or torque converter cover and the oil level sensor wires (if equipped). Refill the engine with the specified grade of oil (Chapter 1).

---

42   Cylinder head — reassembly and installation

Note: *Regardless of whether or not the head was sent to an automotive machine shop for servicing, make sure it is clean before beginning reassembly. If the head was sent out for valve servicing, the valves and related components will already be in place. Begin the reassembly procedure with Step 5.*

1   Lubricate the valve stems with engine assembly lube or moly-based grease, then install the first one in its original location (photo).

2   Install the spring seat, the spring (with the closely wound coils next to the head) and the retainer (photos).

3   Compress the valve spring and install the keepers. **Note:** *The intake and exhaust valves require different style keepers — do not interchange them or engine damage will result. Make sure the keepers are securely locked in their retaining grooves.*

4   Repeat the procedure for each of the remaining valves. Be careful not to mix up the components or install them in the wrong location.

5   Lubricate the rocker arm shaft with clean engine oil, then install the springs, rocker arms and pedestals in the reverse order of removal. Install the clip on the end of the shaft. Make sure that the bolt holes in the pedestals are aligned with the recesses in the shaft and that the pedestal with the oil hole is at the flywheel end of the shaft.

6   Remove the bolts/washers holding the cylinder liners in place and make sure the head and block mating surfaces are perfectly clean. Lay a new gasket on the block (it may be stamped *TOP* — if so, make sure the word *TOP* is facing up) (photo). Do not use any gasket sealant.

7   Make sure there is no oil in the head bolt holes (use a syringe to remove it if there is).

8   Carefully lower the head onto the block (do not disturb the gasket) (photo). Install the bolts and tighten them to the specified torque following the sequence shown in the accompanying illustration. Work up to the final torque in three steps (photo).

9   Install the pushrods in their original locations (photo).

10   Lower the rocker shaft assembly onto the head and make sure the adjusting screw ball ends locate in the pushrod ends. Install the spring washer (convex side up), nuts and bolts and tighten them to the

Fig. 2A.30 The rocker arm pedestal support with the oil hole (arrow) must be installed at the flywheel end of the engine (Sec 42)

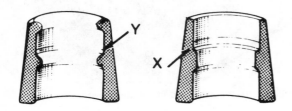

Fig. 2A.29 Note that the intake valve keepers (X) are different than the exhaust valve keepers (Y) — do not mix them up (Sec 42)

42.6   The dowels will hold the head gasket in position

42.8a   Carefully lower the head onto the gasket

42.8b   The head bolts are tightened to the specified torque in three steps, following the prescribed sequence to avoid warping the cylinder head

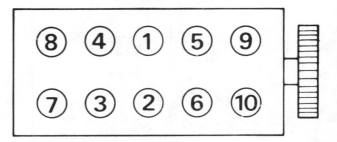

Fig. 2A.31 Cylinder head bolt tightening sequence (Sec 42)

specified torque (photo).
11 Adjust the valve clearances as described in Chapter 1 (use the *COLD ENGINE* specifications at the front of this Chapter).
12 Install the rocker arm cover (use a new gasket) and tighten the bolts/nuts evenly and securely.
13 If the engine is in the vehicle, reverse the removal procedure in Section 8 to complete the installation.

43 Distributor drive gear — installation

1   Position the number 1 piston at TDC (refer to the valve adjustment procedure in Chapter 1 for details).
2   Without moving the crankshaft, position the drive gear with the slots at the 2 o'clock and 8 o'clock positions and the larger offset side facing away from the engine (photo).
3   Now lower the gear into mesh with the camshaft and oil pump shaft. As the gear meshes with the camshaft it will rotate counterclockwise and should end up with its slot at right angles to the crankshaft centerline and the larger offset facing the flywheel. It may take two or three attempts to get it right (photo).

42.9   Install the pushrods in their original locations

42.10   Make sure the pushrods mate with the valve adjustment screws when the rocker arm assembly is installed

43.2   Install the distributor drive gear . . .

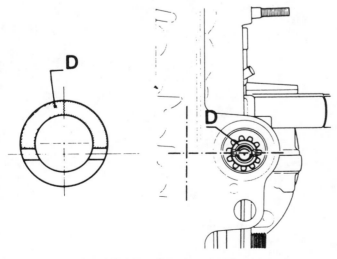

Fig. 2A.32 Distributor drive gear installation (Sec 43)

D = Larger offset side

43.3   . . . so that the slot is at a right angle to the crankshaft centerline and the larger offset side is facing the flywheel

44 Engine — installation

Engine installation is basically the reverse of removal, but note the following points:

    a) Tighten the exhaust pipe-to-manifold bolts as described in Chapter 4.
    b) Refill the cooling system as described in Chapter 1
    c) Adjust the drivebelt tension as described in Chapter 1
    d) Where applicable, refill the transmission and engine with oil as described in Chapter 1.

45 Initial start-up and break-in after overhaul

1   Once the engine has been properly installed in the vehicle, doublecheck the engine oil and coolant levels.

2   With the spark plugs out of the engine and the coil high-tension lead grounded to the engine block, crank the engine over until oil pressure registers on the gauge (if so equipped) or until the oil light goes off.

3   Install the spark plugs, hook up the plug wires and the coil high tension lead.

4   Start the engine. It may take a few moments for the gasoline to reach the injectors, but the engine should start without a great deal of effort.

5   As soon as the engine starts it should be set at a fast idle (to ensure proper oil circulation) and allowed to run for 20 minutes. While the engine is warming up, make a thorough check for oil and coolant leaks.

6   Shut the engine off and recheck the engine oil and coolant levels. Allow the engine to cool for 2 1/2 hours, then refer to Section 42 and retighten the head bolts to the specified torque. Loosen each bolt 1/2-turn, then tighten them again, in the correct sequence to the specified torque. Recheck the valve clearances.

7   Drive the vehicle to an area with minimum traffic, accelerate at full throttle from 30 to 50 mph, then allow the vehicle to slow to 30 mph with the throttle closed. Repeat the procedure 10 or 12 times. This will load the piston rings and cause them to seat properly against the cylinder walls. Check again for oil and coolant leaks.

8   Drive the vehicle gently for the first 500 miles (no sustained high speeds) and keep a constant check on the oil level. It is not unusual for an engine to use oil during the break-in period.

9   At approximately 500 to 600 miles, change the oil and filter and recheck the valve clearances (if applicable).

10   For the next few hundred miles, drive the vehicle normally. Do not either pamper it or abuse it.

11   After 2000 miles, change the oil and filter again and consider the engine fully broken in.

Chapter 2 Part B 1.7 liter engine

Refer to Chapter 13 for information on the 2.0 liter engine and 1986 and later 1.7 liter engines

Contents

Specifications

Note: *To avoid conversion inaccuracies, all specifications are given in metric values, as specified by the manufacturer.*

General

Bore	81 mm
Stroke	83.5 mm
Displacement	1.7 liter
Oil pressure	
Idle speed	2.0 bar
3000 rpm	3.5 bar
Cylinder numbers	1-2-3-4 (from flywheel end)
Number 1 cylinder	Flywheel end of engine
Firing order	1-3-4-2

Cylinder head

Maximum warpage	0.05 mm
Cylinder head height	169.3 to 169.7 mm

Valves and related components

Valve face and seat angle	
Intake	60°
Exhaust	45°
Valve stem diameter	8.0 mm
Valve guide inside diameter	Check with dealer service department or automotive machine shop
Stem-to-guide clearance	Check with dealer service department or automotive machine shop
Valve guide bore diameter	12.99 mm
Valve guide height above joint	42.8 to 42.2 mm
Valve seat width	1.5 to 1.9 mm
Valve margin width (minimum)	1/32 in
Valve spring free length	44.9 mm
Tappet diameter (std.)	34.99 to 35.04 mm
Valve clearances (engine cold)	
Intake	0.20 mm (0.008 in)
Exhaust	0.40 mm (0.016 in)

Crankshaft and connecting rods

Crankshaft end play	0.07 to 0.23 mm
Connecting rod end play (side clearance) ...	0.22 to 0.40 mm
Main bearing journal diameter	54.794 mm
Main bearing journal minimum regrind diameter	54.545 mm
Main bearing oil clearance	Check with dealer service department or automotive machine shop
Connecting rod journal diameter	48 mm
Connecting rod journal minimum regrind diameter	47.75 mm
Connecting rod bearing oil clearance	Check with dealer service department or automotive machine shop
Crankshaft journal taper/out-of-round limit	Check with dealer service department or automotive machine shop

Engine block

Cylinder bore diameter	81.0 mm
Out-of-round/taper limit	Check with dealer service department or automotive machine shop

Pistons and rings

Piston ring side clearance	Check with dealer service department or automotive machine shop
Piston-to-bore clearance	Check with dealer service department or automotive machine shop
Piston ring end gap	Pre-set (do not change)

Camshaft

Bearing journal diameter	Check with dealer service department or automotive machine shop
Bearing oil clearance	Check with dealer service department or automotive machine shop
Camshaft end play	0.048 to 0.133 mm

Oil pump

Gear-to-body clearance	0.02 mm maximum
Gear end play	0.085 mm maximum

Auxiliary shaft

Bushing diameter	
Inner	39.5 mm
Outer	40.5 mm
End play	0.07 to 0.15 mm

Torque specifications	**Ft-lbs**
Cylinder head bolts	
1st step	22
2nd step	52
1st retightening step*	15
2nd retightening step	Turn through 123°
Connecting rod cap nuts	37
Main bearing cap bolts	48
Flywheel bolts	41
Engine mount nuts/bolts	30
Camshaft sprocket bolt	37
Camshaft bearing cap bolts	
8 mm	15
6 mm	7
Crankshaft pulley hub bolt	70
Idler pulley bolt	15
Tensioner pulley nut	30
Oil pan bolt	11
Oil pump mounting bolts	18

Wait 3 minutes, then loosen all bolts

1 General information

The 1.7 liter engine is an in-line, overhead valve four cylinder mounted transversely in the engine compartment. The block is cast iron and the head is aluminum. The crankshaft is supported by five insert-type main bearings. Thrust bearings are installed at the number 2 main to control crankshaft end play.

The connecting rods ride in insert-type bearings at the crankshaft and are attached to the pistons by interference fit pins. The pistons are made of aluminum and are equipped with two compression rings and one oil control ring.

The camshaft, which is mounted directly in the cylinder head, is belt driven from the crankshaft and operates the valves through inverted bucket-type tappets which ride in machined bores in the head. Valve adjustment is done by replacing thin shims which are positioned between the cam lobes and the tappets.

An auxiliary shaft is located alongside the crankshaft and is driven by the timing belt.

Lubrication is provided by a gear-type oil pump driven off the auxiliary shaft and located in the crankcase.

The distributor is driven off the end of the camshaft.

2 Repair operations possible with the engine in the vehicle

Refer to Section 2 in Part A, but note that the timing belt (instead of a timing chain), camshaft and auxiliary shaft can also be removed from the 1.7 liter engine with it in place in the vehicle (in addition to the items mentioned in Chapter 2, Part A).

3 Engine overhaul — general information

Refer to Section 3 in Chapter 2, Part A.

4 Engine rebuilding alternatives

Refer to Section 4 in Chapter 2, Part A

5 Engine removal — methods and precautions

Refer to Section 5 in Chapter 2, Part A. Note that the engine and transmission must be removed as an assembly, as there is not enough room to work if the transmission is left in the vehicle (as an alternative, the transmission could be removed first, but it would definitely be a waste of time).

6 Engine/transmission — removal

1   Disconnect the battery cables and lift out the battery, then remove the hood as described in Chapter 11.
2   Remove the radiator as described in Chapter 3.
3   Remove the air cleaner.
4   Refer to Chapter 1 and drain the transmission.
5   Loosen the hose clamps and disconnect the two heater hoses at the fittings on the engine.
6   Remove the air conditioner compressor, but leave the hoses attached.
7   Disconnect the throttle and cruise control cables.
8   Detach the brake servo vacuum hose from the rear of the intake manifold.
9   Disconnect the engine ground strap under the manifolds and the ground strap at the transmission.
10 Undo the two bolts, remove the springs and release the exhaust pipe from the manifold.
11 Disconnect the fuel lines and remove the gas tank cap.
12 Disconnect the ignition wire from the center of the distributor cap.
13 Detach and label all vacuum hoses and wire connectors.

14 Note the locations of the wires at the rear of the alternator and disconnect them.
15 Note the wire locations at the starter motor solenoid and disconnect them.
16 Disconnect the lead at the coolant temperature sending unit on the cylinder head and the lead at the oil pressure switch on the front side of the block.
17 Undo the two bolts and remove the TDC sensor from the top of the bellhousing.
18 Disconnect the wiring at the horn and at the oil level sensor on the oil pan.
19 All the wiring to the engine should now be disconnected and, after releasing the clips and ties, it should be possible to move the complete wiring harness to one side.
20 Withdraw the spring wire retaining clip securing the speedometer cable to the rear of the transmission and remove the cable. Note the installed direction of the clip.
21 Disconnect the clutch cable from the release fork and the bracket on the bellhousing.
22 Jack up the front of the vehicle and support it on jackstands.
23 Remove the four bolts, one at each corner, and detach the splash shield.
24 Slide back the rubber cover and remove the nut and bolt securing the rod to the fork control shaft. Slide the rod off the shaft and recover the sleeve.
25 Disconnect the wiring at the back-up light switch and, where installed, the gear position sensors on the case.
26 If equipped with an automatic transmission, disconnect the fluid cooler lines from the transmission and plug the fittings.
27 Disconnect and drain the power steering hoses at the pump (if equipped).
28 Drive out the roll pin securing the right-hand driveaxle inner joint to the differential stub shaft. Note that the roll pin is in fact two roll pins, one inside the other.
29 Remove the three bolts securing the left-hand driveaxle inner joint boot and retaining plate to the side of the transmission.
30 Lower the vehicle to the ground and make a final check that all cables, lines and components likely to impede removal have been detached and moved aside.
31 Attach a hoist to the engine using chain at the engine lifting brackets.
32 Remove the nuts and bolts at the front, and the single nut at the rear securing the engine mounting brackets to the rubber mount. Remove the retaining bolts and detach the movement limiter from the

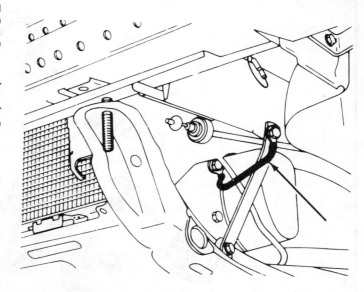

Fig. 2B.1 Location of the transmission ground strap (arrow) that must be disconnected when removing the engine/transmission (Sec 6)

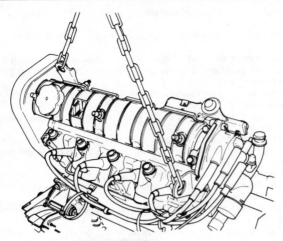

Fig. 2B.2 Attach the engine hoist chains to the lifting eyes (Sec 6)

engine and subframe.

33 Raise the engine and transmission slightly and release the brackets from the rubber mount.

34 Move the engine and transmission assembly to the left as far as possible and tap the right-hand driveaxle inner joint off the stub shaft using a soft-faced hammer.

35 Now move the engine assembly to the right and lift the left-hand driveaxle inner joint spider out of the differential.

36 Slowly lift the engine and transmission assembly, moving it around as necessary to clear all obstructions. When high enough, lift it over the front body panel and lower it.

---

7   Separating the engine and transmission

1 With the assembly removed from the vehicle, undo the retaining bolts and lift off the cover plate at the base of the bellhousing. If equipped with an automatic transmission, remove the driveplate-to-torque converter bolts through the cover plate opening. When the engine and transmission are pulled apart, be sure the torque converter stays on the transmission shaft.

2 Turn the crankshaft as necessary using a socket on the pulley bolt until the notch on the flywheel is in line with the TDC mark on the bellhousing timing scale (see Chapter 1). Now make a reference mark on the block in line with the flywheel notch. This will be useful because once the transmission is removed, the timing marks go with it, and it then becomes difficult to accurately determine the TDC position of the number 1 piston.

3 Remove the support bracket bolt and the three bellhousing bolts securing the starter in position. Detach the starter motor, noting the location of the dowel in one of the bolt holes.

4 Remove the bolts and the two nuts securing the engine to the bellhousing. Support the transmission and withdraw the engine. The engine may be tight due to the locating dowels.

---

8   Engine overhaul — disassembly sequence

Refer to Section 7 in Part A, but note that the distributor on the 1.7 liter engine does not have to be removed — only the cap and wires. Also, the camshaft on the 1.7 liter engine will come off with the cylinder head, there are no pushrods to remove, a belt is used in place of the timing chain and the cylinders are an integral part of the engine block.

---

9   Timing belt — removal

1 If the engine is in the vehicle, first carry out the following operations:
    a) Disconnect the negative battery cable.
    b) Remove the air cleaner assembly.
    c) Remove the alternator drivebelt.

2 Remove the four bolts and detach the timing belt cover.

3 Note the location of the timing mark on the outer edge of the camshaft sprocket. Using a socket and ratchet on the crankshaft pulley bolt, turn the crankshaft until the camshaft sprocket timing mark is uppermost and in line with a corresponding mark or notch on the metal plate behind the sprocket. Note that some earlier engines do not have

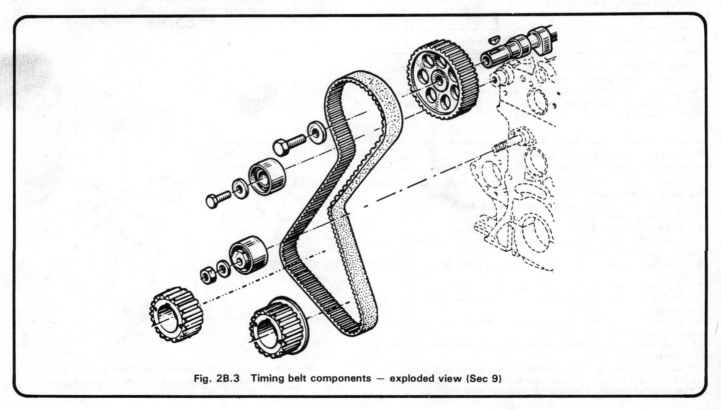

Fig. 2B.3 Timing belt components — exploded view (Sec 9)

a mark or notch on the plate and if this is the case just turn the crankshaft so that the timing mark on the sprocket is roughly near the top. This will do for the time being.

4 Again using a socket and ratchet, remove the crankshaft pulley retaining bolt and withdraw the pulley. If the engine is in the vehicle, the crankshaft can be prevented from turning by engaging top gear and firmly applying the handbrake. If the engine is out of the vehicle, lock the flywheel ring gear using a wide screwdriver or strip of angle iron between the ring gear teeth and the long stud on the side of the block.

5 Remove the plug on the lower front side of the engine, at the flywheel end, and obtain a metal rod which is a snug fit in the plug hole. Turn the crankshaft slightly as necessary to the TDC position, then push the rod through the hole to locate in the slot in the crankshaft web. Make sure that the crankshaft is exactly at TDC for the number 1 piston by aligning the timing notch on the flywheel with the bell-housing mark, or the mark on the camshaft sprocket with the corresponding mark on the metal plate. If the crankshaft is not positioned accurately, it is possible to engage the rod with a balance hole in the crankshaft web (which is not the TDC slot).

6 Double check that the camshaft sprocket timing mark is aligned with the corresponding mark on the metal plate. If the plate does not have a mark, make one now using paint or by accurately scribing a line aligned with the mark on the sprocket. Also make sure that there are arrows indicating the running direction of the belt, located between the auxiliary shaft sprocket and the idler pulley. Some belts also have their own timing mark. If so, these marks should also be aligned with the marks on the sprocket and plate.

7 Loosen the tensioner pulley retaining nut and rotate the tensioner body until the belt is slack.

8 Slip the timing belt off the sprockets and pulleys and remove it from the engine.

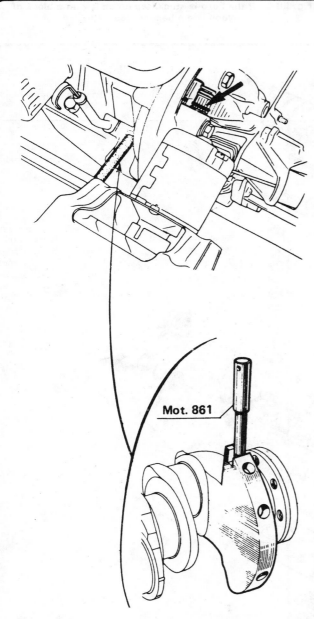

Fig. 2B.4 Using a rod to locate the crankshaft with the number 1 piston in the TDC position (the rod will keep it from moving) (Sec 9)

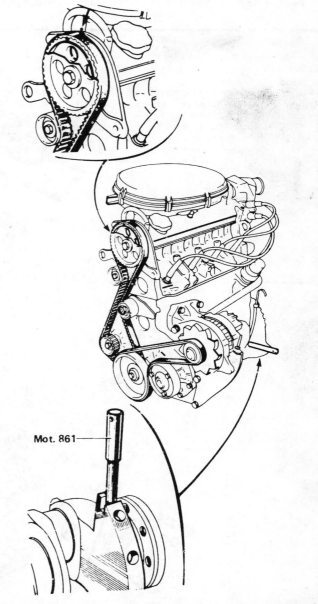

Fig. 2B.5 The timing marks on the belt and sprocket must align with those on the backing plate when the number 1 piston is at TDC on the compression stroke (Sec 9)

10   Cylinder head — removal (engine in vehicle)

1   Refer to the previous Section and remove the timing belt.
2   Refer to Chapter 1 and drain the cooling system.
3   Disconnect the ignition wire at the center of the distributor cap.
4   Disconnect the lead at the coolant temperature sending unit on the cylinder head.
5   Disconnect the fuel lines and plug them.
6   Disconnect the throttle cable.
7   Disconnect the cruise control cable (if equipped).
8   Disconnect the brake servo vacuum hose from the intake manifold.
9   Disconnect the heater hoses, crankcase ventilation hoses and the two nuts securing the support plate to the rear side of the cylinder head. Disconnect all wires attached to the head.
10   Disconnect the top radiator hose from the thermostat housing.
11   Remove the two bolts and withdraw the springs securing the exhaust pipe to the manifold.
12   Remove the three domed nuts, lift off the washers and detach the

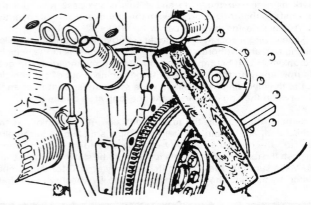

Fig. 2B.6   If the head is stuck, tap up on it with a block of wood and a hammer (Sec 10)

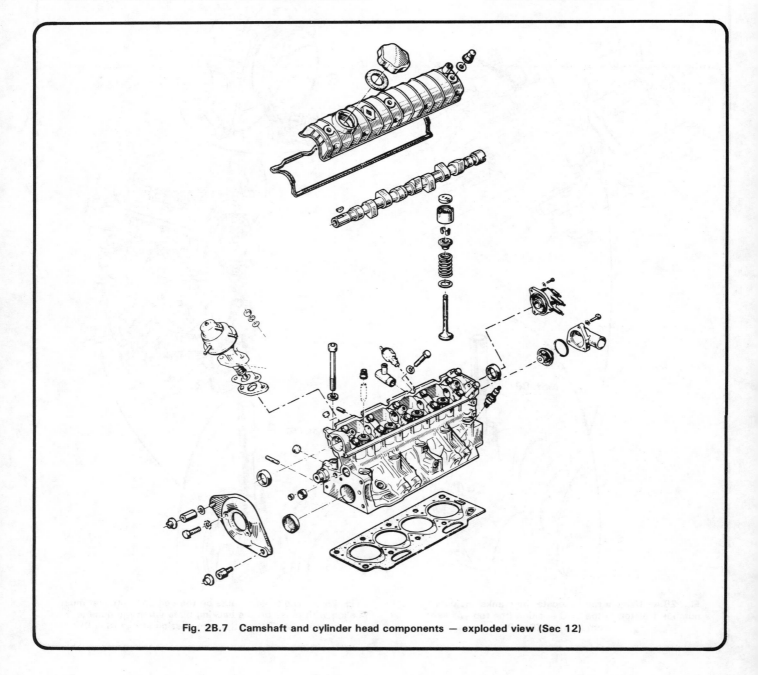

Fig. 2B.7   Camshaft and cylinder head components — exploded view (Sec 12)

camshaft cover from the cylinder head. Recover the gasket.
13 Using a hex-head socket bit, loosen the cylinder head bolts, half a turn at a time in the reverse order to that shown in Fig. 2A.31 (Chapter 2 Part A). When the tension has been relieved, remove all the bolts.
14 Lift the cylinder head, complete with manifolds, up and off the engine. If it is stuck, tap it up using a hammer and block of wood. Do not try to turn it, as it is located by two dowels. Do not, under any circumstances, try to pry it up with a screwdriver or pry bar.

---

11 Cylinder head — removal (engine on stand)

The procedure is the same as the one described in Section 10, beginning with Paragraph 12. Note that the timing belt should be removed first.

---

12 Camshaft and tappets — removal

1   If the engine is in the vehicle, first carry out the following operations:
    a) Remove the timing belt.

    b) Remove the distributor cap.
    c) Remove the camshaft cover.
2   Remove the bolt securing the camshaft sprocket to the camshaft and withdraw the sprocket. The camshaft may be prevented from turning during this operation by holding it between the cam lobes with vise-grips or by wrapping an old timing belt around the sprocket, clamping the belt tight and holding it securely. With the sprocket removed, see if the Woodruff key is likely to drop out of the camshaft groove and if it is, remove it and store it safely.
3   Remove the two bolts securing the metal sprocket backing plate to the cylinder head and remove the plate.
4   Number the camshaft bearing caps 1 to 5 with number 1 nearest the flywheel, and also mark them with an arrow pointing towards the flywheel, to indicate their installed positions.
5   Loosen all the camshaft bearing cap retaining bolts a little at a time and remove them from the caps.
6   Lift off the five bearing caps and then remove the camshaft (complete with oil seals) from the cylinder head.
7   Withdraw the tappet buckets, complete with shims, from the bores in the head. Lay the buckets out on a sheet of cardboard numbered 1 to 8 with number 1 at the flywheel end. It is a good idea to write the shim thickness size on the card alongside each bucket in case the shims are accidentally knocked off their buckets and mixed up. The size is stamped on the shim bottom face.

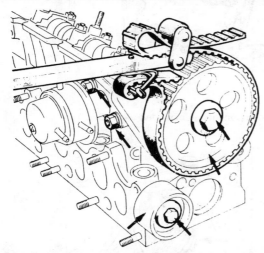

Fig. 2B.8 Hold the sprocket with an old timing belt, then remove the bolt, followed by the idler pulley (Sec 12)

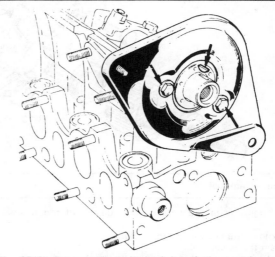

Fig. 2B.9 Remove the bolts and detach the metal sprocket backing plate and the Woodruff key (if loose) (Sec 12)

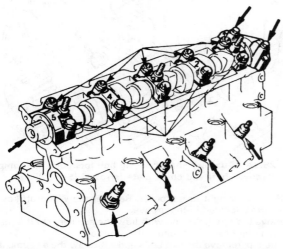

Fig. 2B.10 Mark the cam bearing caps before removing the bolts (Sec 12)

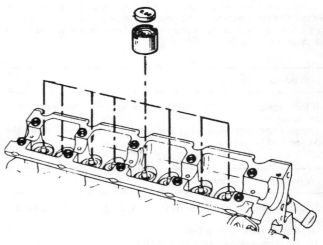

Fig. 2B.11 Be sure to keep the tappets and shims in order so they can be returned to their original positions in the head (Sec 12)

13   Cylinder head — disassembly

Refer to Section 10 in Part A, but note that the 1.7 liter engine must have the camshaft and tappets removed from the head before removing the valves. Also, the manifolds and thermostat can be removed if necessary. Be very careful not to scratch the tappet bores when compressing the valve springs and note that seals are installed on the valve guides (they should be removed).

14   Cylinder head — cleaning and inspection

Refer to Section 11 in Part A, but note that the 1.7 liter engine has no rocker arm components to inspect. Instead, check the camshaft and tappets as described later in this Chapter.

15   Valves — servicing

Refer to Section 12 in Part A.

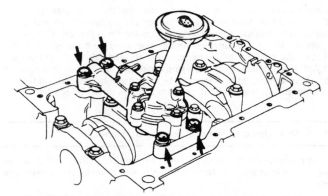

Fig. 2B.12   The oil pump is held in place with four bolts (Sec 17)

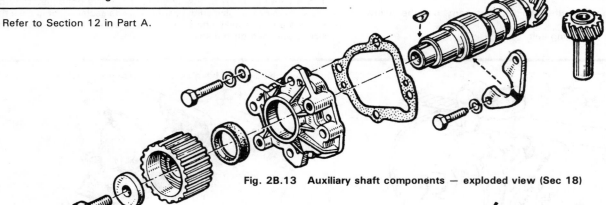

Fig. 2B.13   Auxiliary shaft components — exploded view (Sec 18)

16   Oil pan — removal

1   If the engine is in the vehicle, first carry out the following operations:
   a) Remove the engine splash shield.
   b) Drain the engine oil.
   c) Undo the bolts and remove the flywheel cover plate.
   d) Where applicable, disconnect any electrical wiring at the sensors.
2   Loosen and remove the bolts securing the oil pan to the crankcase. Tap the pan with a soft-faced hammer to break the seal between the flange and crankcase and remove the pan. Note that a gasket is not used, only a sealing compound.

17   Oil pump — removal

1   If the engine is still in the vehicle, refer to Section 16 and remove the oil pan.
2   Remove the mounting bolts and withdraw the pump from the crankcase and drive gear.

18   Auxiliary shaft — removal

1   If the engine is in the vehicle, first carry out the following operations:
   a) Remove the timing belt.
   b) Remove the engine splash shield.
2   Remove the retaining bolt and washer securing the sprocket to the auxiliary shaft. Hold the sprocket with an old timing belt, tightly clamped and securely held while removing the bolt.
3   Withdraw the sprocket using two screwdrivers as levers to ease

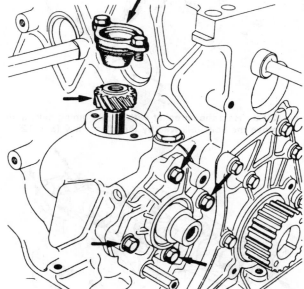

Fig. 2B.14   Auxiliary shaft housing bolt locations, oil pump drive shaft and cover plate (arrows) (Sec 18)

it off. If it is very tight, use a puller. Recover the Woodruff key if it is not securely located in the groove.
4   Remove the four bolts and withdraw the auxiliary shaft housing. Access may be easier from under the vehicle.
5   At the top, remove the two bolts and withdraw the oil pump drive gear cover plate. Screw a bolt into the oil pump drive gear or use a tapered wooden shaft to withdraw the drive gear.
6   Remove the two bolts and washers and lift out the auxiliary shaft retaining plate and shaft.

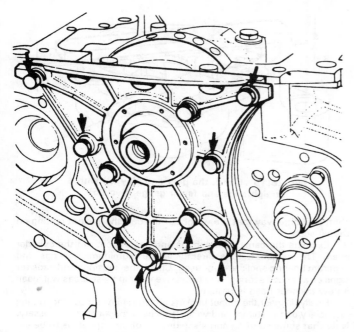

Fig. 2B.15 Crankshaft front plate bolt locations (Sec 19)

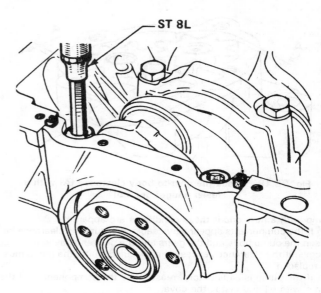

Fig. 2B.16 The number 1 main bearing cap bolts require a large Allen head socket for removal (Sec 22)

20 Piston/connecting rod assembly — removal

Refer to Section 17 in Part A — the procedure is essentially the same as the one described for the 1.4 liter engine. However, note that the 1.7 liter engine does not have removable cylinder liners and the procedure must be modified slightly as a result. On the 1.7 liter engine, use a ridge reamer to remove the wear ridge from the top of each cylinder bore before removing the piston/connecting rod assemblies through the *tops* of the cylinders (follow the instructions provided with the reamer).

21 Flywheel/driveplate — removal

Refer to Section 18 in Part A.

22 Crankshaft — removal

Refer to Section 19 in Part A. Note that the number 1 main bearing cap bolts are unique and require a large Allen head socket for removal.

23 Crankshaft rear oil seal — replacement

Refer to Section 20 in Part A.

24 Engine mounts — replacement

Refer to Section 21 in Part A, but note that an additional movement limiter is used on the 1.7 liter engine between the front of the engine and subframe. Removal is accomplished by removing the bolts.

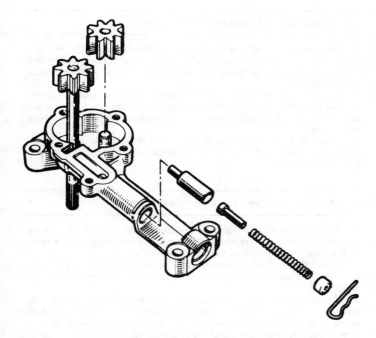

Fig. 2B.17 Oil pump components — exploded view (Sec 25)

19 Crankshaft front plate — removal

1 If the engine is in the vehicle, first carry out the following operations:
   a) Remove the timing belt.
   b) Remove the oil pan.
2 Withdraw the crankshaft sprocket using two screwdrivers carefully as levers, or by using a puller.
3 Remove the bolts securing the front plate to the block and withdraw the plate, noting that it is located by dowels in the two lower bolt hole locations.

25 Oil pump — inspection and repair

1 Remove the retaining bolts and lift off the pump cover.
2 Withdraw the idler gear and the drive gear and shaft.
3 Extract the retaining clip and remove the oil pressure relief valve spring retainer, spring, spring seat and plunger.
4 Clean the components and carefully examine the gears, pump body and relief valve plunger for any signs of scoring and wear. Replace the

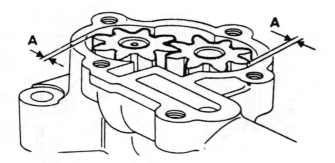

Fig. 2B.18   Check the gear-to-body clearance (A) with a feeler gauge (Sec 25)

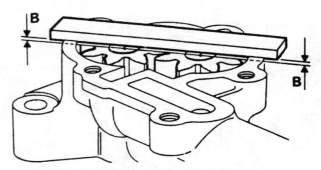

Fig. 2B.19   Check the gear end play (B) with a straightedge and feeler gauge (Sec 25)

pump with a new one if these conditions are apparent.

5   If the components appear serviceable, measure the clearance between the pump body and the gears and the gear endplay with feeler gauges. If the clearances exceed the specified limits, the pump must be replaced.

6   If the pump is satisfactory, reassemble the components, fill the pump with oil and install the cover.

26   Crankshaft — inspection

Refer to Section 23 in Part A.

27   Main and connecting rod bearings — inspection

Refer to Section 24 in Part A.

28   Engine block — cleaning

Use the procedures outlined in Chapter 2A except note that the 1.7 liter engine does not have removable liners so disregard or modify any procedures directly related to them.

29   Engine block — inspection

Refer to Section 26 in Part A. Note that the 1.7 liter engine does not have removable liners so disregard or modify any procedures directly related to them.

30   Piston/connecting rod assembly — inspection

Refer to Section 28 in Part A.

31   Camshaft and tappets — inspection

1   Examine the camshaft bearing surfaces and cam lobes for wear, pitting and scoring. Replace the camshaft if any of these conditions are found.

2   The oil seals at each end of the camshaft should be replaced as a matter of course. To change the oil seal at the flywheel end of the camshaft, the distributor rotor and end plate must be removed first. Unfortunately, the rotor is bonded to the end of the camshaft with a special adhesive and can only be removed by breaking it. Having done this, the seal and end plate can be slid off. With two new oil seals, a new rotor and a quantity of the special adhesive, available from Renault dealers, the new seals can be installed. Lubricate the seal lips, then carefully slip them over the camshaft journals, ensuring that the open sides face the camshaft. Install the end plate, then bond the new rotor to the camshaft. After installing the new oil seals, store the cam-

shaft in such a way that the weight of the camshaft is not resting on the oil seals.

3   Examine the camshaft bearings and bearing caps in the cylinder head. The camshaft runs directly in the aluminum housings and separate bearing shells are not used. Check the housings and caps for signs of wear and scoring. Any excessive wear in these areas will mean a new cylinder head is required.

4   Finally, inspect the tappet buckets and the shims for scoring, pitting (especially on the shims), and wear. Replace components as necessary. Note that some scuffing and discoloration of the tappets is to be expected and is acceptable providing that the tappets are not scored.

32   Timing belt and sprockets — inspection

1   Examine the timing belt carefully for signs of cracking, fraying and general wear, particularly at the roots of the teeth. Replace the belt if there is any sign of deterioration or if there is any oil or grease contamination.

2   Also, inspect the sprockets for cracks or chipping of the teeth. Handle the sprockets with care as they may easily crack if they are dropped or struck sharply. Replace the sprockets if they are damaged in any way.

3   Check that the idler and tensioner pulleys rotate freely with no trace of roughness or harshness and without excessive free play. Replace them if necessary.

33   Auxiliary shaft and bearings — inspection

1   Examine the auxiliary shaft and oil pump drive shaft for pitting, scoring and wear on the bearing journals and for chipping and wear of the gear teeth. Replace parts as necessary.

2   Check the auxiliary shaft bearings in the block for wear and, if worn, have them replaced by your Renault dealer or an automotive machine shop.

3   Clean off all traces of old gasket from the auxiliary shaft housing and tap out the oil seal using a section of pipe. Install the new oil seal using a block of wood and tap it in until it is flush with the outer face of the housing. The open side of the seal must face towards the engine.

34   Crankshaft front plate — inspection

1   Check the front plate for signs of distortion and damage to the threads. If serviceable, clean off all traces of sealant and tap out the oil seal with a section of pipe.

2   Install a new seal flush with the outer face of the front plate using a block of wood and a hammer. Make sure that the open side of the seal is facing the engine.

35   Flywheel/driveplate — inspection and repair

Refer to Section 32 in Part A.

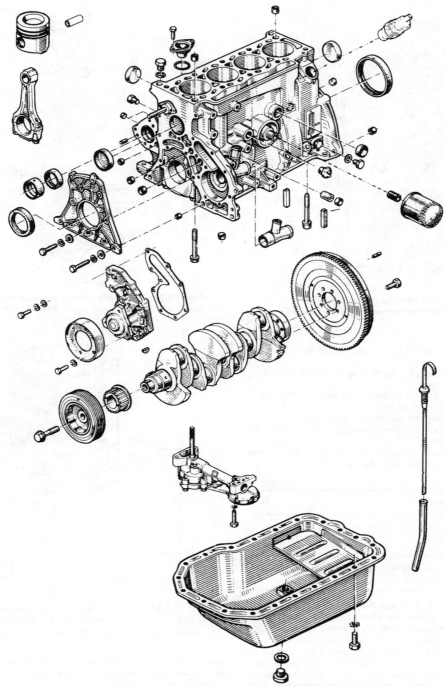

Fig. 2B.20 Engine block components — exploded view (Sec 29)

36 Engine overhaul — reassembly sequence

Refer to Section 33 in Part A, but note that the camshaft is installed after the cylinder head and the front plate is installed before the timing belt and sprockets. Also, the 1.7 liter engine has no pushrods.

37 Crankshaft — installation and main bearing oil clearance check

1   Before installing the crankshaft and main bearings, you must determine the correct thickness of the side seals to be installed with the number 1 main bearing cap. To do this, place the cap in position and tighten the bolts. Locate a drill bit, dowel or steel rod which will just fit in the seal groove, then measure its thickness. This measurement is the seal groove size. If it is less than or equal to 5 mm, a 5.10 mm thick seal is needed. If it is greater than 5 mm, a 5.3 mm thick seal is required. Once the correct size seals have been obtained, refer to Section 34 in Part A, follow Steps 1 through 18 to install bearing caps 1 through 4 (tighten the bolts finger tight only), then follow the procedure described below to install bearing cap number 1. **Note:** *The thrust bearings are installed in the number 2 main on the 1.7 liter engine.*

2   Install the number 1 main bearing side seals with the grooves facing out. Approximately 0.2 mm of each seal should protrude from the bottom of the cap.

3   Apply RTV-type sealant to the block mating surfaces of the cap,

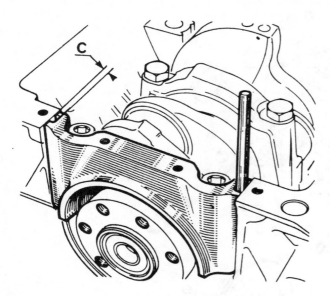

Fig. 2B.21   Use a drill bit to determine the side seal groove width (C) in the number 1 main bearing cap (Sec 37)

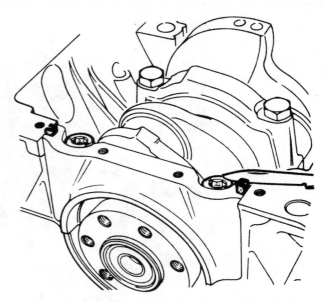

Fig. 2B.22   Trim the side seals flush with the block after the bearing cap is installed (Sec 37)

then install the bolts.

4   Place the cap in position on the block and thread the bolts into the holes about three turns.

5   Press the cap into place, make sure the side seals are still protruding and tighten the bolts finger tight.

6   Press the new rear main oil seal into the recess until it is flush with the cap and block, then tighten all of the main bearing cap bolts to the specified torque by referring to Section 34 in Part A.

7   Make sure the crankshaft turns without binding and check the end play as described in Section 34.

8   After tightening the bolts and checking the end play, trim the protruding ends of the side seals flush with the block.

38   Piston rings — installation

Refer to Section 29 in Part A.

39   Piston/connecting rod assembly — installation and bearing oil clearance check

1   Refer to Section 36 in Part A, but note that on the 1.7 liter engine the pistons are installed through the top of the block, using a piston ring compressor to guide them into the cylinder bores (see the accompanying illustration and note). The procedure used to attach the rods to the crankshaft and check the bearing oil clearance is identical to the procedure in Section 36 (disregard any references to the removable cylinder liners). **Note:** *When using the ring compressor, be sure to lubricate the piston, rings and cylinder wall with clean engine oil before installing the ring compressor. Leave the piston skirt protruding about 1/2-inch to guide the piston into the cylinder. The rings must be compressed as far as possible.*

2   Gently place the piston/connecting rod assembly into the number 1 cylinder bore and rest the bottom edge of the ring compressor on the block. Tap the top edge of the compressor to make sure it is contacting the block uniformly. Carefully tap on the top of the piston with the end of a wooden hammer handle while guiding the end of the connecting rod into place on the crankshaft journal.

3   The piston rings may try to pop out of the ring compressor just before entering the cylinder bore, so keep some downward pressure on the ring compressor.

4   Work slowly, and if any resistance is felt as the piston enters the cylinder, stop immediately. Find out what is hanging up and fix it before proceeding. **Note:** *Do not, for any reason, force the piston into the cylinder or you will break a ring and/or the piston.*

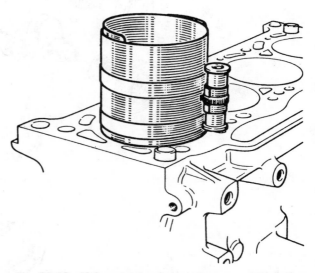

Fig. 2B.23   Make sure the ring compressor contacts the block uniformly around its entire circumference when installing the piston/connecting rod assemblies (Sec 39)

40   Flywheel/driveplate — installation

Refer to Section 38 in Part A.

41   Crankshaft front plate — installation

1   Apply a bead of RTV-type sealant to the mating surface of the front plate and lubricate the oil seal lips.

2   Install the front plate and the retaining bolts. The two bolts around the oil seal opening at the 2 o'clock and 8 o'clock positions should also have a small quantity of the sealant applied to their threads, as they protrude into the crankcase. Progressively tighten the retaining bolts in a diagonal pattern.

3   Make sure that the Woodruff key is located in the crankshaft groove then install the crankshaft sprocket.

4   If the engine is in the vehicle, install the oil pan and timing belt.

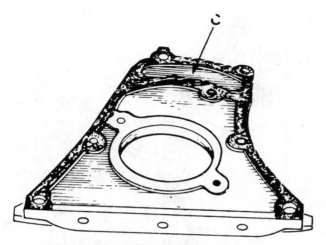

Fig. 2B.24   When applying sealant to the crankshaft front plate, do not block the oilway in area C (Sec 41)

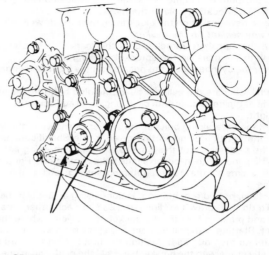

Fig. 2B.25   Apply sealant to the two bolts indicated by the arrows (Sec 41)

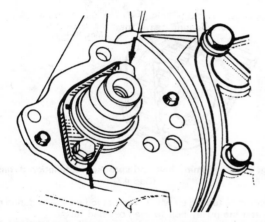

Fig. 2B.26   Install the auxiliary shaft retaining plate with the curved side away from the crankshaft (Sec 42)

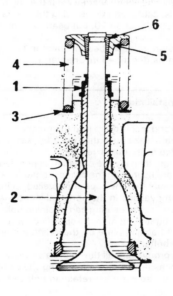

Fig. 2B.27   1.7 liter engine valve components (Sec 45)

1 Oil seal
2 Valve
3 Spring seat
4 Spring
5 Retainer
6 Keepers

42 Auxiliary shaft — installation

1   Liberally lubricate the auxiliary shaft and carefully slide it into the bearings.
2   Place the retaining plate in position with its curved edge away from the crankshaft and install the two retaining bolts. Tighten the bolts.
3   Place a new gasket in position over the dowels in the block. If a gasket was not used previously, apply a bead of RTV-type sealant to the housing mating surface.
4   Liberally lubricate the oil seal lips and then locate the housing in place. Install and tighten the housing retaining bolts progressively in a diagonal pattern.
5   Lubricate the oil pump drive gear and lower the gear into place.
6   Position a new O-ring seal on the drive gear cover plate, install the plate and secure it with the two retaining bolts.
7   With the Woodruff key in place, install the auxiliary shaft sprocket, washer and retaining bolt. Hold the sprocket using the method employed for removal, and tighten the bolt securely.
8   If the engine is in the vehicle, install the timing belt and, if removed, the engine splash shield.

43 Oil pump — installation

1   Position the pump on the block with the drive gear and shaft engaged.
2   Install the bolts and tighten them in a criss-cross pattern.
3   If the engine is in the vehicle, install the oil pan.

44 Oil pan — installation

1   Make sure that the mating faces of the oil pan and block are clean and dry.
2   Apply a bead of RTV-type sealant to the mating surface and place the oil pan in position. Install the retaining bolts and tighten them progressively in a diagonal sequence.
3   If the engine is in the vehicle, reconnect the wiring to the sensor, install the flywheel cover plate and the splash shield, then fill the engine with oil.

45 Cylinder head — reassembly and installation

Note: *Refer to Section 42 in Part A when reassembling the head, but note that the 1.7 liter engine uses valve stem seals that must be installed after the valves and before the springs, retainers and keepers. Use the installation tool with the new seals.*
1   Make sure that the mating faces of the block and head are spotlessly clean, that the head bolt threads are also clean and dry and that they screw easily in and out of the holes.
2   Turn the crankshaft as necessary to bring the number 1 piston to

the TDC position. Retain the crankshaft in this position using a metal rod in the TDC locating hole in the block.

3   Place a new gasket on the block face, over the dowels. **Note:** *Do not use any sealant on the gasket.*

4   Turn the camshaft sprocket until the mark on its outer face is aligned with the mark on the sprocket backing plate.

5   Lower the cylinder head into position on the block and engage the dowels.

6   Lightly lubricate the cylinder head retaining bolt threads and the underside of the bolt heads with clean engine oil and screw in the bolts finger tight.

7   Tighten the retaining bolts in the sequence shown in the illustration, to the 1st tightening setting given in the Specifications. Now repeat the sequence, but this time to the 2nd tightening setting.

8   Wait 3 minutes, then loosen all the bolts completely. Tighten them again, this time to the 1st retightening setting, still in the correct sequence.

9   The final, or 2nd retightening, is done using an angular measurement. To do this, draw two lines at 123° to each other on a sheet of card and punch a hole for the socket at the point where the lines intersect. Starting with bolt number 1, engage the socket through the card and into the bolt head. Position the first line on the card under, and directly in line with the breaker bar. Hold the card, and in one movement tighten the bolt until the breaker bar is aligned with the second line on the car. Repeat this procedure for the remaining bolts in the correct sequence.

10   Install the timing belt and check the valve clearances. If the engine is in the vehicle, install the controls, cables and wires using the reverse of the removal procedure described in Section 10, but bearing in mind the following points:

    a)   Adjust the drivebelt tension as described in Chapter 1.

    b)   Refill the cooling system as described in Chapter 1.

46 Camshaft and tappets — installation

1   Lubricate the tappet buckets and insert them into their respective locations as noted during removal. Make sure that each bucket has the correct (original) shim in place in its upper recess.

2   Lubricate the camshaft bearings, then lay the camshaft in position. Position the oil seals so that they are flush with the cylinder head faces and install the bearing caps. Make sure that the caps are installed facing the same way as noted during removal and in their original locations.

3   Apply thread locking compound to the bearing cap retaining bolts, install the bolts and progressively tighten them to the specified torque.

4   Install the camshaft sprocket backing plate on the cylinder head and secure it with the retaining bolts.

5   With the Woodruff key in the groove, install the camshaft sprocket and retaining bolt. Prevent the camshaft from turning using the same method as for removal and tighten the sprocket retaining bolt to the specified torque.

6   If the engine is in the vehicle, install the timing belt and distributor cap, then check the valve clearances before installing the camshaft cover.

47 Timing belt — installation

1   Make sure that the crankshaft is at the TDC position for the number 1 piston and that the crankshaft is locked in this position using the metal rod through the hole in the block.

2   Make sure that the timing mark on the camshaft sprocket is in line with the corresponding mark on the metal backing plate.

3   Align the timing marks on the belt with those on the sprockets, noting that the running direction arrows on the belt should be positioned between the auxiliary shaft sprocket and the idler pulley.

4   Hold the belt in this position and slip it over the crankshaft, auxiliary shaft and camshaft sprockets in that order, then around the idler tensioner pulleys.

5   Make sure that all the timing marks are still aligned, then temporarily tension the belt by turning the tensioner pulley counterclockwise and tightening the retaining nut.

6   Remove the TDC locating rod.

7   Install the crankshaft pulley and retaining bolt. Prevent the

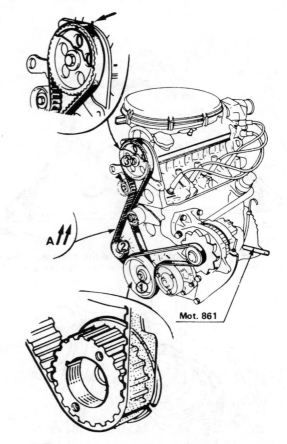

Fig. 2B.28   Timing belt and sprocket installation details (Sec 47)

crankshaft from turning by whichever method was used during removal and tighten the pulley bolt to the specified torque.

8   Using a socket on the pulley bolt, turn the crankshaft at least two complete turns in the normal direction of rotation, then return it to the TDC position with the number 1 piston on compression.

9   Make sure that the timing marks are still aligned. If not, loosen the tensioner, move the belt one tooth (as necessary) on the camshaft sprocket and check again.

10   With the timing correct, tension the belt by turning the tensioner as necessary so that under moderate pressure applied at a point midway between the auxiliary sprocket and idler pulley, the belt deflects 7.5 mm. When the tension is correct, tighten the tensioner pulley retaining nut.

bolts.

12   If the engine is in the vehicle, install the alternator drivebelt and air cleaner, then reconnect the battery.

48 Rejoining the engine and transmission

Refer to Section 7 and follow the procedure in reverse. Lubricate the end of the manual transmission input shaft with moly-based grease.

49 Engine — installation

Refer to Section 6 and follow the procedure in reverse.

50 Initial start-up and break-in after overhaul

Refer to Section 45 in Part A, but note that it is not necessary to retorque the cylinder head bolts on the 1.7 liter engine.

Chapter 3
Cooling, heating and air conditioning systems

Contents

Specifications

Thermostat rating . . . .   Stamped on thermostat
Cooling system capacity . . . .   See Chapter 1

1 General information

The cooling system is a pressurized, pump-assisted thermo-syphon type. It consists of the radiator, water pump, thermostat, electric cooling fan, expansion tank and the connecting hoses and passages.

The system cycle begins as coolant in the bottom of the right-hand radiator tank passes through the bottom hose and into the water pump, which circulates it through the engine block and cylinder head passages. After cooling the cylinders and head, the coolant reaches the underside of the thermostat, which is initially closed when the engine is started cold, and is diverted through passages in the water pump to the heater hose outlet. After passing through the heater, the coolant is returned to the pump.

When the engine is cold, the coolant circulates only through the engine and heater. When the coolant reaches a pre-determined temperature, the thermostat opens and the coolant travels through the top hose and into the radiator. As the coolant flows through the radiator it is cooled by the air passing through it as the vehicle is in motion. The electric cooling fan provides airflow when vehicle motion is inadequate. When the coolant reaches the bottom right-hand side of the radiator, the cycle is complete.

When the engine is at normal operating temperature, the coolant expands and some of it is displaced into the expansion tank. When the engine cools, it is returned to the radiator.

2 Antifreeze — general information

Caution: *Do not allow antifreeze to come into contact with your skin or painted surfaces of the vehicle. Flush contacted areas immediately with plenty of water. Antifreeze can be fatal to children and pets; they like it because it is sweet. Just a small amount can be fatal. Wipe up* *garage floor and drip pan coolant spills immediately. Keep antifreeze containers covered and repair leaks in your cooling system as soon as possible.*

The cooling system should be filled with a distilled water/ethylene glycol-based antifreeze solution, which will prevent freezing down to at least −20°F at all times (borax-based antifreeze must not be used under any circumstances). It also provides protection against corrosion and increases the coolant boiling point.

The cooling system should be drained, flushed and refilled initially at 12000 miles and at the beginning of each winter from then on. The use of antifreeze solutions for periods longer than one year is likely to cause damage and encourage the formation of rust and scale in the radiator.

Before adding antifreeze to the system, check all hose connections (antifreeze tends to search out and leak through very small openings).

The exact mixture of antifreeze-to-water which you should use depends on the relative weather conditions. The mixture should contain at least 50% antifreeze, but should never contain more than 70% antifreeze.

3.3 Removing the thermostat from the upper radiator hose (note how it is installed)

3 Thermostat — replacement

Caution: *The engine must be completely cool before beginning this procedure. Also, when working in the vicinity of the electrical cooling fan, disconnect the negative battery cable from the battery to prevent the fan from coming on accidentally.*

1.4 liter engine

1   The thermostat is located in the water pump end of the upper radiator hose and is held in place with a hose clamp.
2   Drain approximately one (1) quart of coolant out of the radiator (see Chapter 1 for the procedure to follow). Reconnect the bottom hose and tighten the hose clamp.
3   Loosen the two hose clamps on the water pump end of the upper radiator hose. Detach the hose from the water pump outlet and withdraw the thermostat from the hose (photo) (note how it is installed).
4   Refer to the thermostat checking procedure.
5   Installation is the reverse of removal, but be sure to position the thermostat bleed hole in the slot in the end of the water pump housing. Also, be sure to tighten all hose clamps and refill the radiator with coolant before starting the engine (see Chapter 1).
6   Start the engine, allow it to reach normal operating temperature and check carefully for leaks.

1.7 liter engine

7   The thermostat is located in a housing bolted to the left-hand side of the cylinder head, under the distributor.
8   Refer to Chapter 1 and partially drain the cooling system.
9   Loosen the hose clamp and detach the radiator hose from the thermostat housing (use a twisting motion to break the hose seal).
10   Remove the three bolts, detach the housing from the head and lift out the thermostat (note how it is installed).
11   Refer to the thermostat checking procedure.
12   Installation is the reverse of removal. Be sure to clean the mating surfaces of the cylinder head and thermostat housing and replace the seal with a new one.

4 Thermostat — check

1   The best way to check the thermostat is with it removed from the engine. In most cases, if you suspect that the thermostat is faulty, it is easier to simply buy and install a replacement, as they are not very expensive.

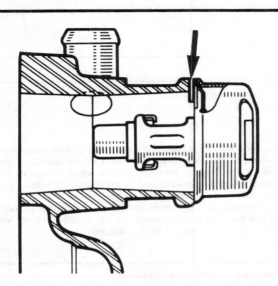

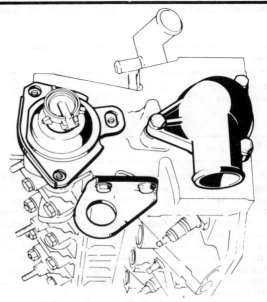

Fig. 3.1 When installing the thermostat on the 1.4 liter engine, the bleed hole must be aligned with the water pump outlet slot (arrow) (Sec 3)

Fig. 3.2 1.7 liter engine thermostat housing location (Sec 3)

2   Begin by removing the thermostat as described in Section 3, then check it for corrosion and damage. Replace it with a new one if either condition is noted.

3   Suspend the thermostat in a pan of water (along with a thermometer), heat the water and note the temperature at which the thermostat begins to open. Continue heating the water and see if the thermostat opens completely by the time the water is boiling. Remove it from the water.

4   The opening temperature is stamped on the thermostat. If it does not start to open at the specified temperature, does not completely open in boiling water or does not close when it is removed from the water and cooled, replace it with a new one.

5   Cooling fan thermostatic switch — check and replacement

1   If the switch, which is installed in the radiator tank (photo), fails to operate properly, it will most likely be the result of an open circuit. When an open circuit occurs, the fan will not operate even when the coolant temperature is excessive.

2   To check the switch, make sure the coolant temperature is at least 195°F, then disconnect the wires from the switch and connect them together (a jumper wire may be required to do this). If the electrical cooling fan operates with the switch bypassed, the switch should be replaced with a new one (keep in mind that the coolant temperature must be as specified earlier or the test results will be inconclusive).

3   The switch can be removed from the radiator after draining the coolant (see the procedure in Chapter 1) and disconnecting the wires. Make sure the engine is completely cool before attempting to remove the switch.

6   Cooling fan assembly — removal and installation

1   Remove the radiator as described in Section 7.

2   Drill the heads off the rivets that secure the shroud or fan motor bracket to the radiator, then tap out the rivets with a small pin punch. The fan/motor and shroud or bracket can now be separated from the radiator.

3   Remove the nut or snap-ring and slide the fan off the shaft (note how the fan is installed to simplify installation). The motor can be removed by drilling out the mounting rivets.

4   Installation is the reverse of removal. Be sure to install the fan correctly or it will blow in the wrong direction.

7   Radiator — removal, servicing and installation

Caution: *The engine must be completely cool before beginning this procedure. Also, when working in the vicinity of the electrical cooling fan, disconnect the negative battery cable from the battery to prevent the fan from coming on accidentally.*

1   Refer to Chapter 1 and drain the cooling system as described there.

2   Loosen the hose clamp and detach the upper hose from the radiator (twist it back-and-forth with large channel-lock pliers, then pull it free).

3   Release the clamp and detach the expansion tank hose from the filler neck (photo).

4   Disconnect the wires from the thermostatic switch on the left-hand side of the radiator and unplug the fan wires (photos).

5   If your vehicle is equipped with an automatic transmission, disconnect the cooler lines from the radiator and plug them.

5.1   Cooling fan thermostatic switch location

7.3   Disconnecting the expansion tank hose from the radiator filler neck

7.4a   Disconnect the thermostatic switch wires . . .

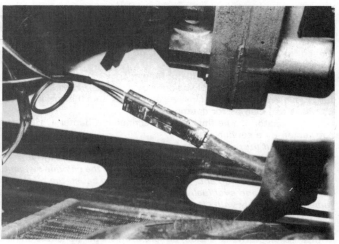

7.4b   . . . and the electric cooling fan wires

7.6a Lift up on the wire retaining clip and move the top of the radiator toward the engine, . . .

7.6b . . . then lift up on it to disengage the lower mounting pegs

9.1 The alternator adjusting bolt/nut must be loosened to remove the drivebelt

9.4 The bolt behind the pulley can be loosened by inserting a socket through the hole

6   Lift up on the large wire retaining clip at the top of the radiator (photo), then move the radiator towards the engine and lift up on it to disengage the lower mounting pegs (photo). As the radiator is removed from the engine compartment, be very careful not to damage the cooling fins or tubes.

7   Carefully examine the radiator for evidence of leaks and damage. Any necessary repairs should be done by a radiator repair shop. Carefully brush accumulations of insects and leaves from the fins and check all hoses and clamps for deterioration.

8   The radiator can be flushed as described in Chapter 1. Have the cap tested by a service station.

9   **Caution:** *If the radiator is to be left out of the vehicle for more than 48 hours, special precautions must be taken to prevent the brazing flux used during manufacture from reacting with the chloride elements remaining from the coolant. The reaction could cause the aluminum core to oxidize and eventually leak. To prevent this, either flush the radiator thoroughly with clean water, dry it with compressed air and seal all openings or refill the radiator with coolant and plug all openings.*

10   Installation is the reverse of removal. If your vehicle is equipped with an automatic transmission, be sure to check the transmission fluid as described in Chapter 1.

8   Water pump — check

1   Water pump failure can cause overheating and serious engine damage because it will not circulate coolant through the engine.

2   There are three ways to check the pump while it is in place on the engine. If it is defective, it must be replaced with a new or rebuilt unit.

3   With the engine running at normal operating temperature, squeeze the upper radiator hose. If the pump is operating properly, a surge of coolant will be felt as the hose is released.

4   Most water pumps are equipped with small vent or 'weep' holes on the underside of the pump body. If a pump seal failure occurs, small amounts of coolant will leak from the hole. In most cases it will be necessary to use a flashlight from under the vehicle to see evidence of leakage from the hole.

5   If the pump shaft bearings fail, a squealing sound will be heard when the engine is running. Shaft wear can usually be felt if the pump pulley is moved up-and-down. Do not mistake drivebelt slippage (which also causes a squealing sound) for water pump failure.

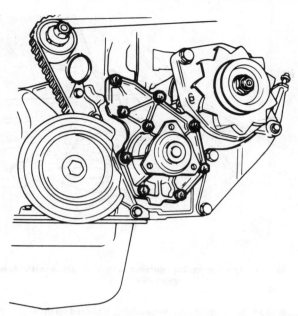

Fig. 3.3 1.7 liter engine water pump bolt locations (Sec 9)

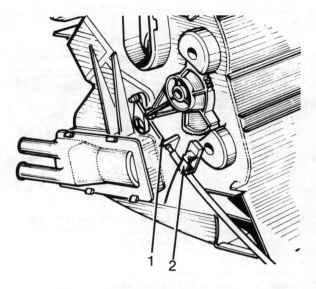

Fig. 3.4 The heater control cable (1) is adjusted by moving the clip (2) (Sec 11)

9 Water pump — removal and installation

Caution: *The engine must be completely cool before beginning this procedure. Also, when working in the vicinity of the electrical cooling fan, disconnect the negative battery cable from the battery to prevent the fan from coming on accidentally.*

1.4 liter engine

1 Drain the cooling system as described in Chapter 1, then loosen the alternator pivot and adjusting bolts (photo) and remove the drivebelt.

2 Remove the bolt, then swing the alternator mounting bracket away from the water pump.

3 Loosen the hose clamps and detach the hoses from the pump, then disconnect the wire from the coolant temperature sending unit on top of the pump.

4 Loosen and remove the bolts that attach the pump to the cylinder head (to loosen the bolt behind the pulley, rotate the pulley until the bolt is visible in the hole, then insert a socket through the pulley and loosen the bolt) (photo).

5 Make sure all the bolts are removed, then separate the pump from the head (if it is stuck, tap it gently with a soft-faced hammer to loosen it — do not pry between the pump and head as the gasket sealing surfaces will be damaged).

6 Using a gasket scraper, carefully remove all traces of the old gasket from the cylinder head. The mating surfaces of the new pump and the cylinder head must be clean and dry (wipe them with a clean rag slightly saturated with lacquer thinner).

7 Attach the new pump and a new gasket to the cylinder head (do not use gasket sealant), then install and tighten the bolts following a criss-cross pattern (do not over tighten the bolts).

8 The remaining installation steps are the reverse of removal (be sure to adjust the drivebelt and refill the cooling system). Start the engine and check carefully for leaks.

1.7 liter engine

9 Disconnect the negative battery cable from the battery. Raise the front of the vehicle and support it securely on jackstands. Apply the parking brake.

10 Remove the splash shield and drain the cooling system (Chapter 1).

11 Remove the right front tire and the inner fender panel.

12 Remove the serpentine drivebelt and loosen the water pump pulley bolts (the pulley cannot be removed until the water pump is removed, so let it hang to gain access to all of the bolts).

13 Remove the pump bolts and withdraw the pump through the opening in the fender.

14 Clean the block gasket mating surfaces.

15 Position a new gasket, then install the pump and pulley and tighten the pump mounting bolts.

16 Install the pulley bolts.

17 Install the drivebelt and tighten the pulley bolts.

18 Install the inner fender panel, tire and splash shield, then lower the vehicle.

19 Refer to Chapter 1 and refill the cooling system.

10 Coolant temperature sending unit — check and replacement

1 The only way to effectively check the sending unit requires an ohmmeter and some way to monitor engine coolant temperature.

2 With the engine coolant temperature at approximately 154 °F, stop the engine and remove the wire from the sending unit. Attach one ohmmeter lead to the sending unit terminal. Ground the remaining ohmmeter lead and note the reading. It should be 340 to 410 ohms.

3 Start the engine and allow it to reach normal operating temperature. The ohmmeter reading should be considerably lower. If it is not, the sending unit is probably faulty and should be replaced with a new one.

4 To replace the sending unit, make sure the engine has completely cooled, then drain approximately one (1) quart of coolant from the radiator (see Chapter 1 for the procedure to follow). Disconnect the wire and unscrew the unit from the water pump (1.4 liter engines) or the cylinder head (1.7 liter engines).

5 Installation is the reverse of removal.

11 Heater control — adjustment

1 Move the temperature control on the heater control panel to the *cold* position.

2 Working under the dash, make sure that the warm/cold air flap on the side of the heater assembly is closed (push up on the lever that the cable is attached to).

3 If it isn't, release the clip securing the cable housing, move the cable until the flap is closed, then reinstall the clip.

Fig. 3.5 Remove the rubber seal (arrow) and the cover-to-plenum screws (1) to gain access to the heater fan
(Sec 12)

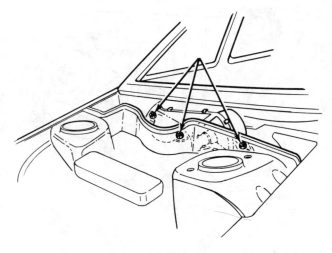

Fig. 3.6 The fan motor housing is held in place with three nuts (Sec 12)

12   Heater fan — removal and installation

1   Disconnect the negative battery cable from the battery.
2   Carefully remove the rubber hood seal from the flange at the top of the firewall.
3   On some models the ignition coil is mounted on the firewall, ahead of the heater. It does not have to be removed, but the wires must be disconnected (label the wires and terminals to avoid confusion during installation).
4   Remove the cover screws and separate it from the heater plenum.
5   Disconnect the fan motor wires and remove the housing mounting nuts, then lift out the fan and housing assembly.
6   Installation is the reverse of removal. When positioning the fan motor housing in the plenum, be sure to align it on the studs before installing the nuts.

13   Air conditioning system — general information

Since servicing and repair of the air conditioning system requires special tools, techniques and precautions, it should be done by a dealer service department or an automotive air conditioning shop.
During times of the year when the air conditioning system is not in regular use, it should be run a few minutes each week to keep the seals from shrinking, cracking and causing leaks.
At regular intervals, check the refrigerant in the sight glass on the receiver/dryer. The appearance of bubbles in the sight glass for the first few minutes of operation is normal, but they should eventually disappear. If they don't, have the refrigerant checked by your dealer. Check and adjust the drivebelt as described in Chapter 1.
Components of the system can be unbolted and moved within the limits of travel of the connecting hoses in order to remove or service other components.
Caution: *Never disconnect any part of the system yourself — the refrigerant is potentially dangerous. If components must be removed, have the system discharged and recharged by your dealer service department or an air conditioning shop. When components are disconnected, the fittings must be plugged to prevent the entry of moisture.*
The fins of the condenser should be periodically cleaned to ensure free movement of air through it.

Chapter 4 Fuel and exhaust systems

Contents

Specifications

Idle speed . . . . See Chapter 1

Fuel pressure
  Multi-point injection . . . . 70 psi
  TBI . . . . 14 to 15 psi

Torque specifications   **Ft-lbs**
Oxygen sensor (multi-point injection) . . . . 28 to 34
Oxygen sensor (TBI) . . . . 20 to 25

1   General information and precautions

Vehicles manufactured for sale in California are equipped with a multi-point fuel injection system, while all other vehicles are equipped with a throttle body injection system (TBI). The two systems have some common components, but most service and repair procedures for each system are unique and handled separately in this Chapter. Keep in mind that the fuel system is integrated with the emission control systems described in Chapter 6 and many fuel system components function as emission system components. Always use the information in Chapter 6 in conjunction with the information included here.

Multi-point fuel injection

The multi-point injection system consists of an electric fuel pump, a fuel filter, a pressure regulator, a cold start injector, the fuel injectors for each cylinder, a control relay, an airflow meter, a supplementary air control valve, an electronic control unit, a thermo-time switch, a throttle position switch, a coolant temperature sensor and an oxygen sensor. The first five components make up the fuel injection system, while the remaining components are part of the control system.

The fuel pump delivers fuel from the tank, through the filter, to the injector ramp assembly. The pressure regulator, which is connected to the tank return hose, maintains a pre-determined pressure at the injectors. The regulator is connected to the intake manifold for pressure compensation based on manifold vacuum. The injectors are controlled by the electronic control unit (ECU). They inject fuel twice per engine cycle, which allows the use of a conventional ignition distributor. The electrical current to the fuel pump is controlled by the ignition switch and the control relay. A ballast resistor in series with the motor reduces the voltage to less than 12 volts. The resistor is bypassed when the starter motor relay is energized.

The ECU controls the fuel injection time and changes it according to input from:

a) The airflow meter, which constantly measures the volume and density of the air coming into the engine by a potentiometer (located on the end of the flap shaft) and a temperature sensor
b) The ignition coil, where the primary winding tachometer voltage is used to determine the engine speed
c) The coolant temperature sensor, which is located on the cylinder head, for mixture enrichment when the engine is cold

d) The throttle position switch located on the throttle plate shaft, which is used to indicate the idle and wide open throttle (WOT) positions

The feedback system operates in one of two modes: open loop or closed loop. In general terms, the system will be in the open loop mode whenever the engine operating conditions do not conform to the programmed in criteria for closed loop operation. During open loop operation the fuel/air mixture is maintained at a preprogrammed ratio that is dependent on the type of engine operation involved. The oxygen sensor feedback is not accepted by the ECU during this mode. The following conditions involve open loop operation:

a) Engine start-up
b) Coolant temperature lower than 63 °F
c) Engine idling, coolant temperature between 63° and 113°F
d) Oxygen sensor temperature low
e) Wide open throttle (WOT)

When all feedback conforms to the programmed criteria for closed loop, the oxygen content output voltage from the oxygen sensor is accepted by the ECU, which results in a fuel/air mixture that will be optimum for the current engine operating condition. Closed loop operation occurs when:

a) The coolant temperature is greater than 113°F (except WOT)
b) The engine is above idle speed and the coolant temperature is between 63° and 113°F

The cold start injector is controlled by the thermo-time switch. When the starter motor is engaged, it provides the extra fuel necessary for cold starts.

The supplementary air regulator is controlled by a bimetallic spring that is warmed by the heat given off by the engine and by an electric heating element. It increases the amount of air bypass to provide a faster idle speed when the engine is cold.

The control relay, located on the right-hand suspension strut tower, controls the voltage input to the fuel pump, the injectors, the ECU, the supplementary air regulator and the throttle position switch.

The throttle plate assembly contains a supplementary air circuit which is in operation when the air conditioner compressor or power steering pump is running. It compensates for the decrease in engine speed at idle when the compressor or power steering pump loads the engine. The compressor clutch or power steering pressure switch provides voltage to energize the solenoid valve, which opens a vacuum circuit to a pneumatic capsule. The capsule diaphragm moves and opens the

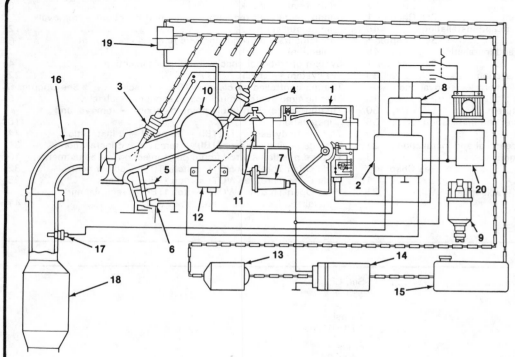

Fig. 4.1 Multi-point fuel injection system components

1   *Airflow meter (with air temperature sensor)*
2   *Electronic Control Unit (ECU)*
3   *Fuel injector*
4   *Cold start injector*
5   *Coolant temperature sensor*
6   *Thermo-time switch*
7   *Supplementary air regulator*
8   *Control relay*
9   *Ignition distributor*
10 *Air intake manifold chamber*
11 *Throttle plate*
12 *Throttle position switch*
13 *Fuel filter*
14 *Fuel pump*
15 *Fuel tank*
16 *Exhaust manifold*
17 *Oxygen sensor*
18 *Catalytic converter*
19 *Fuel pressure regulator*
20 *Ignition control module*

additional air passage. The solenoid is also energized when the starter motor is engaged.

The oxygen sensor, located in the exhaust pipe, provides voltage to the ECU that is related to the oxygen content of the exhaust gases. A lean fuel/air mixture causes greater amounts of oxygen in the exhaust, while a rich fuel/air mixture reduces the oxygen content. The ECU receives the feedback and adjusts the mixture accordingly.

Throttle body injection (TBI)

The throttle body injection system is a pulse time system that injects fuel into the throttle body above the throttle plate. The fuel is metered to the engine by an electronically-controlled fuel injector.

The fuel system consists of an electric fuel pump (in the tank), a fuel filter, a pressure regulator and one fuel injector that supplies all four cylinders. The control system is composed of a manifold air/fuel temperature sensor (MAT), a coolant temperature sensor (CTS), a manifold absolute pressure sensor (MAP), a wide open throttle (WOT) switch, a closed throttle (idle) switch, an oxygen sensor, an electronic control unit (ECU), a gear position indicator (automatic transmission only), a throttle position sensor (automatic transmission only) and an idle speed control (ISC) motor.

The ECU controls the fuel pump, the ISC motor, the ignition advance, the injector, the EGR solenoid and the canister purge solenoid. It controls injection of the fuel based on input from the oxygen sensor, the coolant temperature sensor, the manifold absolute pressure sensor and the throttle and crankshaft position sensors. The desired fuel/air mixtures for various driving and atmospheric conditions are programmed into the ECU. As feedback is received from the sensors and switches, the ECU processes the input and computes the engine fuel requirements. The ECU then activates the injector for a specific time duration (which varies according to engine operating conditions).

When the ignition switch is turned on the following actions occur:
  a) The fuel pump is activated by the ECU (the pump will operate for one second unless the engine is running or the starter motor is engaged)

  b) All engine sensors are activated and begin providing feedback to the ECU
  c) The EGR solenoid is energized to block the vacuum to the EGR valve when the coolant temperature is below 110 °F

When the engine is started, the following actions occur:
  d) The fuel pump operates continuously
  e) The ISC motor will control idle speed (including fast idle) if the TPS is closed at idle
  f) The ignition advance shifts to the ECU programmed curve
  g) The fuel pressure regulator maintains the fuel pressure at approximately 14.5 psi by returning excess fuel to the tank

Precautions

Before blaming the fuel injection system for poor engine performance, make certain that the problem isn't caused by the spark plugs, distributor, ignition timing, air leaks in the intake tract or leaks in the exhaust system upstream of the catalytic converter. Also, make sure that fuel is indeed reaching the injectors.

When checking or replacing components, never disconnect the wires with the ignition switch on.

2   Air intake leak check (multi-point injection)

1   Before blaming the fuel injection system for poor engine performance, the intake tract must be checked carefully for leaks.
2   Disconnect the air intake chamber-to-supplementary air regulator hose (at point *F* in the accompanying illustration). Seal off the end of the exhaust pipe with a rag or an expandable rubber plug.
3   Open the throttle plate and apply compressed air (15 psi maximum) to the air intake chamber at the hose connection.
4   Apply soapy water to all hose connections, joints, seals, etc. with a brush. If bubbles or foam appear, a leak is indicated. Repair the leak(s) before performing any of the system checks outlined in this Chapter.

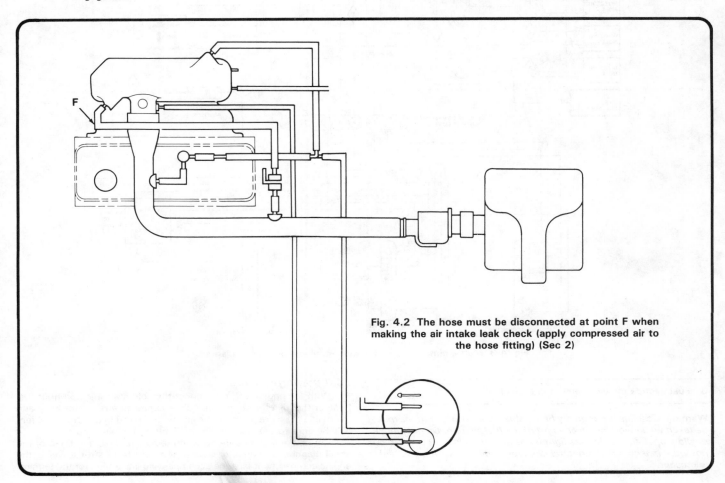

Fig. 4.2 The hose must be disconnected at point F when making the air intake leak check (apply compressed air to the hose fitting) (Sec 2)

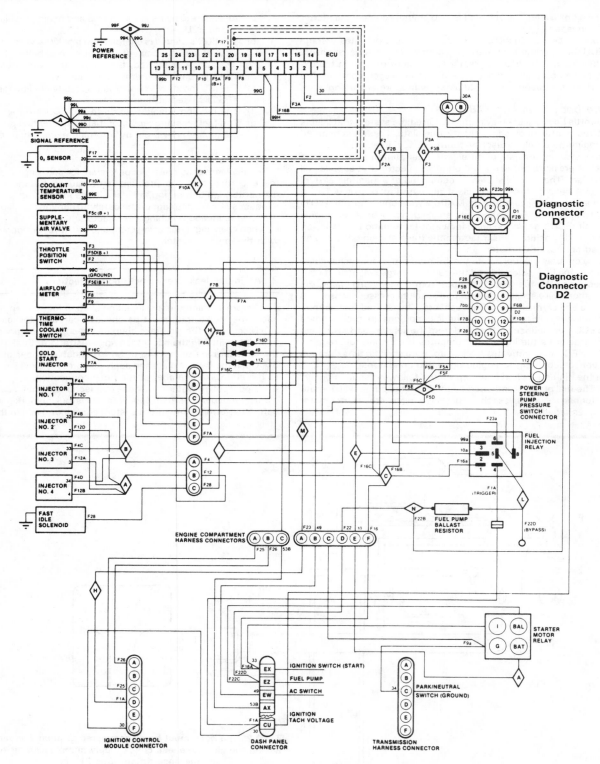

Fig. 4.3 Multi-point fuel injection system electrical wiring diagram

3   Fuel system checks (multi-point injection)

Warning: *Gasoline is extremely flammable, so extra precautions must be taken when working on any part of the fuel system. Do not smoke or allow open flames or bare light bulbs near the work area. Also, do not work in a garage if a natural gas-type appliance with a pilot light is present.*

Fuel pump pressure

1   With the engine off, disconnect the cold start injector input fuel hose or the injector ramp assembly and pressure regulator hose and connect a pressure gauge in the line with a T-fitting (the hose is 8 mm ID). Be sure to use clamps on the T-fitting connections.

2   Connect a jumper wire between terminals D1-5 and D1-6 of the small diagnostic connector next to the right-front strut tower in the engine compartment (see the accompanying illustration for the terminal

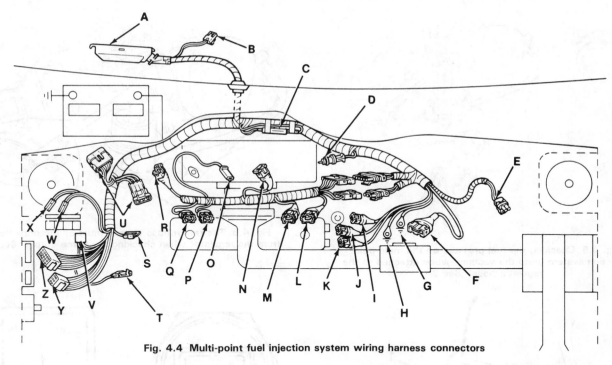

Fig. 4.4 Multi-point fuel injection system wiring harness connectors

A ECU	H Power ground	N Throttle position sensor	T Tach voltage
B IP	I Supplementary air regulator	O Fast idle solenoid	U Engine wire harness
C Diodes	J Thermo-time switch	P Injector	V Control relay
D Oxygen sensor	K Coolant temperature sensor	Q Injector	W Ballast resistor
E Power steering switch	L Injector	R Cold start injector	X Ballast resistor
F Airflow meter	M Injector	S Ballast resistor bypass	Y Diagnostic connector (D1)
G Signal ground			Z Diagnostic connector (D2)

locations). The fuel pump will begin to operate and pressure will be indicated on the gauge.

3   The gauge should read approximately 70 psi. If not, the pump, the filter or the wiring may be faulty.

Pressure regulator operation

4   Using a vacuum pump, apply a vacuum to the pressure regulator (approximately 16 in Hg), then activate the fuel pump as described in Step 2. The pressure on the gauge should drop to 20 ± 3 psi. If it doesn't, the pressure regulator may be faulty.

Injector leakage

5   Disconnect the wires from the injectors, then remove the injector ramp assembly with the injectors (including the cold start injector) in place.

6   Activate the pump as described in Step 2 and look for fuel leakage at the injector tips. If fuel leaks past the injectors, they must be replaced with new ones (slight dampness is acceptable).

Injector operation

7   As a preliminary check, start the engine and disconnect the wire from each injector, one at a time. When each wire is removed, the engine speed should decrease.

8   Position the injector ramp assembly so that each injector can be placed in a container (one injector at a time). Activate the fuel pump as described earlier, then ground the injector body to the engine block with one jumper wire and momentarily apply battery voltage to the injector terminal with another jumper wire. **Warning:** *Be sure to connect the ground wire first. Next attach the wire to the terminal on the injector, then hook it to the battery.*

9   Fuel should spray out of the injector into the container when battery voltage is applied and stop when the wire is disconnected. **Warning:** *Disconnect the jumper wire at the battery — not at the injector.*

10 Repeat the procedure for the remaining injectors. Replace any faulty injectors with new parts.

Fuel pump output

11 Disconnect the fuel return hose from the pressure regulator and attach a length of hose to the regulator fitting. Place the end of the hose in a two quart container. Activate the fuel pump as described earlier.

12 Let the pump run for about one (1) minute, then check the amount of fuel in the container (there should be approximately one quart).

13 If not, the fuel filter, the pressure regulator, the fuel pump or the wiring may be faulty.

4   System operational checks (multi-point injection)

Note: *To locate the terminals and make the voltmeter/ohmmeter connections required for the following checks, refer to the fuel injection system wiring schematic at the front of this Chapter.*

1   With the engine off, the ignition on and the coolant temperature less than 77 °F, check the control relay and ECU ground circuit by connecting the ohmmeter probes between terminals D1-3 and D2-7. The ohmmeter should read zero ohms.

2   Check for battery voltage by connecting the voltmeter probes between terminals D1-5 (+) and D1-3 (−). The voltmeter should read 12 volts. Check for ignition voltage by connecting the probes between D1-2 (+) and D1-3 (−). Again, the meter should read 12 volts.

3   Unplug the ECU wiring connector, then check the coolant temperature sensor by connecting the ohmmeter probes between terminals D2-12 and D2-7. The ohmmeter should read approximately 2.5 K ohms (assuming the coolant temperature is less than 77 °F.)

4   To check the injectors, reconnect the ECU wiring and connect the ohmmeter probes between pins A and B of the injector wiring harness connector. The ohmmeter should indicate approximately 4 ohms.

5   To check the fuel pump, apply battery voltage to terminals D1-5 and D1-6 with jumper wires and listen for noise coming from the pump (indicating that it is running).

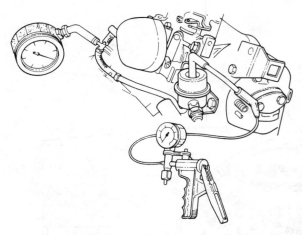

Fig. 4.5 Checking the fuel pressure on the multi-point injection system (note the vacuum gauge attached to the regulator hose) (Sec 3)

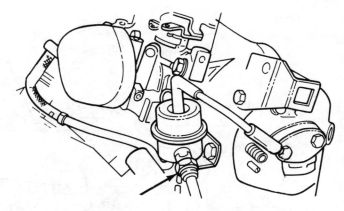

Fig. 4.6 The return hose (arrow) must be disconnected from the regulator when checking the pump output (Sec 3)

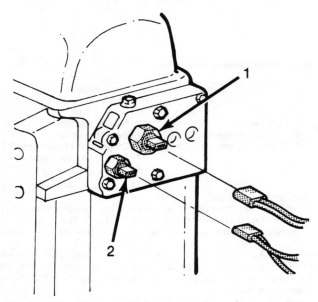

Fig. 4.7 Thermo-time switch (1) and coolant temperature sensor (2) locations (Sec 5)

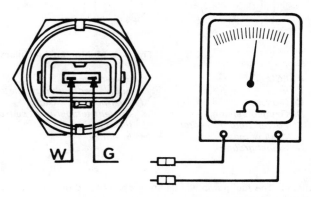

Fig. 4.8 Thermo-time switch terminal locations (Sec 5)

6   To check the throttle position switch, connect the ohmmeter probes between terminals D2-13 and D2-6. The ohmmeter should read infinite ohms. Move the probe from D2-6 to D2-4 and make sure the throttle is at the idle position. The ohmmeter should now read zero ohms. With the probes connected to terminals D2-4 and D2-6 and the throttle wide open, the ohmmeter should also read zero ohms.

7   The thermo-time switch can be checked by connecting the voltmeter probes between terminals D2-9 (+) and D2-7 (−). The voltmeter should read from 8 to 12 volts.

8   With the starter motor engaged (the coolant temperature still less than 77 °F), the start voltage signal can be checked by connecting the voltmeter probes between terminals D1-4 (+) and D1-3 (−). Look for a reading of from 8 to 12 volts. The tach voltage can also be checked under the same conditions by connecting the voltmeter probes to terminals D1-1 (+) and D1-3 (−). The meter should indicate a pulsating or oscillating voltage.

9   Start the engine and check the integrator voltage (open loop) before the coolant and oxygen sensor temperatures rise. Connect the voltmeter probes between terminals D2-2 (+) and D2-7 (−). The meter should read approximately 6.8 volts (the specified voltage is not critical, but be sure to note what it is as it will be required for the remaining tests).

10 With the engine running at 700 ± 100 rpm, the coolant temperature greater than 104 °F and the oxygen sensor temperature more than 480 °F, check the closed loop integrator voltage by connecting the voltmeter probes between terminals D2-2 (+) and D2-7 (−). The voltmeter reading should vary within 0.5 volts of the previous reading (6.3 to 7.3 volts).

11 To check the fuel cut-off during deceleration, increase the engine speed to 3500 rpm and rapidly close the throttle. With the voltmeter probes still connected as described for the previous test, the voltage should read the same as in Step 9 (approximately 6.8 volts).

5   Thermo-time switch (multi-point injection) — check

1   With the coolant temperature less than 86 °F, disconnect the wiring connector from the thermo-time switch. Connect the probes of an ohmmeter between terminal G of the switch and the switch housing (ground). The ohmmeter should read 25 to 40 ohms.

2   Move the ohmmeter probe from terminal G to terminal W and note the ohmmeter reading. It should now be zero (0) ohms.

3   Move the probe from the switch housing to terminal G and note the ohmmeter reading again. It should now be 25 to 40 ohms.

4   Start the engine and allow the coolant temperature to rise above 104 °F, then repeat the resistance checks. With the probes connected to terminal G and the switch housing, the reading should be 50 to 80 ohms. With the probes attached to terminal W and the switch housing, the reading should be 100 to 160 ohms. With the probes attached to both switch terminals, the reading should be 50 to 80 ohms.

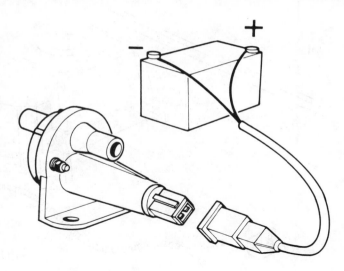

Fig. 4.9 When checking the supplementary air regulator heater, the terminals must be connected to the battery with an insulated connector (Sec 6)

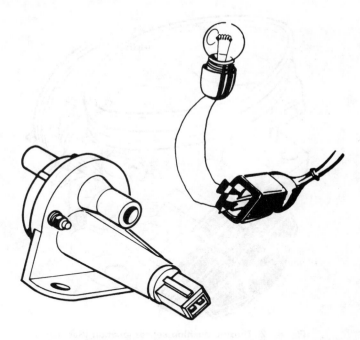

Fig. 4.10 Checking the supplementary air regulator wire harness with a test light (Sec 7)

6 Supplementary air regulator heater (multi-point injection) — check

1 Allow the engine to cool overnight before proceeding with this check (the air regulator assembly must be at approximately 68 °F).
2 Disconnect the air hoses and wires from the air regulator, then look into the inlet fitting and make sure the diaphragm is partly open.
3 Using jumper wires, connect the regulator heater terminals directly to the battery posts (be very careful not to cause a direct short — insulate the ends of the jumper wires that connect to the air regulator heater terminals).
4 After approximately 10 minutes the regulator diaphragm should be completely closed. If it isn't, replace the air regulator with a new one.

7 Supplementary air regulator wiring harness (multi-point injection) — check

1 With the engine completely cold, disconnect the wires from the supplementary air regulator terminals.
2 Connect a test light to the wire connector terminals.
3 Start the engine and see if the light glows. If it doesn't, the wiring harness is defective and should be carefully checked for an open circuit.

8 Coolant temperature sensor (multi-point injection) — check

1 With the engine cold (the temperature of the sensor must be 66 to 70 °F), detach the wiring connector and check the resistance of the sensor by attaching the ohmmeter probes to the terminals. The reading should be 2.1 to 2.9 k ohms.
2 Start the engine and allow the coolant to reach a temperature of 174 to 178 °F, then recheck the resistance. It should now be 250 to 390 ohms. If the readings are not as specified, replace the sensor with a new one.

9 Airflow meter bypass (multi-point injection) — adjustment

Note: *The fuel pressure regulator vacuum source must be connected to the intake manifold port when checking or adjusting the airflow meter.*

1 When, and only when, the engine is overhauled, the airflow meter is replaced with a new one or high idle CO has been detected by a

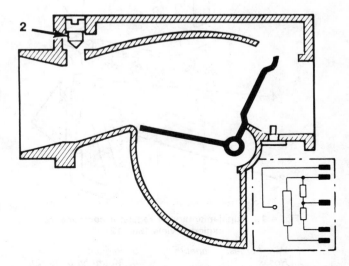

Fig. 4.11 Airflow meter bypass adjustment screw location (2) (Sec 9)

testing station, the bypass adjustment screw (located on the top of the airflow meter housing) must be adjusted to obtain the correct fuel/air mixture.
2 Refer to Chapter 1 and make sure the idle speed is as specified. Remove the tamper resistant cap to gain access to the bypass adjustment screw.
3 Disconnect the oxygen sensor wire connector. Attach the probes of a voltmeter to terminals D2-2 and D2-7 of the large diagnostic connector in the engine compartment and record the voltage reading (it should be 6 to 7 volts).
4 Reconnect the oxygen sensor wire connector. While watching the voltmeter, adjust the bypass screw until the meter needle varies 0.5 volts above and below the previously recorded voltage (a misadjusted screw can cause a voltage variation of plus or minus 3 volts).
5 After the bypass adjustment, check and adjust the idle speed and install a new tamper resistant cap.

Fig. 4.12 Throttle position sensor location (Sec 10)

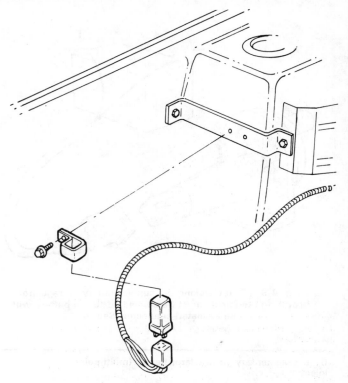

Fig. 4.13 Control relay location (Sec 11)

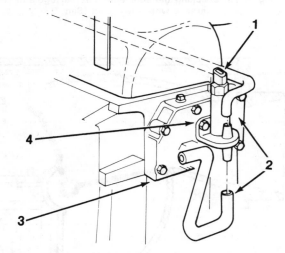

Fig. 4.14 Supplementary air regulator components —
exploded view (Sec 12)

| 1 | Wire harness connector | 3 | Regulator |
| 2 | Hoses | 4 | Mounting bolts (2) |

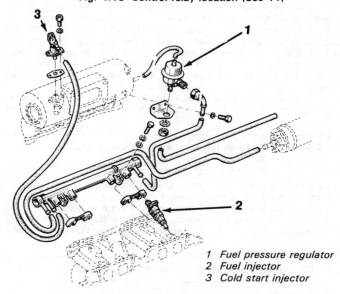

1 Fuel pressure regulator
2 Fuel injector
3 Cold start injector

Fig. 4.15 Fuel injector and related components — exploded
view (Sec 13 through 15)

10 Throttle position switch (multi-point injection) — adjustment

1   Loosen the switch screws (it may be necessary to remove the throttle body to gain access to the screws).
2   With the throttle plate against the idle speed stop, slowly rotate the TPS in the direction of the throttle plate opening until the inner stop can be felt, then retighten the screws. The adjustment can also be made with an ohmmeter (refer to the operational checks).

11 Control relay (multi-point injection) — removal and installation

1   The control relay is attached to the right-hand strut tower in the engine compartment.

2   To replace it, remove the bracket mounting screw, separate the relay from the bracket and detach the wire connector from the relay.
3   Installation is the reverse of removal.

12 Supplementary air regulator (multi-point injection) — removal and installation

1   Disconnect the wires and hoses from the regulator fittings.
2   Remove the mounting bolts and separate the regulator from the cylinder head.
3   Position the new regulator, install the mounting bolts and hook up the hoses and wires.

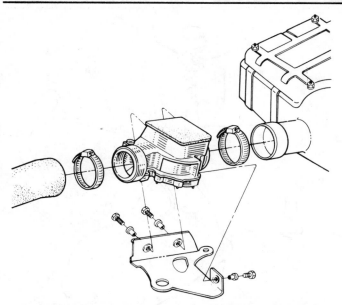

Fig. 4.16 Airflow meter mounting details (Sec 18)

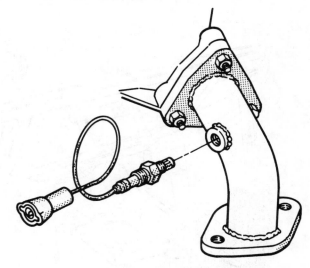

Fig. 4.17 Oxygen sensor location (Sec 19)

13 Fuel pressure regulator (multi-point injection) — removal and installation

Warning: *Gasoline is extremely flammable, so extra precautions must be taken when working on any part of the fuel system. Do not smoke or allow open flames or bare light bulbs near the work area. Also, do not work in a garage if a natural gas-type appliance with a pilot light is present.*

1 Detach the fuel and vacuum hoses from the regulator fittings (it may help to label them to avoid confusion during installation).
2 Unscrew the large nut at the bottom of the regulator and separate it from the bracket.
3 Position the new regulator, install and tighten the nut, then hook up the fuel and vacuum hoses.
4 Start the engine and check carefully for fuel leaks.

14 Injectors (multi-point injection) — removal and installation

Warning: *Gasoline is extremely flammable, so extra precautions must be taken when working on any part of the fuel system. Do not smoke or allow open flames or bare light bulbs near the work area. Also, do not work in a garage if a natural gas-type appliance with a pilot light is present.*

1 Remove the air intake chamber, then disconnect the fuel hoses and wires from the injectors.
2 Remove the injector ramp bolts and separate the ramp from the injectors by pulling on it.
3 The injectors can be pulled out of the cylinder head recesses.
4 Installation is the reverse of removal, but be sure to check the O-ring on each injector for damage (lubricate them with a small amount of gasoline before installing the injectors).

15 Cold start injector (multi-point injection) — removal and installation

Warning: *Gasoline is extremely flammable, so extra precautions must be taken when working on any part of the fuel system. Do not smoke or allow open flames or bare light bulbs near the work area. Also, do not work in a garage if a natural gas-type appliance with a pilot light is present.*

1 Disconnect the wire connector and detach the fuel hose from the injector.
2 Remove the bolts and washers and separate the injector and gasket from the housing.
3 Installation is the reverse of removal (be sure to use a new gasket).

16 Thermo-time switch (multi-point injection) — removal and installation

1 The engine must be completely cool when replacing the thermo-time switch. Refer to Chapter 1 and drain about 2 or 3 quarts of coolant out of the radiator.
2 Disconnect the wire from the switch and unscrew it from the cylinder head.
3 Install the replacement switch and hook up the wire (handle the new switch carefully — if it is dropped it could be damaged).
4 Refill the cooling system (refer to Chapter 1), start the engine and check for leaks at the switch.

17 Coolant temperature sensor (multi-point injection) — removal and installation

The coolant temperature sensor removal and installation procedure is identical to the thermo-time switch removal and installation procedure (Section 16).

18 Airflow meter (multi-point injection) — removal and installation

1 Disconnect the wire connector, then loosen the duct clamps and separate the ducts from the airflow meter.
2 Remove the screws and separate the airflow meter from the bracket.
3 Installation is the reverse of removal. Be sure the wire is securely connected to the terminals.

19 Oxygen sensor (multi-point injection) — removal and installation

The oxygen sensor is threaded into the exhaust pipe and will probably be very tight due to corrosion and repeated heat/cool cycles (a 22 mm crow-foot flare nut wrench should be used for removal and installation).
2 Disconnect the wire and remove the unit from the pipe.
3 Make sure the threads in the pipe are clean (run a tap into the hole if necessary), then apply anti-seize compound to the threads of the new oxygen sensor (don't get the anti-seize compound on any other part of the sensor).
4 Start the sensor into place by hand, then tighten it to the specified torque with the crow-foot wrench.
5 Reconnect the wire.

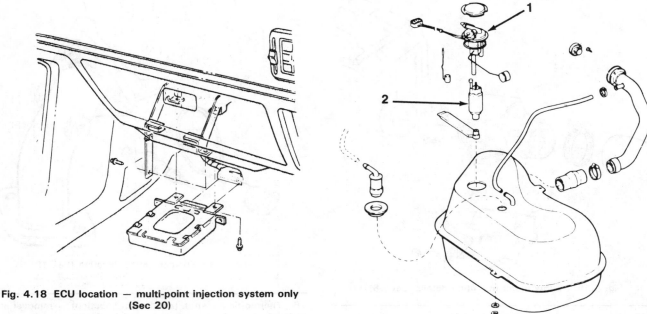

Fig. 4.18 ECU location — multi-point injection system only
(Sec 20)

Fig. 4.19 Fuel tank, pump and sending unit components —
exploded view (Sec 21)

1 Sending unit   2 Fuel pump

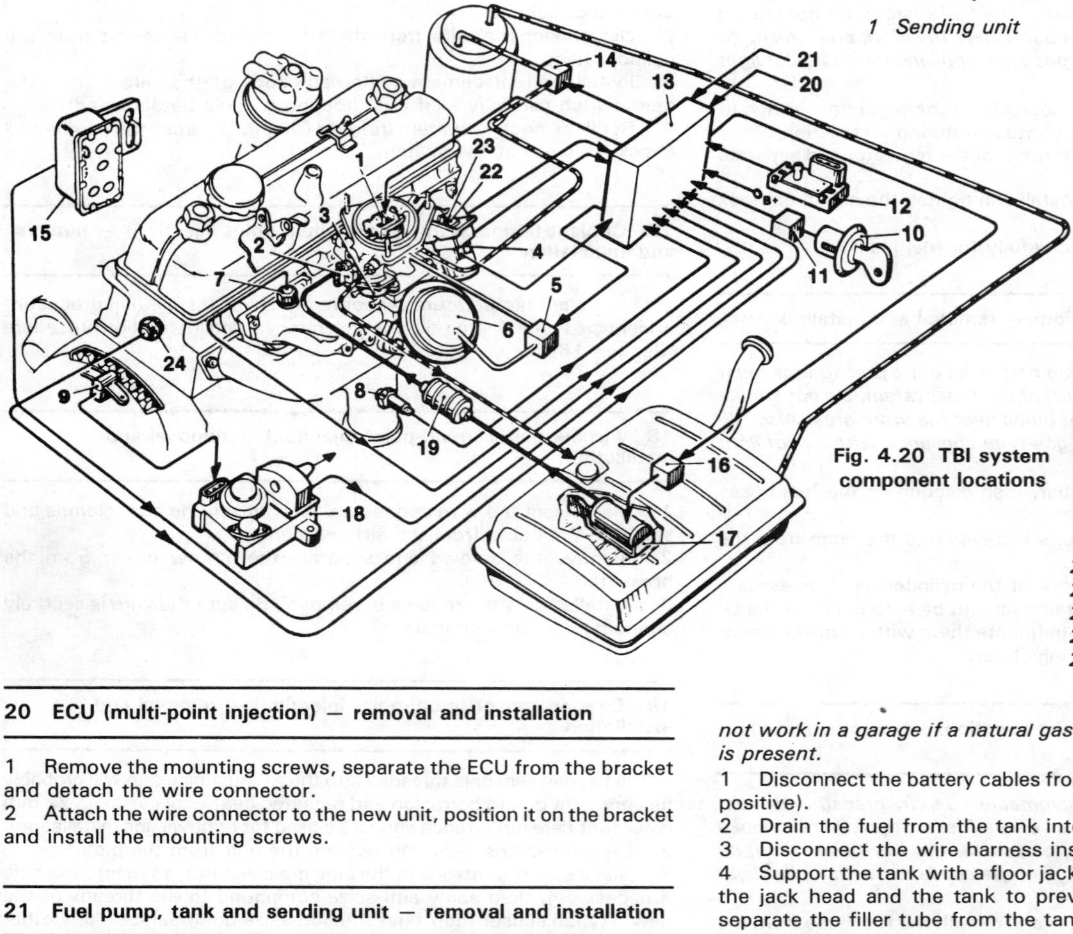

Fig. 4.20 TBI system
component locations

1   Injector
2   Throttle position sensor
3   Fuel pressure regulator
4   ISC motor
5   EGR solenoid
6   EGR valve
7   MAT sensor
8   Oxygen sensor
9   Speed sensor
10 Ignition switch
11 Power relay
12 MAP sensor
13 ECU
14 EVAP canister solenoid
15 Starter motor relay
16 Fuel pump relay
17 Fuel pump
18 Ignition control module
19 Fuel filter
20 Air conditioner on
21 Neutral/Park switch
22 Closed throttle switch
23 WOT switch
24 Coolant temperature sensor

20   ECU (multi-point injection) — removal and installation

1   Remove the mounting screws, separate the ECU from the bracket
and detach the wire connector.
2   Attach the wire connector to the new unit, position it on the bracket
and install the mounting screws.

21   Fuel pump, tank and sending unit — removal and installation

Warning: *Gasoline is extremely flammable, so extra precautions must
be taken when working on any part of the fuel system. Do not smoke
or allow open flames or bare light bulbs near the work area. Also, do*

*not work in a garage if a natural gas-type appliance with a pilot light
is present.*
1   Disconnect the battery cables from the battery (negative first, then
positive).
2   Drain the fuel from the tank into a clean container.
3   Disconnect the wire harness inside the trunk.
4   Support the tank with a floor jack (place a piece of wood between
the jack head and the tank to prevent damage to the tank), then
separate the filler tube from the tank.
5   Remove the tank mounting bolts, then slowly lower the jack and
the tank.
6   Disconnect the hoses from the tank (mark them to prevent confusion during installation).

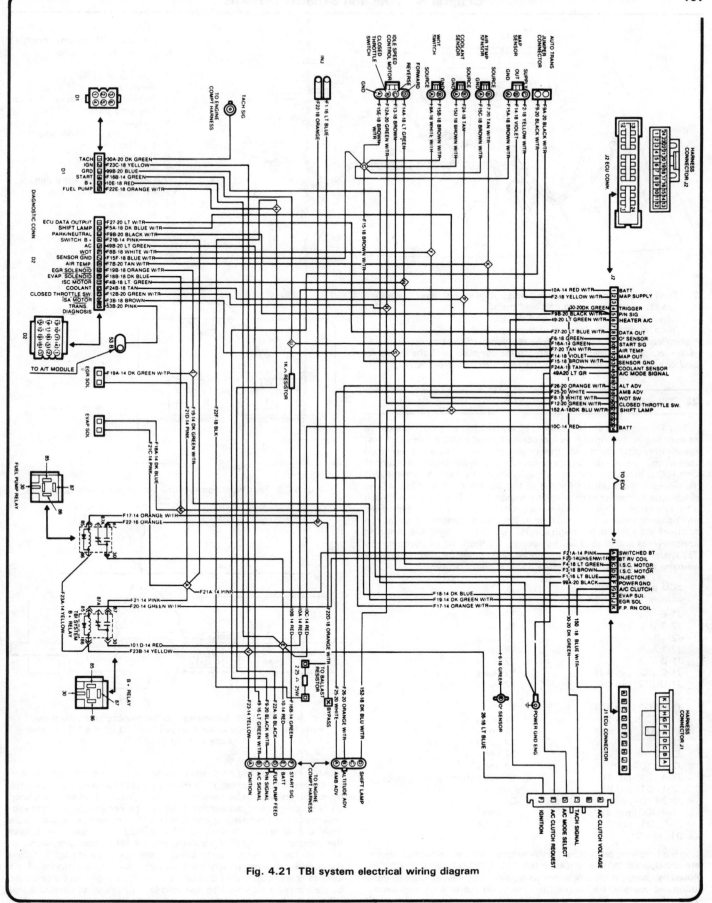

Fig. 4.21 TBI system electrical wiring diagram

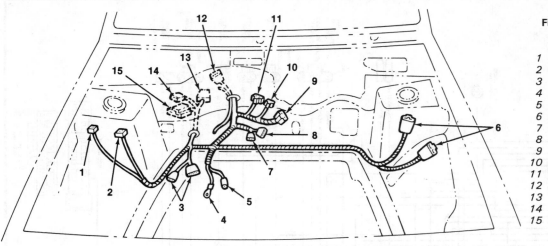

Fig. 4.22 TBI system wiring harness connectors

1   Fuel pump relay
2   Power relay
3   Engine compartment harness
4   Engine ground
5   Oxygen sensor
6   EVAP and EGR solenoids
7   WOT switch
8   ISC motor
9   Fuel injector
10 Coolant temperature sensor
11 Air temperature sensor
12 MAP sensor
13 ECU
14 IP harness
15 ECU

7   Turn the sending unit retaining ring with a screwdriver to remove it, then lift out the sending unit and pump.
8   Separate the sending unit and pump.
9   Installation is the reverse of removal.
Note: *Replacement fuel pumps may require modifications during installation. Be sure to follow the instructions supplied with the new part and consult your dealer parts department before proceeding.*

22   TBI system — check

The TBI injection system should be considered as a possible cause of poor engine performance, fuel economy and exhaust emission test results only after checks of other engine components have been made (see Section 1). A self-diagnostic system within the Electronic Control Unit (ECU) detects common malfunctions in the TBI system and will illuminate a test bulb connected to the trouble code terminal of the diagnostic connector in the engine compartment. The system will flash a trouble code if a malfunction has been detected. The trouble codes and possible causes are listed below. No special equipment is required to check the system, although a VOM, 12 volt test light and assorted jumper wires and probes will be needed. **Caution:** *When checking the TBI system, the following connections must never be made or serious damage to the ECU or the entire system could occur:*

ECU pin/diagnostic connector pin	Connection
J1-E	12 volts or ground
J2-8 (D2, pin 1)	12 volts
J2-18	12 volts
J2-17	12 volts
J1-B	12 volts
J1-C (D2, pin 11)	12 volts or ground
J1-D (D2, pin 14)	12 volts or ground
J1-K	12 volts
J1-H (D2, pin 10)	12 volts
J1-G (D2, pin 2)	12 volts
J1-J (D2, pin 9)	12 volts
J2-2	12 volts or ground
J2-12	12 volts
J2-13 (D2, pin 7)	12 volts
J2-4 (D1, pin 1)	12 volts or ground
J2-1 (D1, pin 5)	Ground
J2-24 (D1, pin 5)	Ground
J1-A (D2, pin 4)	Ground
J1-F (D1, pin 3)	12 volts
D1, pin 6	Ground

In the following procedures, only complete (non-intermittent) failures are considered. In most cases, intermittent failures can also be diagnosed by using the trouble codes as a guide (a certain amount of good judgment will also be required to zero in on the faulty component). The self-diagnostic feature of the ECU provides help for solving system

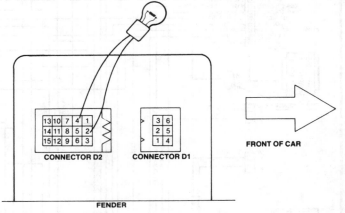

Fig. 4.23 Test light connections for trouble code diagnosis (Sec 22)

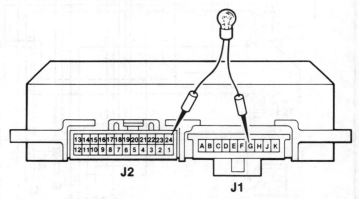

Fig. 4.24 Test light connections for trouble code diagnosis (vehicles with code letter E in position 10 of the VIN — see note in text) (Sec 22)

problems by recording six possible failures if they are encountered during normal engine operation. Additional checks should allow specific failed components to be identified (multiple failures that are not related must be diagnosed separately). It should be noted that the test procedures can cause false interpretations of certain problems and consider them as ECU failures. In the event that an ECU failure is indicated, take the vehicle to a dealer service department for further diagnosis.
1   Poor fuel economy, erratic idling, power surging and engine stalling are common symptoms when a fuel system component has failed. As long as the ECU is working properly, trouble codes can be obtained by connecting a number 158 test light (or equivalent) to pins D2-2 and D2-4 of the large diagnostic connector in the engine compartment (see

the accompanying illustration). **Note:** *On Alliance/Encore models with code letter E in position 10 of the VIN, connect the test light to pins J2-24 and J1-G at the back of the ECU harness connector. Also, before testing air conditioning-equipped models, disconnect the low pressure switch.*

2   With the test light hooked up, push the WOT switch lever on the throttle body, and with the ISC motor plunger (closed throttle switch) also closed, have an assistant turn on the ignition switch while you watch the test light.

3   If the ECU is functioning normally, the test light will light momentarily, then go out. This will occur regardless of the existance of failures.

4   After the initial illumination, the ECU will cycle and flash a single digit code if any system malfunctions have been detected by the ECU during engine operation. **Note:** *The ECU is capable of storing two different trouble codes in its memory. The initial trouble detected will be flashed first, then, followed by a short pause, the second problem code will be flashed. There will be a somewhat longer pause between the second code and the repeat cycle of the first code again.*

5   The trouble codes are:

   1 flash — Manifold Air/Fuel Temperature (MAT) sensor failure

   2 flashes — Coolant Temperature Sensor (CTS) failure

   3 flashes — Simultaneous WOT and closed throttle switch input

   4 flashes — Simultaneous closed throttle switch and high air flow

   5 flashes — Simultaneous WOT and low air flow

   6 flashes — Oxygen sensor failure

6   In a situation where further testing produces no apparent cause for the failure indicated by the ECU self-diagnostic system, an intermittent failure should be suspected.

7   If the trouble code is erased and quickly returns with no other symptoms, the ECU should be suspected. However, in the absence of other symptoms, replacement of the ECU is not advised.

8   Note that the trouble code memory will be erased if the ECU power supply is interrupted by disconnecting the ECU wire harness connector, disconnecting either battery cable or leaving the engine inoperative in excess of five days. Also, whenever a defective fuel system component is replaced with a new one, the memory must be erased by one of the methods mentioned.

9   The following chart contains a list of problems, possible causes and corrective actions for the six trouble codes commonly indicated by the ECU.

10   If the test results are inconclusive or if the repair involves replacement of components, it may be a good idea to have a dealer service department confirm the diagnosis before purchasing parts. Also, remember that the emission control systems are integrated with the fuel system and can affect performance (see Section 1).

Trouble Code	Possible cause	Corrective action
Code 1 (poor low temp. engine performance)	MAT sensor resistance not less than 1000 ohms (hot) or more than 100 K ohms (very cold)	Refer to the MAT sensor check (replace it if necessary)
Code 2 (poor high temp. engine performance — engine lacks power)	Coolant temperature sensor resistance less than 300 ohms or more than 300 K ohms (10 K ohms at room temp.)	Check the MAT sensor and coolant temp. sensor (replace the coolant temp. sensor if necessary)
Code 3 (poor fuel economy, hard starting when cold, stalling and rough idle)	Defective WOT or closed throttle (idle) switch, or both (or wiring harnesses)	Check WOT and closed throttle switches and wire harnesses
Code 4 (poor acceleration, performance and fuel economy)	Simultaneous closed throttle switch and MAP sensor failure	Check the closed throttle switch and MAP sensor and related wires and hoses)
Code 5 (poor acceleration and sluggish performance	Simultaneous WOT switch and MAP sensor failure	Check the WOT switch and MAP sensor (and related wires and hoses)
Code 6 (poor fuel economy, driveability and idle, black smoke from tailpipe)	Oxygen sensor failure	Check the oxygen sensor and fuel system pressure (Chapter 4); the EGR solenoid control, canister purge and PCV system (Chapter 6); the secondary ignition system (Chapter 5)
No test light flash	No battery voltage at ECU; no ground at ECU (J1-A with key on)	Repair or replace the wire harness, connectors or relays
	Simultaneous WOT and CTS switch contact (ground at both D2 pin 6 and D2 pin 13	Repair or replace WOT or CTS switch, wire harness or connectors
	No battery voltage at test light (D2 pin 4)	Repair the harness or connector
	Defective test light	Replace the test light with a known good one
	Low battery voltage (less than 11.5 volts)	Charge or replace the battery; repair the wire harness

23   Manifold Air/Fuel Temperature (MAT) sensor (TBI) — check

1   The MAT sensor is threaded into the top of the intake manifold so it may be helpful to remove the air cleaner assembly to have room to work. Disconnect the wire harness connector from the sensor.

2   Attach the leads of a digital ohmmeter to the MAT sensor wire terminals. The resistance varies between 1000 ohms (engine hot) and 100 K ohms (engine very cold).

3   Replace the sensor if the resistance is outside of the specified range.

4   Check the resistance of the harness wires (terminals J2-11 and J2-13 at the ECU wire harness connector and the MAT sensor wire harness connector terminals). Repair the harness as necessary if the resistance is greater than 1 ohm.

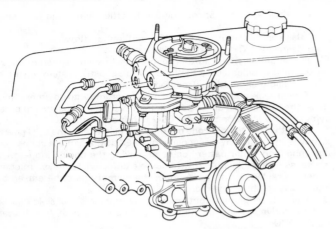

Fig. 4.25 MAT sensor location (Sec 23)

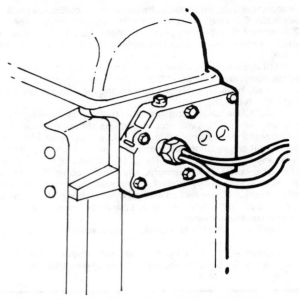

Fig. 4.26 Coolant temperature sensor location (Sec 24)

24 Coolant temperature sensor (TBI) — check

1   The coolant temperature sensor is attached to the end of the cylinder head. The checking procedure is identical to the MAT sensor check (Section 23). The resistance can vary from 300 ohms to more than 300 K ohms (10 K ohms at room temperature).
2   Check the resistance of the harness wires (terminals J2-11 and J2-14 at the ECU wire harness connector and the coolant temperature sensor wire harness connector terminals). Repair the harness if an open circuit is indicated (no resistance).

25 Wide Open Throttle (WOT) switch (TBI) — check

1   The WOT switch is attached to the ISC motor bracket on the right-hand side of the throttle body. Disconnect the wire harness connector from the switch.
2   Attach the ohmmeter leads to the wire terminals in the connector that is attached to the switch wires. Open and close the switch by hand.
3   The resistance should be infinite when the throttle is closed and very low when the throttle is wide open. Make the check several times by opening and closing the throttle or switch with your hand.
4   Replace the switch with a new one if the results are not as described.
5   Reconnect the wire harness connector, then turn the ignition switch on and check the voltage at the diagnostic connector (terminals D2-6 and D2-7). The voltage should be zero (0) at the WOT position and greater than two (2) volts when not at the WOT position.
6   If the voltage is always zero, check for a short to ground in the harness or switch. Also, check for an open circuit between terminal J2-19 at the ECU and the switch connector.
7   If the voltage is always greater than two volts, check for an open circuit in the wire or connector between the switch and ground.

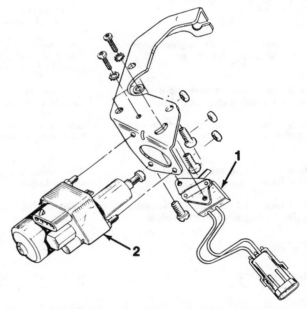

Fig. 4.27 WOT switch (1) and ISC motor (2) locations
(Sec 25)

26 Closed throttle switch (TBI) — check

1   It is important that all testing be done with the idle speed control (ISC) motor plunger in the fully extended position (as it would be after a normal engine shutdown). If it is necessary to extend the motor plunger to check the switch, an ISC motor failure is indicated. Refer to the ISC motor adjustment procedure if necessary.
2   With the ignition switch on, check the voltage at diagnostic connector terminals D2-13 and D2-7 and ground. The voltage should be close to zero (0) at closed throttle and greater than two (2) volts off the closed throttle position.
3   If the voltage is always zero, check for a short to ground in the wire harness or switch. Also, check for an open circuit between ECU connector terminal J2-20 and the switch.
4   If the voltage is always more than two volts, check for an open circuit in the wire harness between the ECU and the switch connector and ground.

27 Manifold Absolute Pressure (MAP) sensor (TBI) — check

1   The MAP sensor is mounted on the passenger side of the firewall. Check the vacuum hose and connections at the MAP sensor and throttle body.
2   Check the sensor output voltage at connector pin B (as marked on the sensor body) with the ignition switch on and the engine off. It should be 4 to 5 volts. **Note:** *The voltage should drop from 0.5 to 1.5 volts under hot, neutral idle speed conditions.*
3   Check the voltage at ECU pin J2-12; it should be the same as the MAP sensor output voltage mentioned above.
4   Check the MAP sensor supply voltage at pin C with the ignition on. It should be 5 ± 0.5 volts. The same voltage reading should be obtained at pin J2-2 of the ECU wire harness connector.
5   Check the ground circuit at connector pin A and ECU connector pin J2-13 (ignition off). Check the resistance between ECU connector pin J2-13 and J1-F with an ohmmeter. If the ohmmeter indicates an

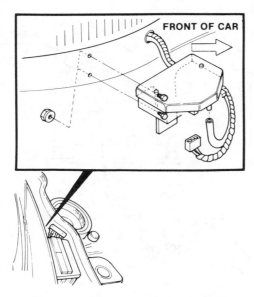

Fig. 4.28 MAP sensor location (Sec 27)

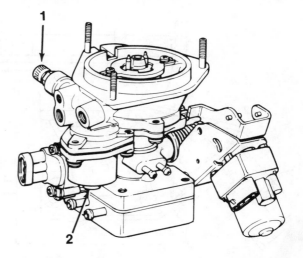

Fig. 4.29 The TBI fuel pressure is checked by attaching a gauge to the fitting on the throttle body (1); the adjusting screw (2) on the pressure regulator is used to change the pressure (Sec 29 and 30)

open circuit (no resistance), check for a good sensor ground connection on the flywheel housing near the starter motor. If the ground connection is good, suspect the ECU.

28 Oxygen sensor (TBI) — check

1   The oxygen sensor is mounted in the exhaust pipe attached to the engine. Check for continuity in the wire harness between the sensor and pin J2-9 of the ECU wire harness connector (make sure the wire is not shorted to ground).
2   Check for continuity between the sensor ground (place the ohmmeter probe on the bare metal of the exhaust manifold) and pin J2-13 of the ECU wire harness connector.
3   Check the fuel system pressure.
4   Check the sensor operation by driving the vehicle with a test light connected between terminals D2-2 and D2-4 of the diagnostic connector. The bulb should light when the engine is cold and go out as it warms up. If the bulb does not go out or if it lights after the engine warms up, the oxygen sensor is not functioning properly. **Note:** *Additional checking may be necessary to locate the cause of an oxygen sensor failure. Check the PCV system, the secondary ignition system, the fuel delivery system and the EGR solenoid and canister purge controls.*

29 Fuel pressure (TBI) — check

Warning: *Gasoline is extremely flammable, so extra precautions must be taken when working on any part of the fuel system. Do not smoke or allow open flames or bare light bulbs near the work area. Also, do not work in a garage if a natural gas-type appliance with a pilot light is present.*
1   The fuel pressure is checked at a throttle body fitting. Remove the air cleaner assembly to gain access to the fitting.
2   With the engine off, remove the cap from the fitting and connect a fuel pressure gauge.
3   Start the engine and note the reading on the gauge. It should be between 14 and 15 psi.
4   If the pressure is low, check the voltage at the fuel pump connector (it should be approximately 7.5 volts). Check the fuel filter for restrictions and make sure the fuel pump ballast resistor is functioning (it can be bypassed using the pigtail connector beneath it).
5   Check the pressure regulator by pinching off the rubber fuel return hose with the engine idling. If the pressure increases considerably with the hose restricted, the regulator is working.
6   If the fuel pressure is high, the return hose could be restricted.

Disconnect the return hose and connect a larger diameter hose to the fitting (direct the hose into a separate closed container). Recheck the fuel pressure as described above. If the pressure drops, the fuel return hose or tank fittings may be restricted. If the pressure does not drop, the regulator may be malfunctioning (it can be rebuilt and/or adjusted).

30 Fuel pressure regulator (TBI) — adjustment

Warning: *Gasoline is extremely flammable, so extra precautions must be taken when working on any part of the fuel system. Do not smoke or allow open flames or bare light bulbs near the work area. Also, do not work in a garage if a natural gas-type appliance with a pilot light is present.*
1   Adjustment of the pressure regulator is necessary after a replacement is installed (to establish the correct system pressure). A fuel pressure gauge, a TORX-head screwdriver and a tachometer will be required to adjust the pressure.
2   Remove the air cleaner assembly and connect the tachometer to terminals D1-1 and D1-3 of the diagnostic connector. Connect the fuel pressure gauge to the fitting on the throttle body.
3   Start the engine and run it at approximately 2000 rpm. **Caution:** *Be very careful when working on a running engine. Do not allow your hands or clothing near the pulleys, belts or fan.*
4   Turn the TORX-head adjustment screw on the bottom of the regulator until the pressure gauge reads 14.5 psi.
5   Shut off the engine and disconnect the pressure gauge and tachometer, then install the air cleaner assembly.

31 Idle Speed Control (ISC) motor (TBI) — adjustment

1   Adjustment of the ISC motor plunger is necessary only to establish the initial position of the plunger after a new motor has been installed.
2   Start the engine and allow it to reach normal operating temperature, then shut it off and remove the air cleaner assembly. Connect a tachometer to terminals D1-1 and D1-3 of the diagnostic connector. Make sure the air conditioner (if equipped) is off.
3   With the ignition off, the ISC motor plunger should move to the fully extended position. With the plunger fully extended, disconnect the ISC motor wire harness connector and start the engine.
4   Under these conditions, the idle speed should be 3500 ± 200 rpm. If the speed is not correct, turn the hex-head screw until the engine speed is 3500 rpm.
5   Retract the ISC motor all the way by holding the closed throttle switch plunger in while the throttle is opened by hand. The closed throttle switch plunger should not be touching the throttle lever when the

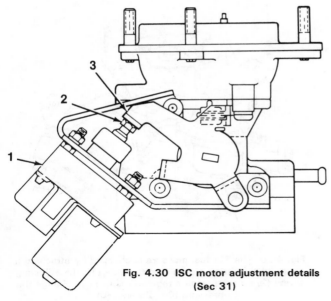

Fig. 4.30 ISC motor adjustment details (Sec 31)

1 ISC motor
2 Hex-head adjustment screw
  (also part of the closed
  throttle switch plunger)
3 Throttle lever

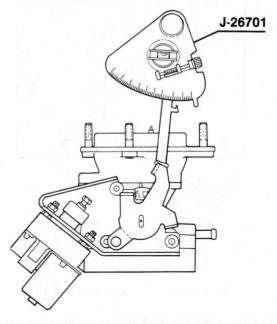

Fig. 4.31 When adjusting the WOT switch, the special angle gauge is attached to the throttle lever (Sec 32)

throttle is returned to the closed position. If contact is noted, check the throttle linkage and/or cable for binding or damage. **Note:** *Holding the closed throttle switch in may cause a trouble code to be stored in the ECU memory. With the ignition switch off, disconnect the negative battery cable for 10 seconds to clear the trouble code from the ECU.*

6   Reconnect the wire harness. Turn the ignition switch off for ten (10) seconds. The ISC motor should move to the fully extended position.

7   Start the engine. It should run at 3500 rpm for a short period of time and then slow down to idle speed. Turn the ignition off and disconnect the tachometer. After final adjustment of the ISC motor, apply Locktite 290 (or equivalent) to the adjustment screw threads. **Warning:** *After the sealant hardens, application of heat with a soldering gun is required to loosen the adjustment screw. Do not apply a flame to soften the sealant or damage to the ISC motor or ignition of gasoline fumes could result.*

8   Reinstall the air cleaner assembly.

32 Wide Open Throttle (WOT) switch (TBI) — adjustment

1   Adjustment of the WOT switch is necessary only after a new switch has been installed. A special angle gauge (no. J-26701) is needed to make the adjustment. For this reason, it may be a good idea to leave the replacement and adjustment to a dealer service department or auto repair shop.

2   Remove the throttle body assembly from the engine and loosen the WOT switch mounting screws.

3   Open the throttle to the wide open position. Attach the alignment gauge to the throttle lever as shown in the accompanying illustration.

4   Rotate the scale on the gauge until the 15 degree mark is aligned with the pointer (throttle body level).

5   Adjust the bubble until it is centered, then rotate the scale to align the zero degree mark with the pointer.

6   Close the throttle slightly to center the bubble on the gauge (the throttle is now at 15 degrees before the WOT position).

7   Position the WOT switch lever on the throttle cam so that the switch plunger is just closed at 15 degrees before the WOT position.

8   Tighten the switch mounting screws and remove the alignment gauge. The throttle body can now be reinstalled on the engine.

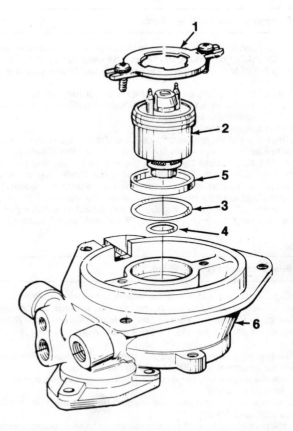

Fig. 4.32 TBI fuel injector components — exploded view (Sec 33)

1 Retainer clip   4 Lower O-ring
2 Injector   5 Back-up ring
3 Upper O-ring   6 Fuel body

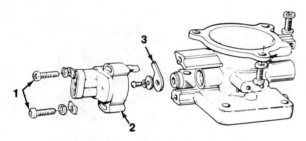

Fig. 4.33 Throttle position sensor mounting details
(Sec 34)

1 Mounting screws   3 Throttle shaft lever
2 Throttle position sensor

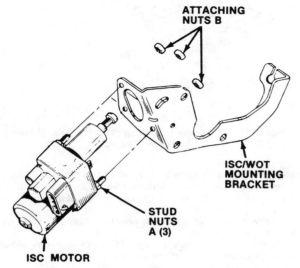

Fig. 4.35 When removing the ISC motor attaching nuts (B),
hold the stud nuts (A) with a wrench to keep the studs
from turning and damaging the ISC motor internally
(Sec 36)

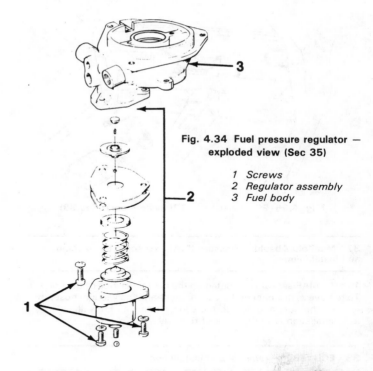

Fig. 4.34 Fuel pressure regulator —
exploded view (Sec 35)

1 Screws
2 Regulator assembly
3 Fuel body

2   Remove the two TORX-head mounting screws and separate the sensor from the shaft lever and throttle body.
3   Installation is the reverse of removal.

35 Fuel pressure regulator (TBI) — removal and installation

Warning: *Gasoline is extremely flammable, so extra precautions must be taken when working on any part of the fuel system. Do not smoke or allow open flames or bare light bulbs near the work area. Also, do not work in a garage if a natural gas-type appliance with a pilot light is present.*
1   Remove the three screws that attach the regulator to the fuel body.
2   Carefully separate the regulator from the fuel body (note the relationship of the parts to one another to simplify installation).
3   Discard the gasket and use a new one during installation.
4   Installation is the reverse of removal. Start the engine and check carefully for fuel leaks when the installation is complete.

36 Idle Speed Control (ISC) motor (TBI) — removal and installation

Note: *The closed throttle (idle) switch is an integral part of the ISC motor.*
1   Remove the air cleaner assembly and disconnect the throttle return spring.
2   Disconnect the wire harness from the ISC motor and the WOT switch, then detach the throttle cable from the mounting bracket and throttle body. Also, remove the cruise control cable (if so equipped).
3   Remove the TORX-head screws and separate the bracket, ISC motor and WOT switch from the throttle body as an assembly.
4   Remove the motor-to-bracket nuts and separate the motor from the bracket. **Note:** *Be sure to hold the stud nuts with an 8 mm wrench to keep the studs from turning (the wrench may have to be ground down to make it thin enough to fit between the ISC motor and bracket).*
5   Installation is the reverse of removal. After the ISC motor is installed, start the engine with the throttle 1/4 open (this prevents the ISC plunger from retracting). Stop the engine. When the ignition switch is turned off, the plunger should extend completely (if the plunger is not extended all the way, the closed throttle switch may open and cause the idle speed to drop to about 400 rpm).

33 Fuel injector (TBI) — removal and installation

Warning: *Gasoline is extremely flammable, so extra precautions must be taken when working on any part of the fuel system. Do not smoke or allow open flames or bare light bulbs near the work area. Also, do not work in a garage if a natural gas-type appliance with a pilot light is present.*
1   Remove the air cleaner assembly and disconnect the injector wire harness.
2   Remove the injector retainer clip screws and detach the retainer clip. Note how the wire terminals are oriented.
3   Using a small pliers, gently grasp the center collar of the injector (between the electrical terminals) and remove it by lifting and twisting.
4   Discard the upper and lower O-rings (use new ones during installation). Note that the back-up ring fits over the upper O-ring.
5   Lubricate the new O-rings with light oil and install them in the housing bore. Install the back-up ring over the upper O-ring.
6   Position the injector in the fuel body and center the nozzle in the lower housing bore. Seat the injector using a pushing/twisting motion.
7   Align the wire terminals and install the retainer clip and screws. Hook up the wires and install the air cleaner assembly.

34 Throttle position sensor (TBI) — removal and installation

1   Remove the air cleaner assembly, then disconnect the wire harness from the sensor.

Fig. 4.36 ECU location — TBI system only (Sec 38)

37 Manifold Absolute Pressure (MAP) sensor (TBI) — removal and installation

1   The MAP sensor is mounted on the passenger side of the firewall. To remove it, disconnect the wire harness and the vacuum hose, then remove the nuts and detach the sensor from the firewall.
2   Installation is the reverse of removal.

38 ECU (TBI) — removal and installation

1   Remove the screws and bracket that support the ECU below the glove box.
2   Detach the ECU and disconnect the wire harnesses.
3   Installation is the reverse of removal.

39 Manifold Air/Fuel Temperature (MAT) sensor (TBI) — removal and installation

1   Remove the air cleaner assembly and disconnect the wire harness connector from the sensor.
2   Unscrew the sensor from the intake manifold and clean the threads in the manifold with a tap and wire brush.
3   Install the new sensor, tighten it securely and connect the wire harness.
4   Install the air cleaner assembly.

40 Oxygen sensor (TBI) — removal and installation

   Refer to Section 19 and follow the procedure there (be sure to use the correct torque for the TBI oxygen sensor).

41 Wide Open Throttle (WOT) switch (TBI) — removal and installation

1   Remove the air cleaner assembly and disconnect the throttle return spring and throttle cable.
2   Remove the ISC motor bracket-to-throttle body screws and disconnect the wire harnesses from the ISC motor and WOT switch.
3   Separate the bracket, with the ISC motor and WOT switch attached, from the throttle body.
4   Remove the ISC motor (Section 36), then remove the WOT switch-to-bracket screws and detach the switch.
5   Installation is the reverse of removal.

42 Coolant temperature sensor (TBI) — removal and installation

1   Refer to Chapter 1 and drain about two quarts of coolant from the

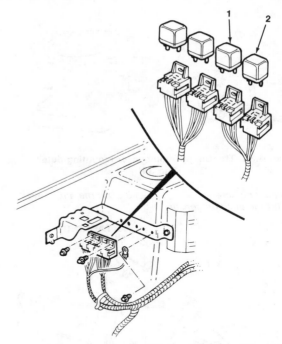

Fig. 4.37 TBI system fuel pump (1) and power (2) relay locations (Sec 43)

radiator (the engine must be cool when this is done).
2   Remove the wire harness connector from the coolant temperature sensor (the sensor is located on the end of the cylinder head, above the flywheel).
3   Unscrew the sensor, install the new one, tighten it securely and hook up the wire harness.
4   Refill the cooling system (Chapter 1), start the engine and check carefully for coolant leaks at the sensor.

43 Power and fuel pump relays (TBI) — replacement

1   Remove the power or fuel pump relay from the group of four relays attached to the right-hand suspension strut tower, then plug in the replacement relay.

44 Throttle body assembly (TBI) — removal and installation

Warning: *Gasoline is extremely flammable, so extra precautions must be taken when working on any part of the fuel system. Do not smoke or allow open flames or bare light bulbs near the work area. Also, do not work in a garage if a natural gas-type appliance with a pilot light is present.*
1   Remove the air cleaner assembly, then detach the throttle cable and return spring.
2   Disconnect the wire harness from the injector, the WOT switch and the ISC motor.
3   Using a flare nut wrench, detach the fuel supply and return lines from the throttle body.
4   Label the vacuum hoses to simplify installation, then remove them from the throttle body.
5   Remove the throttle body-to-manifold stud nuts, then separate the throttle body from the manifold. Discard the old gasket. If any gasket material remains on the manifold or throttle body, carefully remove it with a gasket scraper and lacquer thinner.
6   If a new throttle body assembly is being installed, transfer the ISC motor/WOT switch and bracket assembly to the new throttle body.
7   Lay a new gasket in place, then position the throttle body over the studs and seat it on the manifold. Install the nuts and tighten them evenly and securely (follow a criss-cross pattern).
8   The rest of the installation procedure is the reverse of removal.

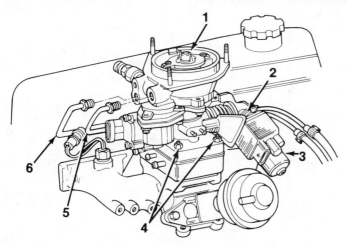

Fig. 4.38 Throttle body assembly removal details (Sec 44)

1 Injector	3 ISC motor	5 Fuel return line
2 WOT switch	4 Fuel supply line	6 Mounting nuts

45 Fuel body assembly (TBI) — removal and installation

1 Refer to Section 44 and remove the throttle body from the intake manifold.
2 Remove the three TORX-head screws and separate the fuel body from the throttle body. Remove and discard the original gasket.
3 Installation is the reverse of removal (use a new gasket and tighten the screws securely).

46 Exhaust system components — replacement

Caution: *Inspection and repair of exhaust system components should be done only after enough time has elapsed after driving the vehicle to allow the system components to cool completely. Also, when working under the vehicle, make sure it is securely supported on jackstands.*

1 The exhaust system consists of the exhaust manifold, muffler, catalytic converter, tailpipe and connecting pipes, brackets, hangers and clamps. The entire system is attached to the body with mounting brackets and rubber hangers. If any one of the parts is improperly installed, excessive noise and vibration will be transmitted to the body.
2 Regular inspections of the exhaust system should be made to keep it safe and quiet. Look for any damaged or bent parts, open seams, holes, loose connections, excessive corrosion and other defects that could allow exhaust fumes to seep into the vehicle. Deteriorated ex-

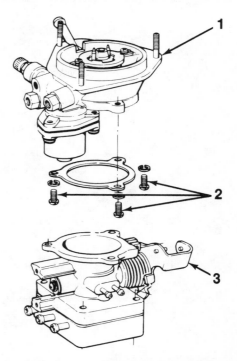

Fig. 4.39 Fuel body assembly removal details (Sec 45)

1 Fuel body	3 Throttle body
2 TORX-head screws	

haust system components should not be repaired; they should be replaced with new parts.
3 If the components are extremely corroded or rusted together, it may be a good idea to have the work performed by a reputable muffler shop, since welding equipment will probably be required to remove the components.
4 Always work from the back to the front when removing exhaust system components. Penetrating oil applied to mounting bolts and nuts will make them much easier to loosen. Always use new gaskets, hangers and clamps and apply anti-seize compound to mounting bolt threads when putting everything back together. Also, when replacing any exhaust system parts, be sure to allow enough clearance from all points on the underbody to avoid contact and possible overheating of the floor pan (which could damage the interior carpet and insulation).
5 When finished, start the engine and check for exhaust leaks and/or rattles caused by misalignment of components.

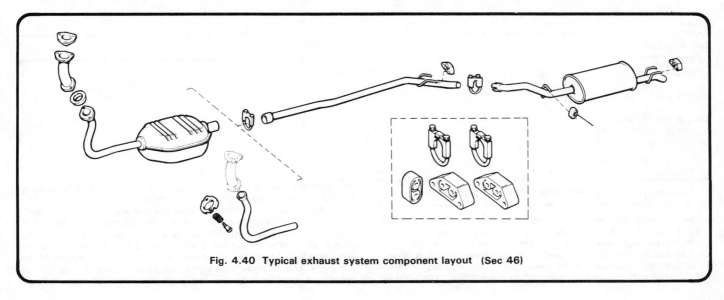

Fig. 4.40 Typical exhaust system component layout (Sec 46)

Chapter 5   Engine electrical systems

Refer to Chapter 13 for information on 1986 and later models

Contents

Specifications

Ignition timing . . . .   See Chapter 1

Spark plug type and gap . . . .   See Chapter 1

Torque specifications	Ft-lbs
Starter motor mounting bolts	32
Starter motor bracket bolt	16

---

1   Ignition system — general information and precautions

The electronic ignition system utilizes a computer module to perform the main functions normally assigned to the distributor.

The system consists of three main components: the computer module, which incorporates an ignition coil and a vacuum advance unit, the distributor, which directs the secondary system voltage received from the coil to the spark plugs, and a Top Dead Center (TDC) sensor, which determines the position and speed of the crankshaft by sensing special magnetic segments in the flywheel.

The computer module receives information related to crankshaft position and engine speed from the TDC sensor and engine load from the vacuum advance unit and MAP sensor (TBI system only). From these constantly changing variables, the computer calculates the precise instant at which the spark plugs should be fired and triggers the coil accordingly. The secondary system voltage passes from the coil to the distributor and then to the spark plug(s). The functions of the

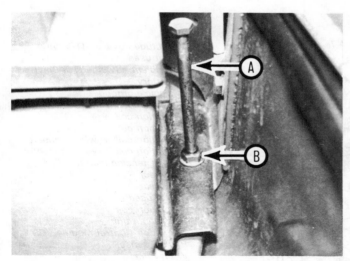

2.4   Battery hold-down clamp bolt (A) and locknut (B)

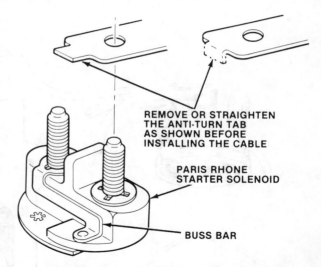

Fig. 5.1 When replacing the battery cables on vehicles equipped with a Paris Rhone starter, the anti-turn tab on the cable end must be bent up or removed to prevent contact with the buss bar on the solenoid (Sec 4)

mechanical and vacuum advance units, as well as the breaker points, normally associated with the distributor, are all handled by the computer (the sole purpose of the distributor is to direct the secondary system voltage from the coil to the spark plugs).

Due to the sophisticated nature of the ignition system, the following precautions must be observed to prevent damage to the system components and reduce the risk of personal injury:

  a) Make sure the switch is in the Off position before disconnecting any ignition system wires.
  b) Make sure the ignition switch is Off before connecting or disconnecting test equipment such as a timing light.
  c) Do not connect a suppression condenser or a test light to the ignition coil negative (−) terminal.
  d) Do not connect any test equipment requiring a 12 volt power supply to the ignition coil positive (+) terminal.
  e) Do not allow a spark plug lead to short out or spark against the computer module body.

2   Battery — removal and installation

1   The battery is located on the right-hand side of the engine compartment, adjacent to the firewall. It is held in place by a hold-down clamp near the bottom of the battery case.
2   Hydrogen gas is produced by the battery, so keep open flames and lighted cigarettes away from it at all times. Always keep the battery in an upright position. Spilled electrolyte should be rinsed off immediately with large quantities of water. Always wear eye protection when working around a battery.
3   Be sure to disconnect the negative (−) battery cable first, followed by the positive (+) cable.
4   After the cables are separated from the battery, loosen the locknut and unscrew the hold-down clamp bolt (photo).
5   Carefully lift the battery out of the engine compartment.
6   Installation is the reverse of removal. The cable clamps should be tight, but do not overtighten them as damage to the battery case could occur. The battery posts and cable ends should be cleaned prior to connection (see Chapter 1).
7   Always connect the positive cable first, then the negative cable (failure to do so could result in a short circuit if the wrench you are using to tighten the clamp bolt contacts the positive cable clamp and a metal part of the vehicle).

3   Battery — emergency jump starting

Refer to the *Booster battery (jump) starting* procedure at the front of this manual.

4   Battery cables — check and replacement

Note: *Alliance/Encore models built between sequence numbers W76499 and W76787 were equipped with a Paris Rhone starter motor. Due to the fact that these starters have a buss bar on the solenoid, the anti-turn tab on the battery cable used in production was modified to prevent contact with the buss bar. When replacing the cable on a vehicle with a Paris Rhone starter, remove or straighten the anti-turn tab as shown in the accompanying illustration before attaching the new cable to the solenoid terminal.*

1   Periodically check the entire length of each battery cable for damage, cracked or burned insulation and corrosion. Poor battery cable connections can cause starting problems and decreased engine performance.
2   Check the cable-to-terminal connections at the ends of the cables for cracks, loose wire strands and corrosion. The presence of white, fluffy deposits under the insulation at the cable terminal connection is a sign that the cable is corroded and should be replaced. Check the terminals for distortion, missing mounting bolts or nuts and corrosion.
3   If only the positive cable is to be replaced, be sure to disconnect the negative cable from the battery first.
4   Disconnect and remove the cable(s) from the vehicle. Make sure the replacement cables are the same length and diameter.
5   Clean the threads of the starter or ground connection with a wire brush to remove rust and corrosion. Apply a light coat of petroleum jelly to the threads to ease installation and prevent future corrosion. Inspect the connections frequently to make sure they are clean and tight.
6   Attach the cable(s) to the starter or ground connection and tighten the mounting nut(s) securely.
7   Before connecting the new cable(s) to the battery, make sure they reach the terminals without having to be stretched.
8   Connect the positive cable first, followed by the negative cable. Tighten the nuts and apply a thin coat of petroleum jelly to the terminal and cable connection.

5   Ignition system — check

Note: *Problems associated with the ignition system can usually be grouped into one of two areas: those caused by the secondary circuit (which includes the spark plugs, plug wires, distributor cap and rotor), and those caused by the primary circuit (which includes the computer module and related components and wires). Refer to Chapter 1 for the spark plug wire, distributor cap and rotor check. In the following procedures, the letters and numbers referred to indicate the terminals and*

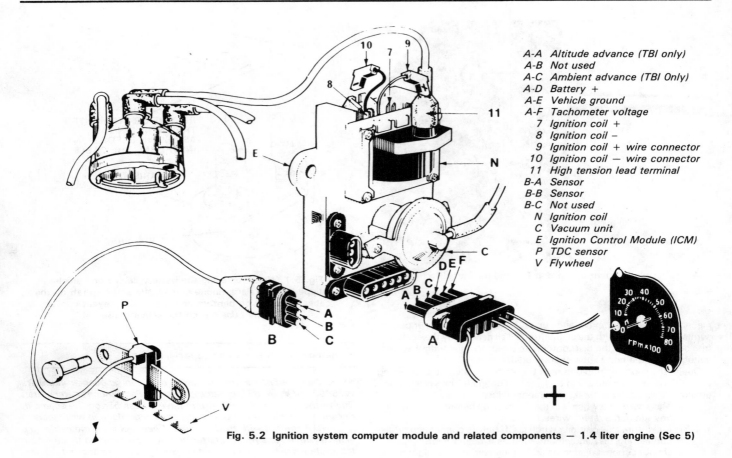

A-A Altitude advance (TBI only)
A-B Not used
A-C Ambient advance (TBI Only)
A-D Battery +
A-E Vehicle ground
A-F Tachometer voltage
7 Ignition coil +
8 Ignition coil –
9 Ignition coil + wire connector
10 Ignition coil – wire connector
11 High tension lead terminal
B-A Sensor
B-B Sensor
B-C Not used
N Ignition coil
C Vacuum unit
E Ignition Control Module (ICM)
P TDC sensor
V Flywheel

Fig. 5.2 Ignition system computer module and related components — 1.4 liter engine (Sec 5)

connectors shown in the accompanying illustration. A voltmeter, ohmmeter and 12 volt test light will be required for the checks.

Engine will not start (no secondary voltage)

All engines

1　With connector A (1.4 liter engine) or 1 (1.7 liter engine) unplugged, the ignition switch On and the starter motor engaged, check the module battery input voltage by connecting the voltmeter between terminals A-D (1.4 liter engine) or 1-A (1.7 liter engine) and a good ground. The voltage should be a minimum of 9.5 volts. If it isn't, check the battery condition and the wire between the battery and module.

2　Turn the ignition switch off, then attach the leads of an ohmmeter between terminal A-E (1.4 liter engine) or 1-B (1.7 liter engine) and a good ground. The meter should read zero (0) ohms. If not, check the module ground wire.

1.4 liter engine only

3　Check for continuity between ignition coil feed wire 9 and terminal A-D. The ohmmeter should read zero (0) ohms. If it doesn't, the module is probably defective and should be replaced with a new one.

4　Reattach connector A to the module, then turn the ignition switch on. Check the voltage at connector A (with the voltmeter leads on terminal A-D and a good ground). It should be a minimum of 9.5 volts. If it isn't, unplug and plug in connector A several times, then recheck the voltage. If it is still incorrect, replace connector A with a new one.

5　With connector B unplugged and the ignition switch off, check the TDC sensor resistance by connecting the ohmmeter leads to terminals B-A and B-B. The ohmmeter should read 150 ± 50 ohms if the engine is cold and 200 ± 75 ohms if the engine is hot. Replace the sensor with a new one if the resistance is not as specified.

6　Connect the ohmmeter leads to terminal B-B and the TDC sensor mounting bracket. The ohmmeter should indicate infinite resistance. If it doesn't, replace the sensor.

7　Connect the ohmmeter leads to terminal B-A and the mounting bracket. The result should be the same as in Step 6.

8　Check the distance between the sensor and the flywheel with a feeler gauge. It should be 0.039 ± 0.020-inch. If the clearance is cor-

rect, clean the sensor face; if it is incorrect, replace the sensor with a new one.

9　With connectors A and B plugged in and the starter motor engaged, connect a test light between wires 9 and 10 (after the wires have been disconnected from the terminals). The light should flash at starter motor speed. If it doesn't, the computer module is probably defective and should be replaced with a new one.

10　Turn the ignition switch off and unplug the high tension lead from the coil. Connect the ohmmeter leads between terminals 7 and 11 (the high tension lead terminal) and check the ignition coil secondary resistance. It should be 4000 ± 1500 ohms. **Note:** *If the resistance reading is infinite, make sure the ohmmeter leads are making good contact with the terminals.*

11　Disconnect wires 9 and 10 (if not already off) and check the coil primary resistance by attaching the ohmmeter leads to terminals 7 and 8. It should be 0.4 to 0.8 ohms. If the resistance readings are not as specified, replace the ignition coil with a new one. **Caution:** *Do not switch wires 9 and 10 when reattaching them to the terminals. The red wire (9) must be connected to the positive terminal (number 7) and the black wire (10) must be connected to the negative terminal (number 8).*

12　If there is still no secondary system voltage to fire the spark plugs after the above checks have been made, the computer module is probably defective and should be replaced with a new one. Since the module is an expensive component, it would be a very good idea to have the checks verified by a dealer service department before replacing the module.

1.7 liter engine only

13　With the ignition coil removed and the starter motor engaged, a test light attached to the coil terminals should flash at starter motor speed. If it doesn't, replace the module only after checking the output from ECU connector 2, terminal B.

14　If it does, check the ignition coil primary and secondary winding resistance (primary resistance should be 0.4 to 0.8 ohms; secondary resistance should be 4000 ± 1500 ohms). If it is not as specified, replace the ignition coil.

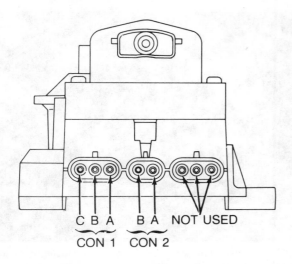

7.5   Disconnect the high tension lead (A), the vacuum hose (B), the wire harness connectors (C) and the mounting nuts (D) to replace the computer module

Connector 1
A - Ignition (+)
B - Ground (−)
C - Tachometer

Connector 2
A – Not Used
B – ECU, Ignition Coil
Interface (+)

Fig. 5.3 Ignition system computer module connector terminals — 1.7 liter engine (Sec 5)

15   If the resistance is correct, the module is probably defective and should be replaced with a new one. Since it is an expensive component, it would be a very good idea to have the checks verified by a dealer service department before replacing the module.

Engine hard to start but runs normally
16   Disconnect the coil wire from the distributor cap and hold the end about 3/4-inch from the engine block (do not hold the wire against the computer module). Operate the starter motor and watch for a continuous succession of bright, blue sparks between the wire end and the engine block. If sparks are noted, proceed to Step 2. If the sparks are not bright, blue and well-defined, refer to the checks at the beginning of this Section.

Engine will not start
17   Refer to Chapter 1 and check the ignition timing. If the timing is correct, check the fuel system and cylinder compression. If the timing is incorrect, the computer module is probably defective (see Step 12 above).

Engine starts but runs poorly
18   With the engine running at 3000 rpm, disconnect the hose from the vacuum unit on the computer module; the engine speed should decrease.
19   If the engine speed decreases, perform the checks under *Engine hard to start but runs normally*. If the speed does not decrease, check the vacuum hose for leaks and correct installation
(replace it with a new one if necessary). If the hose is in good condition and hooked up properly, the computer module is probably defective (see Step 12 above).

---

6   Distributor — removal and installation

1.4 liter engine
1   Remove the screws and detach the cap and spark plug wires from the distributor (fasten them out of the way with a length of string or wire).
2   Release the wire harness from the clip at the base of the distributor.
3   Make a mark on the distributor body directly in line with the rotor end, then remove the bolt and lift up on the distributor to remove it from the engine (be sure to recover the seal).

4   Do not turn the crankshaft with the distributor removed or the ignition timing may be changed.
5   When installing the distributor, line up the rotor with the mark and engage the dog at the bottom of the shaft with the drive shaft in the block. Align the hole and install the bolt, then reinstall the cap and route the wire harness through the clip.

1.7 liter engine
6   The 1.7 liter engine does not have a distributor, as such, but instead the rotor is bonded to the end of the camshaft and the distributor cap is installed over it and secured to the cylinder head.
7   To remove the cap, loosen and remove the screws, then pull it off and position it to one side.
8   If the rotor must be removed, break it off with a pliers.
9   When installing a new rotor it must be bonded to the shaft.

---

7   Ignition module — removal and installation

1   Disconnect the negative cable from the battery.
2   Remove the high tension lead from the coil on the front of the module.
3   Detach the hose from the vacuum unit on the module and release it from the clip.
4   Unplug the two wire harness connectors from the front of the module.
5   Remove the mounting nuts and separate the module from the firewall (photo).
6   Installation is the reverse of removal.

---

8   Ignition coil — removal and installation

1   The ignition coil is not an integral part of the computer module and can be replaced separately if it is defective.
2   To separate the coil from the module, detach the wires and remove the four mounting screws. Installation is the reverse of removal.

---

9   Top Dead Center (TDC) sensor — removal and installation

1   Disconnect the cable from the negative battery terminal.
2   Detach the smaller of the two wire harness connectors from the computer module.
3   Remove the two sensor mounting bolts and separate it from the bellhousing.

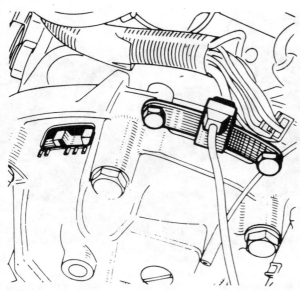

Fig. 5.4 The TDC sensor is attached to the bellhousing with two shouldered bolts (Sec 9)

4   Installation is the reverse of removal. Note that the mounting bolts have a shoulder machined into them — they must not be replaced with ordinary bolts.

10 Charging system — general information and precautions

The charging system consists of the alternator, voltage regulator, battery and connecting wires. These components work together to supply electrical power for the ignition system, lights, power accessories, etc.

The alternator is driven by a belt from the pulley at the front of the crankshaft. When the engine is running, voltage is generated by the internal components of the alternator and routed to the battery for storage.

The purpose of the regulator (which is an integral part of the alternator) is to limit the alternator output to a pre-set value. This prevents voltage surges, circuit overloads, etc., during peak voltage output.

The charging system does not ordinarily require periodic maintenance. The drivebelt, electrical connectors and wire harnesses should, however, be inspected at the intervals recommended in Chapter 1.

Note the following precautions when working on the charging system:

a)   Always label wires before detaching them from the alternator. This will enable you to hook them up correctly later.

b)   Before using electric arc welding equipment to repair any part of the vehicle, disconnect the wires from the alternator and battery.

c)   Always disconnect both battery cables before hooking up a battery charger and never start the engine with a battery charger connected to the battery posts.

11 Charging system — check

1   If a malfunction occurs in the charging system, do not immediately assume that the alternator is causing the problem. **Note:** *If the charging system warning light does not come on when the ignition switch is turned on, check the voltage regulator wire connector to make sure it is securely attached. Try to determine if the warning light bulb is blown by grounding the 1/4-inch terminal on the connector (if the bulb is good, it should light when the terminal is grounded). Check the following items as well:*

a)   The battery cables where they attach to the battery (make sure the connections are clean and tight

12.2   Label the wires and terminals before removing the wires from the alternator

12.4   Alternator mounting bolt (A) and nut (B)

b)   The battery state-of-charge
c)   Alternator wire connections (they must be clean and tight)
d)   Drivebelt condition and tension (see Chapter 1)
e)   Alternator mounting bolt tightness
f)   Abnormal alternator noise 2   Using a voltmeter, check the battery voltage with the engine off. It should be approximately 12 volts.

3   Start the engine and increase the speed until the voltmeter reading stops increasing (it should stabilize at 13.5-to-15 volts). If it does not rise when the engine is started or if it exceeds 15 volts, the alternator or regulator is defective.

4   Turn on all electrical accessories and note the voltage reading (the regulated voltage should remain steady between 13.5 and 15 volts).

5   If the voltmeter indicates battery voltage or a reading greater than 15 volts, the alternator is probably faulty and should be replaced with a new one (since the alternator is an expensive component, it would be a good idea to have the test results verified by a dealer service department or reputable repair shop before buying a new one).

12 Alternator — removal and installation

1   Disconnect the negative battery cable from the battery.
2   Label the wires and terminals at the rear of the alternator, then disconnect the wires (photo).

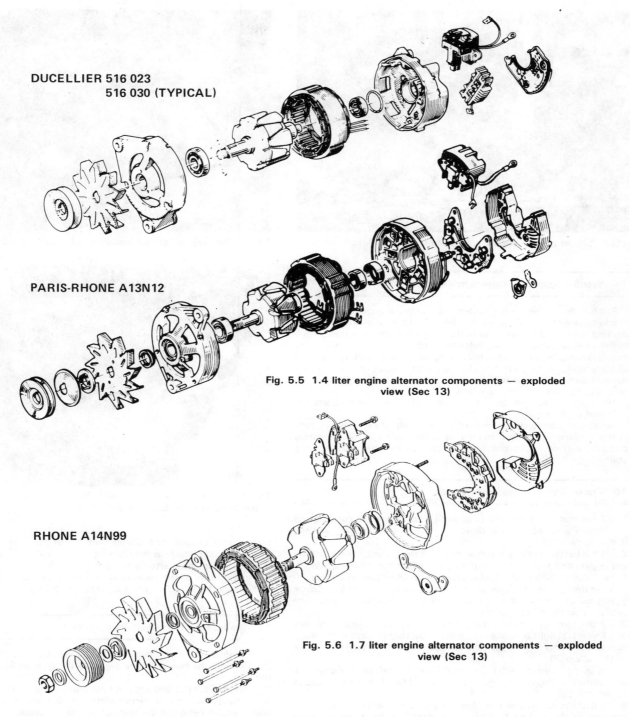

DUCELLIER 516 023
516 030 (TYPICAL)

PARIS-RHONE A13N12

Fig. 5.5 1.4 liter engine alternator components — exploded
view (Sec 13)

RHONE A14N99

Fig. 5.6 1.7 liter engine alternator components — exploded
view (Sec 13)

3 Loosen the drivebelt tensioner bolt (on vehicles equipped with power steering, loosen the idler pulley bolt and the mounting bolt nut, then pivot the alternator toward the engine and slip off the drivebelt.

4 Remove the tensioner and mounting bolts (photo) and separate the alternator from the engine.

5 Installation is the reverse of removal. Be sure to adjust the drivebelt tension as described in Chapter 1.

13 Alternator brushes — replacement

1 The brushes can be replaced without removing the alternator from the vehicle. Disconnect the negative cable from the battery.

2 Label the wires and terminals at the rear of the alternator, then detach the wires.

3 Remove the small bolts or nuts and detach the regulator/brush holder assembly from the rear of the alternator.

4 Note how they are installed, then disconnect the wires from the regulator/brush holder assembly.

5 Make sure that the brushes are not worn down to the holder and see if they move freely (clean them with contact cleaner if they stick in the holder). Both brushes should have the same spring tension. If in doubt as to the condition and serviceability of the brushes, compare them to new ones at a dealer parts department.

6 Clean the slip rings in the alternator and check for wear and damage. If damage is evident, the alternator should be serviced or replaced.

7 Installation is the reverse of removal.

16.3   Starter motor support bracket-to-engine block bolt (arrow)

16.4a   Remove the starter motor-to-bellhousing bolts (arrows) . . .

14   Starting system — general information

The function of the starting system is to crank the engine. The system is composed of the starter motor, solenoid, ignition switch and connecting wires and cables. The battery supplies the electrical energy to the solenoid, which then actuates the starter motor. The actual motor circuit is composed of thick cables designed to carry the large amount of current required by the starter. The control circuit (which includes the ignition switch) is made up of small diameter wires, since the current requirements are considerably less.

The starter motor and solenoid are mounted together at the transmission end of the engine.

Never operate the starter motor for more than 30 seconds at a time without pausing to allow it to cool for at least one minute. Excessive cranking can cause overheating, which can seriously damage the starter.

15   Starter motor — testing in vehicle

1   If the starter motor fails to operate, first check the condition of the battery and cable connections (switch on the headlights and see if they glow brightly).
2   If the battery is not the problem, check the ground connection on the engine and the buss bar and cable connections on the solenoid.
Note: *Some vehicles have fasteners at the solenoid battery cable connection that promote corrosion and subsequent hard starting. Check with your dealer to obtain the new fasteners and repair procedure published in the related service bulletin.*
3   If the terminal connections are tight and clean, use a voltmeter or 12 volt test light to make sure there is battery voltage at the main solenoid terminal (where the positive cable from the battery attaches to the solenoid).
4   With the ignition switch on and the key in position D, make sure that battery voltage is present at the solenoid terminal with the spade connector and at the main starter terminal.
5   If there is no voltage reaching the spade connector, suspect the wires or ignition switch. If voltage is present, but the starter does not operate, then suspect the solenoid or starter motor.
6   Since the starter is an expensive component, it would be a very good idea to have the test results verified by a dealer service department or reputable repair shop before replacing it.

16   Starter motor — removal and installation

1   Disconnect the negative battery cable from the battery.
2   Disconnect the cable and wire from the solenoid.
3   Remove the bolt that secures the motor support bracket to the rear of the engine block (photo).
4   Remove the three bolts that attach the motor to the bellhousing

16.4b   . . . and separate the motor from the block (note the arrow indicating the locating dowel)

(photo) and separate the starter from the engine. Note the position of the locating dowel in the upper bolt hole and make sure that it is in place when the starter is reinstalled (photo).
5   Installation is the reverse of removal. Be sure to tighten the bellhousing bolts before the support bracket bolt.

17   Starter motor brushes — replacement

1   Remove the starter motor from the vehicle (Section 16).
2   Remove the two nuts and separate the bracket from the rear of the motor.
3   Remove the nut and separate the lead from the solenoid terminal.
4   If equipped, remove the cap plate from the rear cover and the bolt and washers between the rear cover and armature.
5   Tap the engagement lever pivot pin out of the drive end housing.
6   Remove the nuts that attch the solenoid to the drive end housing.
7   Remove the through-bolts and withdraw the yoke, armature, solenoid and engagement lever from the drive end housing.
8   Remove the solenoid and engagement lever and the rear cover and brushes, then slide the armature out of the yoke.
9   Slip the brushes out of the holders to release the rear cover.
10   Make sure that the brushes protrude from the holders an equal amount and that all springs provide the same moderate tension. See if the brushes move freely in the holders (clean them with contact cleaner if they stick). If in doubt about the brush length or condition, compare them to new ones at a dealer parts department.
11   Note that new field brushes must be soldered to the leads.
12   Reassemble the motor by reversing the disassembly procedure.

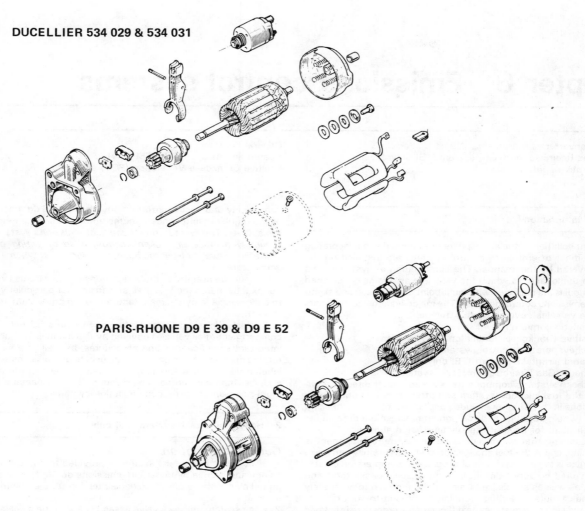

DUCELLIER 534 029 & 534 031

PARIS-RHONE D9 E 39 & D9 E 52

Fig. 5.7 1.4 liter engine starter motor components — exploded view (Sec 17)

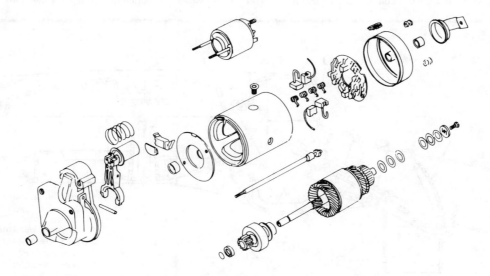

Fig. 5.8 1.7 liter engine starter motor components — exploded view (Sec 17)

Chapter 6   Emissions control systems

Contents

1 General information

To prevent pollution of the atmosphere from burned and evaporating gases, a number of emissions control systems are installed on the vehicles covered by this manual. The combination of systems used depends on the locality to which the vehicle was originally delivered (California models are equipped with multi-point fuel injection and slightly different emissions control devices). The major systems/components used on the vehicles covered by this manual are:

 a) Catalytic converter
 b) Positive Crankcase Ventilation (PCV) system
 c) Fuel evaporative control system
 d) Heated air intake system (TBI only)
 e) Exhaust Gas Recirculation (EGR) system

Each of these systems/components is linked, either directly or indirectly, to the fuel injection system and often affect its operation.

The Sections in this Chapter include general descriptions, checking procedures (where possible) and component replacement procedures (where applicable) for each of the systems listed above.

Before assuming that an emissions control system/component is malfunctioning, check the fuel and ignition systems carefully and make sure the engine is in good mechanical condition (a compression or leak-down test would be very helpful). In some cases, special tools and equipment, as well as specialized training, are required to accurately diagnose the cause(s) of a rough running or difficult-to-start engine. If checking and servicing become too difficult or if a procedure is beyond the scope of the home mechanic, consult your dealer service department. This does not necessarily mean, however, that the emissions control systems are all particularly difficult to maintain and repair. You can quickly and easily perform many checks and do most (if not all) of the regular maintenance at home with common tune-up and hand tools. **Note:** *The most frequent cause of emissions system problems is simply a loose or broken vacuum hose or wiring connection. Therefore, always check the hoses and wires first when a problem is encountered.*

It should be noted that the illustrations of the various systems may not exactly match the system installed on your particular vehicle, due to changes made by the manufacturer during production or from year-to-year.

A vehicle Emissions Control Information label is located in the engine compartment of all vehicles covered by this manual. The label contains important specifications and procedures, as well as a vacuum hose routing diagram. When servicing the engine or emissions systems, the label in your vehicle should be checked for pertinent information.

Unless otherwise noted, the procedures in this Chapter apply to both multi-point and throttle body injection systems.

2 Heated air intake system (TBI only)

General description

1   The heated air intake system is provided to improve engine efficiency and reduce hydrocarbon emissions during the initial warm-up period by maintaining a controlled air temperature at the throttle body assembly.

2   The system utilizes a valve assembly inside the air cleaner snorkel to control the ratio of cold and warm air directed into the throttle body. The valve is controlled by a wax thermostat mounted upstream from the valve and connected to it by a mechanical linkage.

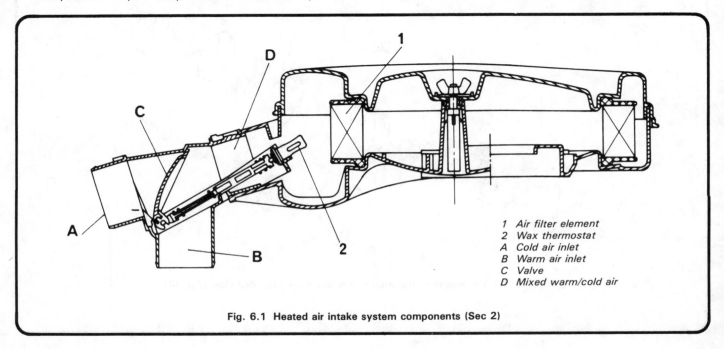

1 Air filter element
2 Wax thermostat
A Cold air inlet
B Warm air inlet
C Valve
D Mixed warm/cold air

Fig. 6.1 Heated air intake system components (Sec 2)

3   At temperatures below 79 °F, the wax thermostat causes the valve to block off the air cleaner snorkel and opens the warm air inlet to allow air heated by the exhaust manifold to enter the air cleaner assembly. As the temperature increases under the hood, the wax thermostat gradually opens the valve and allows cooler air to enter through the air cleaner snorkel and mix with the warm air. At temperatures above 97 °F, the thermostat has expanded enough to virtually close off the warm air duct.

4   Because of this cold-engine-only function, it is important to check the operation of the system periodically to prevent poor engine performance.

Checking

5   To check the operation of the valve, remove the flexible duct from the end of the air cleaner snorkel (cold air inlet). With the engine cold and the air temperature less than 79 °F, look into the cold air inlet and see if the valve is at least partially closing off the passage (a mirror may be helpful for this check). Depending on the actual air temperature, the valve may be in one of many positions.

6   Start the engine and allow it to warm up. As the engine temperature increases, watch the valve to see if it moves down to close off the warm air inlet. If it does not move, the linkage may be stuck or the wax thermostat may be defective.

Component replacement

7   If the valve does not operate as it should and the linkage is not sticking, the wax thermostat is probably faulty and should be replaced with a new one. Check with your dealer concerning the availability of parts.

3   Fuel evaporative control system

General description

1   This system is designed to trap and store fuel that evaporates from the gas tank (the vapor would normally enter the atmosphere as hydrocarbon emissions). The fuel vapors enter a special canister and are then routed to the intake tract when the engine is started.

2   The system consists of a charcoal-filled canister (located in the engine compartment), a pressure/vent gas tank filler cap, a one-way rollover valve in the gas tank and connecting lines and hoses. The lines include a vent line between the tank and canister and a purge line between the intake tract and canister as well as vacuum lines to operate the valve in the canister when the engine is running. An electrically-operated solenoid valve controls the vacuum to the canister.

3   The presence of a strong fuel odor indicates that the system is not working properly.

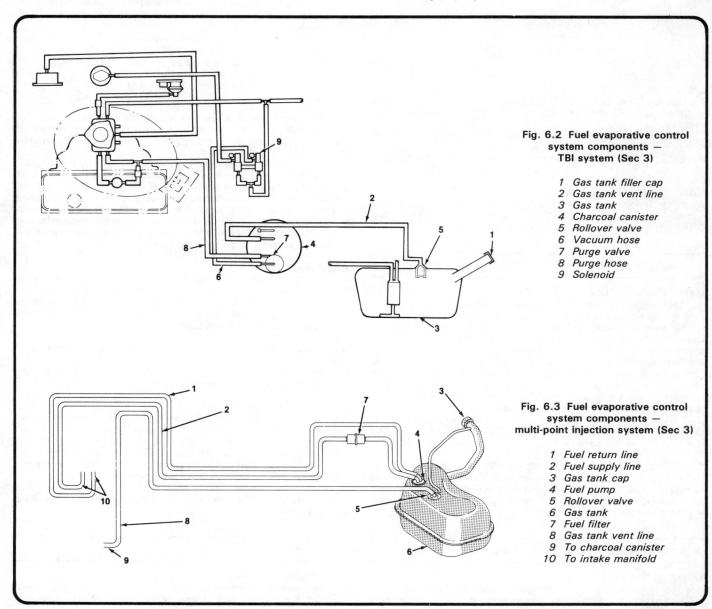

Fig. 6.2 Fuel evaporative control
system components —
TBI system (Sec 3)

1   Gas tank filler cap
2   Gas tank vent line
3   Gas tank
4   Charcoal canister
5   Rollover valve
6   Vacuum hose
7   Purge valve
8   Purge hose
9   Solenoid

Fig. 6.3 Fuel evaporative control
system components —
multi-point injection system (Sec 3)

1   Fuel return line
2   Fuel supply line
3   Gas tank cap
4   Fuel pump
5   Rollover valve
6   Gas tank
7   Fuel filter
8   Gas tank vent line
9   To charcoal canister
10   To intake manifold

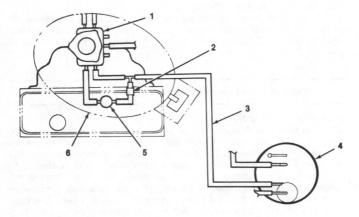

Fig. 6.4 Positive Crankcase Ventilation (PCV) system components — TBI system (Sec 4)

1 *Throttle body assembly*
2 *Orifice*
3 *PCV hose-to-charcoal canister*
4 *Charcoal canister*
5 *PCV outlet*
6 *Air cleaner housing*

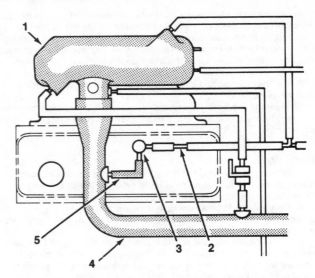

Fig. 6.5 Positive Crankcase Ventilation (PCV) system components — multi-point injection system (Sec 4)

1 *Air intake chamber*
2 *Orifice (0.051-inch)*
3 *PCV outlet*
4 *Air intake duct*
5 *Orifice (0.256-inch)*

Checking

4   Check all lines and hoses in the system for cracks, kinks, leaks and damage along their entire length. Repair or replace them as necessary.
5   Check the gasket in the gas tank cap. If it is dried out, cracked or otherwise damaged, replace it with a new one.
6   Because of the interrelationship of this system with the fuel system, further checks must be done by a dealer service department.

Component replacement

7   When replacing lines and hoses in the system, make sure the replacement is an exact duplicate of the original. The lines are often color-coded to denote the particular use.

4   Positive Crankcase Ventilation (PCV) system

General description

1   This system is designed to reduce hydrocarbon emissions by routing blow-by gases (fuel/air mixture and combustion gases that escape from the combustion chamber past the piston rings into the crankcase) from the crankcase to the intake manifold and combustion chamber where they are burned during engine operation.
2   The system is very simple and consists of rubber hoses and one or two small, fixed orifices, depending on the type of fuel injection system installed on the engine. On multi-point injection systems, one is located in the hose coming from the intake chamber and the other is located in the hose between the PCV outlet and the air intake duct. On TBI systems only one orifice is used (it is located in the hose attached between the PCV outlet and the T-fitting in the hose coming from the fuel evaporative canister).

Checking and component replacement

3   Maintenance of this system consists of checking the hoses and fittings for cracks, kinks and other damage and making sure the orifices are not clogged. Be very careful not to enlarge the orifices when cleaning them (do not use a metal tool).

5   Exhaust Gas Recirculation (EGR) system (TBI only)

General description

1   The EGR system meters exhaust gases into the intake tract, through passages cast into the intake and exhaust manifolds, to lower

the combustion temperatures and reduce the amount of oxides of nitrogen (NOX) formed. The main component of the system is the EGR valve, which is attached to the intake manifold beneath the throttle body assembly.
2   The amount of exhaust gas admitted is controlled by the vacuum-operated EGR valve, based on engine operating conditions (no EGR is present at idle and under certain other operating conditions). The vacuum to the EGR valve is controlled by a solenoid that is opened and closed by an electrical signal from the ECU.
3   Common engine problems associated with the EGR system include rough idle or stalling at idle, rough operation during light throttle application and stalling during deceleration.

Checking

4   To check the EGR valve operation, reach behind the valve housing and push in on the diaphragm with the engine idling (if the engine is warm, wear a glove to prevent burns). The engine should begin to run very rough or stall. If it doesn't, the valve or passages are clogged (the EGR passages can be cleaned out, but the valve will have to be replaced).
5   Check the hoses for cracks, kinks and damage. Replace them if necessary.
6   Since the EGR solenoid is controlled by the ECU, further checks must be done by a dealer service department.

Component replacement

7   To replace the EGR valve, disconnect the vacuum hose and remove the two mounting bolts. Separate the valve from the manifold and remove the gasket (you may have to scrape the gasket off the manifold — if so, be careful not to nick or gouge the mating surface).
8   Clean out the EGR passages in the manifold and make sure the mating surfaces on the new valve and manifold are clean.
9   Position a new gasket on the manifold, then attach the new valve with the mounting bolts (tighten them evenly and securely). Hook up the vacuum hose.

6   Catalytic converter

General description

1   The catalytic converter is designed to reduce hydrocarbon (HC) and carbon monoxide (CO) pollutants in the exhaust. The converter

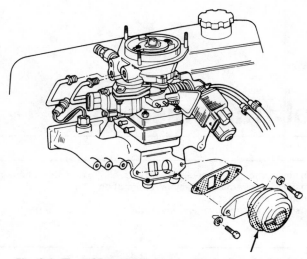

Fig. 6.6 The EGR valve (arrow) is attached to the intake manifold with two bolts (Sec 5)

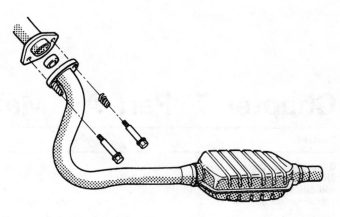

Fig. 6.7 Typical catalytic converter (note the shouldered bolts and springs used to attach the front exhaust pipe to the manifold) (Sec 6)

oxidizes these components and converts them to water and carbon dioxide.

2   The converter is located in the exhaust system and closely resembles a muffler.

3   **Note:** *If large amounts of unburned gasoline enter the catalyst, it may overheat and cause a fire. Always observe the following precautions:*

Use only unleaded gasoline
Avoid prolonged idling
Do not prolong engine compression checks
Do not run the engine with a nearly empty fuel tank
Avoid coasting with the ignition turned Off
Do not dispose of a used catalytic converter along with oily or gasoline soaked parts

Checking

4   The catalytic converter requires little if any maintenance and servicing at regular intervals. However, the system should be inspected whenever the vehicle is raised on a lift or if the exhaust system is checked or serviced.

5   Check all connections in the exhaust pipe assembly for looseness or damage. Also check all the clamps for damage, cracks, or missing fasteners. Check the rubber hangers for cracks.

6   The converter itself should be checked for damage or dents (maximum 3/4 inch deep) which could affect its performance and/or be hazardous to your health. At the same time the converter is inspected, check the metal protector plate under it as well as the heat insulator above it for damage and loose fasteners.

Component replacement

7   Do not attempt to remove the catalytic converter until the complete exhaust system is cool. Raise the vehicle and support it securely on jackstands. Apply some penetrating oil to the clamp bolts and allow it to soak in.

8   Remove the bolts and the hangers, then separate the converter from the exhaust pipes. Remove the old gaskets if they are stuck to the pipes.

9   Installation of the converter is the reverse of removal. Use new exhaust pipe gaskets and tighten the clamp bolts to the specified torque. Replace the rubber hangers with new ones if the originals are deteriorated. Start the engine and check carefully for exhaust leaks.

Chapter 7 Part A   Manual transmission

Contents

Specifications

Model

4-speed	. . . .	JB0
5-speed	. . . .	JB1

Oil type and capacity	. . . .	See Chapter 1

Torque specifications	**Ft-lbs**
Transmission mount nuts/bolts	33
Bellhousing-to-engine nuts/bolts	31
Transmission case-to-clutch	18
Differential housing	18
5th gear-to-input shaft nut	100
5th gear-to-mainshaft bolt	
8 mm	15
10 mm	59

1   General information

The transmission is equipped with either four forward and one reverse gear or five forward and one reverse gear, depending on the model. Gear shifting is handled by a floor mounted lever connected by a remote control housing and linkage rod to the transmission fork contact shaft.

The final drive (differential) unit is an integral part of the main transmission and is located between the mechanism case and the clutch and differential housing. The transmission and differential share the same lubricating oil.

If transmission overhaul is necessary, it would be a good idea to check on availability of rebuilt or used units before buying new parts for your transmission. In most cases, a lot of time and money can be saved by replacing the transmission rather than overhauling it.

2   Shift lever and linkage — removal, installation and adjustment

1   Raise the front of the vehicle and support it securely on jackstands.
2   Working under the vehicle, unhook the spring between the shift linkage rod and the floor pan stud (photo).
3   Loosen the clamp bolt at the shift lever end of the shift linkage rod, then separate the shift lever from the rod.
4   Refer to Chapter 11 and remove the console.
5   Remove the four bolts and separate the remote control assembly and gasket from the floor pan.
6   If necessary, the gearshift lever assembly can be disassembled by referring to the accompanying illustration. Note that the shift knob is glued to the lever and should not be removed.
7   Reassembly and installation are the reverse of removal and disassembly. Be sure to adjust the linkage as described below.

8   Shift the transmission into second gear and make sure the lever on the transmission does not move during the adjustment procedure.
9   Loosen the shift linkage rod clamp bolt, then remove the shift lever rubber boot.
10   Move the shift lever toward the passenger side of the vehicle and insert a 0.0197-inch feeler gauge between the reverse stop release holder and the shift lever housing.
11   Move the shift lever back toward the driver's side of the vehicle until the feeler gauge is held securely in place. Working under the vehicle, tighten the shift linkage rod clamp bolt to 20 ft-lbs. **Note:** *The clamp must be correctly positioned to prevent loosening and loss of*

2.2   Shift linkage rod spring location

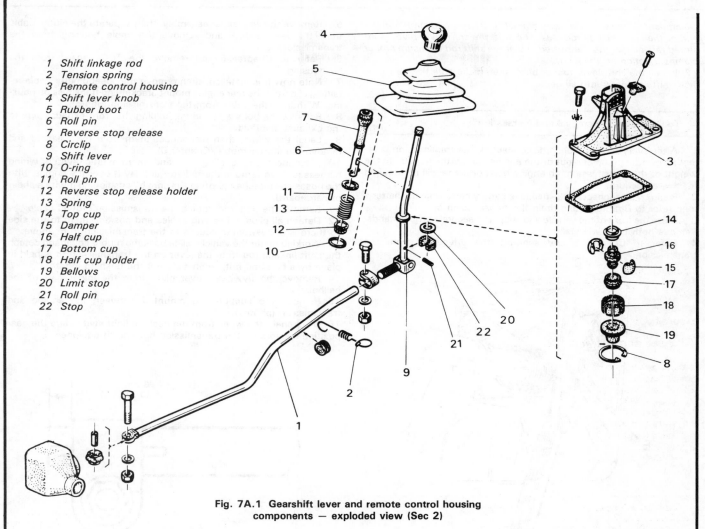

1 Shift linkage rod
2 Tension spring
3 Remote control housing
4 Shift lever knob
5 Rubber boot
6 Roll pin
7 Reverse stop release
8 Circlip
9 Shift lever
10 O-ring
11 Roll pin
12 Reverse stop release holder
13 Spring
14 Top cup
15 Damper
16 Half cup
17 Bottom cup
18 Half cup holder
19 Bellows
20 Limit stop
21 Roll pin
22 Stop

Fig. 7A.1 Gearshift lever and remote control housing
components — exploded view (Sec 2)

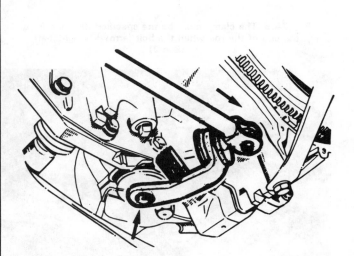

Fig. 7A.2 Move the linkage rod as shown to engage 2nd
gear in the transmission (Sec 2)

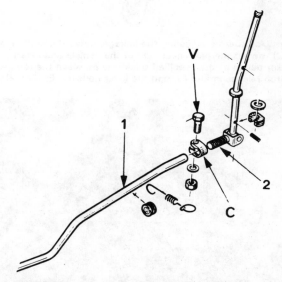

Fig. 7A.3 Linkage adjustment component locations (Sec 2)

1 Shift linkage rod   C Clamp
2 Shift lever pivot   V Clamp bolt/nut

adjustment. Make sure it is approximately 0.313-inch (8 mm) from the end of the shift linkage rod. Also, be sure the shift lever pivot is inserted far enough into the slotted end of the shift rod to ensure proper clamping action on the pivot.
12 Install the shift lever rubber boot, then make sure the transmission shifts properly into all gears.

3 Transmission — removal and installation

1   After everything has been disconnected, the transmission is removed by lifting it up and out of the engine compartment. Due to the weight of the transmission, an engine hoist or crane will be required for this procedure.
2   Begin by disconnecting the negative battery cable from the battery, then refer to Chapter 1 and drain the transmission oil.
3   Raise the front of the vehicle and support it securely on jackstands. Remove both front wheels.
4   Refer to Chapter 8 and separate the driveaxles from the transmission.

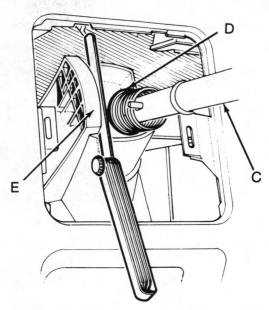

Fig. 7A.4 Before adjusting the linkage, move the shift lever (C) toward the passenger side of the vehicle and insert a feeler gauge of the specified thickness between the reverse stop release holder (D) and the lever housing (E) (Sec 2)

5   Remove the air cleaner assembly, then separate the clutch cable from the release fork and remove the cable housing from the transmission.
6   Refer to Chapter 5 and remove the TDC sensor from the bellhousing.
7   Note how it is installed, then remove the speedometer cable retaining clip from the rear engine mount bracket and transmission housing. Withdraw the cable from the transmission (photo).
8   Remove the bolts and springs holding the front exhaust pipe to the exhaust manifold.
9   Label the wires, then disconnect them from the solenoid and remove the starter motor (Chapter 5).
10 Disconnect the cooling fan and thermostatic switch wiring harnesses, then remove the radiator and lay it over the engine with the hoses still attached (protect the core by cushioning it with a sheet of cardboard).
11 Remove the bolt and detach the transmission ground cable.
12 Detach all clips, wires and cables and position them to the side so there is unobstructed access to the transmission from above.
13 Working under the vehicle, slide back the rubber cover and detach the shift linkage rod from the lever on the transmission (it is held in place by a bolt and nut), then slide out the bushing (photos).
14 Remove the flywheel cover plate from the lower part of the bellhousing.
15 Remove the support rod mounted between the engine and transmission (photos).
16 Disconnect the wires from the back-up light switch and the gear position sensors on the transmission housing (if equipped).

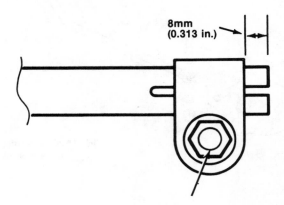

Fig. 7A.5 The clamp must be the specified distance from the end of the rod when the bolt (arrow) is tightened (Sec 2)

3.7   Speedometer cable and retaining clip locations

3.13a   Slide back the linkage rod rubber cover and . . .

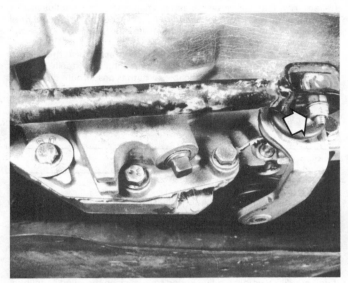

3.13b   . . . remove the nut and bolt (arrow), . . .

3.13c   . . . then slide off the rod and remove the bushing (arrow)

3.15a   The support rod is attached to the engine with a bolt and spacer . . .

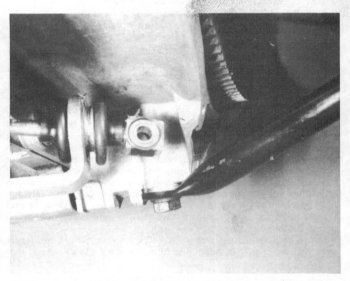

3.15b   . . . and to the transmission with a bolt

3.20a   Transmission front mounting bracket-to-mount bolts

3.20b   Transmission rear mounting bracket stud

17 Position a jack under the engine oil pan to support the engine (place a block of wood between the jack head and the oil pan). Attach the engine hoist to the transmission with chains or cables (depending on the type of hoist used, it may be a good idea to remove the hood).
18 Raise the jack and hoist just enough to take up the weight of the engine and transmission.
19 Remove the engine-to-transmission bolts, then loosen the nuts on the two studs. Thread an additional nut onto each of the studs and hold the inner nut while tightening the outer nut against it. Back the studs out by turning the inner nut with a wrench.
20 Remove the front transmission bracket-to-mount bolts and the rear bracket-to-mount nut (photos).
21 Raise the engine and transmission slightly to clear the mounts, then remove the front bracket (the front engine mounts may have to be loosened as well).
22 Lower the engine and transmission as necessary, then separate the transmission from the engine by moving it sideways and under the left-hand chassis member. When the transmission has cleared the clutch and flywheel, turn it clockwise slightly so the differential will clear the rear of the engine, then raise the hoist. Move the transmission as required to clear the other components, then lift it up and over the front of the vehicle or the fender and lower it carefully to the floor.
23 Installation is basically the reverse of removal, but note the following:
   a) Install the two studs before the remaining engine-to-transmission mounting bolts.
   b) Install the driveaxles as described in Chapter 8.
   c) Be sure to refill the transmission with oil (Chapter 1).

4 Transmission overhaul — general information

Complete disassembly and overhaul of the transmission, especially when it comes to the differential and the bearings in the clutch and differential housing, requires several special tools. For this reason, it is recommended that the home mechanic not attempt a transmission overhaul unless the tools are available and he feels reasonably confident that he can do it after reading through the entire procedure.
Before starting any repair work, clean the outside of the transmission with solvent or a degreaser. Do not use gasoline! Dry it with clean rags or compressed air. Make sure that a clean work area is available and obtain some small containers and trays to store parts. Label everything as it is removed.
Before beginning reassembly, make sure everything is spotlessly clean and use plenty of gear oil to lubricate the parts as they are in-stalled. Always use new roll pins, snap-rings and circlips during reassembly. **Note:** *When installing roll pins, the seam in the pin must always be in line with the centerline of the shaft, not facing one side or the other.*

Other than the additional gear and slight differences in the selector mechanism, the four and five-speed transmissions are virtually identical. The overhaul procedure is applicable to both types (where differences arise, they are noted in the text).

5 Transmission — overhaul

Separating the housings
1 Begin by removing the clutch release bearing and fork (see Chapter 8 if necessary).
2 Remove the rear transmission mounting bracket from the housing.
3 Remove the O-ring from the differential stub shaft (photo).
4 Remove the bolts and separate the mechanism case rear cover from the transmission (photo). Remove the rubber gasket as well.
5 If you are disassembling a four-speed transmission, go to Step 13. If you are disassembling a five-speed transmission, proceed as follows:
6 Support the 5th gear selector shaft with a block of wood between the shaft and gears, then drive out the shift fork roll pin with a hammer and punch.
7 Engage 1st gear by moving the linkage and engage 5th gear by moving the shift fork. With the gears locked, remove the large nut from the end of the input shaft (it holds 5th gear to the shaft).
8 Return the gears to neutral.
9 Remove the 5th speed driven gear, the synchronizer and the shift fork as an assembly with a puller (slide strips of metal under the gear, then engage the puller under the metal strips).
10 Slide the needle bearing, bushing and washer off the input shaft.
11 Where used, remove the bolt and detach the washer and collar over the 5th speed driving gear on the mainshaft.
12 Remove the circlip and dished washer, then pull the gear as described in Step 9.
13 Remove the circlip and dished washer from the end of the input shaft and mainshaft (photos).
14 Lift out the reverse shaft detent retaining plate, then remove the spring and ball (photos). If the ball won't come out, leave it in place but don't forget to remove it after the housings have been separated.
15 Unscrew the limit stop threaded plug (four-speed) (photo) or the detent assembly (five-speed).
16 Remove the back-up light switch (photo).

5.3 Remove the O-ring from the differential stub shaft   5.4 Remove the bolts and separate the cover from the case

17 Loosen and remove the bolts attaching the mechanism case to the clutch and differential housing (note that they are different lengths).
18 Pull the fork control shaft on the side of the transmission out as far as it will go and then lift the mechanism case (with the 5th gear selector shaft on five-speed units) up and off the gears and housing. It may be necessary to tap the input shaft down with a soft-faced hammer to free the case and bearings from the shaft. As soon as the case is free, insert two bolts or rods into the selector shaft holes and push them down firmly. They will retain the detent balls and spring and keep them from flying out as the case is lifted off (photo).

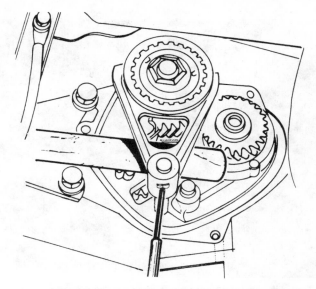

Fig. 7A.6 Drive out the 5th gear shift fork roll pin with a hammer and punch while supporting the shaft with a block of wood (Sec 5)

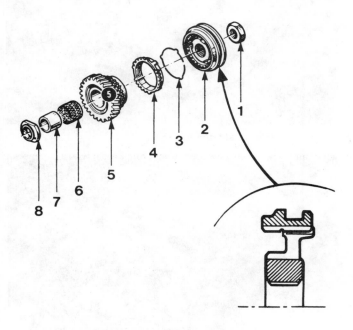

Fig. 7A.7 5th speed driven gear components — exploded view (Sec 5)

1 Retaining nut	5 5th speed driven gear
2 Synchronizer	6 Needle bearing
3 Spring clip	7 Bushing
4 Baulk ring	8 Washer

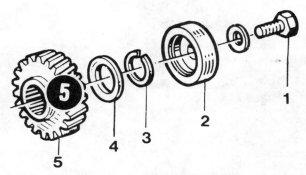

Fig. 7A.8 5th speed driving gear components — exploded view (Sec 5)

1 Bolt (later models only)	4 Dished washer
2 Collar (later models only)	5 5th speed driving gear
3 Circlip	

5.13a   Remove the circlip . . .

5.13b   . . . and dished washer from the input shaft and mainshaft

5.14a Lift out the reverse shaft detent retaining plate, . . .

5.14b   . . . followed by the spring . . .

5.14c   . . . and detent ball

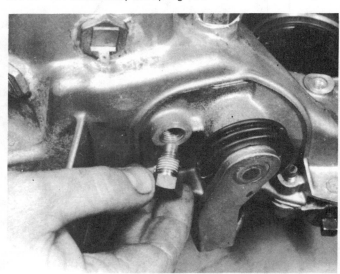

5.15   Unscrew the limit stop threaded plug (four-speed)

5.16   Remove the back-up light switch

5.18   Use two bolts or rods to retain the selector shaft detent balls and springs

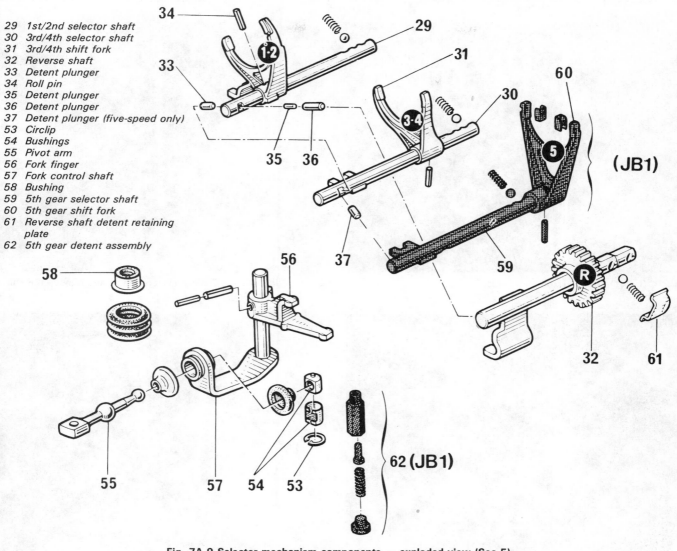

29 1st/2nd selector shaft
30 3rd/4th selector shaft
31 3rd/4th shift fork
32 Reverse shaft
33 Detent plunger
34 Roll pin
35 Detent plunger
36 Detent plunger
37 Detent plunger (five-speed only)
53 Circlip
54 Bushings
55 Pivot arm
56 Fork finger
57 Fork control shaft
58 Bushing
59 5th gear selector shaft
60 5th gear shift fork
61 Reverse shaft detent retaining
     plate
62 5th gear detent assembly

Fig. 7A.9 Selector mechanism components — exploded view (Sec 5)

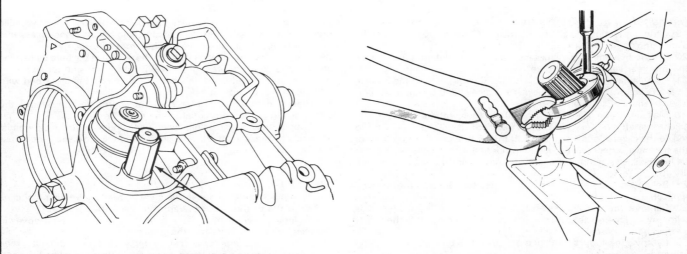

Fig. 7A.10 5th gear detent assembly (arrow) location
(Sec 5)

Fig. 7A.11 Removing the differential stub shaft oil seal
with a punch and pliers (Sec 5)

5.21   3rd/4th shift fork roll pin location

5.22   Withdraw the 3rd/4th selector shaft and remove the shift fork

5.23   Remove the detent plunger after withdrawing the 3rd/4th selector shaft

5.24a   As the 1st/2nd selector shaft is removed, recover the small detent plunger from the hole in the shaft, . . .

Mainshaft, input shaft and differential — removal
19 After separating the housings, the gear train components can be disassembled as follows:
20 On the five-speed transmission, remove the detent plunger from the 5th gear selector shaft bore.
21 Using a hammer and punch, drive out the roll pin from the 3rd/4th shift fork and shaft (photo). Slip a piece of pipe over the shaft to support it while the pin is driven out.
22 Make sure that all gears are in neutral, then withdraw the 3rd/4th selector shaft (the fork will stay in position). It will be necessary to rotate the reverse shaft slightly until the neutral position is found, or the detent plungers will not locate properly in the grooves and it will be impossible to remove the shaft (photo). With the shaft removed, lift out the fork.
23 Remove the detent plunger from the shaft bore in the housing (photo).
24 Remove the 1st/2nd selector shaft and fork. As the shaft is withdrawn, remove the small detent plunger from the hole in the center of the shaft (photos).
25 Remove the long detent plunger from the base of the housing (photo).
26 Grasp the mainshaft, input shaft and reverse shaft gear trains and remove them as an assembly from the housing (photo).
27 Remove the magnet from the housing (photo).

28 The differential can now be removed, if necessary, but a hydraulic press will be needed. The differential should be left alone unless it is absolutely essential to remove it. The procedure follows:
29 Using a small punch and pliers, tip the oil seal in the bore by tapping on one side. As it rotates, grasp it with the pliers and remove it.
30 Place the large differential gear face down on the press bed with a block of wood under it.
31 Press the clutch and differential housing down and remove the circlip securing the differential to the outer bearing.
32 Support the housing on blocks of wood and remove the differential assembly by pressing on the stub shaft. Remove the dished and thrust washers (if equipped).

Mechanism case — overhaul
33 To replace the bearings in the case, spread the retaining circlips and drive the bearings out toward the inside of the case.
34 To install new bearings, first locate the circlips in the grooves in the case with their ends together (photo).
35 Install the bearings in the case by applying force to the outer race only. As they are being installed, spread the circlips to allow the bearings to enter the bore.
36 With the bearings in place, make sure the circlips are seated in the grooves and that the ends are together (photo).

5.24b   . . . then remove the shift fork

5.25   Remove the long detent plunger after removing the 1st/2nd selector shaft

5.26   Remove the mainshaft, the input shaft and the reverse shaft as a unit

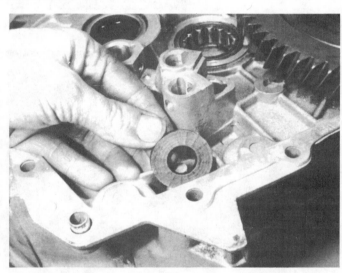

5.27   Remove the magnet from the bottom of the housing

5.34   The mainshaft and input shaft bearings are retained by large circlips

5.36   With the bearings in place, the circlip ends must be next to each other on the same side

5.39   Remove the fork control shaft pivot arm retaining snap-ring . . .

5.40   . . . and the double roll pin

5.46   Input shaft oil seal and bearing assembly location

5.47a   Homemade tool consists of a piece of pipe, a threaded rod, a nut and washers on one side . . .

37 If the selector shaft detent balls and springs are being replaced, remove the bolts or rods used to hold them in place during separation of the housings and withdraw them.

38 Check the condition of the fork control shaft and mechanism (look for wear at the fork ends). Replace parts as necessary using the following procedure:

39 Remove the snap-ring (photo), then slide out the pivot arm bushing and arm.

40 Using a pin punch, remove the roll pins securing the fork finger assembly to the shaft (photo). Withdraw the shaft and remove the fork and oil seal.

41 Reinstall the fork control assembly by reversing the removal procedure.

42 If the oil flow guide on the five-speed transmission is being replaced, bend the retaining lip edge on the guide flat before pushing it into the case.

43 Push the new guide up into position and bend the lip edge over to lock it in place.

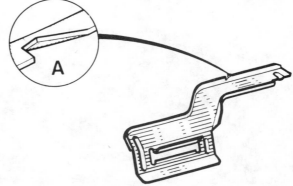

Fig. 7A.12 Oil flow guide retaining lip edge details (five-speed) (Sec 5)

5.47b . . . and a large socket, a nut and a washer on the other side of the housing (required for removing and installing the input shaft oil seal and bearing housing)

5.48   The oil holes in the input shaft bearing and housing must be aligned during installation

Fig. 7A.13 Differential assembly components — exploded view (Sec 5)

38 O-ring
39 Oil seal
40 Circlip
41 Speedometer drive gear
42 Inner bearing
43 Plain thrust washer
44 Dished thrust washer
45 Crownwheel assembly (large gear)
46 Snap-ring
47 Shim
48 Spider gear wheel
49 Shaft
50 Spider gears
51 Thrust washers
52 Stub shaft

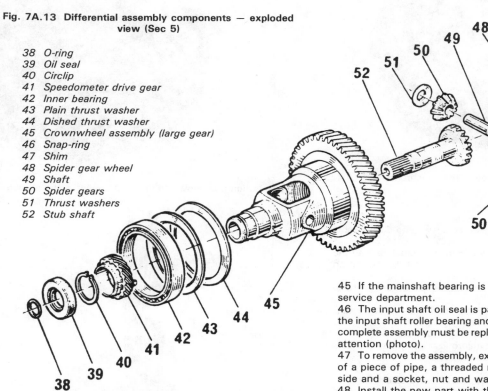

45 If the mainshaft bearing is worn, it must be replaced by a dealer service department.

46 The input shaft oil seal is part of a complete assembly containing the input shaft roller bearing and is contained in a tubular housing. The complete assembly must be replaced if either the seal or bearing require attention (photo).

47 To remove the assembly, extract it with a press or a tool consisting of a piece of pipe, a threaded rod, a nut and a large washer on one side and a socket, nut and washer on the other side (photos).

48 Install the new part with the same tool, but position it with the lubrication holes aligned with the holes in the housing (photo).

Differential — overhaul

49 Do not disassemble the differential unless it is certain that the parts are worn or damaged.

50 Remove the spider gears by referring to the accompanying illustration. Keep the gears and washers together and lay them out in the order of removal.

51 If any of the gears are worn or damaged, replace the entire gear set.

52 Reassemble the gears in the reverse order of disassembly.

Clutch and differential housing — overhaul

44 If a press is available the differential bearings can be removed quite easily. After removing the differential (described earlier), support the housing with the bellhousing face down and press the worn bearing out. If the small bearing must be removed, remove the circlip first. Install the new bearings with the press and use a new circlip to secure the small bearing.

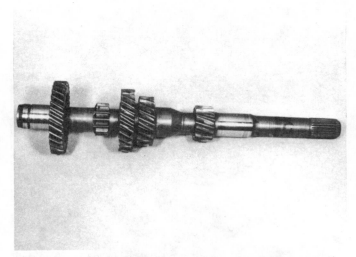

5.58a   Check the shafts for wear and damage on the gear teeth and bearing surfaces

5.58b   Look closely for chipped gear teeth

5.62   Locate the roller and spring key in the synchronizer unit, . . .

5.63   . . . then push down to locate the roller in the groove

Mainshaft — disassembly

53 Support the mainshaft in a vise with soft jaws and disassemble it as follows:

54 Lift off the 3rd/4th and reverse synchronizer, complete with the 4th gear baulk ring, 4th gear and the upper thrust washer as an assembly.

55 Remove the snap-ring and thrust washer, then lift off 3rd gear and the baulk ring.

56 Remove the thrust washer, snap-ring and second thrust washer, then lift off 2nd gear.

57 Remove the thrust washer and snap-ring above the 1st/2nd synchronizer, then lift off 1st gear, the synchronizer and the baulk rings as an assembly.

Shafts, gears and synchronizer units — inspection

58 Check the mainshaft, input shaft and reverse shaft for chipped teeth, wear and score marks (photos). If damage or wear is evident, the shaft must be replaced with a new one.

59 The synchronizers can be disassembled by covering the assembly with a rag and pushing the hub out of the sleeve. Do not interchange parts from one synchronizer to another.

60 Make sure that the hub and sleeve slide easily over each other with a minimum of backlash or axial movement. Check the dog teeth on the sleeve for excessive wear. If the transmission had a tendency to jump out of gear, the synchronizer for that particular gear is the most likely cause and should be replaced with a new one.

5.66   Slide 1st gear onto the mainshaft with the flat face towards the gear on the end of the shaft

5.67a   Install the baulk ring, . . .

5.67b   . . . followed by the 1st/2nd synchronizer unit

5.68a   Position the next baulk ring, . . .

5.68b   . . . then install the snap-ring

5.69a   Lay the thrust washer over the snap-ring, . . .

5.69b   . . . then slide 2nd gear onto the mainshaft

5.70a   Install the first thrust washer, . . .

5.70b   . . . the snap-ring, . . .

5.70c   . . . the second thrust washer . . .

5.70d   . . . and 3rd gear on the mainshaft

5.71a   Place the thrust washer over 3rd gear . . .

5.71b   . . . and install the remaining snap-ring

5.72a Attach the baulk ring to 3rd gear, . . .

5.72b . . . followed by the 3rd/4th synchronizer unit

5.73a Install the 4th gear baulk ring, . . .

5.73b . . . followed by 4th gear . . .

5.73c . . . and the final thrust washer

5.77 Install a new oil seal in the clutch and differential housing

5.80   Push the detent plunger into place with a screwdriver

5.81   Insert the small detent plunger into the hole in the 1st/2nd selector shaft

61   To reassemble the synchronizer, slide the hub into the sleeve (note that for the 1st/2nd synchronizer the shift fork groove in the sleeve and the offset boss on the hub are on opposite sides; for the 3rd/4th unit they are on the same side; for the 5th gear unit the chamfered outer edge is on the same side as the offset hub boss).

62   Place the synchronizer on a bench with the offset side of the hub facing down. Locate the end of the spring key with the two tangs against the hub and position the roller between the loop of the spring key and the side of the sleeve (photo).

63   Push down on the roller and key until they locate correctly with the roller in the internal groove of the sleeve (photo). Repeat the procedure for the remaining rollers and spring keys.

64   Check the baulk rings by sliding them onto the gears. Note if they lock on the taper before reaching the gear shoulder. Also check for cracks and wear on the teeth. It is a very good idea to replace the baulk rings with new ones, regardless of their condition, particularly if the vehicle has a lot of miles on it.

65   Check the shift fork clearance in the synchronizer sleeve groove (it should be minimal). If in doubt, compare the clearance to the clearance of new parts and replace them as necessary. On five-speed transmissions, two contact pads on the fork ends actually engage with the sleeve groove and can be replaced if wear is evident.

Mainshaft — reassembly

66   Place 1st gear on the mainshaft with the flat face on the gear facing the gear on the end of the shaft (photo).

67   Place the baulk ring over 1st gear, then position the 1st/2nd gear synchronizer over it (photos). Make sure the offset side of the hub is facing 1st gear and that the lugs on the baulk ring engage in the roller grooves in the hub.

68   Install the 2nd gear baulk ring and the snap-ring (photos).

69   Lay the thrust washer over the snap-ring, then slide 2nd gear onto the mainshaft with the flat side facing away from the gear on the end of the shaft (photos).

70   Install the first thrust washer, the snap-ring and the second thrust washer, then slide on 3rd gear (flat face toward the gear on the end of the shaft) (photos).

71   Place the thrust washer over 3rd gear, then install the remaining snap-ring (photos).

72   Position the baulk ring over 3rd gear, followed by the 3rd/4th and reverse synchronizer. The offset side of the hub and the groove in the sleeve should face away from 3rd gear. Make sure the lugs on the baulk ring engage with the roller grooves in the hub (photos).

73   Attach the 4th gear baulk ring to the 3rd/4th synchronizer, then slide on 4th gear and the thrust washer (photos).

Mainshaft, input shaft and differential — installation

74   If the differential has been removed, install it as follows:

75   Position the dished thrust washer against the large gear face with the base of the dished face toward the gear. If equipped, place the thrust washer over the dished washer.

76   Place a block of wood under the flat face of the large gear on the press bed. Position the clutch and differential housing over the differential and press the housing on. Keep the housing under pressure (to compress the dished thrust washer) and install a new outer retaining circlip.

77   Remove the assembly from the press and install a new oil seal over the stub shaft (photo). Tap the seal into place with a hammer and a large socket or piece of pipe until it is flush with the case edge.

78   Place the magnet in the bottom of the housing.

79   Hold the assembled mainshaft, input shaft and reverse shaft together and install all three as an assembly in the housing.

80   Insert the long detent plunger into the bore and push it through into contact with the reverse shaft detent grooves with a screwdriver (photo).

81   Locate the 1st/2nd shift fork in the groove in the synchro sleeve and engage the selector shaft in it. Turn the shaft so that the detent grooves at the top are facing the mainshaft, insert the small detent plunger into the hole in the shaft and push the shaft down through the fork (photo). Turn the reverse shaft (in neutral) as required to seat the 1st/2nd selector shaft.

82   Place the 3rd/4th shift fork in the groove in the synchro sleeve with the thicker side facing the differential.

83   Locate the detent plunger in the groove in the housing, then slide the 3rd/4th selector shaft through the fork. Make sure all the shafts are in neutral, then seat the 3rd/4th selector shaft. It may take a few tries to get all the shafts, particularly reverse, in just the right position to allow all the detent plungers to locate in their grooves.

84   Support the selector shafts with a piece of pipe (slip the pipe over the shafts one at a time) and install the roll pins in the shift forks. Tap each pin in until it is flush with the side of the fork (photos).

85   On five-speed models, install the remaining detent plunger in the housing.

Rejoining the housings

86   Make sure the thrust washer is in position on top of the mainshaft (four-speed) and that the 5th gear selector shaft, detent ball and spring are in place in the mechanism case (five-speed).

87   Make sure the mating surfaces are clean (wipe them with a rag soaked with lacquer thinner), then apply a thin bead of appropriate sealer to both surfaces (note that no gasket is used).

88   Make sure that all shafts are in neutral and that the engagement slots on the 1st/2nd and 3rd/4th selector shafts are exactly in line.

89   Pull the fork control shaft in the mechanism case out as far as it will go, then lower the mechanism case into position. Align the selector shafts with the holes in the case and as the shafts protrude remove the bolts or rods used to retain the detent balls and spring (photo).

90   As the input shaft and mainshaft enter the bearings, tap the case with a soft-faced hammer to seat them.

91   Pass a hooked piece of wire through the hole in the top of the case (photo). Lift up the reverse shaft and gear, then install the detent ball, spring and retaining plate.

92   Install two of the housing bolts, then make sure the transmission shifts through all of the gears.

93   If the operation is satisfactory, install the limit stop threaded plug (four-speed) or the 5th gear detent assembly (five-speed).

94   On the four-speed transmission, install the dished washer and circlip on the end of the input shaft, then compress the washer by striking the circlip with a hammer and socket. As the washer compresses, the circlip will seat in the groove (photos). Repeat the procedure for the

5.84a Install the 1st/2nd shift fork roll pin . . .

5.84b . . . and the 3rd/4th shift fork roll pin, . . .

5.84c . . . then tap them in until they are flush with the shift forks (support the shaft when this is done)

5.89 Attaching the mechanism case to the housing

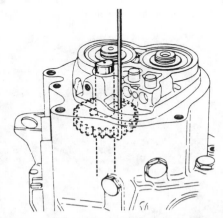

Fig. 7A.14 Using a piece of wire with a hooked end to lift the reverse shaft and gear (Sec 5)

5.91 Use a piece of wire to lift up the reverse shaft

mainshaft, but compress the washer with a socket and bolt screwed into the end of the shaft (photos).

95 Install the remaining housing bolts and tighten all of them to the specified torque in a criss-cross pattern.

96 On the five-speed transmission, apply a few drops of *Loctite 271* or equivalent to the inside of the 5th speed driving gear and install the gear on the mainshaft. Push the gear onto the shaft and seat it with a large socket and a bolt threaded into the end of the shaft (tighten the bolt and the socket will seat the gear).

97 Remove the socket and bolt, install the dished washer and circlip and seat the circlip in the same manner. As the washer is compressed, the circlip will enter the groove.

98 Where used, install the collar, bolt and washer on the end of the mainshaft (use *Locktite* on the bolt threads).

99 Install the washer, bushing and needle bearing on the input shaft, apply *Locktite* to the 5th gear synchro hub splines, then install the driven gear, synchro hub and shift fork as an assembly. Make sure the offset boss on the synchro hub is facing the driven gear.

5.94a Install the dished washer and circlip on the
input shaft, . . .

5.94b . . . then slip a socket over the shaft and tap it down with
a hammer to seat the circlip

5.94c Install the dished washer . . .

5.94d . . . and circlip on the mainshaft

5.94e Compress the dished washer with a socket, bolt and
washer . . .

5.94f . . . until the circlip is seated in the grooveEND.

100 Engage 1st gear by moving the linkage and 5th gear by moving
the shift fork, then install and tighten the 5th gear retaining nut to the
specified torque.
101 Return the gears to neutral, then install the 5th gear shift fork roll
pin.
102 On all models, position a new rubber gasket on the mechanism

case and install the rear cover and bolts.
103 Install a new O-ring over the differential stub shaft.
104 Install the mounting bracket, then refer to Chapter 8 and install
the clutch release bearing and fork.
105 The transmission can now be installed in the vehicle.

Chapter 7 Part B Automatic transmission

Contents

Specifications

Model
1.4 liter engine. MB1
1.7 liter engine. MB3

Fluid type and capacity . . . . See Chapter 1

Torque specifications	Ft-lbs
Transmission mount nuts/bolts	30
Bellhousing-to-engine nuts/bolts	31
Torque converter-to-driveplate bolts	22
Engine mount bolts	25
Front exhaust pipe shoulder bolts	23

---

1 General information

Due to the complexity of the clutches and the hydraulic control system, as well as the special tools and expertise required to perform an automatic transmission overhaul, it should not be attempted by the home mechanic. The procedures in this Chapter are limited to general diagnosis, adjustment and transmission removal and installation.

If the transmission requires major repair work, it should be left to a dealer service department or a reputable automotive or transmission repair shop. You can, however, remove and install the transmission yourself and save the expense, even if the repair work is done by a transmission specialist.

2 Automatic transmission diagnosis — general

Automatic transmission malfunctions may be caused by four general conditions: poor engine performance, improper adjustments, hydraulic system malfunctions and mechanical problems. Diagnosis of transmission troubles should always begin with a check of the easily repaired items: fluid level and condition and shift linkage adjustment. Next, perform a road test to determine if the problem has been eliminated. If the problem persists after the preliminary checks and corrections, additional diagnosis should be done by a dealer service department or a reputable automotive or transmission repair shop.

3 Shift linkage — adjustment

1   Raise the vehicle and support it securely on jackstands, then make sure the shift lever inside the vehicle is in the Park position.

2   Working under the vehicle, loosen the adjustment clamp nuts so the rod is free to move in the clamp.
3   Make sure the selector lever on the transmission is also in the Park position by turning it counterclockwise as far as it will go.
4   Tighten the adjustment clamp nuts, then lower the vehicle to the ground and make sure that all gear positions are functional and that the engine starts in the Park position.

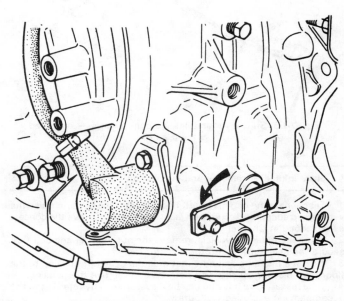

Fig. 7B.1 Move the transmission lever (arrow) in the direction shown to engage Park (Sec 3)

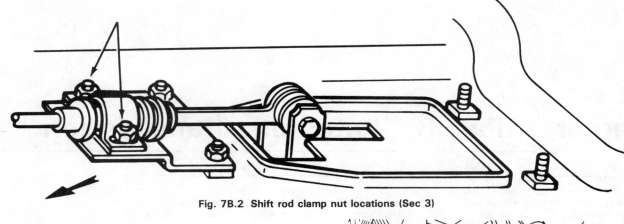

Fig. 7B.2 Shift rod clamp nut locations (Sec 3)

Fig. 7B.3 Shift lever and linkage components — exploded view (Sec 4)

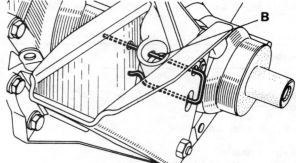

Fig. 7B.4 Speedometer cable retaining clip location (B) (Sec 5)

4 Shift linkage — removal and installation

1   Disconnect the negative battery cable from the battery. Raise the vehicle and support it securely on jackstands, then remove the console as described in Chapter 12.
2   Working under the vehicle, remove the nut, washer and bolt that secure the selector lever to the selector rod.
3   Remove the bolts and nuts that hold the gearshift housing to the floor pan, disconnect the wire harness and remove the housing.
4   If necessary, the housing can be disassembled by referring to the accompanying exploded view drawing.
5   Installation is the reverse of removal. Adjust the shift linkage by referring to Section 3.

5 Automatic transmission — removal and installation

1   After everything has been disconnected, the transmission is removed by lifting it up and out of the engine compartment. Due to the weight of the transmission, an engine hoist or crane will be required for this procedure.
2   Begin by disconnecting the negative battery cable from the battery, then refer to Chapter 1 and drain the transmission fluid.
3   Raise the front of the vehicle and support it securely on jackstands. Remove both front wheels.
4   Refer to Chapter 8 and remove the left-hand driveaxle. Remove the right-hand driveaxle inner joint yoke.
5   Remove the air cleaner assembly.
6   Refer to Chapter 5 and remove the TDC sensor from the bellhousing.
7   Note how it is installed, then remove the speedometer cable retaining clip from the rear engine mount bracket and transmission housing. Withdraw the cable from the transmission.
8   Remove the bolts and springs holding the front exhaust pipe to the exhaust manifold.
9   Label the wires, then disconnect them from the solenoid and remove the starter motor (Chapter 5).
10   Disconnect the cooling fan and thermostatic switch wiring harnesses, then remove the radiator and lay it over the engine with the hoses still attached (protect the core by cushioning it with a sheet of cardboard).
11   Disconnect the transmission linkage selector rod from the bellcrank and bracket.
12   Remove the vacuum hose from the modulator unit on the transmission.
13   Detach the multi-function switch from the transmission.
14   Detach all clips, wires and cables and position them to the side so there is unobstructed access to the transmission from above.
15   Working under the vehicle, remove the lower bellhousing cover plate. Turn the driveplate as needed to remove the three torque converter-to-driveplate bolts. Bolt a small metal tab to the transmission housing to keep the torque converter from falling out of place when the transmission is separated from the engine.

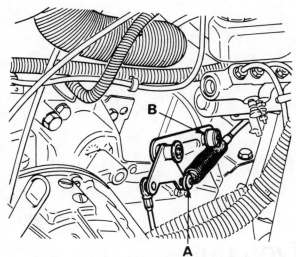

Fig. 7B.5 Disconnect the linkage from the bellcrank at points A and B (Sec 5)

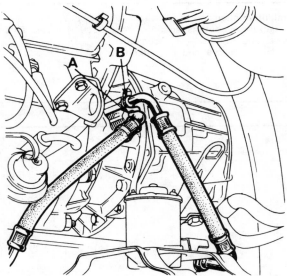

Fig. 7B.7 Fluid cooler line connection points (A and B) (Sec 5)

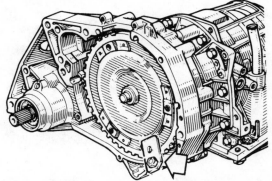

Fig. 7B.6 Bolt a metal strip to the transmission housing to keep the torque converter in place (Sec 5)

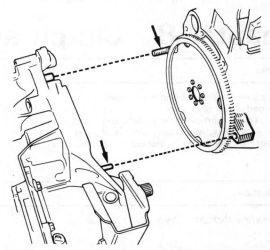

Fig. 7B.8 The two studs (arrows) must be removed in order to separate the transmission from the engine (Sec 5)

Fig. 7B.9 The transmission must be tipped up vertically and the chain attached as shown in order to remove it from the engine compartment (Sec 5)

16   Remove the support rod mounted between the engine and transmission.

17   Detach the fluid cooler lines from the transmission and plug them to prevent contamination of the fluid with dirt.

18   Position a jack under the engine oil pan to support the engine (place a block of wood between the jack head and the oil pan). Attach the engine hoist to the transmission with chains or cables (depending on the type of hoist used, it may be a good idea to remove the hood).

19   Raise the jack and hoist just enough to take up the weight of the engine and transmission.

20   Remove the engine-to-transmission bolts, then loosen the nuts on the two studs. Thread an additional nut onto each of the studs and hold the inner nut while tightening the outer nut against it. Back the studs out by turning the inner nut with a wrench.

21   Remove the transmission bracket-to-mount nuts and bolts, raise the engine and transmission slightly to clear the mounts, then remove the brackets (the engine mounts may have to be loosened as well).

22   Move the engine and transmission as necessary to separate the transmission from the engine. Lower the transmission onto blocks and reposition the chain or cable with the transmission tipped vertically (it must be vertical to provide clearance for removal).

23   Raise the transmission while moving the engine within the limits of the mounts until the transmission can be lifted up and over the front of the vehicle or the fender, then lower it carefully to the floor.

24   Installation is basically the reverse of removal, but note the following:

a)   Lubricate the transmission shaft (where it mates with the crankshaft) with moly-based grease.

b)   Install the two studs before the remaining engine-to-transmission mounting bolts.

c)   Install the driveaxles as described in Chapter 8.

d)   Be sure to refill the transmission with fluid (Chapter 1).

Chapter 8 Clutch and driveaxles

Contents

Specifications

Driveaxle lubricant (see text)

Type	Moly-based grease
Quantity	
Outer joint	6.88 oz
Inner joint	4.94 oz

Torque specifications

	Ft-lbs
Clutch cover bolts	
1.4 liter engine	18
1.7 liter engine	23
Tie-rod balljoint nuts	25
Strut-to-hub bolts	55
Driveaxle retaining nut	154
Left-hand inner boot retaining plate bolts	18

1 General information

All manual transmission models are equipped with a cable-operated, single dry plate diaphragm spring clutch assembly. The clutch cover is dowelled and bolted to the rear face of the flywheel and contains the pressure plate and diaphragm spring.

The clutch plate is free to slide along the splined transmission input shaft and is held in position between the flywheel and pressure plate by the diaphragm spring. The lining material is riveted to the clutch plate, which has a spring-cushioned hub to absorb transmission shocks and ensure smooth clutch engagement.

The clutch is actuated by a cable attached to the clutch pedal. The release mechanism consists of a release arm and throwout bearing which are in permanent contact with the fingers of the diaphragm spring.

Clutch plate lining wear is automatically compensated for by a self-adjusting mechanism attached to the clutch pedal. It consists of a serrated quadrant, a notched cam and a tension spring. One end of the cable is attached to the quadrant, which is free to pivot on the pedal, but is tensioned by the spring. As the pedal is depressed, the notched cam contacts the quadrant and locks it up, allowing the pedal to pull the cable and operate the clutch. As the pedal is released, the spring causes the quadrant to move away from the cam and rotate slightly, taking up any free play that may exist in the cable.

Power is transmitted from the differential to the front wheels by two unequal length solid steel driveaxles. Both driveaxles are equipped with constant velocity (CV) joints at the outer ends. Each joint consists of a stub axle, which is splined to engage in the front hub, and a spider containing roller bearings and cups which engage with the driveaxle yoke. The entire assembly is protected by a rubber boot which is attached to the stub axle and driveaxle.

At the driveshaft inner ends, a different type of joint is used at each side. On the right-hand side a CV-type joint is used. It is attached to the differential stub shaft with a roll pin. A rubber boot covers and protects the entire assembly.

On the left-hand side, the driveaxle engages with a CV-type joint that is an integral part of the differential. The rubber boot is attached to the differential housing with a plate and to the driveaxle with a ball bearing and clamp. The bearing allows the axle to turn within the rubber boot, which does not rotate.

Due to the design and construction of the driveaxlea and CV joints, the only repairs possible include replacement of the rubber boots and inner joints. If the outer CV joints or the driveaxle splines are worn or damaged, the complete driveaxle assembly must be replaced with a new one.

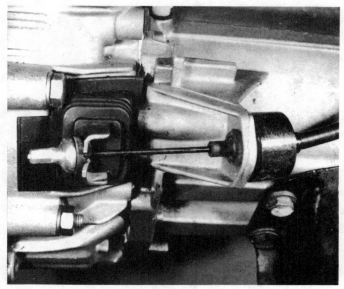

2.2 The clutch cable is attached to the release fork and the housing is held in the bellhousing bracket

3.3 Removing the air duct for access to the clutch pedal assembly

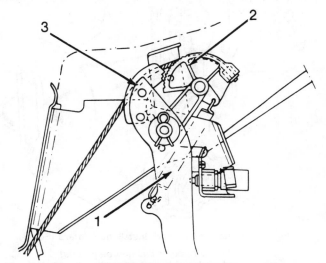

Fig. 8.1 Clutch cable self-adjusting mechanism components (Sec 2)

1 Tension spring   2 Serrated quadrant   3 Notched cam

3.4 The clutch pedal shaft is retained by spring-type clips

2 Clutch cable — removal and installation

1   Disconnect the negative battery cable from the battery.
2   Slip the end of the cable out of the release fork and detach the housing from the bracket on the bellhousing (photo).
3   Working inside the vehicle, remove the plastic cover from the clutch pedal bracket assembly.
4   Depress the clutch pedal to the floor, then release it to free the cable from the quadrant on the self-adjusting mechanism (you may have to hold the cable against the cam as the pedal is released).
5   Separate the cable from the quadrant and push the cable housing through the firewall with a screwdriver.
6   Pull the cable into the engine compartment, detach it from the support clips and remove it from the vehicle.
7   To install the cable, thread it through the hole in the firewall from the engine compartment side, lay it over the self-adjusting cam and connect the end to the quadrant.
8   Slip the other end of the cable through the bellhousing bracket and into the release fork.
9   Depress the clutch pedal to draw the housing into the hole in the

firewall (make sure that it locates properly).
10 Turn the quadrant on the self-adjusting mechanism towards the front of the vehicle to produce some slack in the cable, then depress and release the pedal several times to operate the self-adjusting mechanism.
11 Install the pedal assembly cover, thread the clutch cable through the support clips and attach the cable to the battery.

3 Clutch pedal — removal and installation

1   Disconnect the negative battery cable from the battery.
2   Disconnect the clutch cable from the pedal (Section 2).
3   If necessary, the air duct at the base of the dashboard trim can be removed to provide more room to work. Detach it from the heater unit and vent tube (photo).
4   Remove the retaining clips from both ends of the pedal shaft (photo). Slide the shaft out of the pedal bracket and withdraw the pedal.
5   Check the pedal shaft bushings for wear and replace them if necessary.
6   Installation is the reverse of removal.

4.10a   The clutch throwout bearing fits over the transmission input shaft and is attached to the release fork

4.10b   Remove the throwout bearing spring retainer . . .

4.10c   . . . and lift out the bearing

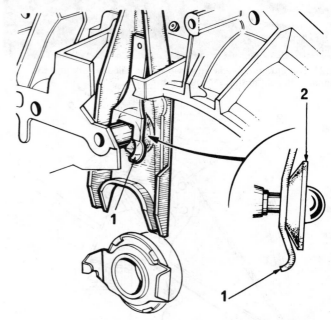

Fig. 8.2 Clutch release fork installation details (Sec 4)

    1   *Spring retainer (located behind flat*
       shoulder of ball pivot stud)
    2   *Rubber cover (where used)*

4   Clutch — removal, inspection and installation

Removal

1   Access to the clutch can be accomplished in one of two ways. Either the engine, or engine/transmission unit, can be removed as described in Chapter 2 and the transmission separated from the engine, or the engine can be left in place and the transmission can be removed as described in Chapter 7. If the engine must be removed for repair, then check and service the clutch at the same time.

2   After the transmission has been separated from the engine, the clutch cover can be detached from the flywheel. If there are no index or alignment marks on the clutch cover and flywheel, use a center punch to mark them (it is not always necessary, but it may simplify installation).

3   Unscrew the clutch cover bolts one turn at a time, following a criss-cross pattern, until they can be removed. Carefully separate the cover from the flywheel (be careful not to allow the clutch plate to fall out).

4   It is not possible to disassemble the pressure plate/clutch cover assembly. **Note:** *Do not get grease or oil on the clutch plate lining or it will have to be replaced with a new one regardless of its condition.*

Inspection

Caution: *The dust on the clutch components contains asbestos, which is harmful to your health. Do not blow it out with compressed air and do not inhale any of it.*

5   If the clutch plate must be replaced with a new one, replace the throwout bearing with a new one as well (this will preclude having

to repeat the clutch removal procedure in the near future). If the pressure plate assembly must be replaced with a new one, check on the availability of rebuilt parts.

6   Examine the clutch plate friction lining for wear and loose rivets and the metal disc for rim distortion, cracks, broken hub springs and worn splines. The lining may be glazed, but as long as the material pattern can be seen and it is not worn down close to the rivet heads, it is usable (compare the lining thickness to a new clutch plate if possible). If it is obvious that oil from the engine or transmission has been leaking onto the clutch, replace the clutch plate with a new one and repair the leak. If in doubt about the clutch condition, replace it with a new one.

7   Check the machined surfaces of the flywheel and pressure plate. If they are worn, scored or discolored, they must be resurfaced by an automotive machine shop or the components must be replaced with new ones.

8   If the pressure plate is distorted or cracked, or if the springs are damaged, new parts will be required.

9   Check the operation of the throwout bearing. If it is noisy or rough and does not turn freely, replace it with a new one. If in doubt about its condition, install a new one.

10   To remove it, tilt the release fork and slide the bearing off the input shaft guide tube (photo). Release the four spring retainer tangs, lift

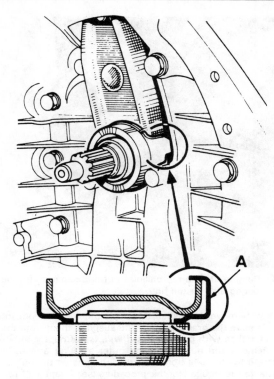

Fig. 8.3 Throwout bearing installation details (tang A locates behind release fork) (Sec 4)

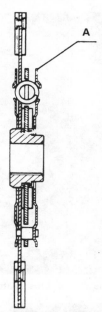

Fig. 8.4 The large offset (A) on the hub must face away from the flywheel when the clutch plate is installed (Sec 4)

off the retainer and remove the bearing (photos).
11 To remove the release fork, disengage the rubber cover and then pull up on the fork to release it from the ball stud pivot.

Installation

12 Lubricate the release fork pivot ball and the bearing-to-diaphragm spring contact areas with a small amount of high-temperature moly-based grease, then install the release fork. The spring retainer must be located behind the flat shoulder of the pivot stud.
13 Slide the throwout bearing onto the input shaft tube and hook the tangs behind the release fork.
14 Be careful not to get any oil or grease on the clutch plate lining, the flywheel or the pressure plate. Always handle the clutch components with clean hands and wipe the flywheel and pressure plate faces with a clean, dry rag before beginning reassembly.
15 Place the clutch plate against the flywheel with the cushion spring assembly (larger offset) facing away from the flywheel (see the accompanying illustration).
16 Align the marks/dowel pins and install the clutch cover/pressure plate assembly. Tighten the bolts finger tight only (the clutch plate must be held in place but free to move).
17 The clutch plate must now be aligned (or centered) so the transmission input shaft will pass through the center of the clutch plate hub when the engine and transmission are rejoined.
18 Use a clutch alignment tool (photos) to center the clutch plate (follow the directions supplied with the tool), then visually check to see if the clutch plate hub and pilot bearing in the end of the crankshaft are concentric.
19 With the tool still in place, tighten the bolts 1/2-turn at a time, following a criss-cross pattern, until they are all at the specified torque.
20 The transmission and engine can now be rejoined.

5 Driveaxles — removal and installation

Removal

1 Raise the front of the vehicle ansd support it securely on jackstands, then remove the wheels.
2 Have an assistant depress the brake pedal and hold it down while you loosen the driveaxle retaining nuts with a breaker bar and a large

4.18a The clutch alignment tool fits through the clutch plate and into the pilot bearing in the end of the crankshaft

4.18b Make sure the clutch plate is centered before tightening the clutch cover bolts

5.2   The driveaxle dished thrust plate fits behind the retaining nut

5.4   Remove the tie-rod balljoint nut and separate the tie-rod from the steering arm on the hub

socket. Remove the dished thrust plate behind the nut (photo).
3   Remove the brake calipers and suspend them from the frame or wheel arches with pieces of stiff wire (see Chapter 9).
4   Remove the nut from each outer steering arm balljoint, then separate the tie-rods from the steering arms on the hubs (photo). A special tool is required for this procedure (see Chapter 11 for additional information).
5   Remove the strut-to-hub nuts/bolts (photo) (see Chapter 11 for more details).
6   From this point on, the procedure is different for right-hand and left-hand driveaxles.

Left-hand driveaxle
7   Refer to Chapter 1 and drain the transmission oil or fluid (depending on transmission type).
8   Remove the three bolts holding the boot retaining plate to the transmission housing (photo).
9   Disengage the hub bracket from the suspension strut and tip the hub/bracket out at the top (photo). At the same time, carefully withdraw the driveaxle inner joint from the transmission (photo). **Caution:** *During removal of the left-hand driveaxle from the transmission, be sure that the three rollers on the CV joint are not dislodged. If this occurs, needle bearings from the joint could fall into the transmission case and cause severe damage. After the shaft is removed, tape the joint to prevent the components from falling apart.*
10   Withdraw the stub axle from the hub to separate the driveaxle from the vehicle. If the axle is tight in the hub, tap it out with a soft-faced hammer or use a puller to remove it.

5.5   Remove the strut-to-hub bolts/nuts

Right-hand driveaxle
11   Using a pin punch and a hammer, drive the roll pin out of the inner joint yoke (photo). Note that the roll pin is actually two roll pins — one inside the other.
12   Disengage the hub bracket from the suspension strut and tip the bracket out at the top.
13   Tap the inner joint off the differential stub shaft with a soft metal drift and a hammer.
14   Withdraw the stub axle from the hub to separate the driveaxle from the vehicle. If the axle is tight in the hub, tap it out with a soft-faced hammer or use a puller to remove it.

Installation
15   Installation is the reverse of removal, but note the following points:
   a) Lubricate the driveaxle joint splines with moly-based grease before installation.
   b) On the right-hand side, position the inner joint splines so that the roll pin holes are aligned when the joint is completely seated. The slots in the roll pins must be 90° apart.
   c) During installation of the left-hand driveaxle, be sure to remove the tape holding the inner joint components together and do

5.8   Remove the bolts and separate the retaining plate from the transmission housing

5.9a   Disengage the bracket from the strut and tip it out slightly, . . .

5.9b   . . . then carefully withdraw the inner joint from the transmission (do not let the roller cups fall off!)

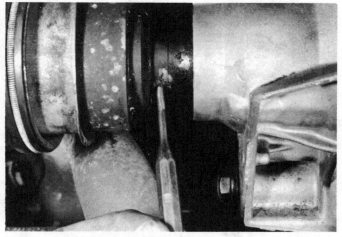

5.11   Removing the roll pin from the inner joint yoke and differential stub shaft (right-hand driveaxle)

not dislodge any of the rollers. If this occurs, needle bearings from the joint could fall into the transmission case and cause severe damage.

d)   Make sure that all nuts and bolts are tightened to the specified torque and that the strut-to-hub bolts are installed with the bolt heads to the rear of the vehicle.

e)   If the left-hand driveaxle has been removed, refer to Chapter 1 and refill the transmission.

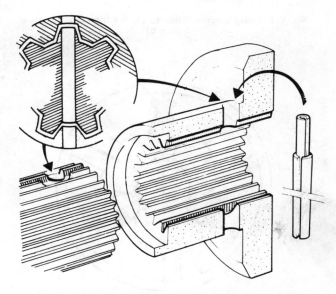

Fig. 8.5 Right-hand driveaxle inner joint yoke roll pin installation details (Sec 5)

6   Constant velocity joints — inspection and repair

Inspection

1   A thorough inspection of the driveaxles and CV joints should be conducted at the same time that the rubber boots are checked (see Chapter 1).

2   If vibration or noise has been noted when making turns, the outer CV joints are probably worn. If vibration has been noted when accelerating, the inner joints are probably at fault. Noise that occurs when the clutch is engaged or the accelerator applied may be caused by worn splines, a loose driveaxle retaining nut or worn CV joints (inner or outer).

3   With the front of the vehicle raised and supported on jackstands, rotate each front wheel and check for damage and distortion of the driveaxles. Check for play in each outer CV joint by holding the driveaxle and attempting to turn the wheel with your hand. Any noticeable play indicates wear in the CV joint, worn splines, a loose driveaxle retaining nut or loose wheel lug bolts. Check for wear at the inner joints by rotating the driveaxle at the differential end.

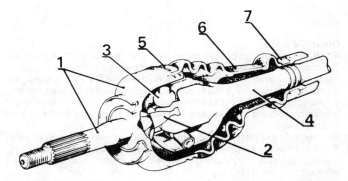

Fig. 8.6 Cutaway view of outer constant velocity (CV) joint (Sec 6)

1   Stub axle
2   Starplate
3   Spider and roller cup
4   Driveaxle yoke
5   Rubber boot clamp
6   Rubber boot
7   Rubber boot clamp

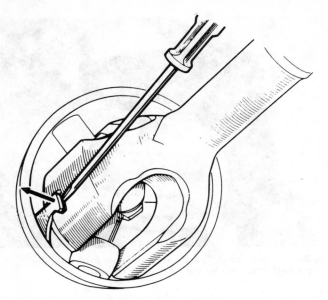

Fig. 8.7 Using a screwdriver to pry up the starplate arms
(Sec 6)

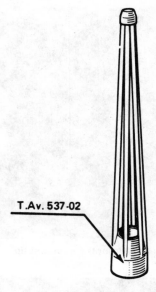

T.Av. 537-02

Fig. 8.8 The manufacturer's tool for installing the rubber
boots looks like this (Sec 6)

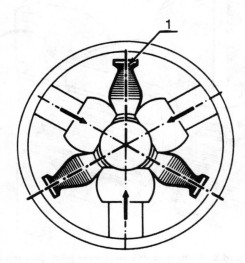

Fig. 8.9 Correct position of starplate arms (1) and roller
cups as driveaxle yoke is installed (Sec 6)

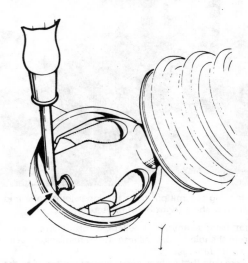

Fig. 8.10 Use a screwdriver to engage the starplate arms in
the driveaxle yoke grooves (Sec 6)

Repair

Outer CV joints

4   If the inspection procedure reveals that the outer CV joint(s) are defective, a new driveaxle assembly must be installed, since the joints cannot be repaired. If the rubber boot on the outer CV joint is damaged, it can be replaced using the following procedure. Before starting, buy a new rubber boot, boot clamps and some special grease for the CV joints (these items are available as a repair kit from your dealer service department).

5   Remove the driveaxle from the vehicle as described in Section 5.

6   If the boot is secured by metal clamps, remove them by releasing the locking tangs or by cutting them with a hacksaw or chisel. If coiled wire clamps are used, pry them off with a screwdriver.

7   Slide the boot down the driveaxle to expose the CV joint, then remove as much of the grease as possible from the joint.

8   Use a screwdriver to pry up the starplate arms until they are clear of the grooves in the driveaxle yoke.

9   Carefully slide the stub axle off the driveaxle, then remove the boot. Recover the thrust ball and spring.

10 Clean the driveaxle yoke and remove as much of the remaining grease as possible from the spider and stub axle with clean rags. **Note:**

Do not use cleaning solvent, gasoline or kerosene — use clean rags only.

11 In order to install the new rubber boot a special tool is required to expand the small end so it will fit over the driveaxle yoke. The manufacturer's tool is shown in the accompanying illustration, but a substitute can be made by bending a piece of sheet metal into a conical shape and fastening the seam with pop rivets. Make sure the seam is covered with tape to protect the new boot.

12 Lubricate the expander tool and the inside of the new boot with clean engine oil.

13 Position the small end of the boot over the small end of the tool and move it up and down the tool several times to make the rubber pliable.

14 Position the large end of the expander against the yoke and pull the boot up the expander and onto the yoke. Make sure the end of the boot does not tuck under and use plenty of lubricant.

15 When the small end of the boot is in place over the yoke, remove the tool and slide the boot up the driveaxle.

16 Install the spring and thrust ball in the spider, move the spider roller cups toward the center and position the starplate arms midway between each cup.

17 Insert the driveaxle yoke into the stub axle and carefully bend the starplate arms until they engage in the grooves in the yoke.

Fig. 8.11 Small diameter tubes can be slipped over the ends of the wire-type clamps to expand and install them (Sec 6)

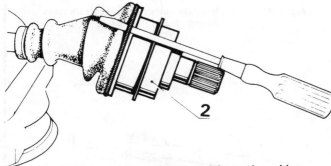

Fig. 8.13 Removing the boot retaining spring with a screwdriver (Sec 6)

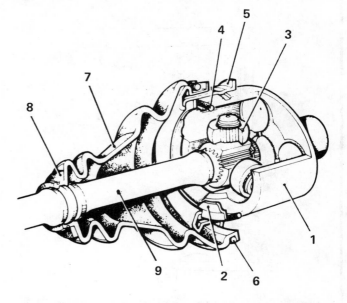

Fig. 8.12 Cutaway view of the right-hand driveaxle inner joint (Sec 6)

1 Yoke
2 Anti-separation plate
3 Spider roller cup
4 Seal
5 Cover
6 Boot retaining spring
7 Rubber boot
8 Boot collar
9 Driveaxle

18 Turn the stub axle in every direction and make sure that it moves freely.
19 Apply all of the grease supplied in the repair kit to the spider and grooves in the driveaxle yoke (make sure everything is thoroughly lubricated).
20 Slide the boot into position in the grooves of the stub axle and driveaxle. Lift up the boot lip with a blunt tool, squeeze the boot slightly to remove any trapped air, then remove the tool.
21 If band-type clamps are included in the repair kit, wrap them tightly around the boot and engage the slot on the one end with the tang on the other end. Squeeze the raised portion with pliers to tighten the clamp.
22 If wire-type clamps have been supplied, they can be installed with short pieces of small diameter tubing or drilled out rods. Slip the tubes or rods over the ends of the clamps and squeeze them together like a pliers. This will expand the clamps enough to allow them to be slipped over the boot.
23 The driveaxle can now be reinstalled.

Right-hand inner joint
24 Remove the driveaxle as described in Section 5. Purchase a CV joint repair kit from your dealer.
25 Using a screwdriver, slip the retaining spring off the rubber boot on the yoke.
26 Release the rubber collar securing the boot to the driveaxle and slide the boot down the shaft.
27 Using pliers, carefully bend back the anti-separation plate tangs, then carefully slide the yoke off the spider. Be prepared to catch the roller cups, which will fall off the spider trunnions as the yoke is withdrawn (they are matched parts and must not be interchanged). Hold the cups in place with tape after removal of the yoke.
28 Remove the circlip holding the spider to the driveshaft. Use a small dab of paint or a file mark to identify the position of the spider in relationship to the shaft (this will ensure correct installation).
29 The spider can now be removed from the shaft. The preferred method is to support the spider under the cups and push on the shaft in a hydraulic press. If a press is not available, support the spider under the center boss in a vise and drive out the shaft with a brass drift. If this method is used, it is important to support only the center of the spider — not the cups. The shock loads imposed could easily damage the inner faces of the cups and spider and the needle bearings.
30 With the spider removed the boot can be slid off the shaft and discarded.

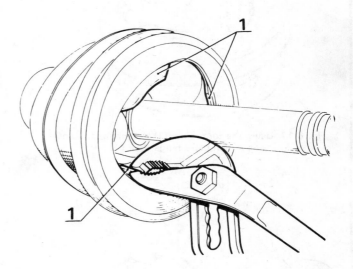

Fig. 8.14 Using a pliers to bend back the anti-separation plate tangs (1) in the yoke (Sec 6)

31 Clean the driveaxle and remove as much of the grease as possible from the spider and yoke with clean rags. **Note:** *Do not use solvent, gasoline or kerosene — use clean rags only.*
32 Check the components for wear and make sure they move smoothly without excess play. If wear or damage is evident, replace the spider assembly and the yoke with new parts.
33 Begin reassembly by lubricating the driveaxle and the inside of the boot with clean engine oil.
34 Place the rubber retaining collar over the driveaxle and install the boot.
35 Slide the spider onto the shaft (be sure to align the marks made during disassembly).

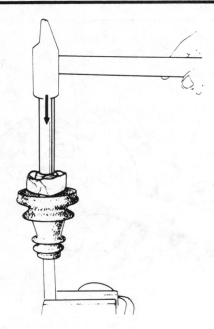

Fig. 8.15 Tapping the spider onto the driveaxle with a hammer and section of pipe (Sec 6)

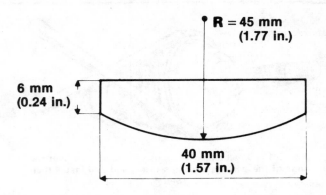

Fig. 8.16 Form plate fabrication diagram (material is 0.100-inch thick) (Sec 6)

R = 45 mm (1.77 in.)

6 mm (0.24 in.)

40 mm (1.57 in.)

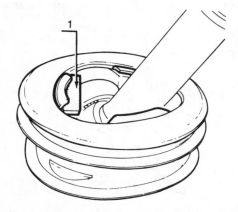

Fig. 8.17 Using the form plate (1) to reshape the anti-separation plate tangs (Sec 6)

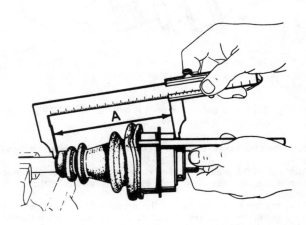

Fig. 8.18 Compress the joint until distance A is as specified in the text (Sec 6)

A

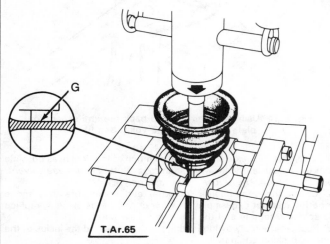

T.Ar.65

Fig. 8.19 Press the bearing/boot assembly onto the driveaxle while supporting the shaft at the machined groove (G) (Sec 6)

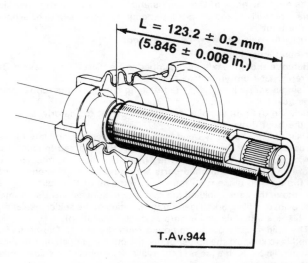

L = 123.2 ± 0.2 mm (5.846 ± 0.008 in.)

T.Av.944

Fig. 8.20 When the manufacturer's tool is used, the distance from the end of the shaft to the inner face of the bearing will be as specified (if a section of pipe is used, the distance will have to be measured) (Sec 6)

36 Drive the spider into place with a hammer and section of pipe, then install the circlip.

37 Apply all of the grease supplied in the repair kit to the spider and grooves in the driveaxle yoke (make sure everything is thoroughly lubricated).

38 Slide the yoke into position over the spider.

39 Using a piece of 0.100-inch thick steel plate, fabricate a form plate like the one shown in the accompanying illustration.

40 Position the form plate under each anti-separation tang in the yoke and tap the tang down onto the plate. Remove the form plate after all tangs have been returned to their original shape.

41 Slide the boot into position in the grooves of the yoke and driveaxle. Slip the rubber retaining collar over the boot.

42 Lift up the boot lip with a blunt tool and squeeze the boot slightly to remove any trapped air. With the tool in position, compress the joint until the distance from the small end to the flat face of the yoke is 6.040-inches (see the accompanying illustration). Hold the yoke in this position and withdraw the tool.

43 Install the new retaining springs on the boot, then install the driveaxle as described in Section 5.

Left-hand inner joint

44 Remove the driveaxle as described in Section 5. Purchase a CV joint repair kit from your dealer.

45 Remove the circlip holding the spider to the driveshaft. Use a small dab of paint or a file mark to identify the position of the spider in relationship to the shaft (this will ensure correct installation).

46 The spider can now be removed from the shaft. The preferred method is to support the spider under the cups and push on the shaft in a hydraulic press. If a press is not available, support the spider under the center boss in a vise and drive out the shaft with a brass drift. If this method is used, it is important to support only the center of the spider — not the cups. The shock loads imposed could easily damage the inner faces of the cups and spider and the needle bearings.

47 Now support the bearing at the small end of the boot and press or drive the shaft out of the boot and bearing assembly.

48 Check the components for wear and make sure they move smoothly without excess play. If wear or damage is evident, replace the parts with new ones.

49 Because of the lip-type oil seal used in the bearing, the bearing and boot must be installed with a press. The seal will most likely be damaged and distorted if a hammer and section of pipe are used to drive the assembly onto the shaft.

50 The accompanying illustration shows the tools required for installing the boot and bearing if a press is being used. The boot and bearing must be positioned so that the distance from the end of the driveaxle to the flat face at the small diameter of the boot is 5.85-inches.

51 Drive or press the spider onto the shaft (align the marks made during disassembly), then install the circlip.

52 Install the driveaxle as described in Section 5.

---

7   Driveaxle rubber boots — replacement

Removal and installation of the boots is an integral part of CV joint repair. Refer to the appropriate part of Section 6 for boot replacement procedures.

Chapter 9 Brakes

Refer to Chapter 13 for additional information

Contents

Specifications

Front brakes
Minimum brake pad thickness . . . . See Chapter 1
Rotor thickness (new) . . . . 0.472 in
Minimum rotor thickness . . . . 0.433 in
Maximum rotor runout (measured at 8.976 in diameter) . . . . 0.003 in

Rear brakes
Maximum allowable drum diameter . . . . 8.060 in
Brake shoe lining minimum thickness . . . . See Chapter 1
Wheel cylinder bore diameter . . . . 0.813 in

Master cylinder
Bore diameter . . . . 0.827 in
Brake fluid type . . . . See Chapter 1

Torque specifications   Ft-lbs
Brake caliper bolts 26
Caliper carrier bolts 74
Master cylinder-to-booster nuts . . . . 11 to 19
Booster-to-firewall nuts 18
Rear stub axle (hub) nut 118
Wheel cylinder mounting bolts . . . . 9 to 13

1 General information

All vehicles covered by this manual are equipped with power-assisted hydraulic brakes. The front brakes are discs and the rear brakes are drums.

The front disc brakes are operated by single piston sliding-type calipers. At the rear, leading and trailing brake shoes are operated by twin piston wheel cylinders. The rear brakes self-adjust when the brake pedal is applied.

The parking brake operates the rear brakes only through a mechanical linkage.

Driver warning lights indicate excessive brake pad wear, low brake fluid level and parking brake application.

After completing any operation involving disassembly of brake system components, always test drive the vehicle to check for proper brake performance before resuming normal driving.

2 Front disc brake pads — replacement

Caution: *Disc brake pads must be replaced on both wheels at the same time. Never replace the pads on only one wheel. Also, brake system dust contains asbestos, which is harmful to your health. Never blow it out with compressed air and do not inhale any of it.*

1 Raise the front of the vehicle and support it on jackstands, then remove the front wheels.

2 Discard two-thirds of the brake fluid from the master cylinder reservoir (do not drain the reservoir completely).

3 Carefully press the piston to the bottom of the caliper bore with a large screwdriver or C-clamp.

4 Remove the caliper mounting bolts and separate the caliper from the carrier. Suspend it from the strut spring with a piece of stiff wire (do not allow it to hang by the rubber brake hose).

5 Hold the anti-rattle clip against the caliper carrier and remove the

Fig. 9.1 If done carefully, a large screwdriver or pry bar can be used to lever the caliper over and depress the piston in the bore (Sec 2)

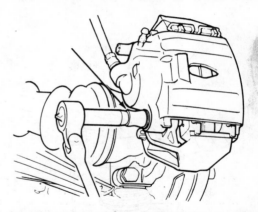

Fig. 9.2 Removing the caliper mounting bolts (arrow) with a socket and ratchet (Sec 2)

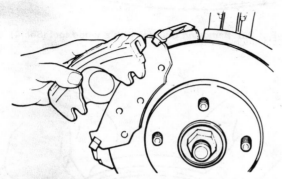

Fig. 9.3 Rotate the caliper up to separate it from the brake pads (Sec 2)

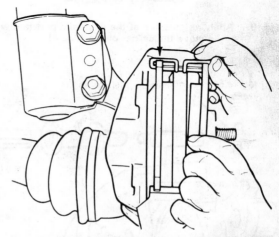

Fig. 9.4 The anti-rattle clip (arrow) must be held up against the carrier when removing the outer brake pad (Sec 2)

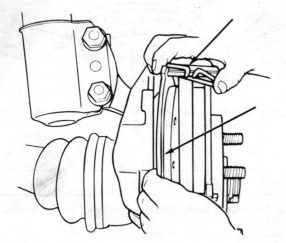

Fig. 9.5 Removing the inner brake pad and the anti-rattle clip (arrows) (Sec 2)

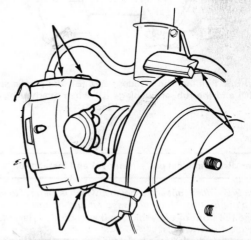

Fig. 9.6 Clean the caliper and carrier mating surfaces (arrows) with a wire brush and apply high-temperature brake grease to ensure free movement of the caliper when the brakes are applied (Sec 2)

outer brake pad.

6 Remove the inner brake pad and the anti-rattle clip, then refer to Section 5 and check the rotor before proceeding.

7 Use a clean, dry rag to wipe off the caliper (do not disturb the rubber dust boot). If the caliper is leaking brake fluid, it should be overhauled by referring to Section 4.

8 Clean the mating surfaces of the caliper and carrier with a wire brush or crocus cloth, then lubricate them with a high-temperature moly-based grease (a small amount will be sufficient here).

9 Attach the anti-rattle clip to the carrier (the split end of the clip

must face away from the rotor).

10 Install the inner and outer brake pads while holding the clip in place.

11 Slip the caliper into place very carefully so the dust boot is not damaged, then install the bolts and tighten them to the specified torque.

12 Add brake fluid to the master cylinder reservoir, then depress the brake pedal firmly to seat the pads.

13 Lower the vehicle and check for proper brake operation.

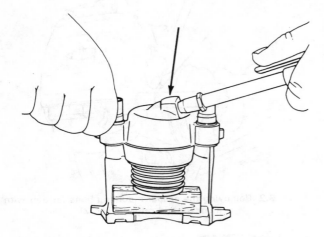

**Fig. 9.7 Apply air pressure at the fluid inlet port (arrow) to
remove the caliper piston (Sec 4)**

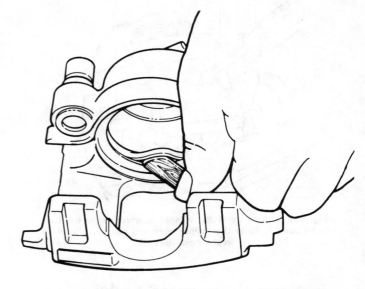

Fig. 9.8 Removing the seal with a wood tool (Sec 4)

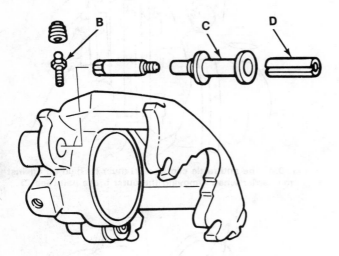

**Fig. 9.9 Remove the bleeder valve (B), the plastic sleeves
(C) and the rubber bushings (D) when overhauling the
caliper (Sec 4)**

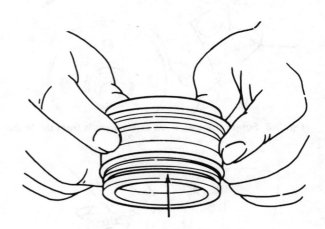

**Fig. 9.10 Make sure the boot lip seats in the piston groove
(arrow) (Sec 4)**

---

3 Front disc brake caliper — removal and installation

Caution: *Brake dust contains asbestos, which is harmful to your health.
Do not blow it out with compressed air and do not inhale any of it.*
1   Raise the front of the vehicle and support it on jackstands, then
remove the front wheels.
2   Discard two-thirds of the brake fluid from the master cylinder reservoir (do not drain the reservoir completely).
3   Carefully press the piston to the bottom of the caliper bore with
a large screwdriver or C-clamp.
4   Disconnect the brake hose from the caliper and plug the hose (use
a flare-nut wrench when disconnecting the hose if you have one
available). If the caliper is being removed for overhaul, see Step 3 of
the following Section regarding the removal of the caliper piston.
5   Remove the caliper mounting bolts and separate the caliper from
the carrier.
6   Installation is the reverse of removal, but be sure to tighten the
bolts to the specified torque, add fluid to the master cylinder reservoir
and bleed the hydraulic system as described later in this Chapter.

4 Front disc brake caliper — overhaul

Note: *Purchase a brake caliper overhaul kit before beginning this
procedure.*
1   Refer to Section 3 and remove the caliper.
2   Clean the exterior of the caliper with brake system solvent,
denatured alcohol or clean brake fluid. **Warning:** *Do not, under any
circumstances, use petroleum-based solvents to clean brake components. Disassemble the caliper on a clean workbench.*
3   Drain any remaining fluid from the caliper, then position a block
of wood inside the casting, in front of the piston. Apply compressed
air at the fluid inlet port to ease the piston out of the bore. **Caution:**
*Never place your fingers in front of the piston in an attempt to catch
or protect it when applying compressed air — serious injury could result!*
If compressed air is not available, brake fluid from the vehicle's hydraulic
system can be used. With the brake hose connected to the caliper and
the caliper suspended from the strut spring, have an assistant slowly
depress the brake pedal which should force the piston out of its bore.
4   Use a screwdriver to pry the dust boot out of the bore, then discard.

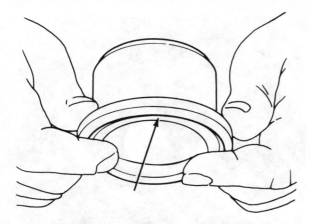

Fig. 9.11 Snap the seal fold (arrow) into place (Sec 4)

5   Using a wood or plastic tool, remove the piston seal from the groove in the caliper bore. Metal tools may cause bore damage.
6   Remove the bleeder valve, then remove and discard the plastic sleeves and rubber bushings from the caliper ears. Also discard all rubber parts.
7   Clean the remaining parts with brake system cleaner and blow them dry with compressed air.
8   If the piston is scored or corroded, replace it with a new one. If the caliper bore is damaged or worn, the caliper must be replaced. If the mounting bolts are corroded or the threads are damaged, replace them with new parts.
9   Lubricate the piston bore and the new seal with clean brake fluid and install the seal in the groove.
10 Lubricate the piston and install the new dust boot. Slide the metal portion of the boot over the open end of the piston and pull the boot to the rear until the lip seats in the piston groove. Push the metal retainer forward until it is flush with the rim at the open end of the piston, then snap the fold into place.
11 Insert the piston squarely into the caliper bore and bottom it (do not unseat the seal).
12 The metal portion of the boot must be seated in the counterbore at the outer end of the caliper bore. A special tool is made for this procedure, but a section of pipe of the correct diameter will work if care is used.
13 Install the bleeder valve and the new plastic sleeves and rubber bushings in the caliper ears.
14 The caliper can now be reinstalled by referring to Section 3.

5   Disc brake rotor — inspection, removal and installation

1   Raise the front of the vehicle and support it on jackstands, then remove the front wheels.
2   Remove the caliper and brake pad assemblies (Section 2).
3   Inspect the rotor surfaces. Light score marks and shallow grooves are normal, but deep grooves, galling and erosion are not. If the brake pedal pulsated during brake application, check the runout as follows.
4   Attach a dial indicator to the caliper carrier with the indicator stem resting on the rotor surface. Turn the rotor in the normal direction of rotation and note the runout. Check both the inner and outer surfaces. If it is greater than the specified limit, or if the rotor is scored or otherwise damaged, remove it and have it resurfaced at an automotive machine shop (have both rotors done at the same time).
5   Measure the rotor thickness with a micrometer. If it is less than the minimum specified, replace it with a new one. Measure the thickness at several points to see if it varies (any variation over 0.0005-inch may cause the pedal to pulsate during brake application). If the thickness is not consistent and the minimum thickness has not been reached, the rotor can be removed and resurfaced.
6   To remove the rotor, remove the caliper carrier bolts and separate the carrier from the hub bracket. Remove the two rotor mounting screws (if used — they have Torx heads and require a special screwdriver) and pull the rotor off the hub. If it is tight, tap very carefully

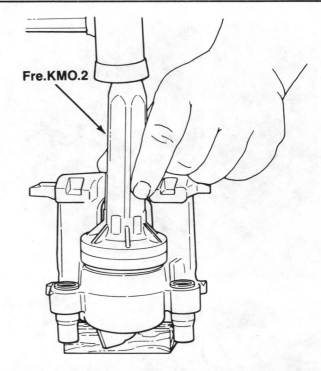

Fig. 9.12 Seat the dust boot metal retainer in the counterbore with the special tool or a section of pipe and a hammer (Sec 4)

6.2   Remove the cap by tapping it from side-to-side and prying with a screwdriver

on the back side with a soft-faced hammer.
7   Installation is the reverse of removal. Make sure the mating surfaces of the rotor and hub are clean before installing the rotor.

6   Rear drum brake shoes — replacement

Caution: *Brake dust contains asbestos, which is harmful to your health. Do not blow it out with compressed air and do not inhale any of it.*
1   Raise the rear of the vehicle and support it on jackstands, then remove the rear wheels.
2   By carefully tapping and prying with a screwdriver, remove the cap from the center of the brake drum (photo).

6.3a   Loosen and remove the stub axle nut . . .

6.3b   . . . and the thrust washer

6.4   The brake drum should come off by hand (if the brake shoes are retracted and the drum is stuck, a puller may be required)

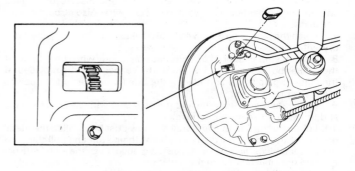

Fig. 9.13 If the drum will not come off, remove the plug from the backing plate, hold the adjuster lever away from the star wheel and turn the star wheel to retract the brake shoes (Sec 6)

3   Using a breaker bar and socket, remove the hub nut and withdraw the thrust washer (photos).
4   Pull the brake drum off of the stub axle. If it is difficult to remove, make sure the parking brake is released. If it is still not loose, retract the brake shoes by removing the access plug from the rear of the backing plate, unseating the automatic adjuster lever with a small screwdriver and backing off the adjuster with a second small screwdriver.
5   **Note:** *All four rear brake shoes should be replaced at the same time, but to avoid mixing up parts, work on only one brake assembly at a time. This will also enable you to use the remaining brake assembly as a guide if problems occur during reassembly.* Remove the return springs, the adjuster assembly and the hold-down springs from the brake shoe assembly.
6   Remove the brake shoes from the backing plate and separate the parking brake cable from the lever with a pliers.
7   Remove the horseshoe retaining clip and spring washer, then separate the lever from the brake shoe.
8   Clean the backing plate and check the shoe pads for wear and burrs. If a ridge has formed, remove it with a file and emery paper. Carefully pull the lower edges of the boots away from the wheel cylinder and look for signs of fluid leakage. Excessive fluid in the boots indicates that wheel cylinder overhaul is needed (see Section 7).
9   Apply a light coat of high-temperature brake grease to the pads where the shoes contact the backing plate.
10   Clean the adjuster mechanism and check it for proper operation.

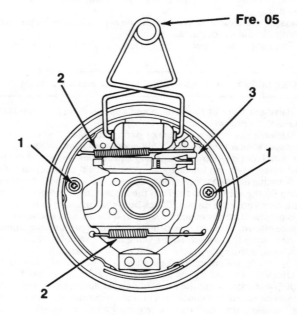

Fig. 9.14 Remove the hold-down springs and pins (1), the return springs (2) and the adjuster assembly (3) before separating the brake shoes from the backing plate (Sec 6)

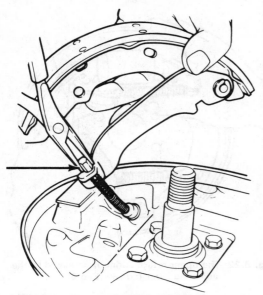

Fig. 9.15 Use a pliers to separate the parking brake cable (arrow) from the lever on the trailing shoe (Sec 6)

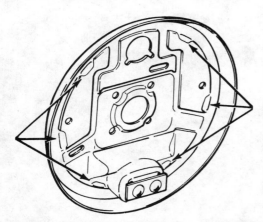

Fig. 9.17 Apply a small amount of high-temperature brake grease to the areas where the brake shoes contact the backing plate (arrows) (Sec 6)

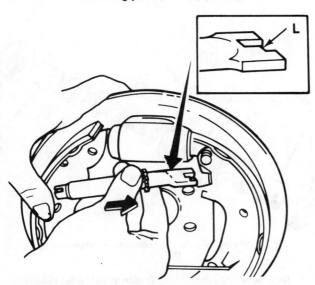

Fig. 9.20 Make sure the marked side of the adjuster socket blade is installed facing the wheel cylinder (Sec 6)

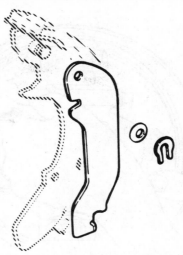

Fig. 9.16 The parking brake lever is secured to the brake shoe pivot with a spring washer and a horseshoe clip (Sec 6)

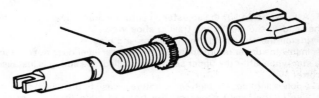

Fig. 9.18 Apply high-temperature brake grease to the adjuster screw threads and the socket end of the adjusting screw (arrows) (Sec 6)

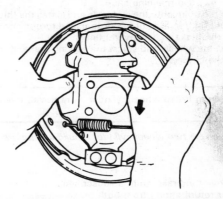

Fig. 9.19 Attach the lower return spring to both shoes, then position the shoe assembly on the backing plate and seat the shoes on the lower pivot (Sec 6)

If the threads are damaged or worn, new parts will be required. Apply high-temperature brake grease to the adjuster screw threads and the socket end of the screw.

11   Install the stainless steel washer and the socket on the end of the adjusting screw. Thread the screw into the adjuster all the way, then back it out one-half turn.

12   Attach the parking brake lever to the trailing shoe, install the washer and crimp a new horseshoe clip over the pin.

13   Attach the cable to the lever.

14   Attach the lower return spring to the shoes, then position the shoe assembly on the backing plate. Install the adjuster assembly (the socket and slot must fit into the trailing shoe and parking brake lever). **Note:** *The socket is marked R or L for right or left brake assemblies. The letter on the flat must face the wheel cylinder to ensure that the deeper slot fits into the parking brake lever.*

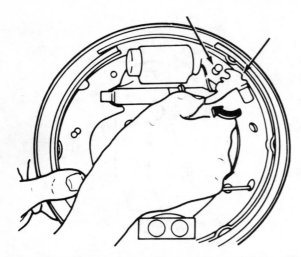

Fig. 9.21 The adjuster lever (arrow) is attached to the pivot (arrow) and the slot in the trailing shoe (Sec 6)

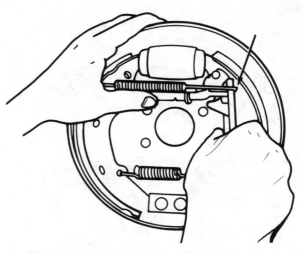

Fig. 9.22 The upper return spring is attached to the adjusting lever (arrow) (Sec 6)

15 Attach one end of the adjuster lever to the brake lever pin and the other end to the slot in the trailing shoe web.
16 Install the shoe hold-down springs and pins.
17 Install the upper return spring. If the adjuster lever does not contact the star wheel after the upper spring is installed, the spring is installed incorrectly.
18 Apply a light coat of high-temperature grease to the wheel spindle.
19 Center the brake shoes on the backing plate (if they are not centered, the drum will be difficult to install).
20 Before reinstalling the drum, it should be checked for cracks, score marks, deep scratches and hard spots (which look like small discolored areas). If the drum is damaged or worn, have both drums resurfaced by an automotive machine shop.
21 Slide the drum onto the stub axle and install the thrust washer and a *new* nut. Tighten the nut to the specified torque and install the cap. Depress the brake pedal several times.
22 Install the wheels and adjust the parking brake, then lower the vehicle to the ground

---

7 Rear drum brake wheel cylinder — removal, overhaul and installation

---

Note: *Purchase two wheel cylinder rebuild kits before beginning this procedure.*

Removal
1 Remove the brake drum as described in Section 6, then remove the upper return spring from both brake shoes.
2 Remove all traces of dirt from around the brake line union at the rear of the backing plate (photo), then loosen the fitting and separate the line from the wheel cylinder (use a flare-nut wrench if you have one available). Plug or cap off the brake line to prevent the entry of dirt.
3 Remove the two wheel cylinder mounting bolts from the backing plate, then move the brake shoes apart at the top and separate the wheel cylinder from the brake assembly.

Overhaul
4 Disassemble the wheel cylinder on a clean workbench to prevent contamination by dirt.
5 Remove the dust covers, the two pistons, the cup seals and the spring/expander assembly. It may help to tap the cylinder body on a block of wood to dislodge the pistons. Unscrew the bleeder valve.
6 Clean the wheel cylinder with brake system solvent, denatured alcohol or clean brake fluid. **Warning:** *Do not, under any circumstances, use petroleum-based solvents to clean brake parts.*
7 Dry the wheel cylinder with compressed air. Check the bore and pistons for scratches, score marks and other visible damage. Replace damaged pistons with new ones and hone the bore if necessary (do

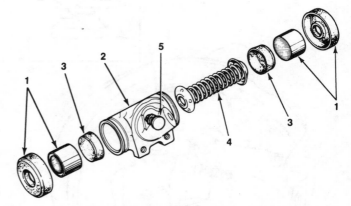

Fig. 9.23 Wheel cylinder components — exploded view (Sec 7)

1 *Dust boot and piston*   4 *Spring/expander assembly*
2 *Wheel cylinder*   5 *Bleeder valve*
3 *Rubber cup seals*

not enlarge the bore more than 0.003-inch when honing). Clean the cylinder again after honing. If the defects cannot be removed easily, replace the wheel cylinder with a new one.
8   Discard all of the rubber parts and use the new ones from the rebuild kit.
9   Dip the new seals and pistons in clean brake fluid and assemble them wet. Insert one of the seals into the bore with the flat face facing out. Insert the piston and install the dust cover.
10 Slide the spring/expander into the bore, then install the second seal with the flat face facing out. Insert the second piston and install the dust cover.
11 Thread the bleeder valve into the hole.

Installation
12 Spread the tops of the brake shoes apart and position the wheel cylinder on the backing plate. Make sure the brake shoes are engaged correctly in the wheel cylinder, then thread the brake line fitting into the hole in the rear of the wheel cylinder.
13 Install the mounting bolts and tighten them to the specified torque, then tighten the brake line fitting.
14 Install the upper brake return spring and the brake drum as described in Section 6. Bleed the hydraulic system as described in Section 15, then install the wheels and lower the vehicle to the ground.

8   Master cylinder — removal and installation

1   Cover the fender and cowling area of the vehicle to avoid damage from spilled brake fluid (it will remove paint). Place rags or newspapers under the master cylinder to catch spilled fluid.
2   Unplug the wires from the master cylinder reservoir (where used), then disconnect the brake lines (use a flare-nut wrench if you have one available).
3   Remove the master cylinder mounting nuts and separate it from the power brake booster.
4   Overhaul procedures are covered in Section 9.
5   Attach the master cylinder to the power brake booster, install the

nuts and tighten them to the specified torque.
6   Connect the brake lines and tighten the fittings (be very careful not to strip the threads).
7   Fill the reservoir to the maximum level with new, clean brake fluid, then bleed the system as described later in this Chapter.
8   If used, hook up the brake fluid level sensor wires.

9   Master cylinder — overhaul

Note: *Purchase a master cylinder rebuild kit before beginning this procedure. The kit will include all the replacement parts necessary for the overhaul. The rubber replacement parts, particularly the seals, are the key to fluid control in the master cylinder. As such, it's very important that they be installed correctly. Be very careful not to let them come in contact with petroleum-based solvents or lubricants.*

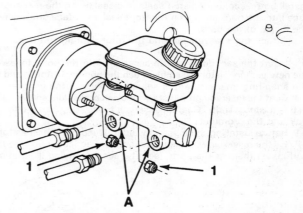

Fig. 9.24 Master cylinder mounting details (Sec 8)

A Brake line mounts   1 Mounting nuts

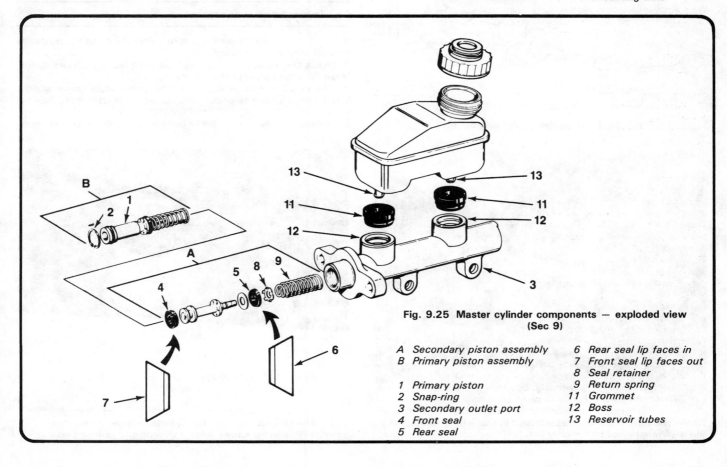

Fig. 9.25 Master cylinder components — exploded view (Sec 9)

A Secondary piston assembly	6 Rear seal lip faces in
B Primary piston assembly	7 Front seal lip faces out
	8 Seal retainer
1 Primary piston	9 Return spring
2 Snap-ring	11 Grommet
3 Secondary outlet port	12 Boss
4 Front seal	13 Reservoir tubes
5 Rear seal	

1   Drain the fluid from the reservoir, then mount the master cylinder in a vise (do not clamp the cylindrical portion — grip the flange).
2   Press in on the primary piston and remove the snap-ring from the end of the bore. Discard the primary piston.
3   Apply air pressure to the secondary outlet port to remove the secondary piston assembly. Remove and discard the front and rear seals.
4   Remove the reservoir by rocking it back-and-forth and lifting up on it.
5   Clean the master cylinder with brake system solvent, denatured alcohol or clean brake fluid and dry it with compressed air. **Warning:** *Do not, under any circumstances, use petroleum-based solvents to clean brake parts.*
6   Check the bore for wear, corrosion and damage. If it is scratched, scored or worn excessively, the master cylinder must be replaced with a new one.
7   Coat the bore and all new rubber parts with clean brake fluid, then install both secondary piston seals (the seal lip on the rear seal must face into the bore; the lip on the front seal must face out, away from the inside of the bore).
8   Attach the seal retainer and the return spring to the secondary piston.
9   Insert the secondary piston assembly into the bore, followed by the new primary piston assembly. Push the primary piston in and install the snap-ring (make sure it is seated properly in the groove).
10 Coat the reservoir grommets with clean brake fluid and install them in the master cylinder. Coat the reservoir tubes also, then slip the reservoir into the grommets.
11 Before installing the master cylinder, bleed out the air as follows:
12 Fill the reservoir with clean brake fluid. Fabricate two bleed tubes and install them in the ports (see the accompanying illustration).

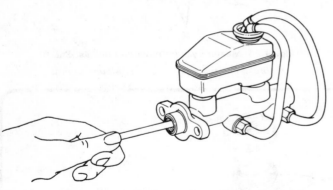

Fig. 9.26 Bleeding the master cylinder (Sec 9)

13 Using a wood dowel, slowly compress and release the piston assemblies (allow the pistons to return under spring pressure). Repeat the procedure until no air bubbles are visible in the fluid leaving the bleed tubes. If necessary, tap the master cylinder lightly with a soft-faced hammer to dislodge air bubbles.
14 Remove the bleed tubes, plug the outlet ports and install the reservoir cap before reinstalling the master cylinder.

10 Hydraulic brake hoses and lines — inspection and replacement

1   About every six months, with the vehicle raised and placed securely on jackstands, the flexible hoses which connect the steel brake lines with the front and rear brake assemblies should be inspected for cracks, chafing of the outer cover, leaks, blisters and other damage. These are important and vulnerable parts of the brake system and inspection should be complete. A light and mirror will enable you to do a thorough job. If the hoses are deteriorated, replace them with new ones.
2   Check the fittings for leaks and the steel lines for corrosion, cracks and dents.
3   Brake line replacement can be accomplished by loosening the fittings at each end and separating the line from the support clips. A flare-nut wrench should be used on the fittings to avoid rounding them off.
4   When removing the flexible hoses, wipe all dirt from the fittings, then loosen them with a flare-nut wrench to avoid rounding them off. Next remove the spring clip and withdraw the end of the hose from the serrated mount (photo). The front brake hoses can be unscrewed from the calipers.
5   Replacement hoses and lines should be obtained from a dealer parts department or an auto parts store. Do not try to fabricate replacements.
6   Installation is basically the reverse of removal. Make sure the lines are supported by the clips and do not kink or stretch rubber hoses. Check to see if suspension components come into contact with the hoses and reposition them if necessary.
7   Be sure to bleed the system when finished replacing lines or hoses.

11 Parking brake — adjustment

Note: *Do not adjust the parking brake unless the brake shoes, cables or lever have been replaced.*
1   Raise the rear of the vehicle and support it securely on jackstands. Make sure the parking brake is released.
2   Working under the vehicle, loosen the primary rod locknut and the knurled adjuster wheel (photo) until considerable slack is produced in the cables.
3   Depress and release the brake pedal several times to ensure opera-

10.4   The rubber brake hoses are held in place by a spring clip and a serrated mount

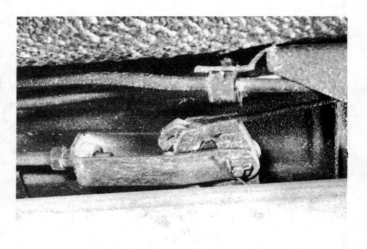

11.2   The locknut (A) must be loosened before the knurled adjuster (B) can be turned when adjusting the parking brake

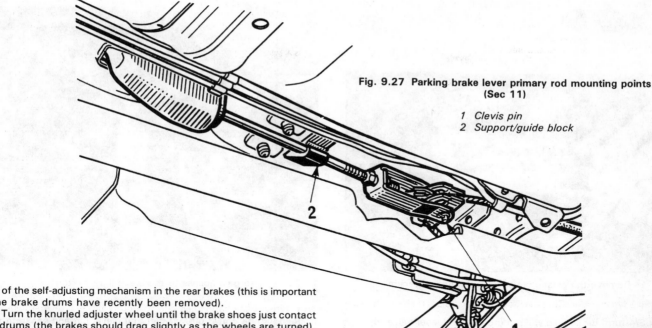

Fig. 9.27 Parking brake lever primary rod mounting points
(Sec 11)

1   Clevis pin
2   Support/guide block

tion of the self-adjusting mechanism in the rear brakes (this is important
if the brake drums have recently been removed).
4   Turn the knurled adjuster wheel until the brake shoes just contact
the drums (the brakes should drag slightly as the wheels are turned).
5   Back off the adjuster wheel until the wheels just turn freely.
6   Turn the adjuster wheel as needed to produce a minimum of 7 or
8 clicks at the parking brake lever before the rear wheels are completely
locked.
7   Tighten the locknut and lower the vehicle to the ground, then check
the operation of the parking brake.

12   Parking brake cable — removal and installation

1   Raise the rear of the vehicle and support it securely on jackstands.
Remove the wheels.
2   Remove the brake drum as described in Section 6.
3   Remove the cotter pin, washer and clevis pin securing the yoke
to the primary rod under the vehicle. Slip the cable end out of the yoke.
4   Disconnect the other end of the cable from the lever on the brake
shoe. Remove the bolt and release the bracket attaching the cable to
the rear suspension arm.
5   Tap the cable housing out of the brake backing plate and support
member, release the rear axle retaining clips and withdraw the cable
from under the vehicle.
6   Installation is the reverse of removal. Be sure to adjust the cable
as described in Section 11.

13   Parking brake lever — removal and installation

1   Raise the rear of the vehicle and support it on jackstands.
2   Working under the vehicle, remove the cotter pin, washer and clevis
pin from the balancer yoke. Disengage the primary rod from the sup-
port/guide block.
3   Working inside the vehicle, remove the two restraint system (seat
belt) anchor bolts.
4   Make a slit in the carpet just to the rear of the lever assembly, then
spread the carpet and disconnect the warning light switch wires.
5   Remove the bolts and separate the lever assembly from the vehicle.
6   Installation is the reverse of removal. Be sure to adjust the cable
as described in Section 11.

14   Power brake booster — inspection, removal and installation

Inspection
1   If the operation of the power brake booster is suspect, carry out
the following test to determine if it is functioning correctly.

2   Depress and release the brake pedal several times, then hold it
down and start the engine. As the engine starts, the brake pedal should
move down. Allow the engine to run for at least two minutes, then
shut it off. Depress the brake pedal again and listen for a hiss at the
booster. After about four or five applications of the pedal, no further
hissing should be heard and the pedal should feel firmer.
3   If the booster does not work as described above, check the vacuum
hose for kinks, cracks and correct installation. Start the engine with
the hose disconnected from the booster and make sure there is vacuum
at the hose. If there is, the booster may be defective.

Removal and installation
4   Disconnect the booster pushrod from the brake pedal inside the
vehicle.
5   Detach the vacuum hose from the booster check valve.
6   Remove the master cylinder mounting nuts, but do not disconnect
the brake lines.
7   Carefully pull the master cylinder forward until it clears the studs
on the booster, then support it so the lines will not get kinked.
8   Working under the dash, remove the booster mounting nuts and
washers, then separate the booster from the firewall.
9   Installation is the reverse of removal. Be sure to check brake operation before driving the vehicle.

15   Hydraulic system — bleeding

1   Whenever air enters the hydraulic brake system, either from component servicing or system damage, all air must be removed from the
brake system in order to maintain proper braking action. Apply the
brakes several times with the engine off to remove the vacuum reserve.
2   Clean the area around the top of the master cylinder and remove
the cap. Keep the reservoir filled with the specified type of brake fluid
during the bleeding operation.
3   You will need an empty, clear plastic container, a length of clear
plastic tubing to fit over the bleeder valve, a wrench to loosen the
bleeder valve and an assistant to depress the brake pedal. The vehicle
should be raised and supported securely on jackstands for access
underneath (it may help to remove the wheels as well).
4   Pour enough new brake fluid into the container to cover the end
of the plastic tubing, then attach the other end of the tubing to the
bleeder valve fitting on the right-rear wheel cylinder (if the bleeder valve
has a dust cover, remove it first).
5   Position the wrench over the bleeder valve, then have your assistant depress the brake pedal and hold it down. Turn the bleeder valve

17.2a   Remove the plastic cover from the pedal bracket . . .

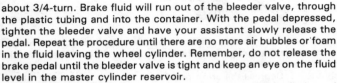

17.2b   . . . to gain access to the brake light switch

about 3/4-turn. Brake fluid will run out of the bleeder valve, through the plastic tubing and into the container. With the pedal depressed, tighten the bleeder valve and have your assistant slowly release the pedal. Repeat the procedure until there are no more air bubbles or foam in the fluid leaving the wheel cylinder. Remember, do not release the brake pedal until the bleeder valve is tight and keep an eye on the fluid level in the master cylinder reservoir.

6   Move to the left-front caliper, then the left-rear wheel cylinder and finally the right-front caliper and repeat the procedure for each wheel.

7   Do not allow the master cylinder to run dry and discard all fluid that is bled from the system. Refill the master cylinder reservoir and check brake operation before driving the vehicle.

16   Brake pedal — removal and installation

1   Working inside the vehicle, detach the plastic cover from the brake pedal assembly under the dash.

2   If the air duct is in the way, detach it from the heater and side vent tube and remove it.

3   Remove the cotter pin, washer and clevis pin and separate the power brake booster pushrod from the pedal.

4   Remove the clips and slide out the pedal shaft (note the positions of any washers installed between the brake and clutch pedals).

5   With the shaft removed, lift out the pedal.

6   If the bushings in the pedal are worn or damaged, replace them with new ones.

7   Installation is the reverse of removal.

17   Brake light switch — removal, installation and adjustment

1   The brake light switch is attached to the brake pedal bracket under the dashboard.

2   To gain access to it, remove the plastic cover around the pedal bracket (photos).

3   Disconnect the wires and unscrew the switch from the bracket.

4   Installation is the reverse of removal. Thread the switch in or out, as required, until the brake light operates after the pedal has moved 1/4-inch.

Chapter 10   Suspension and steering systems

Contents

Specifications

Steering

Front wheel toe-out (vehicle unloaded)

1983	0.5 to 1.5 mm per wheel
1984 on	0 to 1/8 in (0 to 3.3 mm) 0 to 1/4° per wheel

Torque specifications	Ft-lbs
Front suspension	
Driveaxle retaining nut	155
Suspension arm balljoint clamp bolt nut	40
Balljoint-to-suspension arm nuts	55
Suspension arm pivot bolt nuts	59
Suspension strut-to-stub axle carrier bolt/nut	55
Suspension strut top mounting bolt	17
Stabilizer bar clamp nuts	17
Rear suspension	
Suspension arm bracket-to-body bolts	59
Brake drum/hub retaining nut	118
Stabilizer bar mounting bolts	37
Shock absorber lower mount nut	59
Shock absorber upper mount nut	18
Steering	
Steering gear mounting bolts	40
Outer tie-rod stud nut	26
Inner balljoint-to-rack	30
Steering wheel nut	33
Steering shaft U-joint bolts	22

1   General information

The front suspension consists of MacPherson struts and pressed steel suspension arms. The arms are mounted in rubber bushings at their inner ends and attach to the stub axle carriers at the outer ends. A stabilizer bar is atached to both suspension arms and is mounted in rubber bushings at the rear of the front subframe. The front stub axle carriers, which house the wheel bearings, brake calipers and hub/rotor assemblies, are bolted to the struts and attached to the suspension arms with balljoints.

The independent rear suspension consists of trailing suspension arms attached to transverse torsion bars and telescopic, double-acting shock absorbers. A stabilizer bar is also used at the rear and is attached to both trailing arms. The integral rear hub and brake drum assemblies are mounted on stub axles with double-row roller bearings.

Steering may be either manual or power-assisted rack and pinion, depending on the model.

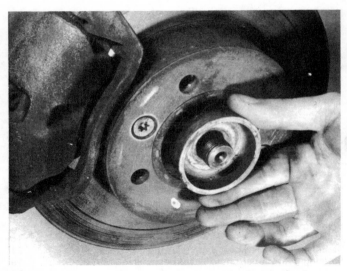

2.2   After removing the driveaxle retaining nut, remove the dished thrust washer from the stub axle

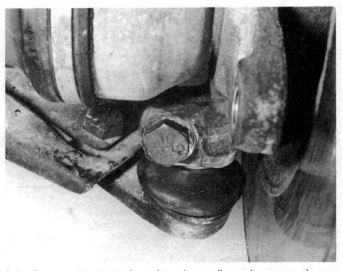

2.5   Remove the nut and washer, then pull out the suspension balljoint clamp bolt

2.7   Disengage the stub axle carrier from the balljoint stud, then carefully withdraw the assembly from the driveaxle

2.8a   Remove the two Torx-type screws (T-40) from the hub . . .

2.8b   . . . then separate the rotor from the hub

2.8c   If the rotor is stuck, suppport it on wood blocks and drive out the hub with a block of wood and a hammer

2 Front stub axle carrier — removal and installation

1   Raise the front of the vehicle and support it on jackstands, then remove the wheel(s).

2   While an assistant applies the brakes, loosen the large nut on the end of the driveaxle(s) with a socket and large breaker bar. Remove the dished thrust washer behind the nut (photo).

3   Refer to Chapter 9 and remove the brake caliper from the axle carrier (you do not have to separate the caliper from the caliper carrier).

4   Refer to Section 17 and separate the tie-rod from the axle carrier arm.

5   Remove the large nut and bolt from the suspension arm balljoint where it mates with the axle carrier (photo).

6   Remove the nuts and washers and separate the strut from the axle carrier.

7   Push down on the suspension arm while lifting on the stub axle carrier to disengage the suspension arm balljoint. Pull out on the carrier to separate it from the driveaxle (photo). If the driveaxle is tight, tap on the back of the carrier with a soft-faced hammer or use a puller as described in Chapter 8.

8   If the hub bearings are in need of attention, the brake rotor must be separated from the hub. Remove the TORX-type screws (size T-40) and pull the rotor off (photos). If the rotor is stuck, support it with wood blocks and drive the hub out of it with a soft-faced hammer (photo).

9   Installation is the reverse of removal, but make sure the mating surfaces of the brake rotor and hub flange are clean before installing the rotor and be sure to tighten all nuts/bolts to the specified torque.

3 Front hub bearings — removal and installation

Note: *The front hub bearings should only be removed from the carrier if they are being replaced with new ones. The removal procedure will damage them and render them unusable.*

1   Remove the stub axle carrier from the vehicle as described in the previous Section.

2   Support the carrier, outer face down, in a large vise or on wood blocks and drive the hub flange out of the bearing with a section of pipe and a hammer. The pipe must be the same diameter as the inner end of the hub flange (photo).

3   The bearing will come apart as the hub flange is removed and one of the inner races will remain on the flange. To remove it, support the flange in a vise and detach the race with a three-jaw puller. Remove the thrust washer from the flange.

4   Remove the snap-ring from the inner end of the stub axle carrier.

5   Turn the carrier over so the outer face is up, then place the previously removed inner race back in position over the balls and cage. Place a section of pipe against the inner race and drive the bearing out with a hammer.

6   Before installing the new bearing, remove the plastic covers protecting the seals from each end.

7   Support the carrier on wood blocks with the outer face down and place the new bearing in position.

8   Use a section of pipe with the same diameter as the bearing *outer* race to drive the bearing into the carrier. Do not hammer on the inner race or the bearing will be damaged. Also, make sure the bearing is

3.2   Hub flange inner end and bearing snap-ring in the stub axle carrier

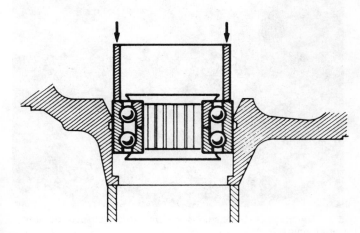

Fig. 10.1 Push or drive the bearing out of the stub axle carrier with a section of pipe the same diameter as the inner race (Sec 3)

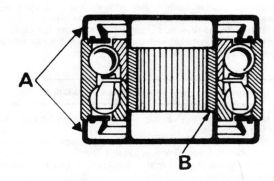

Fig. 10.2 Remove the plastic covers (A) before installing the new bearing; the sleeve (B) should be removed after the bearing is in place (Sec 3)

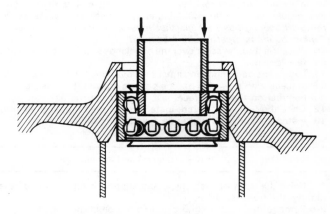

Fig. 10.3 When installing the bearing, apply pressure to the outer race only or the bearing will be damaged (Sec 3)

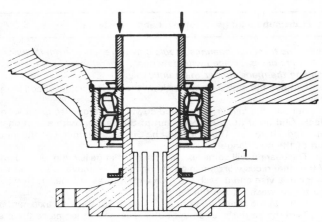

Fig. 10.4 When mating the bearing and hub flange, make sure the thrust washer (1) is in position and apply pressure to the **inner** race only or the bearing will be damaged (Sec 3)

4.3   The front suspension strut mounting bolts are located to the outside of the strut tower

5.2   The stabilizer bar clamp is attached to the suspension arm with a bolt and nut

driven in squarely or the outer race may be damaged.

9   Remove the plastic sleeve from the bearing, then lubricate the seal lips with EP (extreme pressure) moly-based grease. **Note:** *Two different bearings may be used. Some models are equipped with SNR bearings, while others are equipped with Timken bearings (both are interchangeable and have the manufacturer's name stamped on them). Only the SNR bearing has seal lips that must be lubricated. The seal on Timken bearings must* not *be lubricated.*

10   Place the thrust washer over the hub flange and lay it on the bench, flat face down.

11   Locate the carrier bearing inner race over the hub flange and drive it into place with a section of pipe bearing against the *inner* race. Do not hammer on the outer race or it will damage the bearing.

12   Once the flange is seated, install a new snap-ring in the carrier.

13   Install the stub axle carrier as described in the previous Section.

4   Front suspension strut — removal and installation

1   Raise the front of the vehicle and support it on jackstands then remove the front wheel(s).

2   Remove the strut-to-stub axle carrier bolts/nuts.

3   Working in the engine compartment, remove the upper strut mounting bolts (photo).

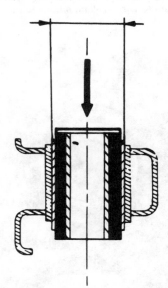

Fig. 10.5 A section of pipe 1.18-inches (30 mm) in diameter must be used when removing and installing the bushings in the front suspension arms (Sec 6)

4   Push the suspension arm down so the strut will not contact the driveaxle rubber boot and tear it, then separate the strut from the upper and lower mounts and withdraw it through the wheel arch.

5   Installation is the reverse of removal. Make sure the strut-to-stub axle carrier bolts are installed with the bolt heads at the rear and tighten the mounting bolts/nuts to the specified torque.

5   Front suspension arm — removal and installation

1   Raise the front of the vehicle and support it on jackstands, then remove the front wheel(s).

2   Loosen and remove the nut, bolt and washer attaching the stabilizer bar clamps to each suspension arm (photo). Disengage the clamps from the slots in the arms, then pivot the stabilizer bar down and away from the suspension arms.

3   Remove the balljoint-to-stub axle carrier bolt/nut.

4   Loosen and remove the two nuts, washers and pivot bolts that attach the suspension arm to the frame.

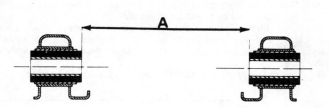

Fig. 10.6 The distance (A) between the inner edges of the bushings must be maintained at 5.79 ± 0.020-inches (Sec 6)

5   Pull down on the outer end of the arm to disengage it from the balljoint, then lever the arm out of the inner mounts. Recover the ball-joint washer.

6   If the pivot bushings are worn out, they can be replaced by pushing them out with sections of pipe (30 mm in diameter) and a hydraulic press or a large vise. Remove and replace the bushings one at a time so their central location in relationship to the pivot bolt is not disturbed. When pressing the last one into the arm, make sure it stops when the distance between the bushings is 5.79 ± 0.02-inches.

7   Installation is the reverse of removal. Make sure the plastic washer is in position over the balljoint stud before rejoining it to the axle carrier. Tighten all nuts/bolts to the specified torque, but leave the arm pivot bolts and the stabilizer bar clamp bolts loose until the vehicle has been lowered to the ground and rolled back-and-forth to settle the suspension.

6 Front suspension balljoint — removal and installation

1   Raise the front of the vehicle and support it on jackstands, then remove the front wheels.

2   Remove the balljoint-to-stub axle carrier bolt and nut (photo).

3   Remove the balljoint-to-suspension arm bolts/nuts, then pull down on the balljoint to disengage it from the carrier. Remove the washer from the balljoint stud.

4   Installation is the reverse of removal. Be sure to tighten the nuts/bolts to the specified torque.

7 Front stabilizer bar — removal and installation

Note: *The front suspension must be under a load during this operation. If a lift or hoist is not available, drive the front of the vehicle onto ramps.*

1   Loosen and remove the nut, bolt and washer attaching the stabilizer bar clamps to each suspension arm (photo 5.2). Disengage the clamps from the slots in the arms and remove them.

2   Remove the stabilizer bar clamp-to-frame bolts (photo), then disengage the clamps from the slots in the frame and remove them.

3   Manipulate the bar to clear the exhaust and gearshift linkage, then withdraw it from under the vehicle to the side.

4   If the rubber bushings are deteriorated, replace them with new ones (lubricate them with silicone spray or rubber grease).

5   Installation is the reverse of removal. Be sure to tighten the bolts/nuts to the specified torque.

8 Rear hub bearings — removal and installation

1   Raise the rear of the vehicle and support it on jackstands, then remove the wheels.

2   Refer to Chapter 9, Section 6, and remove the brake drum/hub assemblies from the rear axles.

3   Remove the bearing snap-ring from one hub.

4   Support the hub/drum assembly on wood blocks with the outer face down, then drive out the bearing with a section of pipe (1.9-inches in diameter) and a hammer.

5   Turn the hub over and position the new bearing in the bore. Drive

6.2   Suspension balljoint clamp bolt/nut and mounting bolts

7.2   The stabilizer bar is attached to the frame by two clamps and bolts

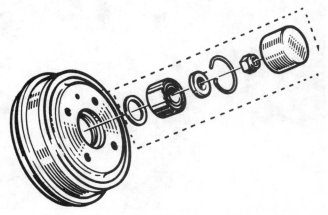

Fig. 10.7 Rear hub bearing and related components — exploded view (Sec 8)

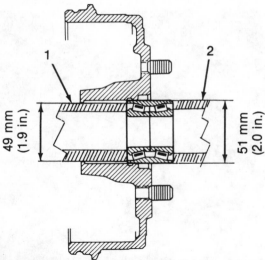

Fig. 10.8 When removing the rear hub bearing (1), apply pressure to the inner race (when installing the bearing [2], apply pressure to the outer race only or the bearing will be damaged) (Sec 8)

it into place with a section of pipe (2.0-inches in diameter) and a hammer. Make sure the pipe contacts the *outer* race only and drive the bearing in squarely or it will be damaged.
6   Install the bearing snap-ring (make sure it is seated in the groove).
7   Make sure the inner thrust washer is in place on the stub axle, then refer to Chapter 9 and reinstall the brake drum/hub assembly on the axle.
8   Repeat the procedure for the remaining hub and bearing.

9   Rear shock absorber — removal and installation

1   Raise the rear of the vehicle and support it on jackstands. Place a jack under the suspension arm on one side and raise it slightly (use a jackstand or wood blocks to ensure that the arm is securely supported).
2   Working in the luggage compartment or trunk, remove the rubber cover from the upper shock mount (photo).
3   Hold the shock strut to keep it from turning by gripping the flats on the upper end with an adjustable wrench or locking pliers. Remove the upper mount nut (photo).
4   Separate the upper mount washers and rubber bushing from the strut.
5   Working under the vehicle, remove the lower shock mount nut and

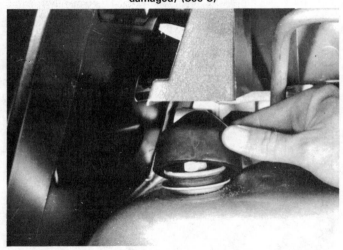

9.2   Remove the rubber cover to expose the rear shock absorber upper mounting nut

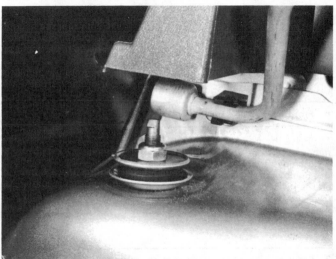

9.3   Remove the nut, the first washer, the rubber bushing and the second washer from the upper mount

9.5   The shock absorber is attached to the suspension arm mounting stud by a single nut

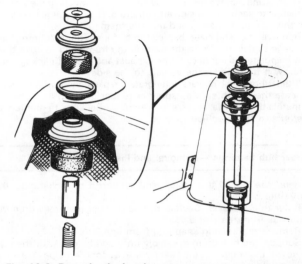

Fig. 10.9 Rear shock absorber upper mount components — exploded view (Sec 9)

washer (photo).

6   Pull the shock off the lower mounting stud, then withdraw it from the upper mounting hole. Note the arrangement of the rubber bushing and washer on the upper end.

7   To install the new shock, pull the strut all the way out, then slide the sleeve, rubber bushing and lower washer over the upper end.

8   Position the upper end in the mounting hole from under the vehicle, then install the lower mounting washer and nut (do not compress the shock any more than is necessary). Tighten the lower mounting nut to the specified torque.

9   Working inside the trunk or luggage compartment, install the washer, rubber bushing, the second washer and the nut. Tighten the nut securely and install the rubber cover.

10   Repeat the procedure for the remaining shock.

10   Rear stabilizer bar

1   Raise the rear of the vehicle and support it on jackstands.

2   Release the parking brake cable retaining clips from the stabilizer bar (photo).

3   Remove the two bolts attaching the stabilizer bar to the suspension arms on each side and remove the bar from under the vehicle (photo).

4   Installation is the reverse of removal. Make sure that the parking

brake cable guide clips are installed under the rear mounting bolts on each side and that the offset edges of the stabilizer bar brackets face the front of the vehicle. Tighten the bolts to the specified torque.

11   Rear torsion bar — removal and installation

1   Raise the rear of the vehicle and support it on jackstands, then remove the rear wheel(s).

2   Refer to Section 10 and remove the stabilizer bar.

3   Refer to Section 9 and remove the shock absorber(s).

4   Slowly lower the jack used to support the suspension arm during shock removal until the arm is hanging unsupported.

5   Pry off the cap (where used) from the outer face of the suspension arm mounting bracket (photo).

6   The torsion bar can now be withdrawn from the arm with a slide hammer puller (the puller should have an adapter that will thread into the hole in the end of the torsion bar). If a slide hammer is not available, thread a long bolt into the hole in the end of the torsion bar, slip a wrench over the bolt and slide it up against the bottom of the bolt head, then rap on the inside of the wrench with a hammer to try to dislodge the torsion bar.

7   Once the splines of the bar are free, pull it completely out. Note that the torsion bars are not interchangeable from side to side (they

10.2   The parking brake cable is attached to the rear stabilizer bar with clips

10.3   The rear stabilizer bar is attached to each suspension arm with two bolts (note the parking brake cable guide held in place by the rear bolt)

11.5   Thread the slide hammer puller shaft into the threaded hole in the end of the torsion bar

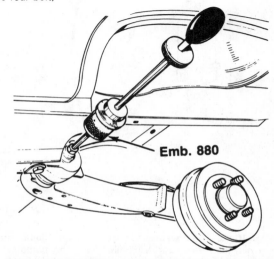

Fig. 10.10   The factory special tool (shown) or a slide hammer puller is needed to remove the rear torsion bars (Sec 11)

are marked on the end to ensure correct installation). Bars with two marks are used on the left-hand side and bars with three marks are used on the right-hand side.

8   Before installation of the torsion bar, the suspension arm must be positioned correctly or the vehicle height will be altered.

9   Support the arm so that the distance from the center of the lower shock mounting stud to the edge of the upper shock mounting hole is exactly 24.040-inches (this dimension is critical, so fabricate a support from a section of threaded rod and install it in place of the shock absorber if necessary).

10   With the suspension arm secured as described above, apply moly-

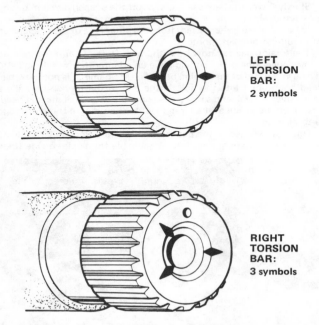

Fig. 10.11 The torsion bars are marked to ensure correct installation (Sec 11)

LEFT
TORSION
BAR:
2 symbols

RIGHT
TORSION
BAR:
3 symbols

based grease to the torsion bar splines and insert it into the mount. Jiggle the bar around until the inner and outer splines engage in the mount. Recheck the suspension arm height to be sure it is correct, then drive the torsion into the mount with a soft drift punch and a hammer.

11   Install the cap in the suspension arm outer face (if used).

12   Refer to the appropriate Sections and install the shock absorber(s) and stabilizer bar, then lower the vehicle and check the vehicle height as described in Section 23. If it is incorrect, the torsion bar(s) may have to be removed and reinstalled.

12   Rear suspension arm — removal and installation

1   Raise the rear of the vehicle and support it on jackstands, then remove the rear wheel(s).

2   Refer to the appropriate Sections and remove the stabilizer bar, the shock absorber and torsion bar on the side that the suspension arm is being removed from.

3   Refer to Chapter 9, Section 6 and remove the brake drum/hub assembly and detach the parking brake cable from the brake assembly.

4   Clean the brake line-to-hose union on the suspension transverse member, then unscrew the union. Carefully withdraw the line, then slip off the hose retaining clip and separate the hose from the bracket. Plug or cap off the line and hose ends to prevent contamination and loss of brake fluid.

5   Position a jack under the suspension arm that is being removed (under the stabilizer mount) and raise the jack until it contacts the arm.

6   Remove the rear seat cushion and the trim panel beside the cushion to expose the suspension arm mounting bracket nutplate.

7   Working under the vehicle, remove the mounting bracket bolts (photo).

8   Lower the jack until the bracket is clear of the body, then pull the arm and transverse member sideways to remove them (if they are tight, tap on the arm with a soft-faced hammer).

9   The assembly can be dismantled further, if necessary, by separating the brake line from the clips and removing the four bolts securing the brake backing plate to the suspension arm. Detach the backing plate and brake line and note the position of the thrust washer on the stub axle.

10   Refer to Section 13 and replace the suspension arm bushings if necessary. Replace the nutplate with a new one if it is damaged.

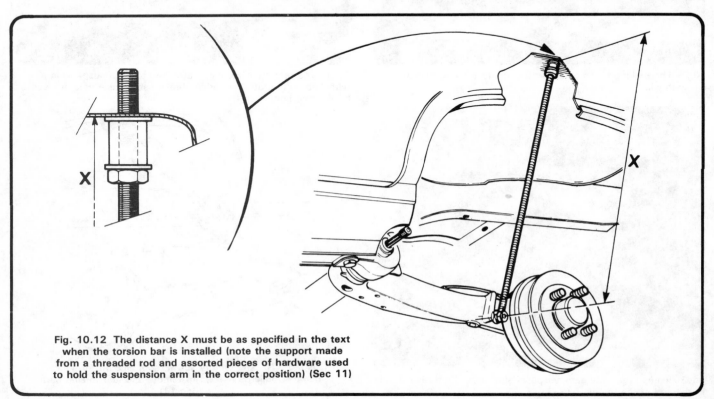

Fig. 10.12 The distance X must be as specified in the text when the torsion bar is installed (note the support made from a threaded rod and assorted pieces of hardware used to hold the suspension arm in the correct position) (Sec 11)

11 To install the suspension arm, lubricate the tube bushings with moly-based grease, slide it into position and align the mounting bracket and body bolt holes. Support the assembly with a jack and install the bolts. Tighten them to the specified torque.

12 Install the trim panel and the rear seat cushion.

13 The remaining installation steps are the reverse of removal. Refer to Chapter 9 when installing the various brake components and be sure to bleed the brake hydraulic system when finished.

13 Rear suspension arm bushings — replacement

Note: *The rear suspension arms pivot on outer bushings located in the mounting brackets and inner bushings located in the left-hand side of the transverse suspension member. If the inner bushings must be replaced, the left-hand suspension arm must be removed. If the outer bushings must be replaced, the suspension arm on the affected side must be removed. The outer bushings are integral with the bracket — if replacement is necessary, the bracket must be replaced with a new one. If the bushing retainers are damaged or worn, the right suspension arm and tube assembly must be replaced.*

1 Remove the appropriate suspension arm as described in Section 12.

Inner bushings

2 A special tool is required to remove the bushings. If the factory tool is not available, take the suspension arm(s) to a dealer service department and have the bushings replaced.

3 If the tool, or a substitute, is available, pull the old bushings out

12.7 The suspension arm mounting bracket is attached to the body with two bolts

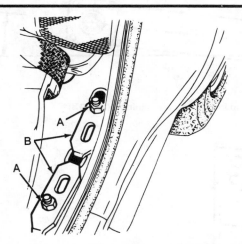

Fig. 10.13 The suspension arm bracket mounting bolts thread into nuts (A) that are held in place by the nutplates (B) (Sec 12)

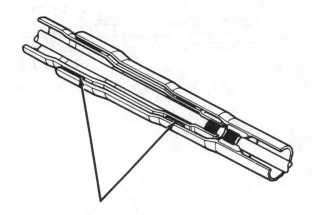

Fig. 10.14 Apply moly-based grease to the tube bushings (arrows) before installing the suspension arm (Sec 12)

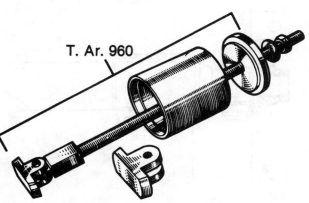

T. Ar. 960

Fig. 10.15 The factory special tool (shown) or a substitute is required to remove and install the rear suspension arm tube bushings (Sec 13)

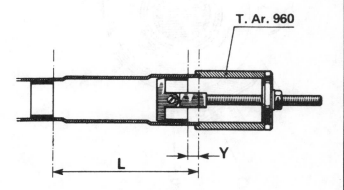

T. Ar. 960

Fig. 10.16 Make sure the bushings are the specified distance from the end of the tube (Sec 13)
L = 7.008 ± 0.078-inches
Y = 0.590 ± 0.078-inch

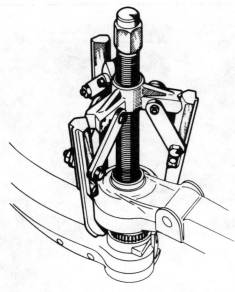

Fig. 10.17 Using a three-jaw puller to separate the mounting bracket from the suspension arm (Sec 13)

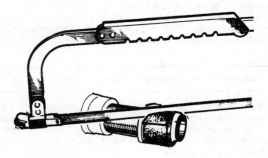

Fig. 10.18 The old bushing must be cut off the suspension arm (Sec 13)

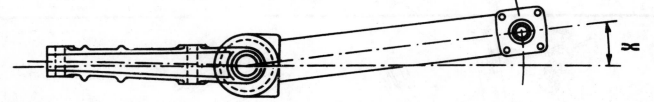

Fig. 10.19 X must be 7° when the bracket and suspension arm are rejoined (Sec 13)

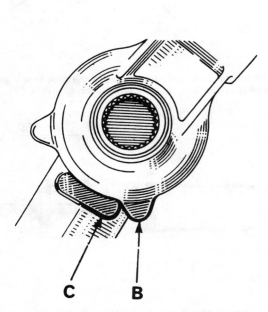

Fig. 10.20 With the arm and bracket correctly positioned, the projection on the bracket (B) should be aligned as shown with the casting mark (C) on the arm (Sec 13)

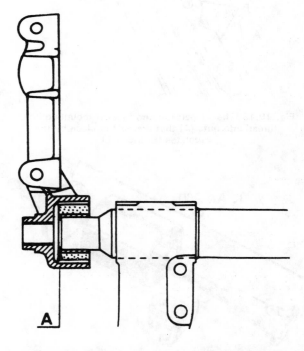

Fig. 10.21 The end of the suspension arm must be flush with the end of the mounting bracket bushing (A) after installation (Sec 13)

and install the new ones. Be sure to lubricate the new bushings before pulling them into place and make sure they are positioned in the tube as shown in the accompanying illustration.

4   The suspension arm can now be installed by referring to Section 12.

Outer bushings

5   Coat the bushing in the mounting bracket with plenty of clean brake fluid and allow it to soak in. This will soften the bushing rubber and make removal easier.

6   Draw the mounting bracket off the suspension arm with a three-jaw puller. The bracket will not come off without tearing the rubber bushing.

7   Using a hacksaw, very carefully cut through the rubber and metal backing of the bushing remaining on the arm. Be careful not to cut the arm itself. After splitting the bushing, pry it off the arm.

8   Align the new mounting bracket and bushing assembly with the arm so that the arm is at an angle of 7° to the bracket. The marks on the arm and bracket must be positioned as shown in the accompanying illustration. Make sure the arm and bracket are right side up.

9   Hold the two components in this position and press or drive the bracket onto the arm until the end of the arm is flush with the bushing.

10   The arm can now be installed by referring to Section 12.

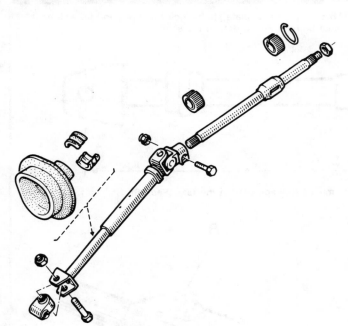

Fig. 10.22 Steering column shaft components — exploded view (Sec 15)

14   Steering wheel — removal and installation

1   Set the front wheels in the straight ahead position.

2   Carefully pry up the steering wheel pad to expose the mounting nut.

3   Using a socket and breaker bar, loosen and remove the nut and washer.

4   Mark the steering wheel hub and the shaft to ensure correct alignment during installation, then pull the steering wheel off. If it is tight, tap it up from behind with the palm of your hand (thread the nut back onto the shaft so the wheel won't fly off). Do not hammer on the shaft to dislodge the steering wheel.

5   Installation is the reverse of removal. Be sure to align the marks on the hub and shaft as the wheel is installed and tighten the nut to the specified torque.

15   Steering column assembly — removal and installation

1   Disconnect the negative cable from the battery.

2   Remove the steering wheel as described in Section 14.

3   Remove the screws, release the clips and separate the lower shroud from the steering column. Lay it aside, but avoid straining the wires or connections.

4   Remove the screws and separate the wiper/washer switch from the upper shroud. Remove the mounting screws and separate the upper shroud from the column.

5   Remove the turn signal switch from the column bracket.

6   Disconnect the ignition switch, turn signal switch and any other switch wire harnesses at the multi-plug connectors. Label the connectors to avoid confusion during reassembly. Release the wire harness cable clips from the steering column and move the wires and switches aside.

7   Mark the steering column shaft in relationship to the intermediate shaft upper U-joint. Remove the nut/bolt securing the shaft to the U-joint.

8   Remove the steering column bracket upper retaining bolts and screws and loosen the lower bolts. Pull the column up to disengage the shaft from the U-joint and the lower mounting bracket from the bolts, then remove the assembly from the vehicle.

9   To replace the steering column bushings, remove the snap-ring from the top of the column.

10   Temporarily install the steering wheel and screw the nut on finger tight.

11   Pull up sharply on the steering wheel to free the shaft and release the upper bushing. Make sure the ignition key is in the switch and the steering lock is released before doing this.

12   Tilt the shaft and push in on the steering wheel to release the lower bushing. Remove the steering wheel and withdraw the shaft and bushings from the column.

13   Lubricate the new lower bushing with moly-based grease and install it in the column with a section of pipe and a hammer. Slide the shaft into position and install the upper bushing in the same manner. Make sure that both bushings locate between the indentations in the column. Install the snap-ring in the top of the column.

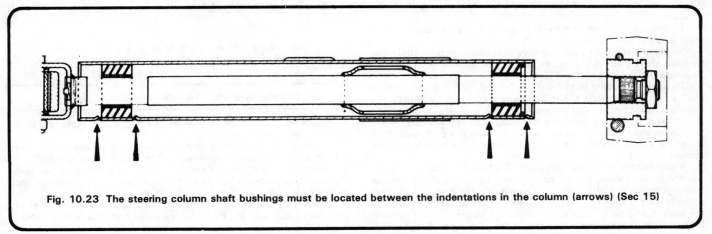

Fig. 10.23 The steering column shaft bushings must be located between the indentations in the column (arrows) (Sec 15)

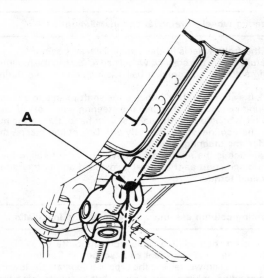

Fig. 10.24 Correct position of the flat (A) on the steering column shaft (Sec 15)

16.5 The intermediate shaft U-joint bolt/nut and firewall boot must be removed to detach the shaft

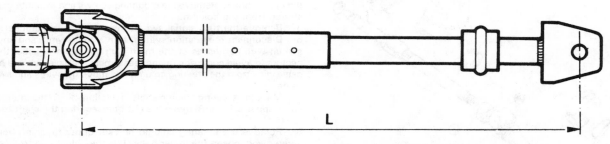

Fig. 10.25 The intermediate shaft length (L) must be as specified in the text (Sec 16)

14 Installation is basically the reverse of removal. Make sure that the flat on the steering column shaft splined end faces the clamp bolt in the U-joint when engaging the shaft. Tighten the upper column retaining bolts first, followed by the lower bolts.

16 Steering column intermediate shaft — removal and installation

1 Raise the front of the vehicle and support it on jackstands, then disconnect the negative battery cable from the battery.
2 Working inside the vehicle, remove the screws, release the clips and separate the lower shroud from the steering column. Lay it aside, but avoid straining the wires and connections.
3 Turn the steering wheel so that the wheels are in the straight ahead position.
4 Remove the nut/bolt from the U-joint between the steering column shaft and the intermediate shaft.
5 Working under the vehicle, remove the nut/bolt securing the intermediate shaft yoke to the upper part of the lower U-joint (photo). Separate the yoke from the U-joint.
6 Release the rubber boot from the firewall, pull the intermediate shaft down to disengage it from the upper U-joint, then withdraw the shaft and boot from inside the vehicle.
7 Replace the rubber boot if it is damaged or deteriorated.
8 Check the shaft for damage and make sure the collapsible joint is secure. Check the shaft length and replace it if it is less than the specified length.
9 Installation is the reverse of removal. Make sure the wheels are pointed straight ahead before installation. The flat on the end of the steering column must face the clamp bolt hole in the intermediate shaft upper U-joint. Tighten the upper U-joint clamp bolt first, followed by the lower clamp bolt. The lower U-joint must be positioned as shown in the accompanying illustration before the clamp bolt is tightened.

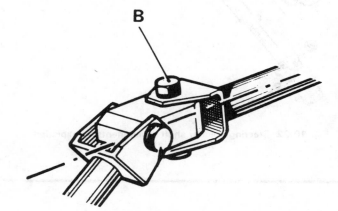

Fig. 10.26 The intermediate shaft U-joint must be positioned as shown here when tightening bolt B (Sec 16)

17 Tie-rod outer balljoint — replacement

1 Raise the front of the vehicle and support it on jackstands, then remove the front wheel(s).
2 Loosen the outer balljoint locknut 1/4-turn. Hold the tie-rod with a wrench on the flats at the inner end to keep it from turning.
3 Remove the nut from the balljoint stud so it can be separated from the stub axle carrier arm. Use a balljoint separator to disengage the balljoint tapered stud from the arm (photo).
4 To replace the outer balljoint, begin by counting the number of exposed threads between the end of the balljoint and the locknut (record it for future use).

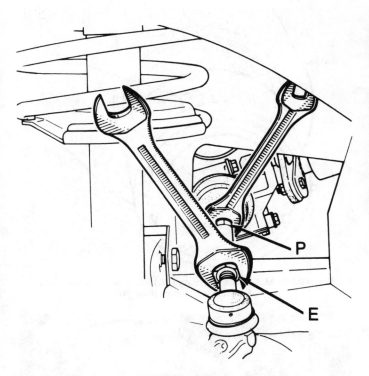

Fig. 10.27 Hold the tie-rod with a wrench (P) when loosening the outer balljoint locknut (E) (Sec 17)

5   Remove the balljoint from the tie-rod and remove the locknut from the balljoint.
6   Thread the locknut onto the new balljoint until the same number of threads are exposed (see Step 4).
7   Thread the balljoint into the tie-rod until the locknut just contacts it, then tighten the nut while holding the tie-rod as described earlier.
8   Position the balljoint stud in the stub axle carrier arm and install the nut. Tighten the nut to the specified torque (if the balljoint stud turns, place a jack under the balljoint and raise it enough to push the tapered stud completely into the arm — the taper on the stud should lock into the arm and prevent it from turning as the nut is tightened).
9   Repeat the procedure for the balljoint on the opposite side of the vehicle.
10   Install the wheel(s), lower the vehicle and have the front wheel alignment checked as soon as possible.

18   Tie-rod and inner balljoint — removal and installation

Note: *If the tie-rod is removed from a vehicle equipped with manual steering for any reason, the inner balljoint will be damaged and the tie-rod should not be reinstalled — a new one must be used. On vehicles equipped with power steering, the tie-rods may be attached to the steering rack with jam nuts and/or roll pins and may be reusable (check with your dealer service department for specific information).*

1   Refer to Section 17 and separate the outer balljoint from the stub axle carrier arm, then refer to Section 19 and remove the rubber boot from the inner end of the tie-rod.
2   Hold the thrust washer with a pin-type spanner wrench or locking pliers and turn the inner balljoint housing with a small pipe wrench to separate the tie-rod from the steering rack.
3   To begin installation, slip the new lock washer and thrust washer over the new tie-rod inner balljoint threaded stud. Make sure the tangs on the inside of the lock washer engage in the slots in the thrust washer.
4   Apply Loctite 271 to the balljoint threads, then thread the tie-rod into the steering rack. Make sure the tabs on the thrust washer align with the flats on the end of the rack.
5   Tighten the balljoint housing securely, then install the rubber boot and attach the outer balljoint to the stub axle carrier.

17.3   Using a balljoint separator to detach the outer tie-rod balljoint from the stub axle carrier arm

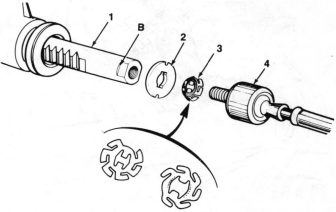

Fig. 10.28 Tie-rod inner balljoint components — exploded view (manual steering only) (Sec 18)

1 Steering rack   4 Balljoint housing
2 Thrust washer   B Flats on rack
3 Lock washer

19   Steering gear rubber boots — replacement

1   Refer to Section 17 and separate the outer balljoint from the stub axle carrier arm.
2   Release the boot clamps and slide it off the steering gear housing and the tie-rod.
3   If the boot was torn or otherwise damaged, check the steering rack carefully for wear and damage.
4   Lubricate the inner part of the new boot with silicone spray or rubber grease, then slip it over the tie-rod and into place on the steering gear housing.
5   Make sure the boot is properly seated, then install the new clamps and tighten them securely.
6   Refer to Section 17 and install the outer balljoint.

20   Steering rack support bearing — replacement

1   Refer to Section 18 and separate the right-hand tie-rod from the steering rack.
2   Turn the steering wheel to full left lock to move the rack out of

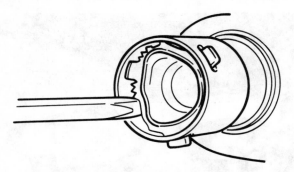

Fig. 10.29 Removing the rack support bearing with a screwdriver (Sec 20)

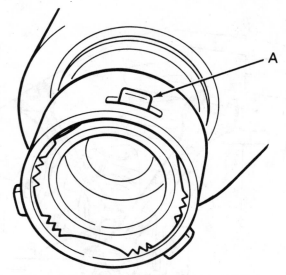

Fig. 10.30 Make sure the tangs (A) are seated in the slots of the rack housing (Sec 20)

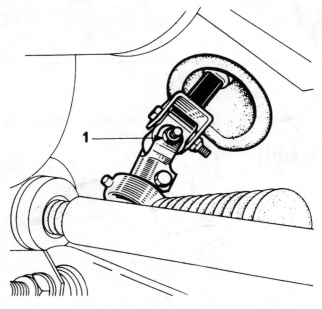

Fig. 10.31 Remove the nut and bolt (1) and separate the lower U-joint from the steering gear yoke (Sec 21)

21.4 The manual steering gear is attached to the frame with two bolts

the way, then carefully pry the bearing out with a screwdriver.

3   Clean the rack and housing, then apply moly-based grease to both components.

4   Install the new bearing and make sure the tangs engage correctly in the slots in the rack housing.

5   Apply moly-based grease to the bearing surface, then turn the steering wheel from lock-to-lock several times to settle the bearing and distribute the grease.

6   Refer to Section 18 and reinstall the tie-rod.

21 Steering gear — removal and installation

Note: *This procedure is for manual steering-equipped vehicles only. In the case of power steering-equipped vehicles, the procedure will be very similar, but the fluid lines will have to be detached from the steering gear and the ends plugged or capped. Also, the mounts may be slightly different than the manual steering gear mounts (consisting of clamps and rubber bushings).*

1   Refer to Section 17 and separate the outer balljoints from the stub axle carrier arms.

2   Mark the position of the intermediate shaft lower U-joint in relationship to the rack housing and the two halves of the U-joint in relationship to each other.

3   Remove the nut and bolt securing the lower part of the U-joint to the steering gear yoke.

4   Remove the steering gear mounting bolts (photo). Separate the

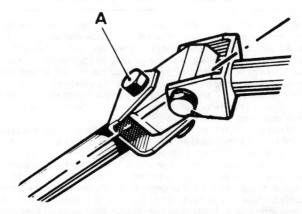

Fig. 10.32 The steering gear yoke and lower U-joint must be positioned as shown here when the bolt (A) is tightened (Sec 21)

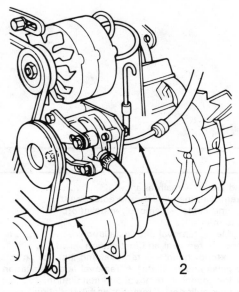

Fig. 10.33 The power steering pump input hose (1) must be pinched off before removal (the outlet hose [2] can be removed without loss of fluid) (Sec 22)

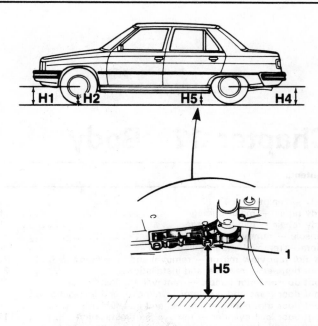

Fig. 10.34 Vehicle height checking points (Sec 23)

U-joint and withdraw the steering gear to the side, through the wheel arch.
5   Installation is the reverse of removal. When rejoining the U-joint and steering gear yoke, align the marks made during removal (if new components are being installed, set the steering wheel and steering gear to the straight ahead position before installation). Tighten the U-joint bolt with the joint positioned as shown in the accompanying illustration. Tighten all bolts to the specified torque.
6   Have the front wheel alignment checked as soon as possible.

22   Power steering pump — removal and installation

1   Clamp the pump input hose to prevent loss of fluid from the reservoir.
2   Place a drip pan under the vehicle, then disconnect the hoses from the pump.
3   Loosen the pump mounting and adjustment bolts, then remove the drivebelt.
4   Remove the bolts and separate the pump from the bracket.
5   If a new pump is being installed, transfer the pulley to the new pump.
6   Installation is the reverse of removal. Be sure to add fluid to the system and adjust the drivebelt as described in Chapter 1.

23   Vehicle height — check and adjustment

1   Before carrying out the following checks, make sure the fuel tank is full and the tires are correctly inflated. The vehicle must be on a level surface as well.
2   Refer to the accompanying illustration and take measurements at the points shown, noting that H1 is from the front axle centerline, H2 is the distance from the bottom of the sill to the ground (measured in line with the wheel centers), H4 is from the rear axle centerline and H5 is the distance from the rear suspension arm mounting bracket rear bolt to the ground.
3   The measurements should be:
    H1 minus H2 = 3.25 ± 0.40-inches
    H4 minus H5 = 1.5 ± 0.40-inches
    Maximum difference from side-to-side [5] 0.40-inch
4   Only the rear underbody height is adjustable by repositioning the torsion bars in the mounting bracket splines. Moving the torsion bars one spline either way will alter the height on the side involved by 0.120-inch. The procedure is described in Section 11.
5   If the front body height is incorrect, the front springs are probably sagged. To correct it, replace the front springs on both sides.
6   If the body height is changed, have the headlight aim checked and adjusted as soon as possible.

Chapter 11   Body

Contents

Specifications

Torque specifications	Ft-lbs
Front seat rail mounting bolts	21
Seat belt mounting bolts	15

1   General information

The body and subframe is of welded steel construction, incorporating progressive crumple zones at the front and rear and a rigid center safety cell. The assembly and welding of the main body unit is completed by computer-controlled robots and is checked for dimensional accuracy using computer and laser technology.

The front and rear bumpers are collapsible to minimize minor accident damage and the front fenders are bolted in place to facilitate accident damage repair.

Component replacement and repair procedures capable of being done by the home mechanic are included in this Chapter.

2   Body — maintenance

1   The condition of your vehicle's body is very important, because it is on this that the second-hand value will mainly depend. It is much more difficult to repair a neglected or damaged body than it is to repair mechanical components. The hidden areas of the body, such as the fender wells, the frame, and the engine compartment, are equally important, although obviously do not require as frequent attention as the rest of the body.

2   Once a year, or every 12000 miles, it is a good idea to have the underside of the body and the frame steam cleaned. All traces of dirt and oil will be removed and the underside can then be inspected care-fully for rust, damaged brake lines, frayed electrical wiring, damaged cables, and other problems. The front suspension components should be greased after completion of this job.

3   At the same time, clean the engine and the engine compartment using either a steam cleaner or a water soluble degreaser.

4   The fender wells should be given particular attention, as under-coating can peel away and stones and dirt thrown up by the tires can cause the paint to chip and flake, allowing rust to set in. If rust is found, clean down to the bare metal and apply an anti-rust paint.

5   The body should be washed once a week (or when dirty). Wet the vehicle thoroughly to soften the dirt, then wash it down with a soft sponge and plenty of clean soapy water. If the surplus dirt is not washed off very carefully, it will in time wear down the paint.

6   Spots of tar or asphalt coating thrown up from the road should be removed with a cloth soaked in solvent.

7   Once every six months, give the body and chrome trim a thorough wax job. If a chrome cleaner is used to remove rust from any of the vehicle's plated parts, remember that the cleaner also removes part of the chrome, so use it sparingly.

3   Upholstery and carpets — maintenance

1   Every three months, remove the carpets or mats and clean the interior of the vehicle (more frequently if necessary). Vacuum the upholstery and carpets to remove loose dirt and dust.

2   If the upholstery is soiled, apply upholstery cleaner with a damp sponge and wipe it off with a clean, dry cloth.

4   Hinges and locks — maintenance

Every 3000 miles or three months, the door, hood and rear hatch hinges and locks should be lubricated with a few drops of oil. The door and rear hatch striker plates should also be given a thin coat of grease to reduce wear and ensure free movement.

5   Body repair — minor damage

See color photo sequence on pages 190 and 191.

Repair of minor scratches

If the scratch is very superficial and does not penetrate to the metal of the body, repair is very simple. Lightly rub the scratched area with a fine rubbing compound to remove loose paint and built-up wax. Rinse the area with clean water.

Apply touch-up paint to the scratch, using a small brush. Continue to apply thin layers of paint until the surface of the paint in the scratch is level with the surrounding paint. Allow the new paint at least two weeks to harden, then blend it into the surrounding paint by rubbing with a very fine rubbing compound. Finally, apply a coat of wax to the scratch area.

If the scratch has penetrated the paint and exposed the metal of the body, causing the metal to rust, a different repair technique is required. Remove all loose rust from the bottom of the scratch with a pocket knife, then apply rust-inhibiting paint to prevent the formation of rust in the future. Using a rubber or nylon applicator, coat the scratched area with glaze-type filler. If required, the filler can be mixed with thinner to provide a very thin paste, which is ideal for filling narrow scratches. Before the glaze filler in the scratch hardens, wrap a piece of smooth cotton cloth around the tip of a finger. Dip the cloth in thinner and then quickly wipe it along the surface of the scratch. This will ensure that the surface of the filler is slightly hollow. The scratch can now be painted over as described earlier in this section.

Repair of dents

When repairing dents, the first job is to pull the dent out until the affected area is as close as possible to its original shape. There is no point in trying to restore the original shape completely as the metal in the damaged area will have stretched on impact and cannot be restored to its original contours. It is better to bring the level of the dent up to a point which is about 1/8-inch below the level of the surrounding metal. In cases where the dent is very shallow, it is not worth trying to pull it out at all.

If the back side of the dent is accessible, it can be hammered out gently from behind using a soft-faced hammer. While doing this, hold a block of wood firmly against the opposite side of the metal to absorb the hammer blows and prevent the metal from being stretched out.

If the dent is in a section of the body which has double layers, or some other factor that makes it inaccessible from behind, a different technique is required. Drill several small holes through the metal inside the damaged area, particularly in the deeper sections. Screw long, self-tapping screws into the holes just enough for them to get a good grip in the metal. Now the dent can be pulled out by pulling on the protruding heads of the screws with locking pliers.

The next stage of repair is the removal of paint from the damaged area and from an inch or so of the surrounding metal. This is easily done with a wire brush or sanding disk in a drill motor, although it can be done just as effectively by hand with sandpaper. To complete the preparation for filling, score the surface of the bare metal with a screwdriver or the tang of a file (or drill small holes in the affected area). This will provide a very good grip for the filler material. To complete the repair, see the Section on filling and painting.

Repair of rust holes or gashes

Remove all paint from the affected area and from an inch or so of the surrounding metal using a sanding disk or wire brush mounted in a drill motor. If these are not available, a few sheets of sandpaper will do the job just as effectively. With the paint removed, you will be able to determine the severity of the corrosion and decide whether to replace the whole panel, if possible, or repair the affected area. New body panels are not as expensive as most people think and it is often quicker to install a new panel than to repair large areas of rust.

Remove all trim pieces from the affected area (except those which will act as a guide to the original shape of the damaged body, i.e. headlight shells, etc.). Then, using metal snips or a hacksaw blade, remove all loose metal and any other metal that is badly affected by rust. Hammer the edges of the hole in to create a slight depression for the filler material.

Wire brush the affected area to remove the powdery rust from the surface of the metal. If the back of the rusted area is accessible, treat it with rust-inhibiting paint.

Before filling is done, block the hole in some way. This can be done with sheet metal riveted or screwed into place, or by stuffing the hole with wire mesh.

Once the hole is blocked off, the affected area can be filled and painted (see the following sub-section on filling and painting).

Filling and painting

Many types of body fillers are available, but generally speaking, body repair kits which contain filler paste and a tube of resin hardener are best for this type of repair work. A wide, flexible plastic or nylon applicator will be necessary for imparting a smooth and contoured finish to the surface of the filler material.

Mix up a small amount of filler on a clean piece of wood or cardboard (use the hardener sparingly). Follow the manufacturer's instructions on the package, otherwise the filler will set incorrectly.

Using the applicator, apply the filler paste to the prepared area. Draw the applicator across the surface of the filler to achieve the desired contour and to level the filler surface. As soon as a contour that approximates the original one is achieved, stop working the paste. If you continue, the paste will begin to stick to the applicator. Continue to add thin layers of filler paste at 20-minute intervals until the level of the filler is just above the surrounding metal.

Once the filler has hardened, the excess can be removed with a body file. From then on, progressively finer grades of sandpaper should be used, starting with a 180-grit paper and finishing with 600-grit wet-or-dry paper. Always wrap the sandpaper around a flat rubber or wooden block, otherwise the surface of the filler will not be completely flat. During the sanding of the filler surface, the wet-or-dry paper should be periodically rinsed in water. This will ensure that a very smooth finish is produced in the final stage.

At this point, the repair area should be surrounded by a ring of bare metal, which in turn should be encircled by the finely feathered edge of good paint. Rinse the repair area with clean water until all of the dust produced by the sanding operation is gone.

Spray the entire area with a light coat of primer. This will reveal any imperfections in the surface of the filler. Repair the imperfections with fresh filler paste or glaze filler and once more smooth the surface with sandpaper. Repeat this spray-and-repair procedure until you are satisfied that the surface of the filler and the feathered edge of the paint are perfect. Rinse the area with clean water and allow it to dry completely.

The repair area is now ready for painting. Spray painting must be carried out in a warm, dry, windless and dust-free atmosphere. These conditions can be created if you have access to a large indoor work area, but if you are forced to work in the open, you will have to pick the day very carefully. If you are working indoors, dousing the floor in the work area with water will help settle the dust which would otherwise be in the air. If the repair area is confined to one body panel, mask off the surrounding panels. This will help minimize the effects of a slight mismatch in paint color. Trim pieces such as chrome strips, door handles, etc., will also need to be masked off or removed. Use masking tape and several thicknesses of newspaper for the masking operations.

Before spraying, shake the paint can thoroughly, then spray a test area until the spray painting technique is mastered. Cover the repair area with a thick coat of primer. The thickness should be built up using several thin layers of primer rather than one thick one. Using 600-grit wet-or-dry sandpaper, rub down the surface of the primer until it is very smooth. While doing this, the work area should be thoroughly rinsed with water and the wet-or-dry sandpaper periodically rinsed as well. Allow the primer to dry before spraying additional coats.

Spray on the top coat, again building up the thickness by using several thin layers of paint. Begin spraying in the center of the repair area and then, using a circular motion, work out until the whole repair area and about two inches of the surrounding original paint is covered. Remove all masking material 10 to 15 minutes after spraying on the final coat of paint. Allow the new paint at least two weeks to harden, then use a very fine rubbing compound to blend the edges of the new paint into the existing paint. Finally, apply a coat of wax.

7.4 Hood hinge mounting bolt locations (trace around the hinges to ensure correct alignment during installation)

6 Body repair — major damage

1   Major damage must be repaired by an auto body shop specifically equipped to perform unibody repairs. These shops have available the specialized equipment required to do the job properly.
2   If the damage is extensive, the underbody must be checked for proper alignment or the vehicle's handling characteristics may be adversely affected and other components may wear at an accelerated rate.
3   Due to the fact that all of the major body components (hood, fenders, etc.) are separate and replaceable units, any seriously damaged components should be replaced rather than repaired. Sometimes these components can be found in a wrecking yard that specializes in used vehicle components (often at considerable savings over the cost of new parts).

7 Hood — removal, installation and adjustment

1   Open the hood and support it with the prop.
2   Drill out the head of the rivet securing the safety cable to the hood (if equipped). Tap out the rivet with a punch and hammer and remove the cable.
3   Disconnect the windshield washer hose at the reservoir.
4   Trace around the hinges with a soft pencil, then loosen the mounting bolts (photo).
5   With the help of an assistant, steady the hood, remove the prop, unscrew the bolts and separate it from the vehicle. Store it where it will not be damaged.
6   Installation is the reverse of removal. Position the hinges within the marks made during removal, but move them as necessary to provide a uniform gap on all sides. Adjust the lock mechanism height as described in Section 8.

8 Hood lock and cable — removal, installation and adjustment

1   With the hood open, disconnect the cable eye from the lock lever and withdraw the cable from the lock.
2   Remove the two mounting bolts and separate the lock from the firewall.
3   Installation is the reverse of removal. Be sure to adjust the lock height so that the hood is flush with the fenders and shuts securely without excessive force.
4   To completely remove the cable, separate it from the lock as described in Step 1, then remove the two bolts that attach the release lever to the side panel inside the vehicle.
5   Release the cable from the engine compartment clips, then pull it through the firewall from inside the vehicle.
6   Installation is the reverse of removal.

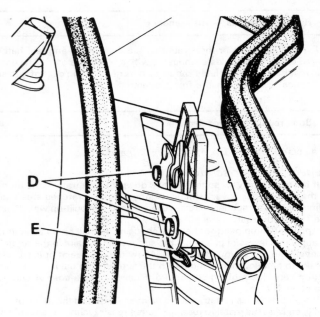

Fig. 11.1 Disconnect the cable from the lock lever (E) and remove the mounting bolts (D) to detach the hood lock mechanism (Sec 8)

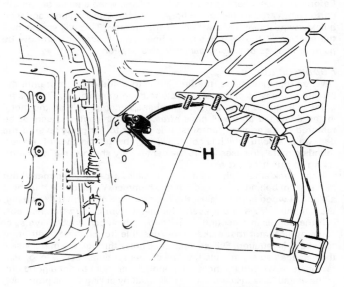

Fig. 11.2 The hood release lever is attached to the side panel under the dash (Sec 8)

Fig. 11.3 Hood release cable and lever assembly (Sec 8)

9.3   The hatch hinge mounting nuts are accessible through an opening in the headlining after removal of a cover plate

10.3   Pry out the retainer with a screwdriver,...

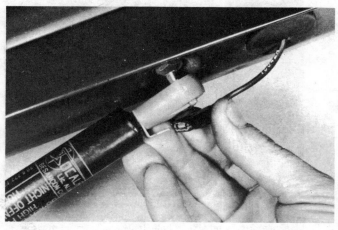

10.2   Disconnect the wires at the hatch support strut terminals

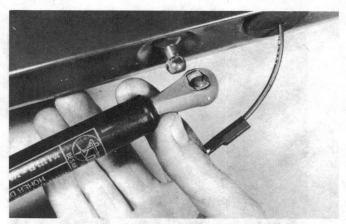

10.4   ...then separate the strut from the ball pivot

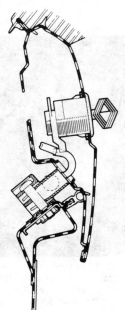

Fig. 11.4   Cross-section view of hatch lock assembly (Sec 11)

9   Hatch — removal and installation

1   Remove the support struts from the ball mounts as described in Section 10.
2   Disconnect the wiper wire harness connector (if equipped).
3   Using a socket, extension and ratchet, remove the hatch hinge mounting bolts from inside the vehicle (they are accessible through an opening on each side of the headlining) (photo). **Note:** *Make sure the hatch is supported by an assistant as the bolts are removed.*
4   Separate the hatch from the vehicle very carefully to avoid scratching the paint.
5   Installation is the reverse of removal. Adjust the hatch position by referring to Section 12.

10   Hatch support struts — removal and installation

1   With the hatch open, unhook the parcel shelf support cords and support the hatch with a wood prop.
2   Disconnect the wires from the strut terminals (photo).
3   Using a screwdriver, carefully pry out the retainer from each of the strut ball pivot fittings (photo).
4   Separate each strut from the ball pivot (photo).
5   Installation is the reverse of removal.

11   Hatch lock cylinder — removal and installation

1   Open the hatch, reach in through one of the openings and

This sequence of photographs deals with the repair of the dent and paintwork damage shown in this photo. The procedure will be similar for the repair of a hole. It should be noted that the procedures given here are simplified — more explicit instructions will be found in the text

In the case of a dent the first job — after removing surrounding trim — is to hammer out the dent where access is possible. This will minimise filling. Here, the large dent having been hammered out, the damaged area is being made slightly concave

Now all paint must be removed from the damaged area, by rubbing with coarse abrasive paper. Alternatively, a wire brush or abrasive pad can be used in a power drill. Where the repair area meets good paintwork, the edge of the paintwork should be 'feathered', using a finer grade of abrasive paper

In the case of a hole caused by rusting, all damaged sheet-metal should be cut away before proceeding to this stage. Here, the damaged area is being treated with rust remover and inhibitor before being filled

Mix the body filler according to its manufacturer's instructions. In the case of corrosion damage, it will be necessary to block off any large holes before filling — this can be done with aluminium or plastic mesh, or aluminium tape. Make sure the area is absolutely clean before ...

... applying the filler. Filler should be applied with a flexible applicator, as shown, for best results; the wooden spatula being used for confined areas. Apply thin layers of filler at 20-minute intervals, until the surface of the filler is slightly proud of the surrounding bodywork

Initial shaping can be done with a Surform plane or Dreadnought file. Then, using progressively finer grades of wet-and-dry paper, wrapped around a sanding block, and copious amounts of clean water, rub down the filler until really smooth and flat. Again, feather the edges of adjoining paintwork

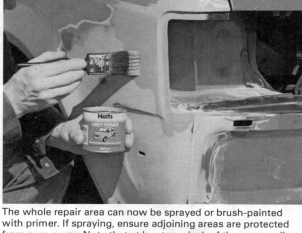

The whole repair area can now be sprayed or brush-painted with primer. If spraying, ensure adjoining areas are protected from over-spray. Note that at least one inch of the surrounding sound paintwork should be coated with primer. Primer has a 'thick' consistency, so will find small imperfections

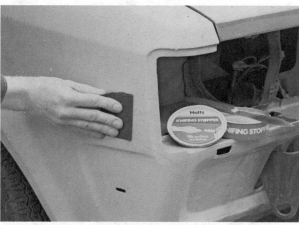

Again, using plenty of water, rub down the primer with a fine grade wet-and-dry paper (400 grade is probably best) until it is really smooth and well blended into the surrounding paintwork. Any remaining imperfections can now be filled by carefully applied knifing stopper paste

When the stopper has hardened, rub down the repair area again before applying the final coat of primer. Before rubbing down this last coat of primer, ensure the repair area is blemish-free — use more stopper if necessary. To ensure that the surface of the primer is really smooth use some finishing compound

The top coat can now be applied. When working out of doors, pick a dry, warm and wind-free day. Ensure surrounding areas are protected from over-spray. Agitate the aerosol thoroughly, then spray the centre of the repair area, working outwards with a circular motion. Apply the paint as several thin coats

After a period of about two weeks, which the paint needs to harden fully, the surface of the repaired area can be 'cut' with a mild cutting compound prior to wax polishing. When carrying out bodywork repairs, remember that the quality of the finished job is proportional to the time and effort expended

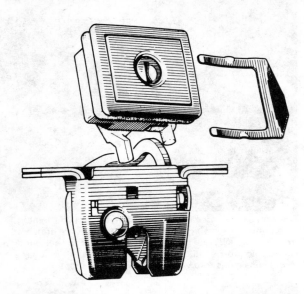

Fig. 11.5 The lock cylinder is held in place by a retaining clip that fits into slots in the lock (grasp the lip with pliers and pull it to the side to release it) (Sec 11)

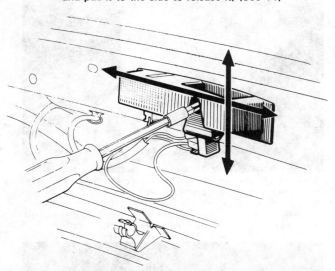

Fig. 11.7 Hatch lock striker plate adjustment details (Sec 12)

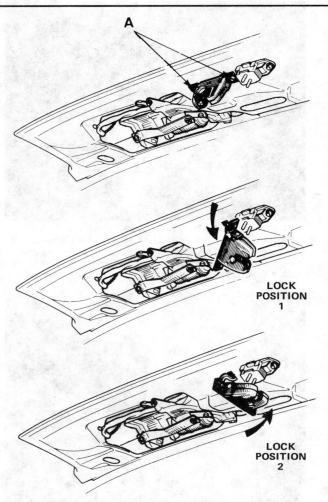

Fig. 11.6 Hatch lock removal sequence. Turn the lock counterclockwise to positions 1 and 2 to remove it (Sec 12)

A Lock mounting bolts.

disengage the lock cylinder retaining clip. A bent needle-nose pliers will be very helpful when removing the clip.
2   Pull the lock cylinder out from the outside.
3   Installation is the reverse of removal.

12   Hatch lock mechanism — removal, installation and adjustment

1   Open the hatch and remove the two lock mounting bolts. Turn the lock mechanism counterclockwise until the lever can be withdrawn through the opening in the sheet metal.
2   Installation is the reverse of removal. Adjust the striker plate by loosening the bolt and moving the plate as required to provide a flush fit all the way around the hatch.

13   Trunk lid — removal, installation and adjustment

1   Open the trunk and trace around the hinges with a soft pencil.
2   Have an assistant support the trunk while you remove the hinge-to-trunk lid bolts (it would be a good idea to cover the painted surface ahead of the trunk lid to avoid scratching the paint if the trunk is dropped).
3   Installation is the reverse of removal. Align each hinge inside the marks made during removal, but be prepared to move the trunk lid, if necessary, to provide a uniform gap all the way around.

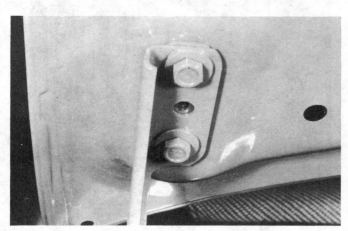

13.2   Trunk lid hinge mounting bolt locations (trace around the hinges to ensure correct alignment during installation)

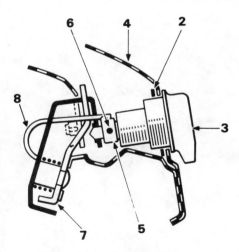

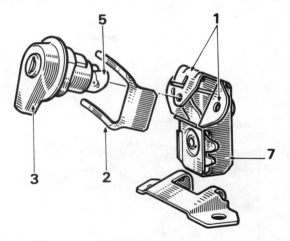

Fig. 11.8 Cross-section view of trunk lock assembly (Sec 14)

2 Retaining clip   6 Pin
3 Lock   7 Lock mechanism
4 Trunk lid   8 Spring wire
5 Locking finger

Fig. 11.9 Trunk lid lock components — exploded view (Sec 14)

1 Mounting holes   5 Locking finger
2 Retaining clip   7 Lock mechanism
3 Lock cylinder

15.1   The trunk lid lock mechanism is held in place with two nuts

15.2   After loosening the bolts, the striker plate can be repositioned so the trunk lid shuts correctly

14 Trunk lid lock cylinder — removal and installation

1   Open the trunk, reach through one of the openings and disengage the lock cylinder retaining clip. Pull the lock cylinder out of the trunk lid from the outside.
2   Installation is the reverse of removal. Make sure the spring wire on the trunk lid locates over the locking finger on the lock cylinder.

16.1a   The door bin is held in place with one screw . . .

15 Trunk lid lock mechanism — removal, installation and adjustment

1   Open the trunk and remove the two mounting nuts (photo), then separate the lock mechanism from the trunk lid.
2   Installation is the reverse of removal. Make sure that the spring wire locates over the locking finger on the lock cylinder. Adjust the striker plate (photo) so the trunk lid shuts and locks without excessive force.

16 Front door trim panel — removal and installation

1   Remove the door bin mounting screw, then lift the bin up to disengage it from the retaining buttons and separate it from the door (photos). Some models are not equipped with the door bin.

16.1b   . . . and retaining buttons at each end

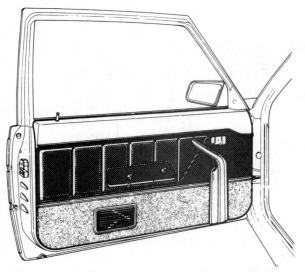

Fig. 11.10 Pivot the armrest down 90° to remove it from the door (Sec 16)

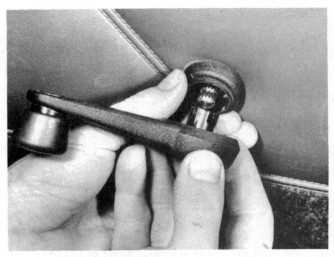

16.3   The window regulator handle can be pried off the spindle with a thin, flat tool

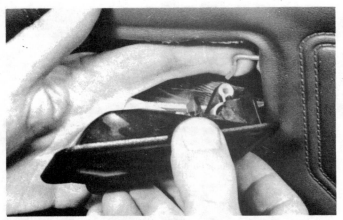

16.4 Disengage the operating rod from the door handle

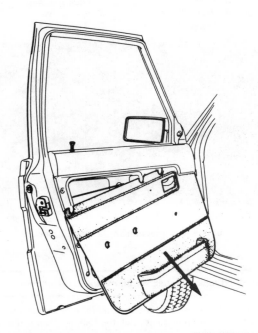

Fig. 11.11 On models with a separate top molding, the trim panel must be pulled down to remove it (Sec 16)

2   Remove the two armrest mounting screws, pivot the armrest down at the rear to disengage the upper mounting peg and separate it from the door.

3   Carefully pry off the window regulator handle (which is a press fit on the spindle) with a flat tool, then separate the trim piece (photo).

4   Remove the screw, ease the door handle to the rear to free the catches, then disengage the operating rod and remove the handle (photo).

5   Starting at one corner, carefully pry the trim panel away from the retaining buttons with a putty knife or flat pry bar (photo). When all the buttons have been released, remove the panel by lowering it at the top to free it from the top molding (where used). **Note:** *On models that do not have a separate top molding (later models), simply lift up on the panel to remove it after the retaining buttons have been released.*

6   Remove the top molding by unscrewing the interior lock button, easing the molding out at the bottom and lifting it up to separate it from the door.

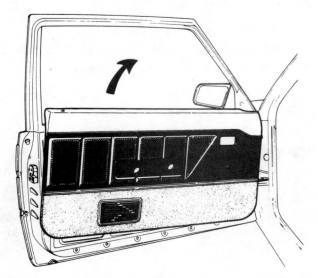

Fig. 11.12 On models with an integral top molding, pull the trim panel up to remove it (Sec 16)

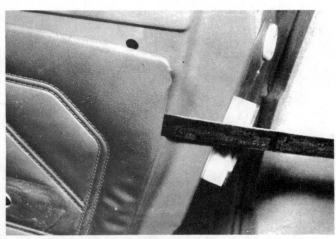

16.5 Use a flat, thin tool (such as a putty knife) to carefully pry the trim panel away from the door and release the retaining buttons

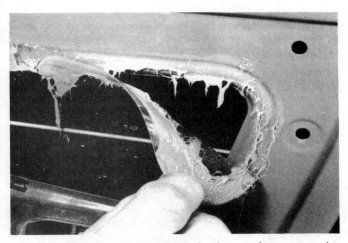

16.7 Peel back the plastic moisture barrier to gain access to the internal door components

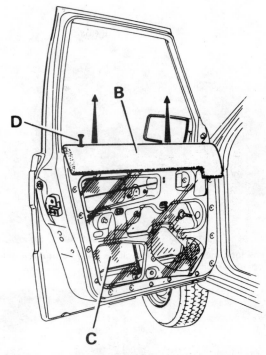

Fig. 11.13 The separate molding can be removed by pulling it straight up after unscrewing the door lock button (Sec 16)

B Top molding   D Lock button
C Plastic moisture barrier

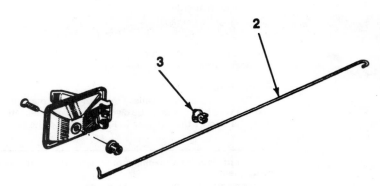

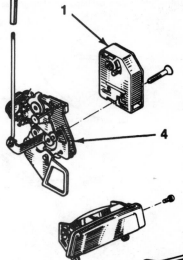

Fig. 11.14 Front door handle and lock mechanism components — exploded view (Sec 17)

1 Latch mechanism
2 Control rod
3 Plastic clip
4 Lock mechanism

7   If the trim panel has been removed to gain access to the internal parts of the door, carefully peel back the plastic moisture barrier as necessary (photo).
8   Installation is the reverse of removal.

17 Front door lock cylinder — removal and installation

Manual locks
1   Refer to Section 16 and remove the door trim panel.
2   Reach inside the door and disengage the retaining clip (photo) from

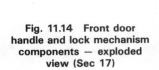

17.2 The lock cylinder retaining clip is easy to remove with a bent needle-nose pliers

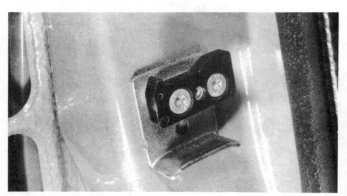

18.5 The striker plate can be moved after loosening the bolts slightly

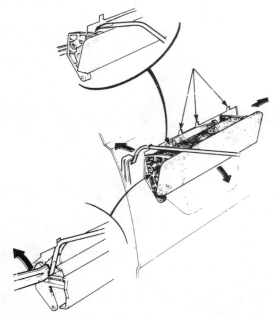

Fig. 11.16 The door handle must be moved forward and tipped down to disengage the lugs from the slots (arrows) (the inset shows the piece of welding rod being used to release the lock lever) (Sec 19)

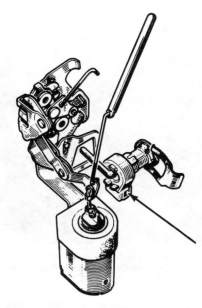

Fig. 11.15 The wire harness and activator (arrow) must be removed from the lock cylinder before the retaining clip is disengaged (Sec 17)

19.1 The front door exterior handle is held in place with a screw in the end of the door

the lock cylinder. Withdraw the lock from the outside.
3   Installation is the reverse of removal.

Electric locks
4   The procedure is essentially the same as for manual locks, but note that the wire harness must be disconnected and the activator removed from the end of the cylinder before removing the retaining clip.

18 Front door lock mechanism — removal, installation and adjustment

1   Open the door and close the window completely. Refer to Section 16 and remove the front door trim panel.
2   If electric locks are used, reach inside the door and disconnect the wire from the solenoid.
3   Separate the remote control rod from the plastic clip on the door.
4   Remove the three latch assembly screws and separate it from the end of the door. The lock mechanism can be removed through one of the openings in the door.
5   Installation is the reverse of removal. Adjust the lock striker (photo) so the door will shut and lock without slamming (make sure the door fits flush all the way around).

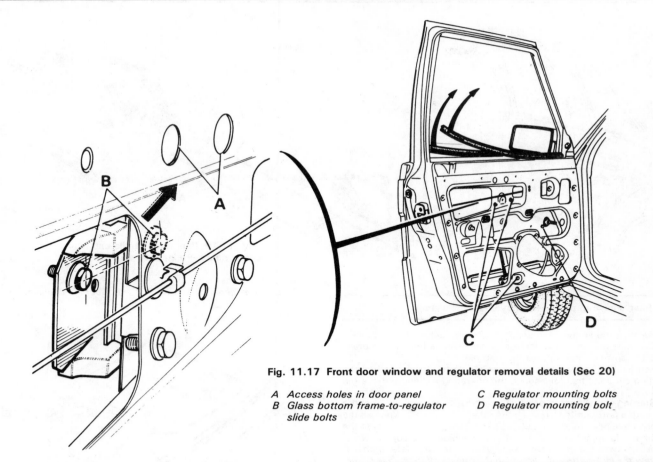

Fig. 11.17 Front door window and regulator removal details (Sec 20)

A Access holes in door panel
B Glass bottom frame-to-regulator
   slide bolts

C Regulator mounting bolts
D Regulator mounting bolt

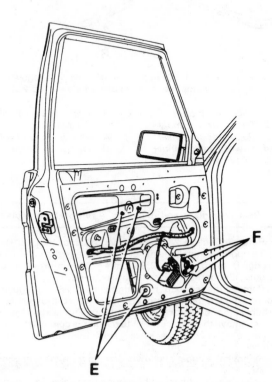

Fig. 11.18 Electric window regulator removal details
(Sec 20)

E Regulator mechanism bolts   F Motor mounting bolts

19 Front door exterior handle — removal and installation

1 Remove the door handle mounting screw from the end of the door (photo).
2 Slide the handle forward to release the retaining lugs, then tip it down (out at the top).
3 Insert a piece of welding rod through the slot at the rear and push the lock lever out of the handle, pull out the screwdriver and separate the handle from the door.
4 Installation is the reverse of removal. Be sure to hold the lock lever up with the welding rod when the handle is inserted into the door.

20 Front door glass and regulator — removal and installation

1 Open the door and close the window completely.
2 Refer to Section 16 and remove the door trim panel. Remove both rubber sealing strips at the top of the door by pulling them straight up (no clips are used).
3 Support the window in the raised position and remove the two bolts securing the bottom frame to the regulator slide. The bolts are accessible through the holes in the inner door panel.
4 On models with manually-operated windows, remove the four regulator mounting bolts and manipulate the regulator out through the opening in the inner panel.
5 On models with electrically-operated windows, disconnect the motor wiring harness, remove the three motor mounting bolts and the three mechanism mounting bolts, then manipulate the assembly out through the opening in the inner panel.
6 Carefully tilt the window to free it from the channels and lift it out from the outside.
7 Installation is the reverse of removal. Tighten all bolts finger tight only until all components have been installed. Center the glass in the closed position before tightening the bottom frame-to-regulator slide bolts.

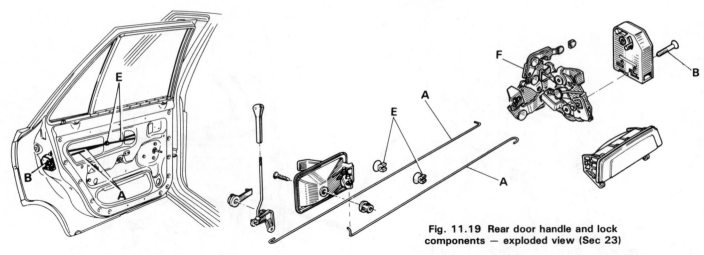

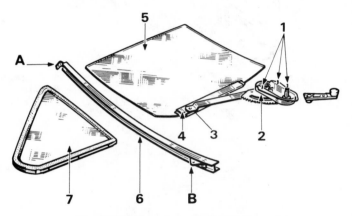

Fig. 11.19 Rear door handle and lock components — exploded view (Sec 23)

A Control rods   E Plastic clips
B Latch mechanism screw   F Lock mechanism

21 Rear door trim panel — removal and installation

1 Remove the screws and separate the armrest from the door.
2 Carefully pry off the window regulator handle (which is a press fit on the spindle) and remove the trim piece.
3 Remove the screw, ease the door handle to the rear to free the retaining catches, then disengage the operating rod and remove the handle.
4 Starting at one corner, carefully pry the trim panel away from the door with a putty knife to release the retaining buttons. When all the buttons have been released, pull the panel away from the door at the bottom and lower it to free it from the top molding (if equipped). **Note:** *On models which do not have a separate top molding (later models), unscrew the lock button and lift up on the trim panel to remove it from the door.*
5 To remove the top molding, unscrew the lock button, then ease the molding out at the bottom, up at the top and off the door.
6 If the panel has been removed for access to the door internal parts, carefully peel back the plastic moisture barrier as necessary.
7 Installation is the reverse of removal.

22 Rear door lock cylinder — removal and installation

The procedure for the rear door lock cylinder is essentially the same as for the front door lock cylinder. Refer to Section 17.

23 Rear door lock mechanism — removal, installation and adjustment

1 Open the door and close the window completely.
2 Refer to Section 21 and remove the door trim panel.
3 Unscrew the lock button. If electric locks are used, reach inside the door and disconnect the wire harness from the lock solenoid.
4 Remove the three screws and separate the latch assembly from the end of the door.
5 Release the remote control rod from the plastic clip on the door and separate the lock button rod from the support clip and bellcrank.
6 Withdraw the lock assembly through the opening in the inner panel.
7 Installation is the reverse of removal. Adjust the striker plate so that the door shuts and locks without slamming (it must fit flush all the way around).

24 Rear door exterior handle — removal and installation

The procedure for the rear door handle is essentially the same as for the front door handle. Refer to Section 19.

Fig. 11.20 Rear door window and regulator components — exploded view (Sec 25)

1 Regulator mounting studs   6 Rear guide channel
2 Regulator assembly   7 Fixed window
3 Regulator arm roller   A Rear guide channel mount
4 Lower glass channel   B Rear guide channel mount
5 Window glass

25 Rear door glass and regulator — removal and installation

1 Refer to Section 21 and remove the door trim panel.
2 Temporarily install the handle and position the window so that the top edge is approximately 7.9-inches (200 mm) from the top edge of the door. Support the glass in this position.
3 Remove the regulator mounting bolts, push the regulator into the door and detach the regulator arm roller from the lower glass channel. Withdraw the regulator through the opening in the inner panel.
4 To remove the glass, allow it to rest in the completely open position, then remove the two upper sealing strips from the top edge of the door by pulling them straight up.
5 Remove the upper and lower screws from the rear window guide channel.
6 Remove the rubber guide channel from the door frame.
7 Tilt the rear guide channel forward and withdraw the fixed window. Separate the rear guide channel from the door.
8 Tip the window forward and lift it up and out of the door.
9 Installation is the reverse of removal.

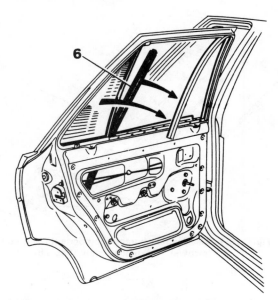

Fig. 11.21 Detach the rear guide channel (6), remove the rubber channel and pull the fixed window out of the door (Sec 25)

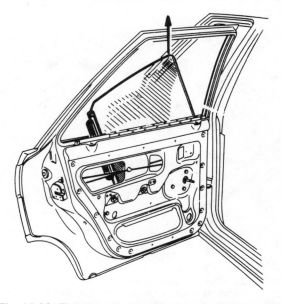

Fig. 11.22 The glass must be tilted as shown here before lifting it out of the door (Sec 25)

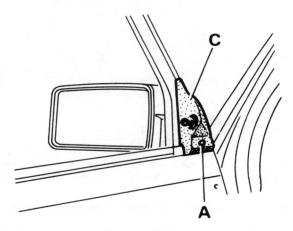

Fig. 11.23 Remove the screw (A) and detach the panel (C) from the inside of the mirror (Sec 26)

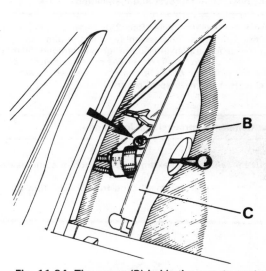

Fig. 11.24 The screw (B) holds the remote control mechanism to the panel (C) (Sec 26)

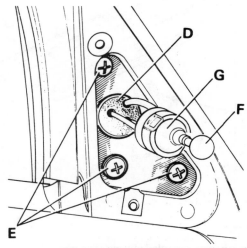

Fig. 11.25 Remote control mirror grommet (D), mounting screws (E), ball end (F) and socket (G) locations (Sec 26)

26   Exterior rear view mirror — removal and installation

Standard mirror
1   Unclip and remove the door trim strip.
2   Carefully pry off the triangular facing panel to expose the mirror mounting screws.
3   Remove the screws and separate the mirror from the door.
4   Installation is the reverse of removal.

Remote control mirror
5   Unclip and remove the door trim strip.
6   Remove the screw from the base of the triangular facing panel.
7   Open the window completely, remove the screw securing the remote control mechanism to the panel and separate them.
8   Push in on the rubber grommet in the center of the mount with a screwdriver.
9   Remove the three screws and separate the mirror and control mechanism from the door.
10   Installation is the reverse of removal.

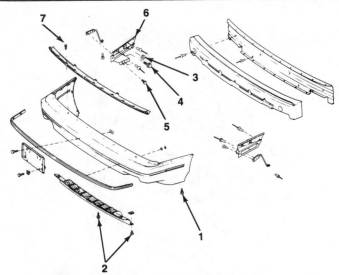

Fig. 11.26 When detaching the front bumper, remove the fasteners in the order shown here (Sec 27)

27 Front bumper — removal and installation

1   Remove the radiator grille (Sec 29). Refer to Chapter 12 and separate the turn signal lens assembly from the bumper.
2   Refer to the accompanying illustration and remove the numbered fasteners in order, from 1 to 7. **Note:** *The reinforcement bracket bolts (5) on the left side also hold the charcoal canister in place.*
3   Installation is the reverse of removal.

28 Rear bumper — removal and installation

Alliance
1   Remove the rear fender extension bolts from the underside of the extension.
2   Remove the plastic retaining clips from the bottom of the rear fascia.

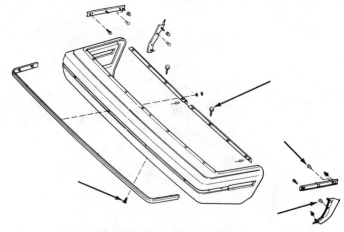

Fig. 11.27 Alliance rear bumper components and fasteners (arrows) — exploded view (Sec 28)

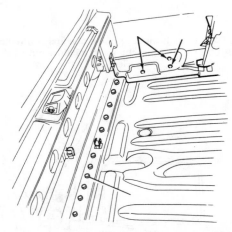

Fig. 11.28 When removing the Alliance rear bumper, some fasteners (arrows) are accessible only from inside the trunk (Sec 28)

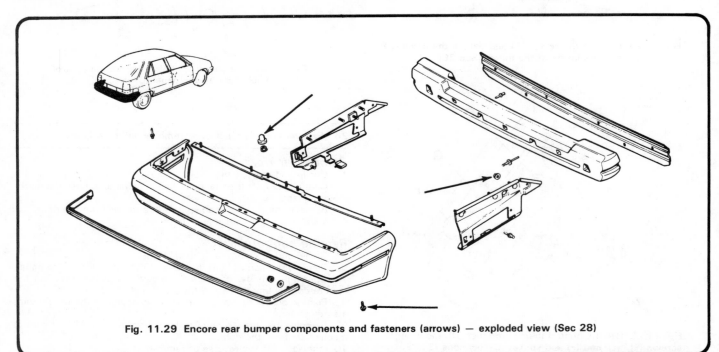

Fig. 11.29 Encore rear bumper components and fasteners (arrows) — exploded view (Sec 28)

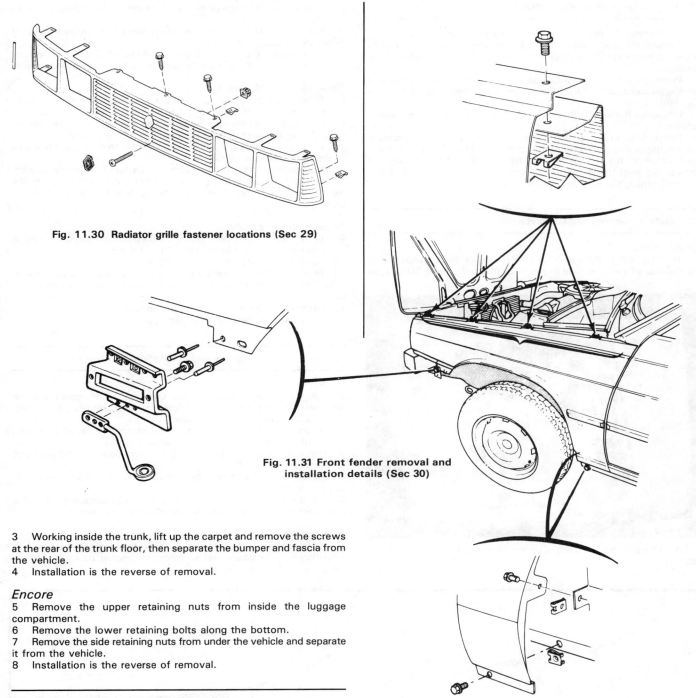

Fig. 11.30 Radiator grille fastener locations (Sec 29)

Fig. 11.31 Front fender removal and installation details (Sec 30)

3   Working inside the trunk, lift up the carpet and remove the screws at the rear of the trunk floor, then separate the bumper and fascia from the vehicle.
4   Installation is the reverse of removal.

Encore
5   Remove the upper retaining nuts from inside the luggage compartment.
6   Remove the lower retaining bolts along the bottom.
7   Remove the side retaining nuts from under the vehicle and separate it from the vehicle.
8   Installation is the reverse of removal.

29   Radiator grille — removal and installation

1   Open the hood and remove the bolts securing the grille to the upper radiator crossmember and the bolts at the lower inside corners.
2   Remove the screws from the front face of the grille, then tilt the grille forward to disengage it from the slots.
3   Installation is the reverse of removal. Do not overtighten the bolts or the grille may crack.

30   Front fender — removal and installation

1   Open the hood and prop it up.
2   Refer to Chapter 12 and remove the turn signal lens assembly from the bumper, then remove the bumper by referring to Section 27.
3   Refer to the accompanying illustration and remove the bolts from the top edge of the fender and from the pillar in front of the door.
4   Remove the pop rivets from the front lower mount, then remove the two screws and separate the lower mud deflector from under the fender.
5   Using a heat gun or a powerful hair dryer, soften the sealant along the front and upper edge joints, then carefully remove the fender.
6   Installation is the reverse of removal. Be sure to use caulking along the front and upper edge joints.

31 Console — removal and installation

1   Disconnect the negative battery cable from the battery.
2   Remove the clock and switches by carefully prying out the sides or the top to release the catches and unplugging the wire harness connector(s).
3   Press in on the right-hand side of the heater control panel and release the catches on the left-hand side with a feeler gauge or other thin tool.
4   Lift up on the shift lever boot and remove the console mounting screws (photo).
5   Reach through the openings in the top of the console and release the catches, then lift the rear of the console and free it from the dash.
6   Disconnect the radio wires and the cigarette lighter wire and lift the console over the shift lever to remove it.
7   Installation is the reverse of removal.

32 Seats — removal and installation

Front seats
1   Slide the seat all the way forward and remove the two bolts securing the rear of the seat rails to the floor (the bolts have TORX-type

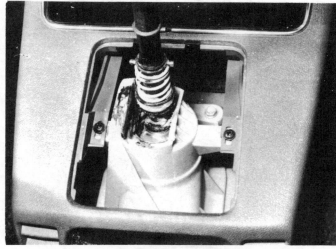

31.4   The console is attached to the gearshift housing with two screws

heads and require a special tool for removal).
2   Slide the seat all the way back and remove the front seat rail mounting bolts.
3   Remove the seat and recover the spacers and washers installed between the seat rails and floor.
4   Installation is the reverse of removal. Be sure to install the washers and spacers correctly and tighten the bolts to the specified torque.

Rear seat — Alliance
5   To remove the seat cushion, withdraw the two retaining tabs securing the legs to the floor fittings (use a pliers to grasp the tabs).
6   Lift the front of the cushion to release the legs from the fittings, then lift out the cushion and remove it from the vehicle.
7   To remove the seat back, simply lift it up to disengage the tabs at the back from the slots.
8   Installation is the reverse of removal. Be sure to push the cushion in completely before pushing down firmly on the front to locate the legs in the floor fittings. Make sure the retaining tabs snap into place correctly.

Rear seat — Encore
9   To remove the rear seat cushion, raise it and remove the retaining clip and pin from the hinges, then lift out the cushion.
10 Installation is the reverse of removal.
11 To remove the seat back, raise the cushion and separate the seat belts from the restraining straps, then remove the seat back mounting bolts.
12 Lift the seat back up and out of the retaining pin.
13 Installation is the reverse of removal.

33 Seat belts — removal and installation

Front
1   Carefully pry off the trim buttons, then remove the upper and lower side seat belt mounting bolts. Note the arrangement of spacers, washers and sleeves at each mount.
2   Remove the rear seat cushion, then detach the center pillar trim pieces (they are held in place with several screws).
3   Remove the retractor mounting bolt and separate the seat belt assembly from the pillar.
4   Installation is the reverse of removal. Be sure to tighten the bolts to the specified torque.
5   The center mounts are held in place with bolts which are accessible only after removing trim panels and lifting the carpeting.

Rear
6   Raise or remove the rear seat cushion, then remove the seat belt mounting bolts. Installation is the reverse of removal. Be sure to tighten the bolts to the specified torque.

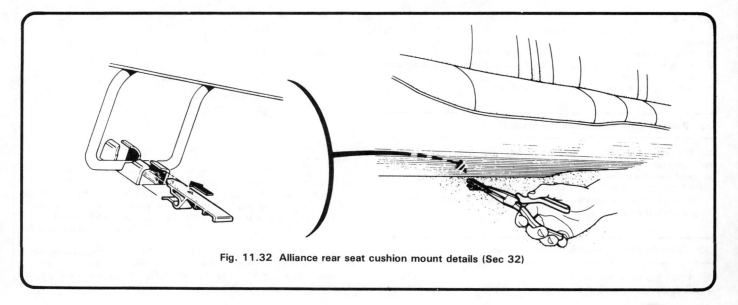

Fig. 11.32 Alliance rear seat cushion mount details (Sec 32)

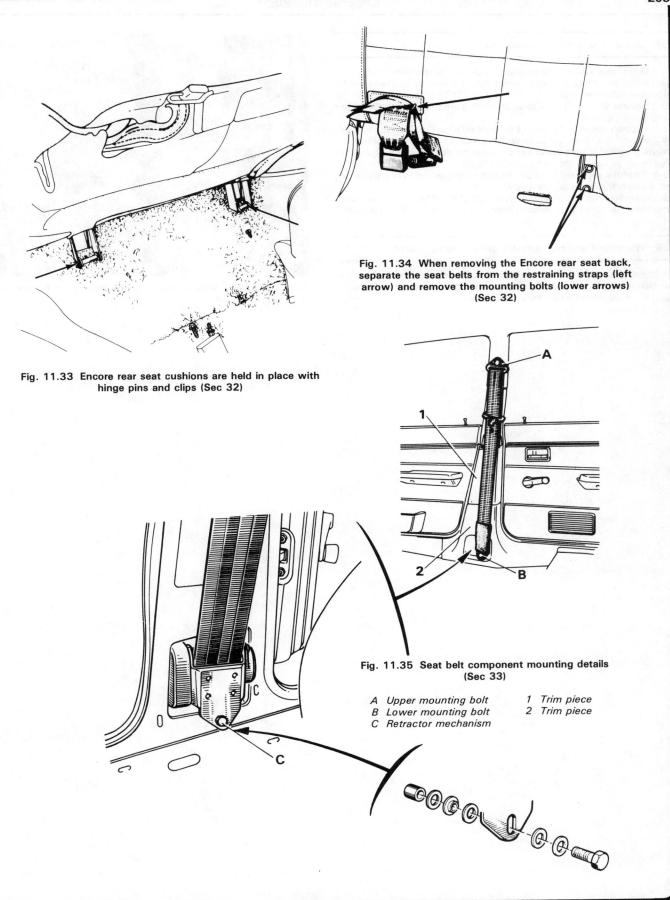

Fig. 11.33 Encore rear seat cushions are held in place with hinge pins and clips (Sec 32)

Fig. 11.34 When removing the Encore rear seat back, separate the seat belts from the restraining straps (left arrow) and remove the mounting bolts (lower arrows) (Sec 32)

Fig. 11.35 Seat belt component mounting details (Sec 33)

A Upper mounting bolt
B Lower mounting bolt
C Retractor mechanism

1 Trim piece
2 Trim piece

34   Doors — removal and installation

1   On models with electric windows or door locks, remove the trim panel (Section 16 or 21), disconnect the wire harness and remove the harness from the door.
2   Release the door check strap by driving out the pin with a hammer and punch (photo).
3   Support the door on blocks or have an assistant hold it securely.
4   Pry off the hinge pin caps with a screwdriver, then drive out the hinge pins. Note that the lower pin must be driven up and the upper pin must be driven down to remove them.
5   Carefully separate the door from the hinges (be very careful not to scratch the paint on the body).
6   Installation is the reverse of removal. If the door is not flush with the body, the hinge arms must be bent with a slotted bar to adjust them.

35   Windshield and rear window glass — replacement

Because of the special tools and expertise required to replace the windshield and rear window glass it should be done by a dealer service department or an auto glass shop.

34.2   The check strap and door hinge pins can be driven out with a hammer and punch

Chapter 12 Chassis electrical system

Contents

Specifications

Bulb application
Interior

	Type
Courtesy light	89
Dome light	C11-7W
Dome/reading light	C11-7W
Cargo light*	194
Lighted vanity mirror	74
Climate control panel	161
Glove box light	C11-5W
Instrument cluster warning lights	74
Instrument cluster illumination	194

Exterior

	Type
Back-up/turn signal light	1156
Brake/taillight/front turn signal light	2057 NA
Side marker light	194
License plate light	C11-5W
Headlights	
High beam	H4651
Low beam	H4652
Underhood light	105
Trunk light**	105

* Encore only
** Alliance only

---

1 General information

The electrical system is a 12-volt, negative ground type with power for the lights and other electrical accessories provided by a lead/acid battery which is charged by the alternator.

This Chapter covers repair and service procedures for the various electrical components not associated with the engine. Information on the battery, alternator, ignition system and starter motor can be found in Chapter 5.

When working on the electrical system, be sure to disconnect the negative battery cable from the battery to prevent short circuits and related problems.

Note: *If problems arise in the* Systems Sentry *monitoring and warning system, have it checked by a dealer service department.*

2   Electrical troubleshooting — general information

A typical electrical circuit consists of an electrically-operated component, any switches and relays used to control the component and the wiring and connectors that hook the component to the battery and the chassis. To help locate a problem in an electrical circuit, wiring diagrams are included at the end of the manual.

Before tackling any electrical problem, first study the appropriate wiring diagram to determine what components and connections make up the affected circuit. Trouble spots, for instance, can often be narrowed down by noting if other components related to the circuit are operating properly or not. If several components or circuits fail at one time, chances are the problem lies in the fuse or ground connection, as several circuits are often routed through the same fuses or ground connections.

Electrical problems often stem from simple causes, such as loose or corroded connections or a blown fuse. Prior to any troubleshooting, visually check the fuse, wires and connections of the problem circuit.

If test equipment will be utilized, use the diagrams to determine ahead of time where the connections should be made to pinpoint the problem.

The basic tools needed for electrical troubleshooting include a circuit tester or voltmeter (a 12-volt bulb with a set of leads attached can also be used), a continuity tester (self-powered test light) and a jumper wire, preferably with a circuit breaker incorporated, which can be used to bypass portions of a circuit.

Voltage checks should be performed if a circuit is not functioning properly. Connect one lead of a circuit tester to either the negative battery terminal or a known good ground. Attach the other lead to a connector in the circuit being tested, preferably near the battery or fuse. If the tester bulb lights, voltage is reaching that point (which means that the part of the circuit between the connector and battery is problem free). Continue checking the entire circuit in the same manner. If you reach a point where no voltage is present, the problem lies between that point and the last good test point. Most of the time the problem is due to a loose connection. Keep in mind that some circuits receive voltage only when the ignition key is in the Acc or Run position.

One method of finding shorts in a circuit is to remove the fuse and connect a test light or voltmeter in its place at the fuse terminals. There should be no load in the circuit. Move the wiring harness from side-to-side and watch the test light. If the bulb lights, there is a short to ground in that area (probably where insulation has rubbed off a wire). The same check can be performed on the rest of the circuit, including any switches.

A ground check should be done to see if a component is grounded properly. Disconnect the battery and connect one lead of a self-powered test light to a known good ground. Connect the other lead to the wire or ground connection being checked. If the bulb lights, the ground is good. If not, the ground is faulty.

A continuity check is done to see if a circuit, wire or component is passing electricity through it properly. Disconnect the battery and connect one lead of a self-powered test light to one end of the circuit. Connect the other lead to the other end of the circuit. If the bulb lights, the circuit is complete (which means that electricity can pass through it). Switches can be checked in the same way.

Remember that an electrical circuit passes current from the battery, through the wires, switches, relays, etc. to the electrical component (light bulb, motor, etc.). From the component it is routed to the body (ground) and back to the battery through the ground cable. An electrical problem is basically an interruption in the flow of current to and from the batttery.

3   Fuses and relays — general information

The fuses and relays are located under the glove compartment. The relays are attached to the fuse panel cover and the fuses are up under the dash. The cover can be released by depressing the clips on the outer corners and pulling it down.

Each of the fuses is designed to protect a specific circuit (the circuits are identified on the fuse panel). The compact fuses with blade-type terminals allow fingertip removal and installation.

If an electrical component fails, check the fuse first. A fuse which has 'blown' is easily identified by the burned and broken element inside the clear plastic body. Also, the terminals are exposed in the fuse body,

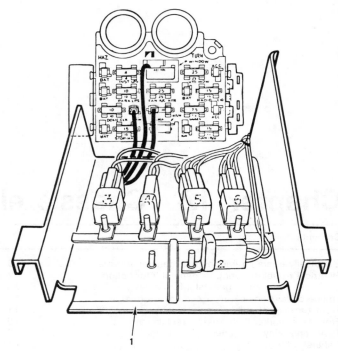

Fig. 12.1 The fuse panel and relays are exposed by pulling the fuse panel cover down after releasing the clips (Sec 3)

1 Fuse panel cover
2 Windshield wiper motor circuit breaker
3 Power window relay
4 Headlight circuit breaker
5 Ignition On relay
6 AC and heater blower motor Off relay

allowing continuity checks.

It is very important that the correct fuse be installed. The different circuits require differing amounts of protection, indicated by the amperage rating molded into the fuse body.

Never bypass the fuse with a piece of metal. Serious damage to the circuit could result.

If the replacement fuse fails immediately, do not replace it again until the cause of the problem is isolated and corrected. In most cases, the problem will not require extensive repair.

If a circuit or system controlled by one of the relays fails to operate, listen for a 'click' at the relay when the switch is operated. If a sound is not heard, then the wiring, connections and relay should be checked.

4   Turn signals and hazard flashers — general information

The hazard flasher is mounted on the fuse panel and the turn signal flasher is attached to a separate block under the left-hand side of the instrument panel (some models have separate right and left side turn signal flashers — the right side flasher is located in the wire harness under the left side of the instrument panel).

If a problem occurs in either of these systems, check the bulbs, wire connections and bulb contacts as well as the fuse(s). If only a part of the circuit is functioning, the bulb is the likely cause. If the entire circuit is dead, the flasher may be defective or the fuse may be blown.

5   Instrument panel — removal and installation

1   Disconnect the battery cables from the battery (negative first, then positive).
2   Remove the two screws from the underside of the housing.
3   Press in at each end of the housing to detach the side clips and press down on the top to detach the two upper clips.

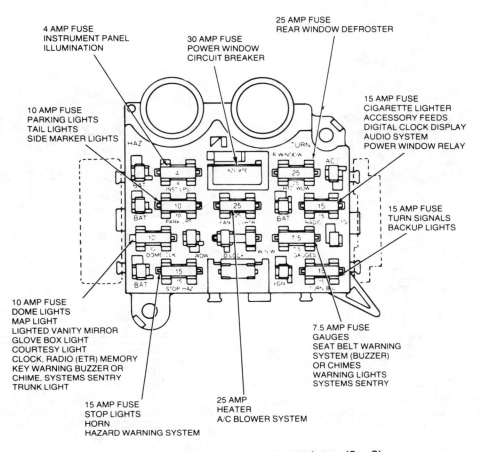

4 AMP FUSE
INSTRUMENT PANEL
ILLUMINATION

30 AMP FUSE
POWER WINDOW
CIRCUIT BREAKER

25 AMP FUSE
REAR WINDOW DEFROSTER

10 AMP FUSE
PARKING LIGHTS
TAIL LIGHTS
SIDE MARKER LIGHTS

15 AMP FUSE
CIGARETTE LIGHTER
ACCESSORY FEEDS
DIGITAL CLOCK DISPLAY
AUDIO SYSTEM
POWER WINDOW RELAY

15 AMP FUSE
TURN SIGNALS
BACKUP LIGHTS

10 AMP FUSE
DOME LIGHTS
MAP LIGHT
LIGHTED VANITY MIRROR
GLOVE BOX LIGHT
COURTESY LIGHT
CLOCK, RADIO (ETR) MEMORY
KEY WARNING BUZZER OR
CHIME, SYSTEMS SENTRY
TRUNK LIGHT

7.5 AMP FUSE
GAUGES
SEAT BELT WARNING
SYSTEM (BUZZER)
OR CHIMES
WARNING LIGHTS
SYSTEMS SENTRY

15 AMP FUSE
STOP LIGHTS
HORN
HAZARD WARNING SYSTEM

25 AMP
HEATER
A/C BLOWER SYSTEM

Fig. 12.2 Typical fuse panel component layout (Sec 3)

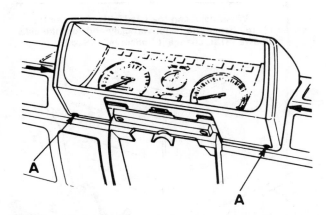

Fig. 12.3 The instrument cluster housing is held in place
with two screws (A) (Sec 5)

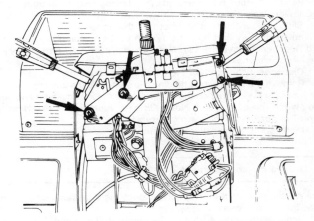

Fig. 12.4 After the lower part of the shroud is removed,
the steering column switches are exposed (the arrows point
to the mounting screws for the various switches) (Sec 6)

4   Remove the three mounting screws and pull the panel out far
enough to reach behind it and disconnect the wire harness plugs and
the speedometer cable.
5   Installation is the reverse of removal. When hooking up the battery
cables, connect the positive first, followed by the negative.

6   Steering column switches — removal and installation

1   Disconnect the negative battery cable from the battery.
2   Remove the screws holding the lower half of the steering column

shroud in place. Release the catches and separate the lower portion
of the shroud (place it aside but do not strain the wiring connections
— if applicable).
3   Remove the upper shroud mounting screws but leave it in place.
4   If the light/turn signal switch is being removed, take out the screws,
lift the upper shroud to provide clearance and withdraw the switch,
then disconnect the wires.
5   The windshield wiper/washer switch is removed in the exact same
manner.
6   Both switches are sealed and cannot be disassembled and repaired.
7   Installation is the reverse of removal.

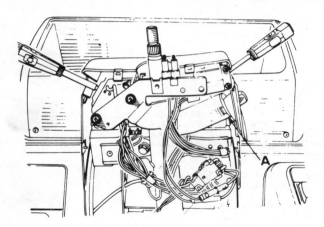

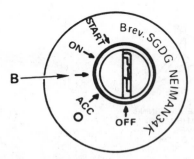

Fig. 12.5 When removing the ignition switch, the key must be placed in the position between Acc and On and the small screw (A) must be removed (Sec 7)

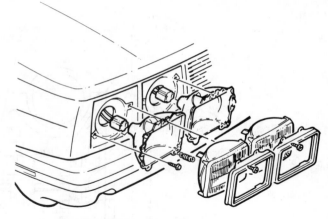

Fig. 12.6 Headlights — exploded view (Sec 8)

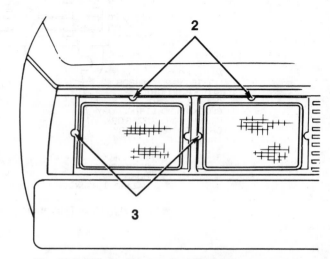

Fig. 12.7 When adjusting the headlights, turn the top screws (2) to change the beam vertically and turn the side screws (3) to change it horizontally (Sec 9)

7   Ignition switch — removal and installation

1   Refer to Section 6 and separate the steering column shrouds (upper and lower) from the column as described there.
2   Slide the switch trim plate out of the upper shroud.
3   Insert the key and turn the switch to the position between Acc and On, then remove the key. **Note:** *On early models, turn the key to the Off position and remove it.*
4   Disconnect the ignition switch wiring connector.
5   Remove the small screw holding the switch to the column, depress the retaining pin located on the upper side of the lock cylinder and push the switch out of position. **Note:** *On early models, the retaining pin is on the bottom of the switch assembly.*
6   Installation is the reverse of removal.

8   Headlight — replacement

1   Working under the hood, disconnect the wire harness from the headlight sealed beam unit.
2   Remove the screws from the headlight trim ring and separate the ring from the headlight (do not mistake the adjustment screws for the trim ring screws).
3   Pull out the headlight, position the new one and install the trim ring, then plug in the wire harness connector.

9   Headlight aim — adjustment

1   Any headlight adjustments made by the home mechanic should be considered temporary only. After adjustment, have the beams checked by a state-approved headlight aiming facility as soon as possible.
2   Adjustment screws are provided at the front of each headlight to alter the beam horizontally (side screw) and vertically (top screw).

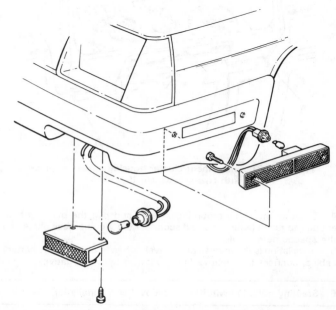

Fig. 12.8 Front side marker lights and parking/turn signal lights — exploded view (Sec 10)

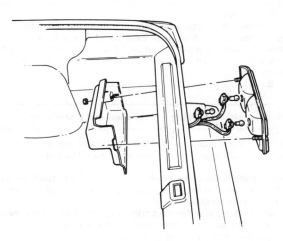

Fig. 12.9 Rear cluster lights — exploded view (Sec 12)

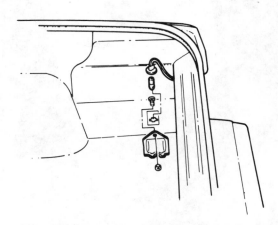

Fig. 12.10 Rear side marker light — exploded view (Sec 13)

10 Front side marker light bulb — replacement

1   The bulb is accessible through the bottom of the front fender inner liner.
2   Turn the socket 1/4-turn counterclockwise and pull it out of the lens assembly.
3   Remove the bulb from the socket and install the new bulb.
4   Push the socket into the lens and turn it 1/4-turn clockwise to lock it in place.

11 Front turn signal bulb — replacement

1   The parking/turn signal bulbs are attached to the bottom of the front bumper on each side.
2   Reach behind the lens assembly, turn the socket counterclockwise and pull the socket and bulb out of the lens.
3   Depress and turn the bulb to remove it from the socket.

12 Rear cluster bulbs — replacement

1   Working inside the trunk/luggage compartment, remove the nuts and separate the cover from the taillight assembly.
2   Depress the tab on the socket and turn the socket counterclockwise to remove it from the lens assembly.
3   Remove the bulb from the socket and install the new one, then insert the socket and turn it clockwise to lock it in place.
4   Install the cover.

13 Rear side marker light bulb — replacement

1   Working inside the trunk/luggage compartment, remove the nut and detach the side marker light cover.
2   Turn the socket 1/4-turn counterclockwise and pull it out of the lens assembly.
3   Remove the bulb, install the new one, insert the socket into the lens assembly and turn it 1/4-turn clockwise to lock it in place.
4   Install the cover and tighten the nut.

14 Windshield wiper motor and linkage — removal and installation

Note: *Before beginning this procedure, be aware that the evaporator on air conditioned models must be moved out of the way to withdraw the wiper assembly.*

14.2   Carefully detach the hood sealing rubber from the firewall

14.3   The cover is held in place with plastic wing nuts

1   Remove the wiper arms by lifting the cover, removing the mounting nuts and carefully prying the arms off the spindles.
2   Carefully detach the hood sealing rubber at the base of the windshield (photo).
3   Unscrew the retaining nuts and remove the cover over the wiper motor and linkage (photo).
4   Withdraw the rubber washer, remove the nut and slip off the second washer from each wiper arm spindle.

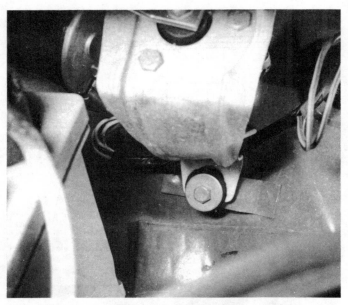

14.5   Wiper motor mounting bracket retaining bolt location

5   Remove the bolt and washer attaching the motor mount bracket to the firewall (photo).
6   Disconnect the motor wire harness connector, push the spindles through to the inside, then withdraw the motor and linkage.
7   Note the number and location of the washers and spacers on the spindles and make sure they are in place when the motor and linkage is reinstalled.
8   Installation is the reverse of removal.

15   Rear hatch wiper motor — removal and installation

1   Remove the wiper arm as described in Section 14.
2   Open the hatch and remove the cover panel to gain access to the motor.
3   Remove the nut from the wiper arm spindle, then lift off the washer, the window washer nozzle and the rubber pad. Separate the tubing from the washer nozzle as it is removed.
4   Disconnect the wire harness connector and remove the mounting bolts/nuts, then separate the motor from the hatch.
5   Installation is the reverse of removal.

16   Speedometer cable — removal and installation

1   Refer to Section 5 and disconnect the cable from the rear of the speedometer as described there.

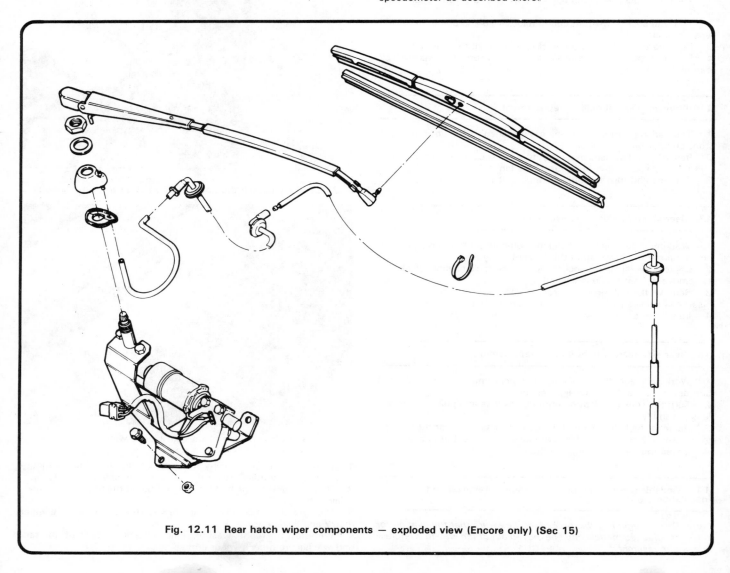

Fig. 12.11 Rear hatch wiper components — exploded view (Encore only) (Sec 15)

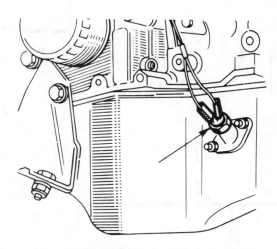

Fig. 12.12 The oil level sensor is threaded into a mount in the oil pan (Sec 17)

2   Pry out the firewall grommet and pull the cable through into the engine compartment, then release it from the clips.
3   Working at the rear of the transmission, withdraw the cable retaining clip through the engine mount and separate the cable from the transmission.
4   Installation is the reverse of removal.

17   Engine oil level indicator — general information

Some models are equipped with an engine oil level sensor, which enables oil level checks by glancing at a gauge in the instrument panel. Later models may be equipped with an elaborate monitoring and warning system known as 'Systems Sentry', which not only electronically monitors engine oil level but also keeps tabs on the coolant, transmission oil, power steering fluid, brake fluid, windshield washer fluid and brake pad wear. Consult your owner's manual for more information on the system.

The gauge is controlled by an electronic circuit located in the instrument panel which receives information from a sensor located in the engine oil pan. The sensor contains a high resistance wire whose thermal conductivity changes according to how far it is immersed in oil.

If the indicator fails to function, check the components as follows:
 a) Remove the sensor from the oil pan by disconnecting the two wires and unscrewing the sensor from the mount.
 b) Connect the leads from an ohmmeter between the sensor terminals. A resistance reading other than infinite should be indicated (if not, the sensor is probably faulty and should be replaced with a new one).
 c) If the sensor is in satisfactory condition, refer to Section 5 and remove the instrument panel. Check for continuity in the wires between the sensor and the gauge wire harness connector. If no continuity exists, trace the wire(s) until the break or bad connection is located and make the necessary repairs.
 d) If the wires are in good condition, attach the ohmmeter leads to the gauge terminals on the back of the instrument panel. The ohmmeter should indicate a resistance other than infinite (if it does not, the gauge is probably faulty).

18   Electric door locks — general information

An electro-mechanical door locking system is installed on some models. The system enables all doors to be locked or unlocked from the outside by locking or unlocking either front door. By depressing a switch on the console, all doors can be locked or unlocked from the inside. The locks can also be operated manually.

Each lock is operated by a solenoid which is connected to the lock mechanism inside the door. A safety device consisting of an inertia switch and thermal cut-out automatically unlocks all the doors in the event of an impact or heat build-up. These components are located in the steering column lower shroud. A reset button is also provided in the shroud to enable the system to be reset in the event of a malfunction.

Removal and installation of the door locks is basically the same as for conventional locks (see Chapter 11).

On some models the door locks are operated by remote control using a small hand-held infra-red transmitter. The transmitter signal is decoded by a receiver mounted above the rear view mirror, which activates the solenoid to lock or unlock the doors.

The transmitter is powered by three 1.5 volt alkaline batteries which have a life of approximately 1 year under normal use. The batteries can be replaced by removing the screws that hold the case together.

If the door lock system malfunctions, have it checked by a dealer service department.

19   Electrically-operated windows — general information

Electrically-operated windows are installed on some models. They are controlled by switches mounted in the center console.

Removal and installation of the door glass and motor assemblies is covered in Chapter 11.

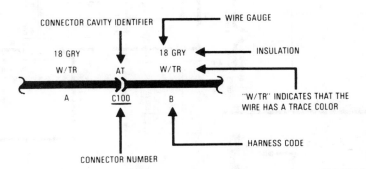

WIRE COLOR CODES

CODE	COLOR	CODE	COLOR	CODE	COLOR
BLK .... Black		GRY .... Gray		VIO .... Violet	
BLU .... Blue		ORN ..... Orange		WHT .... White	
BRN .... Brown		PNK .... Pink		YEL .... Yellow	
GRN ...... Green		RED .... Red			

FUEL TANK UNIT

FUEL PUMP

C101 C100 C200 C301 T5 C2 C3 T5 C301 G300
C A D ORN EZ ORN D N ORN E 14 ORN 18 BLK 18 BLK 12 BLK

16 ORN
18 ORN 18 ORN
C 14 ORN
6

DIAGNOSTIC CONNECTOR D1

TACHOMETER FROM START RELAY ZONE B2

(to "B" next illustration)

A

BALLAST RESISTOR
1.1 OHMS 25 WATT

C106 FUSE LINK G

18 RED   14 RED   14 RED   14 RED
C   C

2
30

87
87a
5
18 ORN
BY PASS CONNECTOR
18 ORN   16 ORN

FUEL INJECTOR RELAY

DIAGNOSTIC CONNECTOR D1
3 6
5
1 2 4
FUEL INJECTION RELAY

5

ELECTRONIC CONTROL UNIT (ECU)

RELAY CONTROL
ENGINE SPEED INPUT (RPM)
SOLID STATE

C109 C100 C201
CU D C
18 GRN W/TR   18 ORN W/TR
TRIGGER SIGNAL

16 LT BLU   18 LT BLU
C
16 LT BLU   18 GRN W/TR   18 ORN W/TR   18 LT BLU

IGNITION CONTROL MODULE

TACH OUTPUT
COIL CONTROL
ENGINE RPM INPUT
RED
WHT

COIL
TO PLUGS
TO PLUGS

DISTRIBUTOR

TDC SENSOR

IGNITION SWITCH

C224 C100 C101 C
2 D A A C
RED 14 YEL   14 YEL   14 YEL   14 YEL   14 YEL
START
ACC ON
OFF

FUSE BLOCK
FUSE BLOCK DETAILS

14 YEL   14 YEL
D
DIAGNOSTIC CONNECTOR D1
2

POWER INPUT
CRANK INPUT
GROUND
SOLID STATE
15   31
50

DIAGNOSTIC CONNECTOR D1
C
3   G110

SOLID STATE
GROUND
E
G103
14 BLK   12 BLK

A

D
POWER
14 YEL

AUTOMATIC TRANSAXLE COMPUTER

CLOSED IN PARK OR NEUTRAL
C   E

IGNITION CONTROL MODULE
WITH AUTOMATIC TRANSAXLE

START RELAY

C101
A   (NOT USED)
14 BLK W/TR   C

C110
A   C
14 BLK W/TR
WITH MANUAL TRANSAXLE
R1

C110
E   G109
14 BLK

FUSE LINK A

18 RED

12 RED

R2

C100
A   C224
DT   3   PNK
12 RED W/TR   12 RED
D

C224 C100
4   A
GRY   14 GRN   14 DK GRN
EX
START
ACC ON
OFF

A
14 ORN
TO C100 (EZ) ZONE C3

C101
14 LT GRN
C
B
TO IDLE DIODE ASSEMBLY ZONE C3

14 LT GRN   14 LT GRN
C

BAL
BAT

SOL

START SOLENOID

14 DK GRN W/TR

C102
B
14 DK GRN W/TR

STARTER MOTOR
M
GRN

ELECTRONIC CONTROL UNIT (ECU)
START
4

C101
F
14 DK GRN W/TR
14 LT GRN

DIAGNOSTIC CONNECTOR D1
4
14 LT GRN
C

C108
A
14 LT GRN
18 LT GRN

COLD START INJECTOR
COLD START INJECTOR INJECTS FUEL DURING COLD STARTS
A   B

R3
C108
F
18 BLK W/TR   18 BLK W/TR

DIAGNOSTIC CONNECTOR D2
10
18 BLK W/TR

THERMO TIME COOLANT SWITCH SHOWN COLD
B
COLD
50 Ω
HOT
50 Ω
50 Ω

THERMO TIME COOLANT SWITCH

4 RED
R2

BATTERY

G112
G100
4 BLK   R2
8 BLK   R2

4 BRAID
R4

FUSE LINK E

G101

ALTERNATOR

R3

18 TAN

DIAGNOSTIC CONNECTOR D2
9
C
18 TAN

C
E
18 TAN   18 TAN
C   A

Typical engine wiring diagram — Calif. models only (1 of 2)

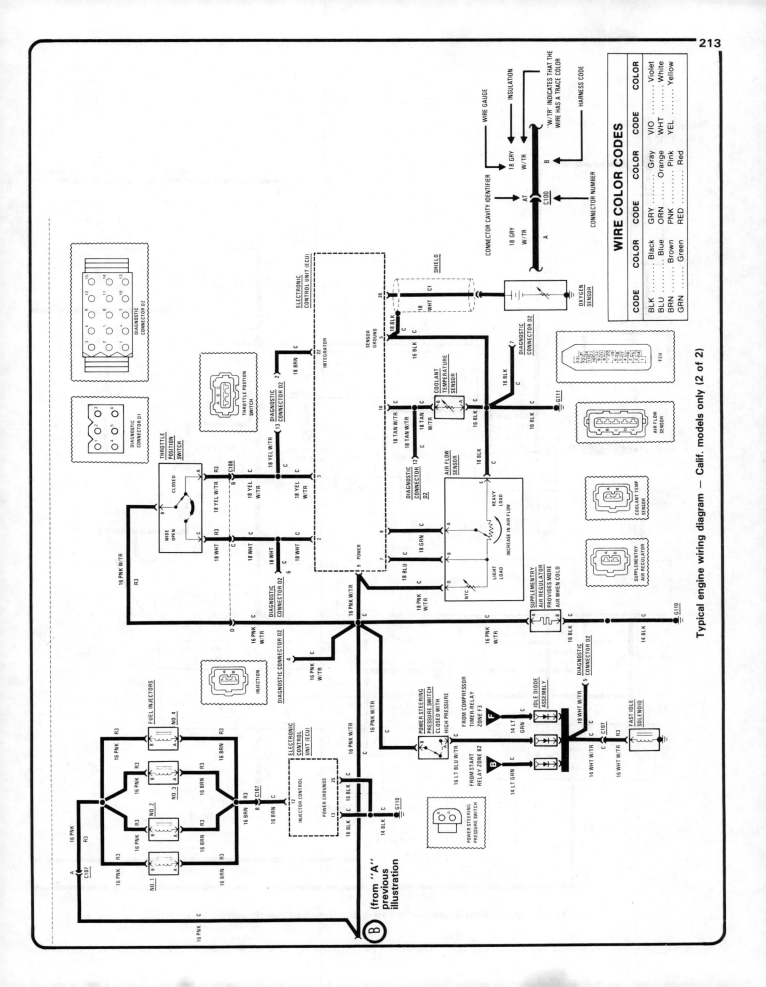

Typical engine wiring diagram — Calif. models only (2 of 2)

Typical engine wiring diagram — 49-state and Canadian models only (1 of 3)

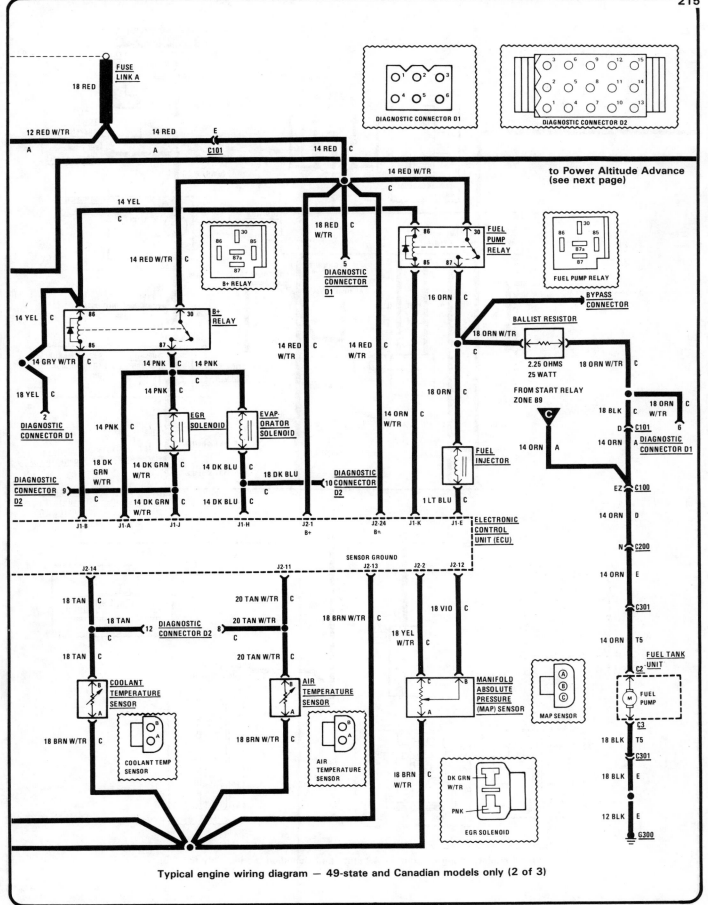

Typical engine wiring diagram — 49-state and Canadian models only (2 of 3)

HOT IN RUN OR START
FROM FUSE LINK A

FUSE
BLOCK

GAUGES
FUSE
7.5A

DISTRIBUTOR
TO PLUGS

18 WHT W/TR   D

SEATBELT
TIMER/
BUZZER

18 WHT W/TR   D

SEE FUSE
BLOCK DETAILS

20 WHT W/TR   D

F
E
D
C
B
A

IGNITION CONTROL
MODULE

14 YEL   A

C1
13

INSTRUMENT
CLUSTER

UP
SHIFT

D
POWER
ALTITUDE   AMBIENT
GROUND   ADVANCE   ADVANCE
E   A   C

COIL

IGNITION
CONTROL
MODULE

TACH SIGNAL
F

2   C1

14 BLK   A

18 GRN W/TR   D

18 GRN W/TR

20 PNK   D

AX   C100

20 PNK   C

(NOT USED)

20
WHT   A

WHT   RED

TACHOMETER

A

CU   C100   C109

20 PNK   A   A   C105

20
ORN
W/TR

20
ORN
W/TR   A

18 GRN
W/TR   D   20 DK GRN   C

A   C111

18 PNK   R1

TDC
SENSOR

1

UPSHIFT
SWITCH
CLOSED IN
FOURTH GEAR

4 SPEED MANUAL
TRANSMISSION
ONLY

C105   B   A

DIAGNOSTIC
CONNECTOR D1

18 BLU   R1

20 ORN
W/TR   C

18 GRN W/TR   A

B   C111

18 BLU   A

20
WHT   C

C   C201

D   C105

18 DK BLU W/TR   C

18 DK BLU W/TR

DIAGNOSTIC
2   CONNECTOR D2

20 DK GRN   C

18 DK BLU W/TR   C

J2-17   J2-18

J2-4

J2-21

ELECTRONIC
CONTROL
UNIT (ECU)

J2-9

J1-F

18 GRY   C

14 BLK   C

A B C D E F G H J K

ECU J1

OXYGEN
SENSOR

18 BLK
C

DIAGNOSTIC
3   CONNECTOR D1

G110

DK BLU

LT
BLU

ORN

PNK

EVAPORATOR
SOLENOID

FUEL INJECTOR

1   24

12   13

ECU J2

Typical engine wiring diagram — 49-state and Canadian models only (3 of 3)

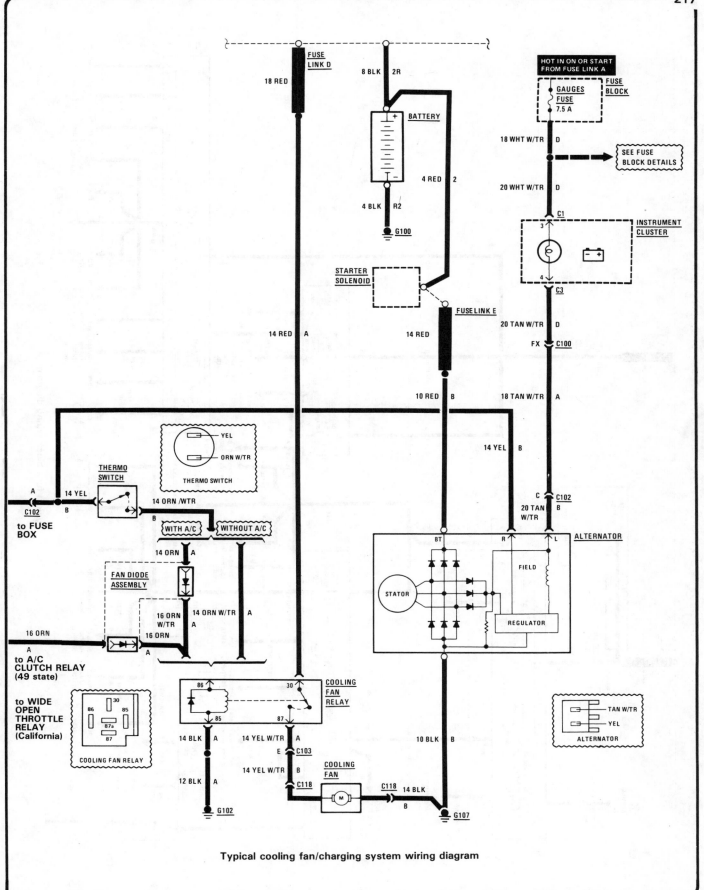

Typical cooling fan/charging system wiring diagram

Typical fuse block wiring diagram

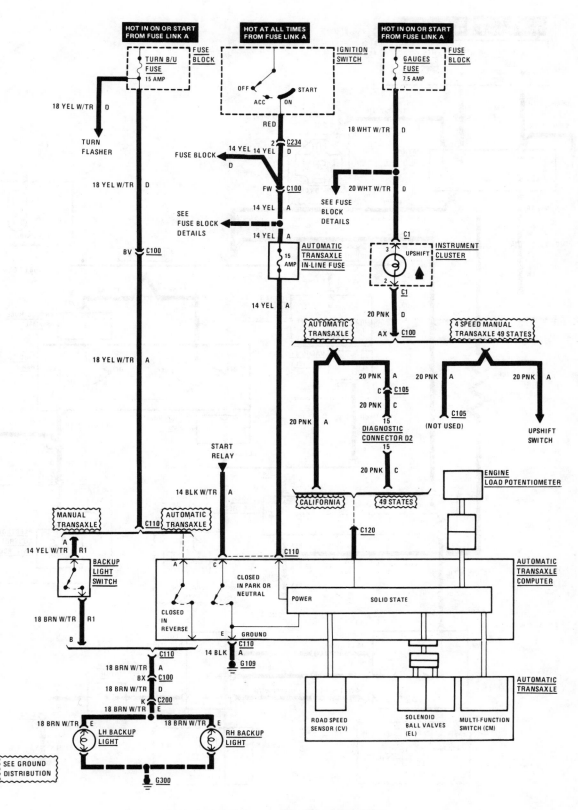

Typical automatic transmission wiring diagram

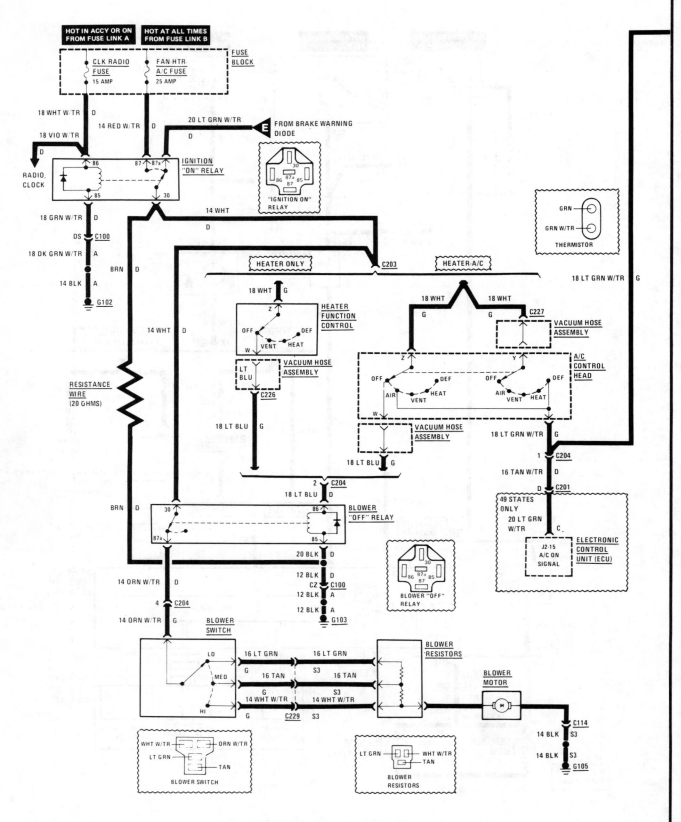

Typical heater blower motor wiring diagram

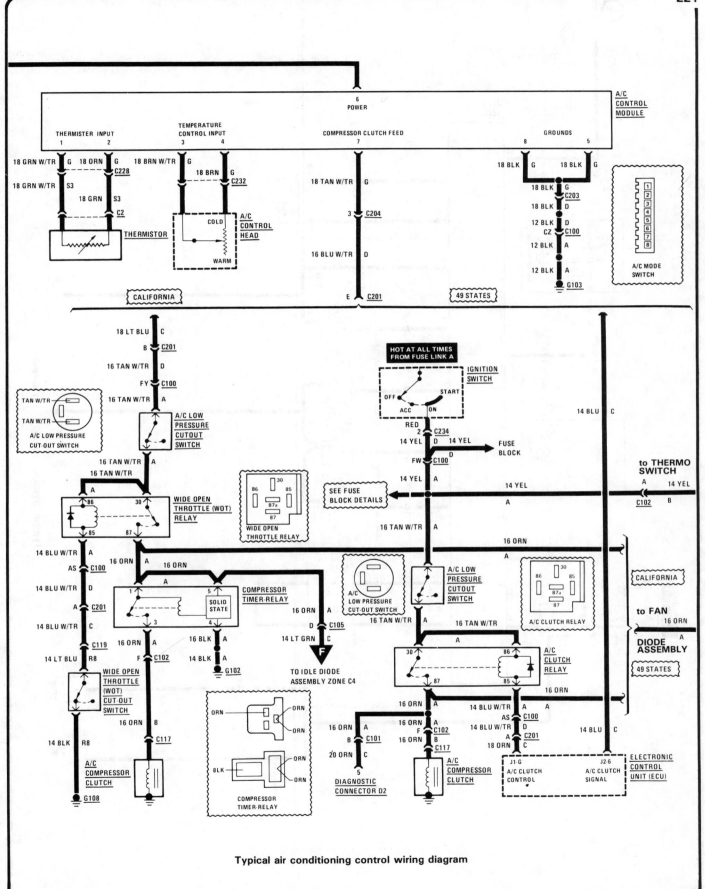

Typical air conditioning control wiring diagram

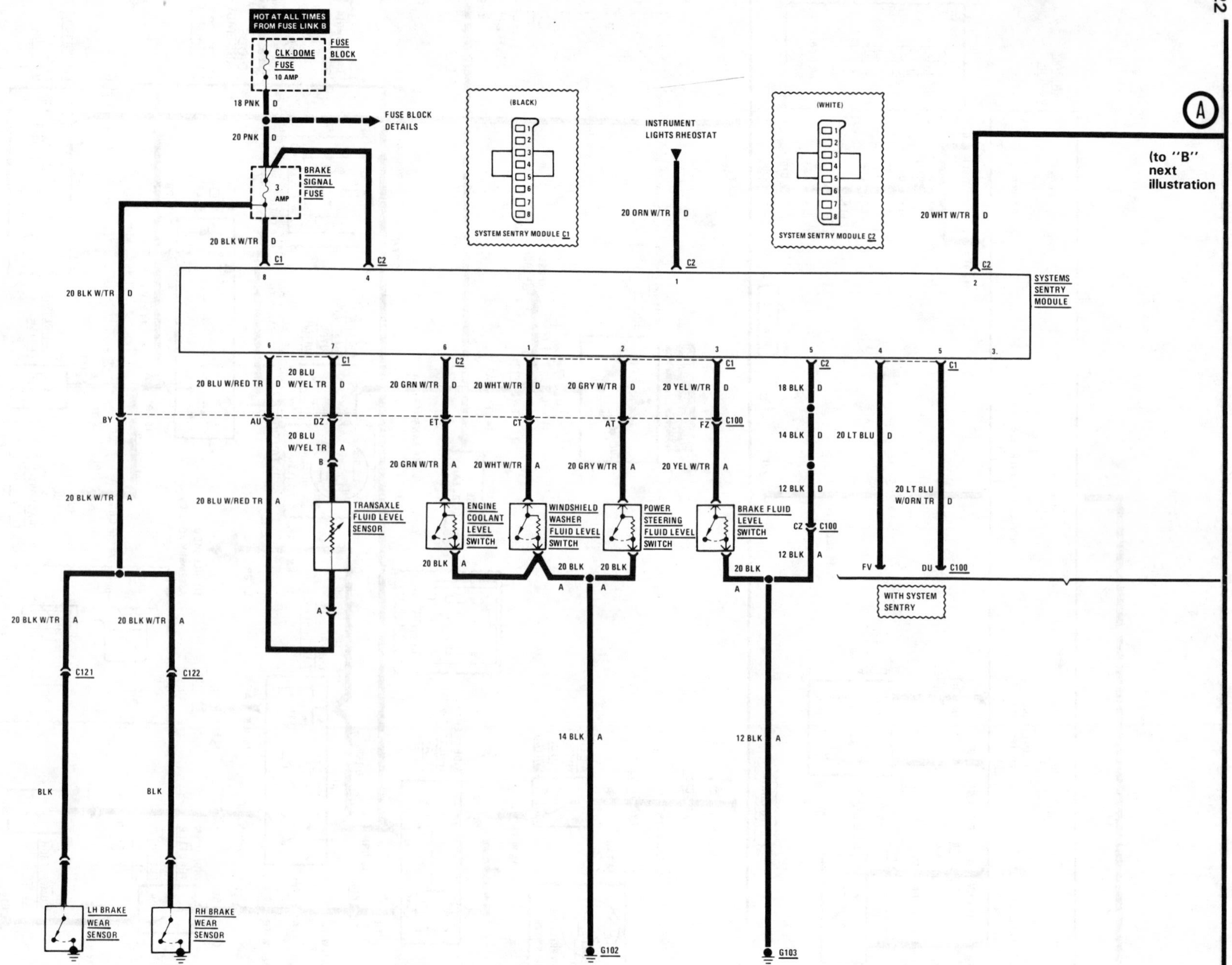

Ⓐ (to "B" next illustration)

SYSTEMS SENTRY MODULE

20 WHT W/TR

(WHITE) SYSTEM SENTRY MODULE C2

INSTRUMENT LIGHTS RHEOSTAT

20 ORN W/TR

(BLACK) SYSTEM SENTRY MODULE C1

HOT AT ALL TIMES FROM FUSE LINK B

FUSE BLOCK

CLK-DOME FUSE 10 AMP

FUSE BLOCK DETAILS

BRAKE SIGNAL FUSE 3 AMP

18 PNK

20 PNK

20 BLK W/TR

C2

C1

C100

WITH SYSTEM SENTRY

20 LT BLU W/ORN TR

20 LT BLU

18 BLK

14 BLK

12 BLK

12 BLK

BRAKE FLUID LEVEL SWITCH

20 BLK

12 BLK

G103

20 YEL W/TR

20 YEL W/TR

POWER STEERING FLUID LEVEL SWITCH

20 BLK

20 GRY W/TR

20 GRY W/TR

WINDSHIELD WASHER FLUID LEVEL SWITCH

20 BLK

14 BLK

G102

20 WHT W/TR

20 WHT W/TR

ENGINE COOLANT LEVEL SWITCH

20 BLK

20 GRN W/TR

20 GRN W/TR

TRANSAXLE FLUID LEVEL SENSOR

20 BLU W/YEL TR

20 BLU W/YEL TR

20 BLU W/RED TR

20 BLU W/RED TR

20 BLK W/TR

C122

BLK

RH BRAKE WEAR SENSOR

20 BLK W/TR

20 BLK W/TR

C121

BLK

LH BRAKE WEAR SENSOR

20 BLK W/TR

Typical 'Systems Sentry' wiring diagram

223

to IGNITION POWER

18 WHT W/TR

INSTRUMENT CLUSTER

18 WHT W/TR

FUEL INJECTOR RELAY

ELECTRONIC CONTROL UNIT (ECU)

C209

CALIFORNIA

49 STATES

16 LT BLU

C

16 LT BLU

DIAGNOSTIC CONNECTOR D1

20 DK GRN

CHARGE INDICATOR

TACHOMETER

IGNITION CONTROL MODULE

18 GRN W/TR

18 GRN W/TR

C3

D

C100

A

CU

18 GRN W/TR

18 GRN W/TR

F TACH SIGNAL

RED

WHT

TDC SENSOR

COOLANT TEMPERATURE GAUGE

C1

4

18 VIO

AU

18 VIO

C100

A

C

C103

B

18 VIO

COOLANT TEMPERATURE SENDER

Typical instrument cluster wiring diagram

HOT IN ON OR START FROM FUSE LINK A

FUSE BLOCK

GAGES FUSE 7.5 AMP

D

D

SEE FUSE BLOCK DETAILS

20 WHT W/TR

C1

D

3

G103

C2

1

FUEL GAUGE

FUEL TANK UNIT

FUEL PUMP

M

FUEL LEVEL SENDER

LOW FUEL SWITCH

C1

D

5

20 TAN

J

C200

E

20 TAN

C301

T5

18 TAN

C1

T5

C3

T5

C301

E

18 BLK

E

18 BLK

12 BLK

E

G300

18 WHT W/TR

20 WHT W/TR

C3

D

10

20 VIO

D

L

C200

E

20 VIO

C301

T5

18 VIO

"BRAKE"

ENGINE OIL LEVEL GAGE

SOLID STATE

WITHOUT SYSTEM SENTRY

PARKING BRAKE CLOSED WITH BRAKE ON

C2

8

20 LT GRN W/TR

C202

B

18 LT GRN W/TR

T3

20 LT GRN W/TR

C4

D

20 LT BLU W/TR

C100

DU

D

C100

A

BRAKE PRESSURE SWITCH CLOSED WITH ONE SYSTEM BAD

3

1

20 LT BLU W/TR

FV

CS 20 GRN W/TR

DY

A

20 GRN W/TR

D

BRAKE WARNING DIODE

D

E

TO "IGNITION ON" RELAY, ZONE D1

C2

D

9

20 LT BLU W/TR

CX

C100

A

18 LT BLU

C103

B

18 LT BLU

OIL PRESSURE SWITCH CLOSED WITH LOW OIL PRESSURE

DU

C100

D

C103

B

20 LT GRN W/TR

ENGINE OIL LEVEL SENSOR

20 LT GRN W/TR

C2

D

20 LT BLU W/TR

FV

D

18 LT BLU W/TR

C102

D

20 LT BLU W/TR

(from "A" previous illustration)

B

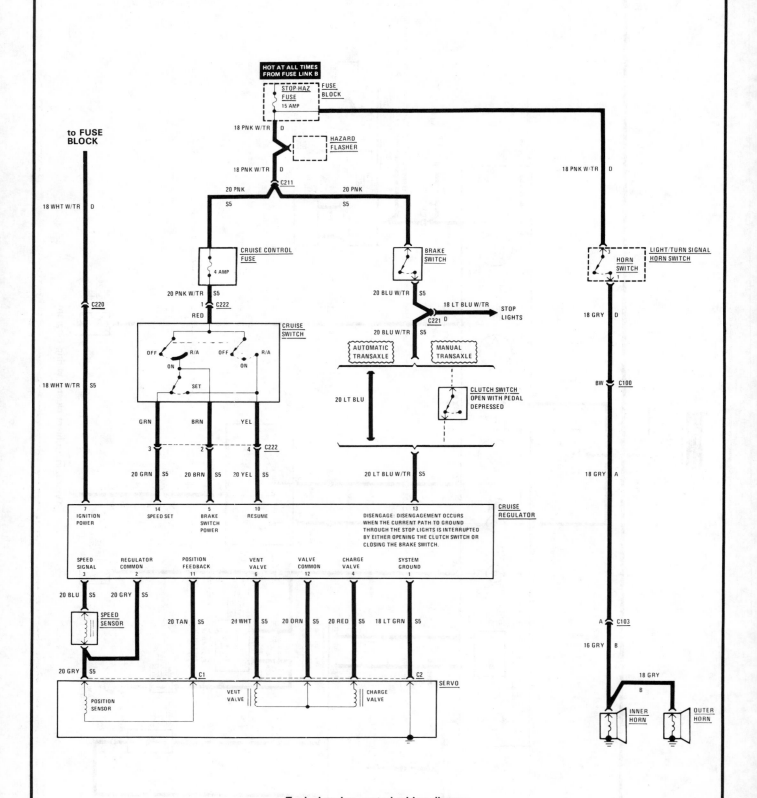

Typical cruise control wiring diagram

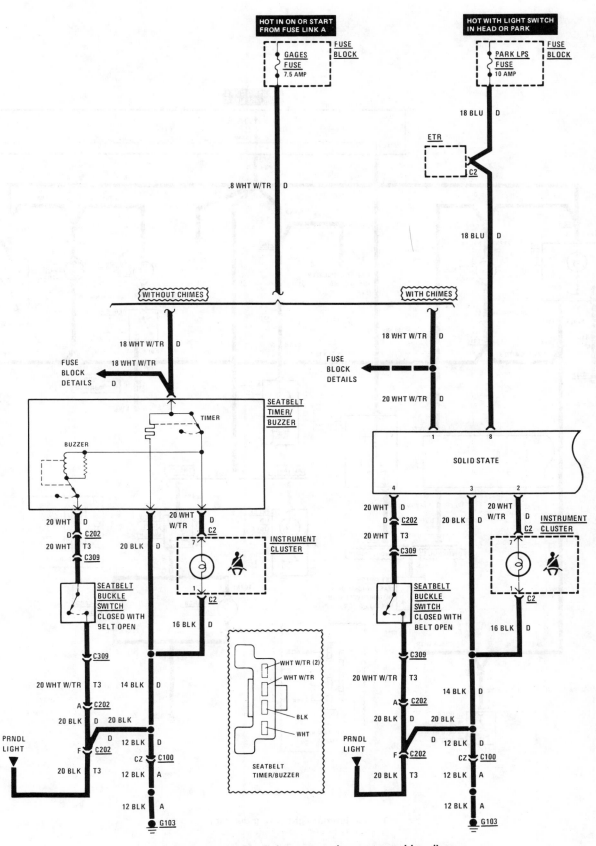

Typical seatbelt/ignition key/lights-on warning system wiring diagram

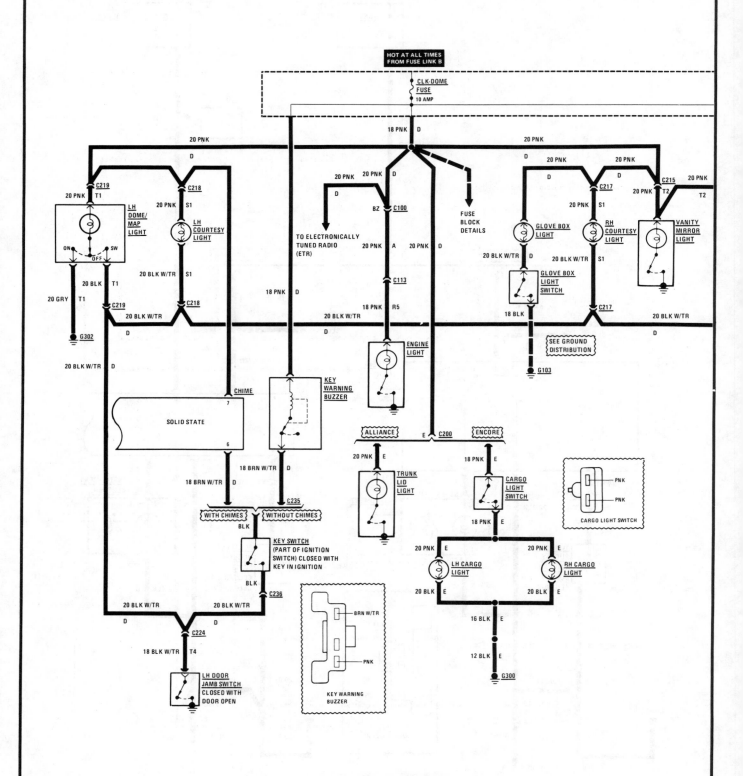

Typical interior light wiring diagram

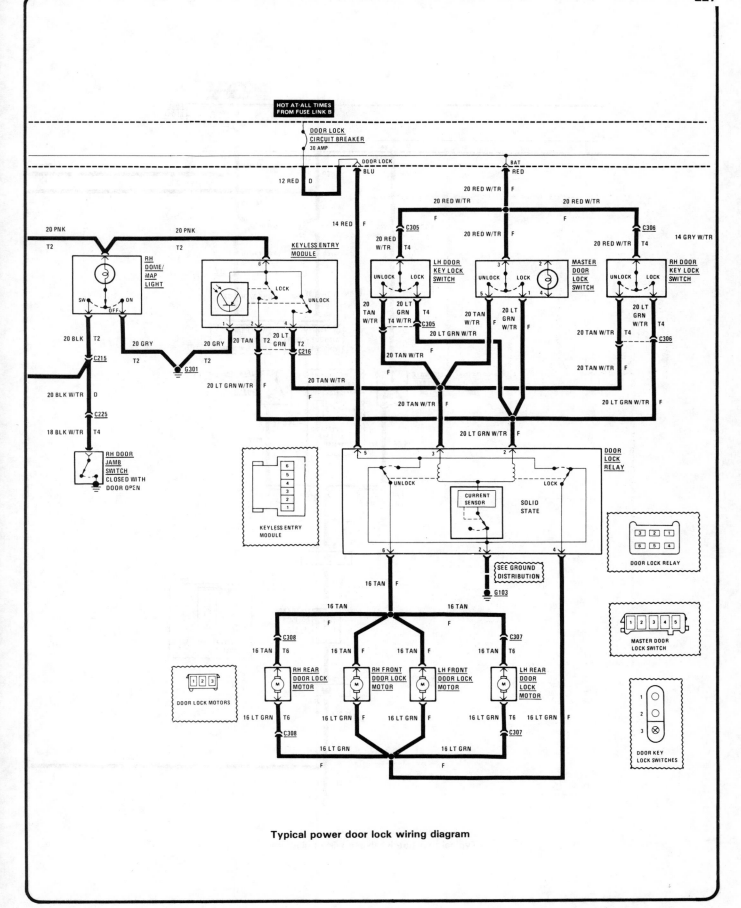

Typical power door lock wiring diagram

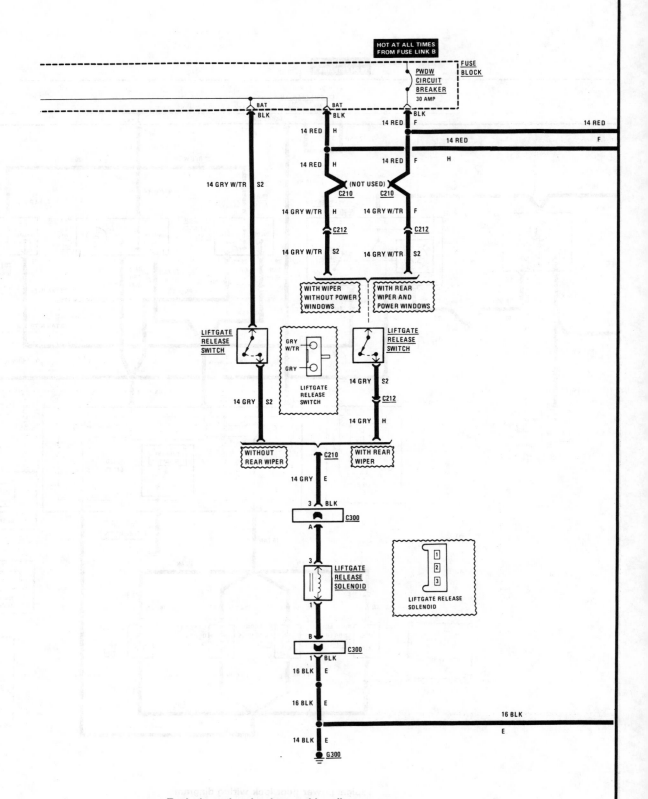

Typical rear hatch release wiring diagram

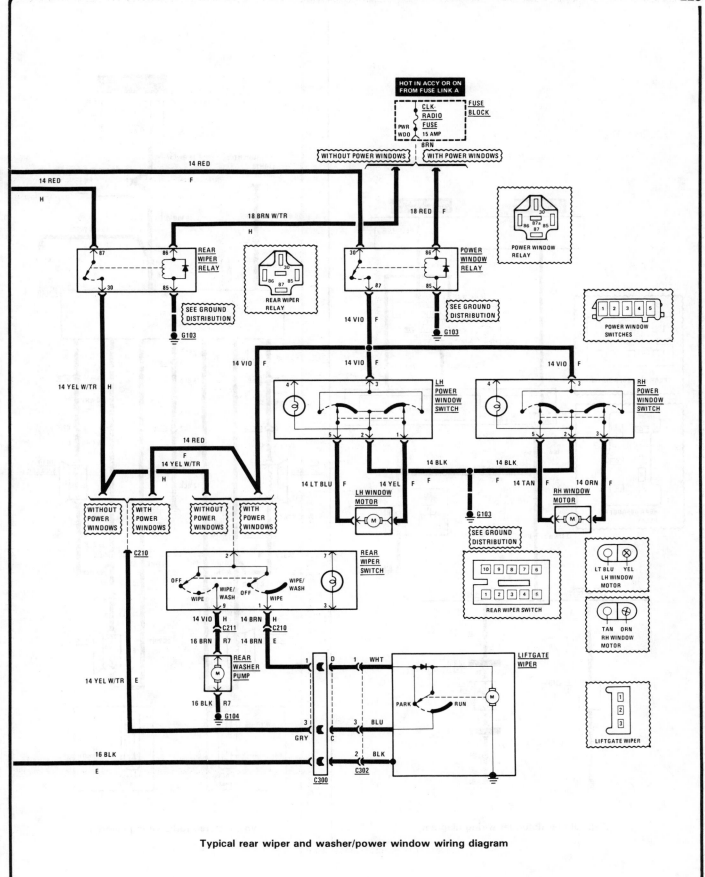

Typical rear wiper and washer/power window wiring diagram

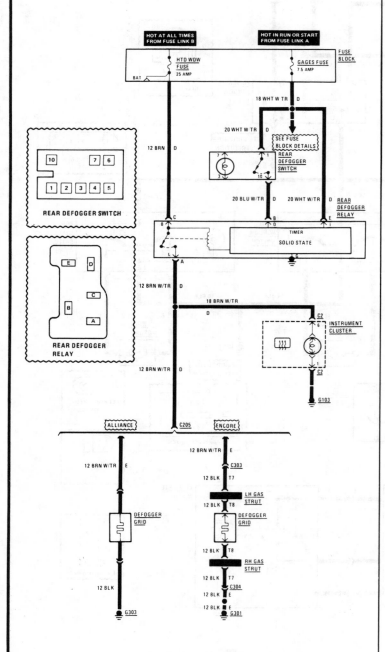

Typical rear defogger wiring diagram

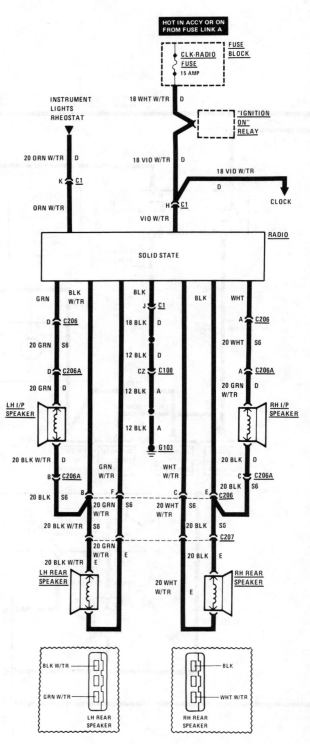

Typical stereo radio wiring diagram

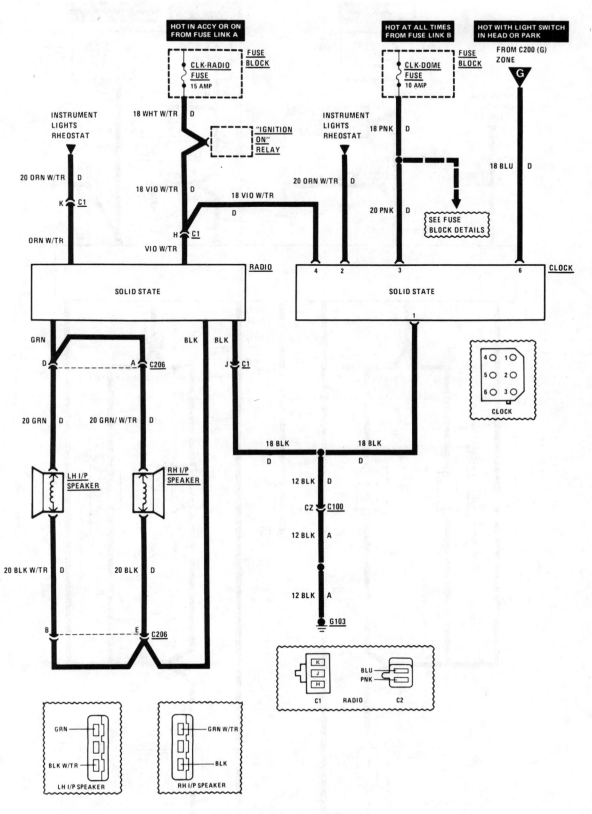

Typical mono radio/clock wiring diagram

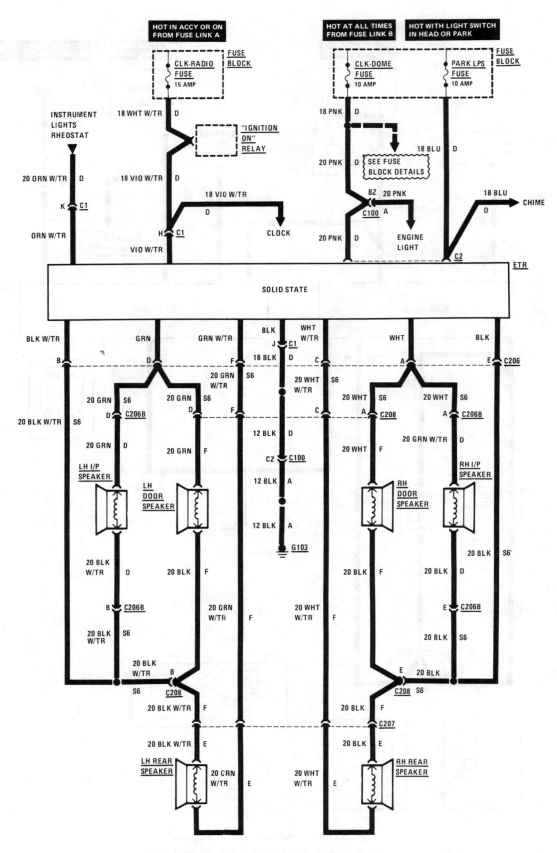

Typical electronically tuned radio wiring diagram

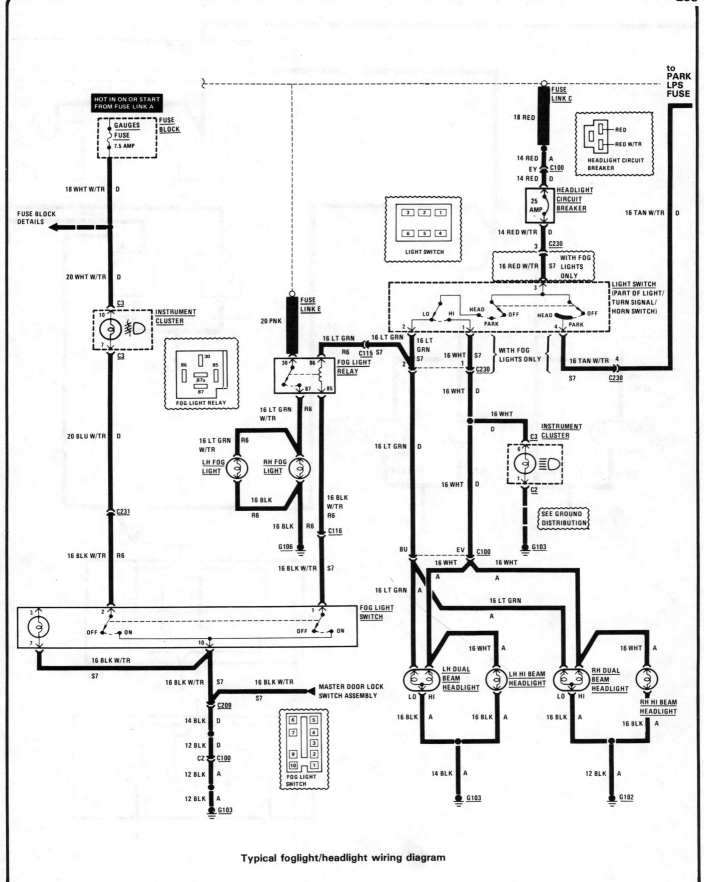

Typical foglight/headlight wiring diagram

PARK LPS
FUSE
10 AMP

18 BLU D

18 BLU D

C2   ETR
RADIO

18 BLU D

8   CHIME

18 BLU D

20 ORN W/TR

20 ORN W/TR D

20 ORN W/TR D

DX   C100

7   HAZARD
SWITCH

2   6   CLOCK

3   1

20 BLK D

18 BLK D

G103

18 BLU D

18 BLU A

18 BLU A

18 BLU D

18 BLU A

18 BLU A

18 BLU A

18 BLU A

LH FRONT
PARK/TURN
LIGHTS

FRONT
SIDEMARKER
LIGHTS

RH FRONT
PARK/TURN
LIGHTS

PARK   TURN

LH

RH

PARK   TURN

16 BLK A

18 BLK A

18 BLK A

16 BLK A

12 BLK A

14 BLK A

G103

G102

18 BLU D

G   C200   G   C200
20 BLU E

20 BLU E

20 BLU E

20 BLU E   20 BLU E

20 BLU E

20 BLU E   HH REAR
MARKER
LIGHT

ALLIANCE

LH REAR
MARKER

LH REAR
PARK/STOP
LIGHT

LICENSE
LIGHTS

RH REAR
PARK
STOP
LIGHT

LH   RH   PARK   STOP

20 BLK E   20 BLK E

20 BLK E   20 BLK E

18 BLK E

G300

G   C200
18 BLU E

18 BLU E   18 BLU E

18 BLU E   18 BLU E   18 BLU E   18 BLU E

ENCORE

LH REAR
MARKER
LIGHT

LH REAR
PARK, STOP AND
TURN LIGHT

LICENSE
LIGHTS

RH REAR
PARK, STOP, AND
TURN LIGHT

RH REAR
MARKER
LIGHT

PARK   STOP/
TURN

LH   RH   PARK   STOP/
TURN

18 BLK E   18 BLK E

16 BLK E

18 BLK E   20 BLK E

12 BLK E

G300

Typical parking light wiring diagram

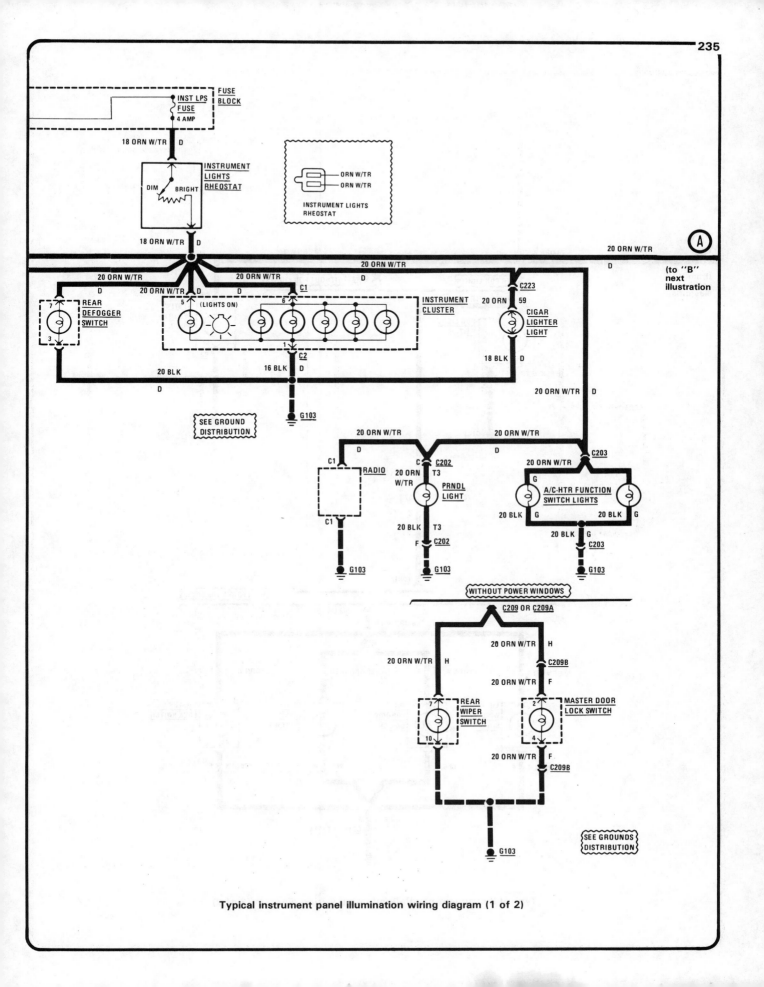

Typical instrument panel illumination wiring diagram (1 of 2)

236

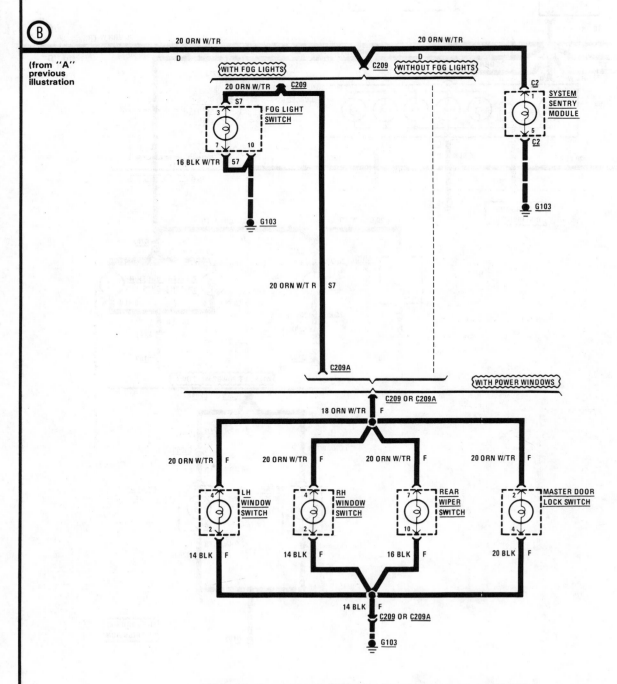

Typical instrument panel illumination wiring diagram (2 of 2)

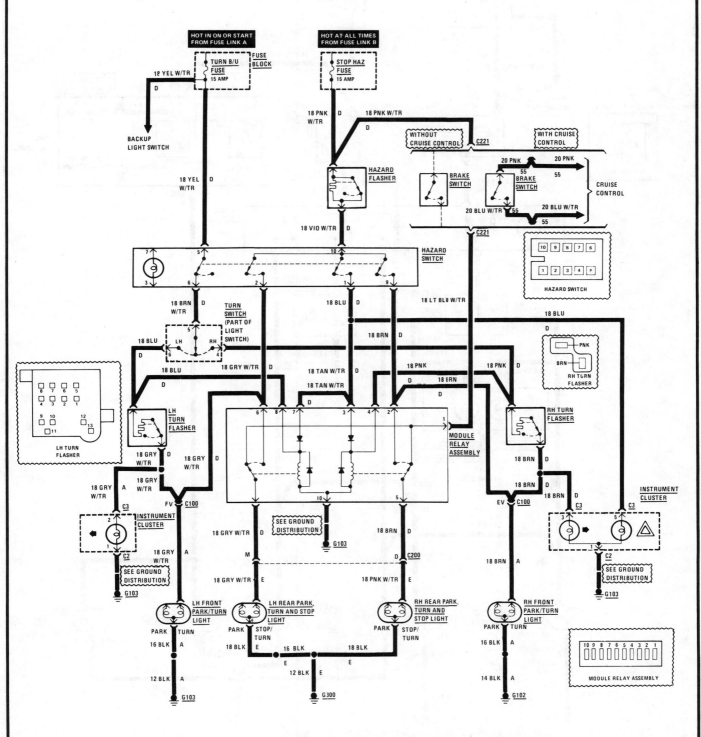

Typical brake/turn signal/hazard warning light wiring diagram (Encore only)

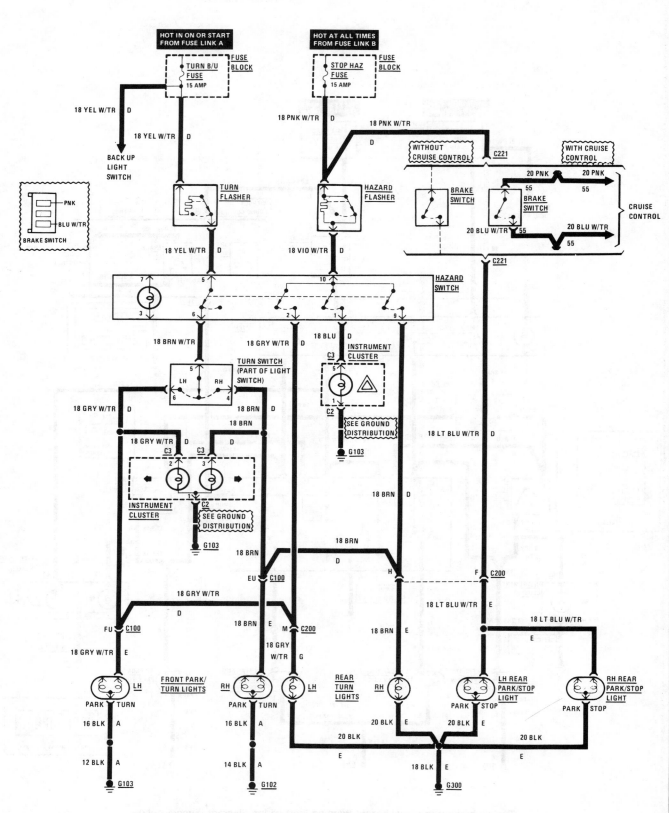

Typical brake/turn signal/hazard warning light wiring diagram (Alliance only)

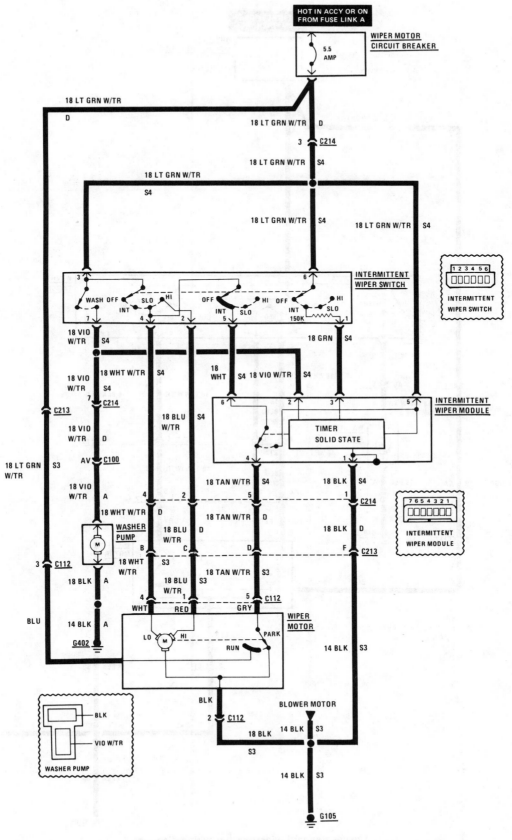

Typical intermittent wiper/washer wiring diagram

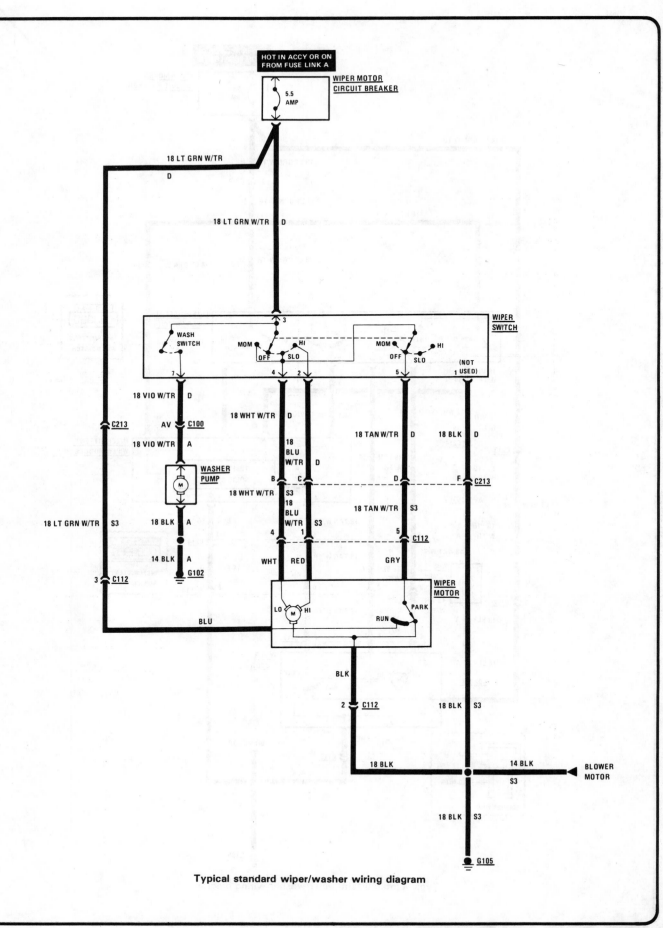

Typical standard wiper/washer wiring diagram

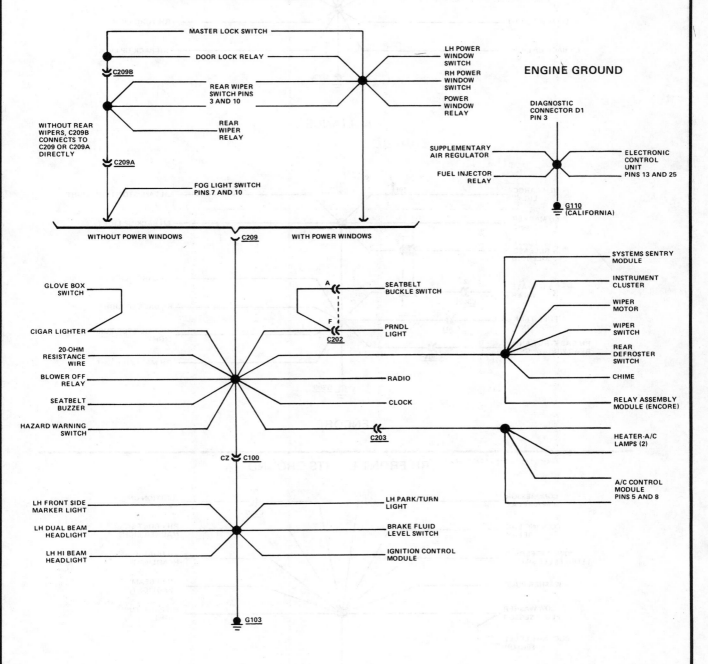

Ground connection wiring diagram (1 of 2)

REAR LIGHTS GROUND

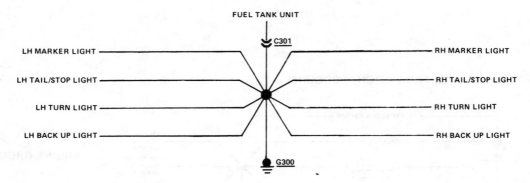

FUEL TANK UNIT

C301

LH MARKER LIGHT	RH MARKER LIGHT
LH TAIL/STOP LIGHT	RH TAIL/STOP LIGHT
LH TURN LIGHT	RH TURN LIGHT
LH BACK UP LIGHT	RH BACK UP LIGHT

G300

ALLIANCE

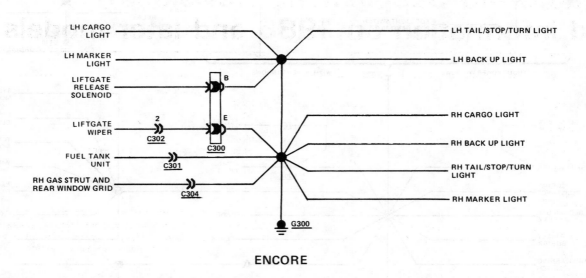

LH CARGO LIGHT — LH TAIL/STOP/TURN LIGHT

LH MARKER LIGHT — LH BACK UP LIGHT

LIFTGATE RELEASE SOLENOID — B

LIFTGATE WIPER — 2 — C302 — E — C300 — RH CARGO LIGHT

FUEL TANK UNIT — C301 — RH BACK UP LIGHT

RH GAS STRUT AND REAR WINDOW GRID — C304 — RH TAIL/STOP/TURN LIGHT

RH MARKER LIGHT

G300

ENCORE

RH FRONT LIGHTS GROUND

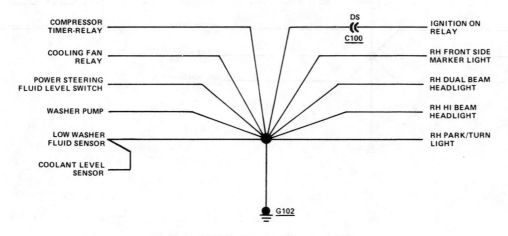

COMPRESSOR TIMER-RELAY — DS — C100 — IGNITION ON RELAY

COOLING FAN RELAY — RH FRONT SIDE MARKER LIGHT

POWER STEERING FLUID LEVEL SWITCH — RH DUAL BEAM HEADLIGHT

WASHER PUMP — RH HI BEAM HEADLIGHT

LOW WASHER FLUID SENSOR — RH PARK/TURN LIGHT

COOLANT LEVEL SENSOR

G102

Ground connection wiring diagram (2 of 2)

Chapter 13 Supplement: Revisions and information on 1986 and later models

Contents

1 Introduction

This Supplement contains Specifications and service procedure changes that apply to all AMC/Renault Alliance and Encore models produced in 1986 and 1987, as well as information related to previous models which was not available at the time of original publication of this manual.

Where no differences (or very minor differences) exist between 1986 and 1987 models and earlier models, no information is given. In those instances, the original material included in Chapters 1 through 12 should be used.

2 Specifications

2.0 liter engine

General

Bore	82 mm (3.22 in)
Stroke	93 mm (3.66 in)
Displacement	1965 cc (120 cu in)
Compression ratio	9.5:1)
Firing order	1-3-4-2)

Camshaft

End play	0.048 to 0.133 mm (0.001 to 0.005 in)

Pistons and connecting rods

Piston-to-bore clearance	0.023 to 0.047 mm (0.0009 to 0.0018 in)
Piston pin diameter	21 mm (0.826 in)
Rod side clearance	0.22 to 0.40 mm (0.008 to 0.015 in)

Crankshaft

End play	0.07 to 0.23 mm (0.002 to 0.009 in)
Main journal diameter	54.795 mm (2.157 in)
Rod journal diameter	48 mm (1.889 in)

2.0 liter engine (continued)

Cylinder head*

Valve arrangement	E-I-E-I-I-E-I-E
Valve guide diameter	8 mm (0.314 in)
Intake valve seat angle	60°
Exhaust valve seat angle	45°
Valve seat width	1.752 ± 0.2 mm (0.066 ± 0.007 in)
Valve seat diameter	
intake	39 mm (1.53 in)
exhaust	33.6 mm (1.32 in)
Valve spring free length	44.9 mm (1.767 in)

* Note: *The cylinder head cannot be resurfaced.*

Intermediate shaft

End play	0.07 to 0.15 mm (0.002 to 0.005 in)

Torque specifications

	Nm	Ft-lbs *(unless otherwise indicated)*
Air cleaner mounting bracket-to-cylinder head	10.3	92 in-lbs
Air cleaner-to-throttle body studs	12.2	108 in-lbs
Alternator bracket-to-block	38	28
Alternator pivot-to-A/C bracket	38	28
Alternator-to-adjustment bracket	12.5	9
Camshaft bearing cap bolts		
6 mm	10	7
8 mm	20	15
Camshaft sprocket bolt	53	39
Closing plate-to-cylinder block	7	5
Connecting rod bearing cap nuts	48	35
Main bearing cap bolts	64	47
Crankshaft cover-to-housing bolts	15	11
Crankshaft pulley bolt	95	70
Cylinder head bolts		
1st step	30	22
2nd step	70	52
3rd step	Loosen all bolts	
4th step (after loosening)	20	15
5th step	123° ± 2°	
Cylinder head cover nuts	5	44 in-lbs
Cylinder head cover studs	7	5
ERG tube-to-exhaust manifold	17	12
ERG valve-to-intake manifold	20	15
Exhaust manifold nuts	22	16
Exhaust pipe adapter-to-exhaust manifold	33	24
Flywheel-to-crankshaft bolts	53	39
Front exhaust pipe-to-manifold stud and nut	34	25
Idler pulley-to-mounting bracket bolts	38	28
Idler pulley nut	20 minimum	15 minimum
Intake manifold nuts	22	16
Oil pan drain plug	27	20
Oil pan bolts	14	10
Oil pump bolts		
6 mm	10	7
8 mm	23	17
Starter motor-to-transmission	42	31
Starter motor bracket-to-block	22.5	16.5
Tensioner pulley nut	40	30
Throttle body-to-intake manifold	20	15
Timing belt tension adjustment nut	10	7.5

---

3 Engine

Timing belt cover — removal and installation

On later model engines the design of the timing belt cover has been changed, with an increase in the number of mounting bolts and a change in their locations (Fig. 13.1). The removal and installation procedure remains essentially the same as the earlier model engine timing belt cover.

Cylinder head — removal (1987 only)

On 1987 models equipped with a 1.7 or 2.0 liter engine, be sure to remove bolt A (Fig. 13.2) before removing the cylinder head bolts.

2.0 liter engine — general information

Later model vehicles may be equipped with an optional 2.0 liter (120 cubic inch) engine. This engine supplements, but does not replace, the 1.7 liter engine. The design of the engine, and the service

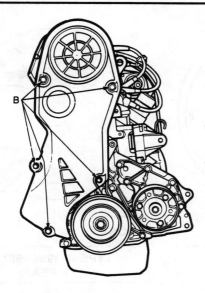

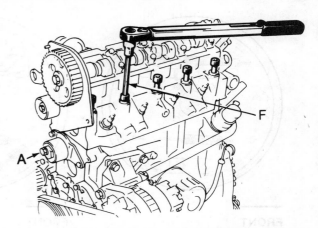

Fig. 13.2 Be sure to remove bolt A before removing any of the cylinder head bolts (F) on later model engines (Sec 3)

Fig. 13.1 Later model engines have a redesigned timing belt cover with five mounting bolts (B) (Sec 3)

procedures applying to it, are essentially the same as the 1.7 liter engine, with the exceptions noted in the Specifications Section of this Supplement.

---

4 Engine electrical systems

Ignition system — general information

Beginning with the 1986 model year, the ignition system used on

the 1.7L engine is also used on the 1.4L engine. Therefore the service procedures included in Chapter 5 for the 1.7L engine will also apply to all 1.4L engines built from 1986 on.

Starting system — general information

All models built after 1985 are equipped with a Bosch starter motor. It utilizes permanent magnets instead of field coils for current induction and a planetary gear set to drive the starter overrunning clutch (Fig. 13.3).

Starter motor brushes — replacement

Because of the design of the Bosch starter motor, which requires extensive disassembly to reach the brush holder, and the special tools required, replacement of the starter motor brushes is beyond the scope of the home mechanic. If the starter motor requires servicing or brush

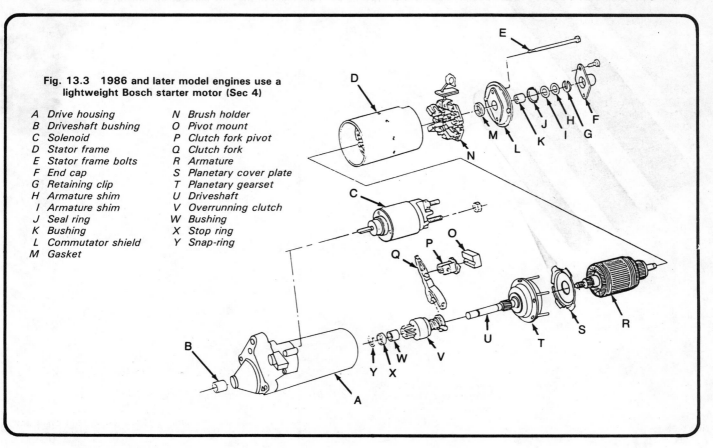

Fig. 13.3 1986 and later model engines use a lightweight Bosch starter motor (Sec 4)

A Drive housing
B Driveshaft bushing
C Solenoid
D Stator frame
E Stator frame bolts
F End cap
G Retaining clip
H Armature shim
I Armature shim
J Seal ring
K Bushing
L Commutator shield
M Gasket
N Brush holder
O Pivot mount
P Clutch fork pivot
Q Clutch fork
R Armature
S Planetary cover plate
T Planetary gearset
U Driveshaft
V Overrunning clutch
W Bushing
X Stop ring
Y Snap-ring

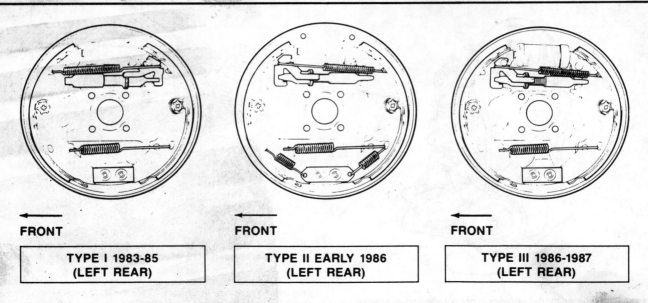

FRONT

FRONT

FRONT

TYPE I 1983-85 (LEFT REAR)	TYPE II EARLY 1986 (LEFT REAR)	TYPE III 1986-1987 (LEFT REAR)

Fig. 13.4   Three different types of rear brakes are used, all similar in design but using non-interchangable components (Sec 5)

replacement, a rebuilt unit should be installed or the original should be taken to a professional mechanic for overhaul.

5 Brakes

Rear drum brakes — identification

Three different rear brake assemblies were used on 1983 and later models. Type I brakes were used on 1983 through 1985 models, Type II brakes were used on early 1986 models and Type III brakes were used on late 1986 and all 1987 models (see Fig. 13.4).

Although service procedures for the three brake assembly types remain essentially the same as those in Chapter 9, note that the components used on the three types, with the exception of the wheel cylinders, are NOT interchangable. When purchasing brake shoes and other parts it is essential that you identify which type of brake assembly you have. It would be a very good idea to take the parts with you and compare them to the new parts at the time of purchase.

Conversion factors

Length (distance)

Inches (in)	X	25.4	=	Millimetres (mm)	X	0.0394	=	Inches (in)
Feet (ft)	X	0.305	=	Metres (m)	X	3.281	=	Feet (ft)
Miles	X	1.609	=	Kilometres (km)	X	0.621	=	Miles

Volume (capacity)

Cubic inches (cu in; in^3)	X	16.387	=	Cubic centimetres (cc; cm^3)	X	0.061	=	Cubic inches (cu in; in^3)
Imperial pints (Imp pt)	X	0.568	=	Litres (l)	X	1.76	=	Imperial pints (Imp pt)
Imperial quarts (Imp qt)	X	1.137	=	Litres (l)	X	0.88	=	Imperial quarts (Imp qt)
Imperial quarts (Imp qt)	X	1.201	=	US quarts (US qt)	X	0.833	=	Imperial quarts (Imp qt)
US quarts (US qt)	X	0.946	=	Litres (l)	X	1.057	=	US quarts (US qt)
Imperial gallons (Imp gal)	X	4.546	=	Litres (l)	X	0.22	=	Imperial gallons (Imp gal)
Imperial gallons (Imp gal)	X	1.201	=	US gallons (US gal)	X	0.833	=	Imperial gallons (Imp gal)
US gallons (US gal)	X	3.785	=	Litres (l)	X	0.264	=	US gallons (US gal)

Mass (weight)

Ounces (oz)	X	28.35	=	Grams (g)	X	0.035	=	Ounces (oz)
Pounds (lb)	X	0.454	=	Kilograms (kg)	X	2.205	=	Pounds (lb)

Force

Ounces-force (ozf; oz)	X	0.278	=	Newtons (N)	X	3.6	=	Ounces-force (ozf; oz)
Pounds-force (lbf; lb)	X	4.448	=	Newtons (N)	X	0.225	=	Pounds-force (lbf; lb)
Newtons (N)	X	0.1	=	Kilograms-force (kgf; kg)	X	9.81	=	Newtons (N)

Pressure

Pounds-force per square inch (psi; lbf/in^2; lb/in^2)	X	0.070	=	Kilograms-force per square centimetre (kgf/cm^2; kg/cm^2)	X	14.223	=	Pounds-force per square inch (psi; lbf/in^2; lb/in^2)
Pounds-force per square inch (psi; lbf/in^2; lb/in^2)	X	0.068	=	Atmospheres (atm)	X	14.696	=	Pounds-force per square inch (psi; lbf/in^2; lb/in^2)
Pounds-force per square inch (psi; lbf/in^2; lb/in^2)	X	0.069	=	Bars	X	14.5	=	Pounds-force per square inch (psi; lbf/in^2; lb/in^2)
Pounds-force per square inch (psi; lbf/in^2; lb/in^2)	X	6.895	=	Kilopascals (kPa)	X	0.145	=	Pounds-force per square inch (psi; lbf/in^2; lb/in^2)
Kilopascals (kPa)	X	0.01	=	Kilograms-force per square centimetre (kgf/cm^2; kg/cm^2)	X	98.1	=	Kilopascals (kPa)
Millibar (mbar)	X	100	=	Pascals (Pa)	X	0.01	=	Millibar (mbar)
Millibar (mbar)	X	0.0145	=	Pounds-force per square inch (psi; lbf/in^2; lb/in^2)	X	68.947	=	Millibar (mbar)
Millibar (mbar)	X	0.75	=	Millimetres of mercury (mmHg)	X	1.333	=	Millibar (mbar)
Millibar (mbar)	X	0.401	=	Inches of water (inH$_2$O)	X	2.491	=	Millibar (mbar)
Millimetres of mercury (mmHg)	X	0.535	=	Inches of water (inH$_2$O)	X	1.868	=	Millimetres of mercury (mmHg)
Inches of water (inH$_2$O)	X	0.036	=	Pounds-force per square inch (psi; lbf/in^2; lb/in^2)	X	27.68	=	Inches of water (inH$_2$O)

Torque (moment of force)

Pounds-force inches (lbf in; lb in)	X	1.152	=	Kilograms-force centimetre (kgf cm; kg cm)	X	0.868	=	Pounds-force inches (lbf in; lb in)
Pounds-force inches (lbf in; lb in)	X	0.113	=	Newton metres (Nm)	X	8.85	=	Pounds-force inches (lbf in; lb in)
Pounds-force inches (lbf in; lb in)	X	0.083	=	Pounds-force feet (lbf ft; lb ft)	X	12	=	Pounds-force inches (lbf in; lb in)
Pounds-force feet (lbf ft; lb ft)	X	0.138	=	Kilograms-force metres (kgf m; kg m)	X	7.233	=	Pounds-force feet (lbf ft; lb ft)
Pounds-force feet (lbf ft; lb ft)	X	1.356	=	Newton metres (Nm)	X	0.738	=	Pounds-force feet (lbf ft; lb ft)
Newton metres (Nm)	X	0.102	=	Kilograms-force metres (kgf m; kg m)	X	9.804	=	Newton metres (Nm)

Power

Horsepower (hp)	X	745.7	=	Watts (W)	X	0.0013	=	Horsepower (hp)

Velocity (speed)

Miles per hour (miles/hr; mph)	X	1.609	=	Kilometres per hour (km/hr; kph)	X	0.621	=	Miles per hour (miles/hr; mph)

*Fuel consumption**

Miles per gallon, Imperial (mpg)	X	0.354	=	Kilometres per litre (km/l)	X	2.825	=	Miles per gallon, Imperial (mpg)
Miles per gallon, US (mpg)	X	0.425	=	Kilometres per litre (km/l)	X	2.352	=	Miles per gallon, US (mpg)

Temperature

Degrees Fahrenheit = (°C x 1.8) + 32

Degrees Celsius (Degrees Centigrade; °C) = (°F - 32) x 0.56

**It is common practice to convert from miles per gallon (mpg) to litres/100 kilometres (l/100km), where mpg (Imperial) x l/100 km = 282 and mpg (US) x l/100 km = 235*

Index

HAYNES AUTOMOTIVE MANUALS

NOTE: New manuals are added to this list on a periodic basis. If you do not see a listing for your vehicle, consult your local Haynes dealer for the latest product information.

ALFA-ROMEO
531   **Alfa Romeo Sedan & Coupe** '73 thru '80

AMC
     Jeep CJ – see JEEP (412)
694   **Mid-size models,** Concord, Hornet, Gremlin & Spirit '70 thru '83
934   **(Renault) Alliance & Encore** all models '83 thru '87

AUDI
162   **100** all models '69 thru '77
615   **4000** all models '80 thru '87
428   **5000** all models '77 thru '83
1117   **5000** all models '84 thru '88
207   **Fox** all models '73 thru '79

AUSTIN
049   **Healey 100/6 & 3000** Roadster '56 thru '68
     Healey Sprite – see MG Midget Roadster (265)

BLMC
260   **1100, 1300 & Austin America** '62 thru '74
527   **Mini** all models '59 thru '69
*646   **Mini** all models '69 thru '88

BMW
276   **320i** all 4 cyl models '75 thru '83
632   **528i & 530i** all models '75 thru '80
240   **1500 thru 2002** all models except Turbo '59 thru '77
348   **2500, 2800, 3.0 & Bavaria** '69 thru '76

BUICK
     Century (front wheel drive) – see GENERAL MOTORS A-Cars (829)
*1627   **Buick, Oldsmobile & Pontiac Full-size (Front wheel drive)** all models '85 thru '90
     Buick Electra, LeSabre and Park Avenue; **Oldsmobile** Delta 88 Royale, Ninety Eight and Regency; **Pontiac** Bonneville
*1551   **Buick Oldsmobile & Pontiac Full-size (Rear wheel drive)**
     Buick Electra '70 thru '84, Estate '70 thru '90, LeSabre '70 thru '79
     Oldsmobile Custom Cruiser '70 thru '90, Delta 88 '70 thru '85, Ninety-eight '70 thru '84
     Pontiac Bonneville '70 thru '86, Catalina '70 thru '81, Grandville '70 thru '75, Parisienne '84 thru '86
627   **Mid-size** all rear-drive **Regal & Century** models with V6, V8 and Turbo '74 thru '87
     Skyhawk – see GENERAL MOTORS J-Cars (766)
552   **Skylark** all X-car models '80 thru '85

CADILLAC
     Cimarron – see GENERAL MOTORS J-Cars (766)

CAPRI
296   **2000 MK I Coupe** all models '71 thru '75
283   **2300 MK II Coupe** all models '74 thru '78
205   **2600 & 2800** V6 Coupe '71 thru '75
375   **2800 Mk II** V6 Coupe '75 thru '78
     Mercury in-line engines – see FORD Mustang (654)
     Mercury V6 & V8 engines – see FORD Mustang (558)

CHEVROLET
*1477   **Astro & GMC Safari Mini-vans** all models '85 thru '90
554   **Camaro** V8 all models '70 thru '81
*866   **Camaro** all models '82 thru '89
     Cavalier – see GENERAL MOTORS J-Cars (766)
     Celebrity – see GENERAL MOTORS A-Cars (829)

625   **Chevelle, Malibu & El Camino** all V6 & V8 models '69 thru '87
449   **Chevette & Pontiac T1000** all models '76 thru '87
550   **Citation** all models '80 thru '85
*1628   **Corsica/Beretta** all models '87 thru '90
274   **Corvette** all V8 models '68 thru '82
*1336   **Corvette** all models '84 thru '89
704   **Full-size Sedans** Caprice, Impala, Biscayne, Bel Air & Wagons, all V6 & V8 models '69 thru '90
319   **Luv Pick-up** all 2WD & 4WD models '72 thru '82
626   **Monte Carlo** all V6, V8 & Turbo models '70 thru '88
241   **Nova** all V8 models '69 thru '79
*1642   **Nova and Geo Prizm** all front wheel drive models, '85 thru '90
*420   **Pick-ups** '67 thru '87 – Chevrolet & GMC, all V8 & in-line 6 cyl 2WD & 4WD models '67 thru '87
*1664   **Pick-ups** '88 thru '90 – Chevrolet & GMC all full-size (C and K) models, '88 thru '90
*831   **S-10 & GMC S-15 Pick-ups** all models '82 thru '90
*345   **Vans** – Chevrolet & GMC, V8 & in-line 6 cyl models '68 thru '89
208   **Vega** all models except Cosworth '70 thru '77

CHRYSLER
*1337   **Chrysler & Plymouth Mid-size** front wheel drive '82 thru '88
     K-Cars – see DODGE Aries (723)
     Laser – see DODGE Daytona (1140)

DATSUN
402   **200SX** all models '77 thru '79
647   **200SX** all models '80 thru '83
228   **B-210** all models '73 thru '78
525   **210** all models '78 thru '82
206   **240Z, 260Z & 280Z** Coupe & 2+2 '70 thru '78
563   **280ZX** Coupe & 2+2 '79 thru '83
     300ZX – see NISSAN (1137)
679   **310** all models '78 thru '82
123   **510 & PL521 Pick-up** '68 thru '73
430   **510** all models '78 thru '81
372   **610** all models '72 thru '76
277   **620 Series Pick-up** all models '73 thru '79
235   **710** all models '73 thru '77
     720 Series Pick-up – see NISSAN Pick-up (771)
376   **810/Maxima** all gasoline models '77 thru '84
124   **1200** all models '70 thru '73
368   **F10** all models '76 thru '79
     Pulsar – see NISSAN (876)
     Sentra – see NISSAN (982)
     Stanza – see NISSAN (981)

DODGE
*723   **Aries & Plymouth Reliant** all models '81 thru '88
*1231   **Caravan & Plymouth Voyager Mini-Vans** all models '84 thru '89
699   **Challenger & Plymouth Saporro** all models '78 thru '83
236   **Colt** all models '71 thru '77
419   **Colt** (rear wheel drive) all models '77 thru '80
610   **Colt & Plymouth Champ** (front wheel drive) all models '78 thru '87
*556   **D50 & Plymouth Arrow Pick-ups** '79 thru '88
234   **Dart & Plymouth Valiant** all 6 cyl models '67 thru '76
*1140   **Daytona & Chrysler Laser** all models '84 thru '88
*545   **Omni & Plymouth Horizon** all models '78 thru '89
*912   **Pick-ups** all full-size models '74 thru '90
*349   **Vans** – Dodge & Plymouth V8 & 6 cyl models '71 thru '89

FIAT
080   **124 Sedan & Wagon** all ohv & dohc models '66 thru '75
094   **124 Sport Coupe & Spider** '68 thru '78
087   **128** all models '72 thru '79
310   **131 & Brava** all models '75 thru '81
038   **850 Sedan, Coupe & Spider** '64 thru '74
479   **Strada** all models '79 thru '82
273   **X1/9** all models '74 thru '80

FORD
*1476   **Aerostar Mini-vans** all models '86 thru '88
788   **Bronco and Pick-ups** '73 thru '79
*880   **Bronco and Pick-ups** '80 thru '90
014   **Cortina MK II** all models except Lotus '66 thru '70
295   **Cortina MK III** 1600 & 2000 ohc '70 thru '76
268   **Courier Pick-up** all models '72 thru '82
789   **Escort & Mercury Lynx** all models '81 thru '90
560   **Fairmont & Mercury Zephyr** all in-line & V8 models '78 thru '83
334   **Fiesta** all models '77 thru '80
754   **Ford & Mercury Full-size,** Ford LTD & Mercury Marquis ('75 thru '82); Ford Custom 500, Country Squire, Crown Victoria & Mercury Colony Park ('75 thru '87); Ford LTD Crown Victoria & Mercury Gran Marquis ('83 thru '87)
359   **Granada & Mercury Monarch** all in-line, 6 cyl & V8 models '75 thru '80
773   **Ford & Mercury Mid-size,** Ford Thunderbird & Mercury Cougar ('75 thru '82); Ford LTD & Mercury Marquis ('83 thru '86); Ford Torino, Gran Torino, Elite, Ranchero pick-up, LTD II, Mercury Montego, Comet, XR-7 & Lincoln Versailles ('75 thru '86)
*654   **Mustang & Mercury Capri** all in-line models & Turbo '79 thru '90
*558   **Mustang & Mercury Capri** all V6 & V8 models '79 thru '89
357   **Mustang V8** all models '64-1/2 thru '73
231   **Mustang II** all 4 cyl, V6 & V8 models '74 thru '78
204   **Pinto** all models '70 thru '74
649   **Pinto & Mercury Bobcat** all models '75 thru '80
*1026   **Ranger & Bronco II** all gasoline models '83 thru '89
*1421   **Taurus & Mercury Sable** '86 thru '90
*1418   **Tempo & Mercury Topaz** all gasoline models '84 thru '89
1338   **Thunderbird & Mercury Cougar/XR7** '83 thru '88
*344   **Vans** all V8 Econoline models '69 thru '90

GENERAL MOTORS
*829   **A-Cars** – Chevrolet Celebrity, Buick Century, Pontiac 6000 & Oldsmobile Cutlass Ciera all models '82 thru '89
*766   **J-Cars** – Chevrolet Cavalier, Pontiac J-2000, Oldsmobile Firenza, Buick Skyhawk & Cadillac Cimarron all models '82 thru '89
*1420   **N-Cars** – Pontiac Grand Am, Buick Somerset and Oldsmobile Calais '85 thru '87; Buick Skylark '86 thru '87

GEO
     Tracker – see SUZUKI Samurai (1626)
     Prizm – see CHEVROLET Nova (1642)

GMC
     Safari – see CHEVROLET ASTRO (1477)
     Vans & Pick-ups – see CHEVROLET (420, 831, 345, 1664)

(continued on next page)

Listings shown with an asterisk (*) indicate model coverage as of this printing. These titles will be periodically updated to include later model years — consult your Haynes dealer for more information.

Haynes Publications Inc., P.O. Box 978, Newbury Park, CA 91320 ● (818) 889–5400 ● (805) 498–6703

HAYNES AUTOMOTIVE MANUALS (continued from previous page)

NOTE: New manuals are added to this list on a periodic basis. If you do not see a listing for your vehicle, consult your local Haynes dealer for the latest product information.

HONDA
138	**360, 600 & Z Coupe** all models '67 thru '75
351	**Accord CVCC** all models '76 thru '83
*1221	**Accord** all models '84 thru '89
160	**Civic 1200** all models '73 thru '79
633	**Civic 1300 & 1500 CVCC** all models '80 thru '83
297	**Civic 1500 CVCC** all models '75 thru '79
*1227	**Civic** all models except 16-valve CRX & 4 WD Wagon '84 thru '86
*601	**Prelude CVCC** all models '79 thru '89

HYUNDAI
*1552	**Excel** all models '86 thru '89

ISUZU
*1641	**Trooper & Pick-up**, all gasoline models '81 thru '89

JAGUAR
098	**MK I & II,** 240 & 340 Sedans '55 thru '69
*242	**XJ6** all 6 cyl models '68 thru '86
*478	**XJ12 & XJS** all 12 cyl models '72 thru '85
140	**XK-E** 3.8 & 4.2 all 6 cyl models '61 thru '72

JEEP
*1553	**Cherokee, Comanche & Wagoneer Limited** all models '84 thru '89
412	**CJ** all models '49 thru '86

LADA
*413	**1200, 1300. 1500 & 1600** all models including Riva '74 thru '86

LANCIA
533	**Lancia Beta** Sedan, Coupe & HPE all models '76 thru '80

LAND ROVER
314	**Series II, IIA, & III** all 4 cyl gasoline models '58 thru '86
529	**Diesel** all models '58 thru '80

MAZDA
648	**626** Sedan & Coupe (rear wheel drive) all models '79 thru '82
*1082	**626 & MX-6 (front wheel drive)** all models '83 thru '90
*267	**B1600, B1800 & B2000 Pick-ups** '72 thru '90
370	**GLC Hatchback (rear wheel drive)** all models '77 thru '83
757	**GLC (front wheel drive)** all models '81 thru '86
109	**RX2** all models '71 thru '75
096	**RX3** all models '72 thru '76
460	**RX-7** all models '79 thru '85
*1419	**RX-7** all models '86 thru '89

MERCEDES-BENZ
*1643	**190 Series** all four-cylinder gasoline models, '84 thru '88
346	**230, 250 & 280** Sedan, Coupe & Roadster all 6 cyl sohc models '68 thru '72
983	**280 123 Series** all gasoline models '77 thru '81
698	**350 & 450** Sedan, Coupe & Roadster all models '71 thru '80
697	**Diesel 123 Series** 200D, 220D, 240D, 240TD, 300D, 300CD, 300TD, 4- & 5-cyl incl. Turbo '76 thru '85

MERCURY
See FORD Listing

MG
475	**MGA** all models '56 thru '62
111	**MGB** Roadster & GT Coupe all models '62 thru '80
265	**MG Midget & Austin Healey Sprite** Roadster '58 thru '80

MITSUBISHI
Pick-up – *see Dodge D-50 (556)*

MORRIS
074	**(Austin) Marina 1.8** all models '71 thru '80
024	**Minor 1000** sedan & wagon '56 thru '71

NISSAN
*1137	**300ZX** all Turbo & non-Turbo models '84 thru '86
*1341	**Maxima** all models '85 thru '89
*771	**Pick-ups/Pathfinder** gas models '80 thru '88
*876	**Pulsar** all models '83 thru '86
*982	**Sentra** all models '82 thru '90
*981	**Stanza** all models '82 thru '90

OLDSMOBILE
	Custom Cruiser – *see BUICK Full-size (1551)*
658	**Cutlass** all standard gasoline V6 & V8 models '74 thru '88
	Cutlass Ciera – *see GENERAL MOTORS A-Cars (829)*
	Firenza – *see GENERAL MOTORS J-Cars (766)*
	Ninety-eight – *see BUICK Full-size (1551)*
	Omega – *see PONTIAC Phoenix & Omega (551)*

OPEL
157	**(Buick) Manta Coupe 1900** all models '70 thru '74

PEUGEOT
161	**504** all gasoline models '68 thru '79
663	**504** all diesel models '74 thru '83

PLYMOUTH
425	**Arrow** all models '76 thru '80 *For all other PLYMOUTH titles, see DODGE listing.*

PONTIAC
	T1000 – *see CHEVROLET Chevette (449)*
	J-2000 – *see GENERAL MOTORS J-Cars (766)*
	6000 – *see GENERAL MOTORS A-Cars (829)*
1232	**Fiero** all models '84 thru '88
555	**Firebird** all V8 models except Turbo '70 thru '81
*867	**Firebird** all models '82 thru '89
	Full-size Rear Wheel Drive – *see Buick, Oldsmobile, Pontiac Full-size (1551)*
551	**Phoenix & Oldsmobile Omega** all X-car models '80 thru '84

PORSCHE
*264	**911** all Coupe & Targa models except Turbo '65 thru '87
239	**914** all 4 cyl models '69 thru '76
397	**924** all models including Turbo '76 thru '82
*1027	**944** all models including Turbo '83 thru '89

RENAULT
141	**5 Le Car** all models '76 thru '83
079	**8 & 10** all models with 58.4 cu in engines '62 thru '72
097	**12 Saloon & Estate** all models 1289 cc engines '70 thru '80
768	**15 & 17** all models '73 thru '79
081	**16** all models 89.7 cu in & 95.5 cu in engines '65 thru '72
598	**18i & Sportwagon** all models '81 thru '86
	Alliance & Encore – *see AMC (934)*
984	**Fuego** all models '82 thru '85

ROVER
085	**3500 & 3500S Sedan** 215 cu in engines '68 thru '76
*365	**3500 SDI V8** all models '76 thru '85

SAAB
198	**95 & 96** V4 all models '66 thru '75
247	**99** all models including Turbo '69 thru '80
*980	**900** all models including Turbo '79 thru '88

SUBARU
237	**1100, 1300, 1400 & 1600** all models '71 thru '79
*681	**1600 & 1800** 2WD & 4WD all models '80 thru '88

SUZUKI
*1626	**Samurai/Sidekick and Geo Tracker** all models '86 thru '89

TOYOTA
*1023	**Camry** all models '83 thru '90
150	**Carina Sedan** all models '71 thru '74
229	**Celica ST, GT & liftback** all models '71 thru '77
437	**Celica** all models '78 thru '81
*935	**Celica** all models except front-wheel drive and Supra '82 thru '85
680	**Celica Supra** all models '79 thru '81
1139	**Celica Supra** all in-line 6-cylinder models '82 thru '86
201	**Corolla 1100, 1200 & 1600** all models '67 thru '74
361	**Corolla** all models '75 thru '79
961	**Corolla** all models (rear wheel drive) '80 thru '87
*1025	**Corolla** all models (front wheel drive) '84 thru '88
*636	**Corolla Tercel** all models '80 thru '82
230	**Corona & MK II** all 4 cyl sohc models '69 thru '74
360	**Corona** all models '74 thru '82
*532	**Cressida** all models '78 thru '82
313	**Land Cruiser** all models '68 thru '82
200	**MK II** all 6 cyl models '72 thru '76
*1339	**MR2** all models '85 thru '87
304	**Pick-up** all models '69 thru '78
*656	**Pick-up** all models '79 thru '90
787	**Starlet** all models '81 thru '84

TRIUMPH
112	**GT6 & Vitesse** all models '62 thru '74
113	**Spitfire** all models '62 thru '81
028	**TR2, 3, 3A, & 4A** Roadsters '52 thru '67
031	**TR250 & 6** Roadsters '67 thru '76
322	**TR7** all models '75 thru '81

VW
091	**411 & 412** all 103 cu in models '68 thru '73
036	**Bug 1200** all models '54 thru '66
039	**Bug 1300 & 1500** '65 thru '70
159	**Bug 1600** all basic, sport & super (curved windshield) models '70 thru '74
110	**Bug 1600 Super** all models (flat windshield) '70 thru '72
238	**Dasher** all gasoline models '74 thru '81
*884	**Rabbit, Jetta, Scirocco, & Pick-up** all gasoline models '74 thru '89 & **Convertible** '80 thru '89
451	**Rabbit, Jetta & Pick-up** all diesel models '77 thru '84
082	**Transporter 1600** all models '68 thru '79
226	**Transporter 1700, 1800 & 2000** all models '72 thru '79
084	**Type 3 1500 & 1600** all models '63 thru '73
1029	**Vanagon** all air-cooled models '80 thru '83

VOLVO
203	**120, 130 Series & 1800 Sports** '61 thru '73
129	**140 Series** all models '66 thru '74
244	**164** all models '68 thru '75
*270	**240 Series** all models '74 thru '90
400	**260 Series** all models '75 thru '82
*1550	**740 & 760 Series** all models '82 thru '88

SPECIAL MANUALS
1479	**Automotive Body Repair & Painting Manual**
1654	**Automotive Electrical Manual**
1480	**Automotive Heating & Air Conditioning Manual**
482	**Fuel Injection Manual**
299	**SU Carburetors** thru '88
393	**Weber Carburetors** thru '79
300	**Zenith/Stromberg CD Carburetors** thru '76

See your dealer for other available titles

6-1-90

Over 100 Haynes motorcycle manuals also available

Haynes Publications Inc., P.O. Box 978, Newbury Park, CA 91320 ● (818) 889-5400 ● (805) 498-6703